A HISTORY OF
AUTOBIOGRAPHY
IN ANTIQUITY

VOLUME I

INTERNATIONAL LIBRARY OF SOCIOLOGY
AND SOCIAL RECONSTRUCTION

Editor : Dr. Karl Mannheim

A HISTORY OF
AUTOBIOGRAPHY
IN ANTIQUITY

by
GEORG MISCH

PROFESSOR OF PHILOSOPHY AT GÖTTINGEN
UNIVERSITY

VOLUME I

GREENWOOD PRESS, PUBLISHERS
WESTPORT, CONNECTICUT

Library of Congress Cataloging in Publication Data

Misch, Georg, 1878-1965.
    A history of autobiography in antiquity.

    Translation of Geschichte der Autobiographie.
    Reprint of the 1950 ed. published by Routledge &
Paul, London, in series: International library of
sociology and social reconstruction.
    1. Autobiography. I. Title.
CT25.M514 1974   920'.009'01   73-13406
    ISBN 0-8371-7053-2

GESCHICHTE DER AUTOBIOGRAPHIE first published by
B. G. Teubner, Leipzig and Berlin, 1907. Second edition 1931;
third edition (A. Francke AG., Berne, and Gerhard Schulte-Bulmke,
Frankfort), Vol. I, first part 1949; second part 1950

HISTORY OF AUTOBIOGRAPHY IN ANTIQUITY
Translated in collaboration with the Author by E. W. DICKES
and first published in England

by ROUTLEDGE & KEGAN PAUL LTD.

This edition originally published in 1950 by Routledge &
Kegan Paul Limited, London

Reprinted with the permission of Routledge & Kegan Paul
Limited.

Reprinted in 1973 by Greenwood Press
A division of Congressional Information Service, Inc.
88 Post Road West, Westport, Connecticut 06881

Library of Congress catalog card number 73-13406
ISBN 0-8371-7053-2 (SET)
ISBN 0-8371-7178-4 (Vol. I)
ISBN 0-8371-7179-2 (Vol. 2)

Printed in the United States of America

10 9 8 7 6 5 4 3 2

PREFACE TO THE ENGLISH EDITION

This book is the English version of a work that appeared in Germany over forty years ago. Its publication now in England is connected with the political events which led to the destruction of the German Reich and, at the same time, diverted to the Anglo-Saxon countries currents of the intellectual life that was suppressed in Germany. The success beyond all expectations of the Library of Sociology and Social Reconstruction bears witness to that notable process. When Dr. Mannheim suggested that my attempt at a history of autobiography should be included in that collection, at first I regarded the plan less with the eyes of an author than with those of an editor of literary remains ; but then it became plain how great was the difficulty of the labour involved in putting into English a German work of these dimensions, a product of German philosophy and cultural history. The best solution of the task seemed to be by means of collaboration between translator and author. The book profited by this collaboration ; for it led to an association, which I hope has been fruitful, of the German philosophical tendency, from which this book of my youth proceeded as a matter of course, with the English practical sense which I have learnt in later years to appreciate. Thus there has resulted, instead of a simple translation, an enlarged version of the book—an undertaking from which I had deliberately refrained when revising the German book some twenty years ago.

I am particularly indebted to Mr. E. W. Dickes for undertaking and carrying through the laborious task. My own task was greatly facilitated by the opportunity for study and discussion afforded to me in St. Deiniol's Library at Hawarden, near Chester ; I should like to thank the Warden, Rev. Dr. Vidler, for the kind hospitality I enjoyed for two years (1944–6) at that unique place, and the then Librarian, Mr. Hugh Buss, M.A., for the suggestions he made when we were discussing some passages difficult to translate. Finally, I should like to take this opportunity to thank the Society for the Protection of Science and Learning, which enabled me to continue my work in hospitable England during the period of Nazi domination.

GÖTTINGEN,   GEORG MISCH.

March, 1948.

NOTE

Thanks are due to Messrs. William Heinemann, Ltd., and to the Editors of the Loeb Classical Library, for permission to make extensive quotations, mentioned in the notes to this book, from volumes of that Library ; and to the Clarendon Press, Oxford, for permission to quote at some length from A. S. L. Farquharson's *The Meditations of the Emperor Marcus Antoninus*, and from Nestorius' *The Bazaar of Heracleides*, translated from the Syriac by G. R. Driver and L. Hodgson.

FROM THE PREFACE TO THE FIRST EDITION

At the suggestion of Professor Walter Simon, a member of the City Council of Königsberg (the City of Kant), the Berlin Academy of Science formulated the theme of a history of autobiography.* That provided the occasion for the writing of this book. Of the three volumes proposed to the Academy, this book represents the first. The second volume, which will follow shortly, deals with the development of autobiography in mediæval and more modern times, down to the seventeenth century; the third volume will carry down to the present day. Appearing in isolation as they do, autobiographies demand for their appreciation, and, indeed, for their description, a comprehensive view of the development of the human mind. This could not be found, as was done in the positivist school of history that culminated in Taine, in the natural conditions of human existence, which, after all, lead only to uniformities; the effort had to be made to grasp the unseen conditions and interconnexions at work in the history of the mind in this special section of intellectual life; these led mainly to the consideration of the growth in Western civilization of man's awareness of personality. In attacking this problem the author was started on his way by the German conception of a universal history of man's religious, philosophical, and moral ideas, the methodical foundation of which is associated with the name of Wilhelm Dilthey. The present book is dedicated to him in gratitude and veneration.

In undertaking to define the limits of a literary *genre* for the first time, the complete freedom of movement had its disadvantages; in the almost unexplored field the discovery of material was largely dependent on chance. Much will have escaped me, and in view of the wide range of literature dealing with autobiography I should be thankful for any information sent to me. I am indebted already to various scholars for information, including Gustav Gröber, Friedrich Leo, A. Morel-Fatio, and Vittorio Rossi. For this volume I am, however, especially indebted to Professor Paul Wendland, who read the manuscript and made many valuable contributions, and to Dr. Herman Nohl, who very kindly attended to the proofs.

CHARLOTTENBURG,   GEORG MISCH.

August, 1907.

* *Sitzngsberichte der Kgl. Preuss. Akad. der Wiss.*, 1900, p. 55; 1905, pp. 686-7.

FROM THE PREFACE TO THE SECOND EDITION

This new edition of the present volume appears almost a quarter of a century after the first edition. Apart from corrections and a few additions, it is a reissue unchanged, to make the book available again after being out of print for some years. To touch a completed work after so long a period would have involved either wholesale changes or complete rewriting. And I was not prepared for either. The present state of the German book market demands, moreover, the utmost economy, so that it was desirable to keep alterations to the minimum.

This is not the place for an enumeration of the various contributions to the literature of the subject. But I must make mention of the work of Friedrich Leo. Anyone who reads the pages devoted to autobiographical writings in the comprehensive account of " archaic literature " that formed the first volume of his *History of Roman Literature* (vol. I, 1913, pp. 341 *sqq.*) will have realized what a wealth of profound discussion would have been accorded to us if Leo had lived to complete the work. And in the matter of general principles we see how that true philologist was occupied with the essential difference between Roman and Greek self-portrayal. He expressed it thus : " Original matter " (*Das Ursprüngliche* as he called it, meaning the fundamental elements of human existence) " was to the Greek mind merely material with which daily life went to work ; it attained to an existence of its own only when it had passed through the retorts of art," or when scientific interest was brought to play on it. " In this inclination of the Greek mind to the typical lies the reason why the Greeks had no autobiography . . . The Romans did not feel the same aversion " (to dealing with those elements).

Such statements tempted me to define that difference, with which I, too, was concerned, with greater precision. But if the whole work was to remain unaltered, I had to do without the additions which I should have liked to make. This applies especially to Plato's epistles, and the Seventh Epistle above all, which would not have been left out of account originally but for the view then held that the epistles were not genuine and for the imposing authority for the opinion that the rightness of that view had been established by philological research. Cæsar's Commentaries, too, ought to have been dealt with more fully, in spite of the principle adopted that memoirs should be excluded from the scope of a history of autobiography ; this had been pointed out at once by Friedrich Gundolf in his review of this volume (*Preussische Jahrbücher*, 1908, pp. 336–7), which remains in my memory as a sign of our common efforts at that time. And then there were the many suggestions set forth by the famous classical scholar Ulrich von Wilamowitz-Moellendorff when he presented the young author with a long review of the book in which the main results arrived at and the main features of the work were summarized (" Die Autobiographie im Altertum," *Internat. Wochenschrift für Wissenschaft* usw. (1907), I, pp. 1105 *sqq.*). One of his most instructive indications concerning " the limits of Greek thought " in the conception of human individuality should not remain unavailed of. " We must not overlook the fact," declared von Wilamowitz, " that just as the Hellenes produced no real historical works, they were unable to conceive an individual man in the full reality of his existence." And he added : " We will not ask here how it is that the Hellenes developed in that way : in those of the sixth and fifth centuries lay the capacity for an entirely different development." That was a call for the more thorough investigation of the early Greek " archaic " poetry with regard to its awareness of personality. And it is hard to refrain from tackling that task, for which all the material is now available. The opportunity will come, however, for returning to it in the continuation of our history. For the poetic self-portrayals of the early Middle Ages are in fact comparable with those Greek works, and in mediæval poetry we can observe the course that led from that primitive type of self-portrayal to autobiographical compositions which also were of poetic character.

GEORG MISCH.

GÖTTINGEN,
January, 1931.

CONTENTS OF VOLUME I

Part II

AUTOBIOGRAPHY IN THE HELLENISTIC AND GRECO-ROMAN WORLD

INTRODUCTION

I

CONCEPTION AND ORIGIN OF AUTOBIOGRAPHY

Since the epoch of the Enlightenment in England, France, and Germany, various writers have recognized the importance of the literature of autobiography and have made it the subject of learned works. In the age of the Renaissance some humanists, drawn to the study of this literature by their interest in the auto-biographers of ancient times, whom they took as their models in their own art of self-portrayal, had been the first to arrive at an objective view of the cultural phenomenon of autobiography, treating it both from a bibliographical and from a psychological standpoint. In the eighteenth century, which had before it as a complete body of works the great autobiographies of the Renaissance, the sense of the value of autobiographies grew under the influence both of inner experience and of historical reflection. There was a demand for the " confessions " of outstanding men, and collections of these were issued ; the more familiar works were surveyed and the attempt was made to classify them. In these efforts historians, philosophers, and poets, some of them of the very highest eminence, took part. Gibbon, Herder, Goethe themselves excelled as autobiographers.

In the course of this process various points of view emerged in regard to the assessment of autobiographical literature. Its documentary value for knowledge of the world and of man was accorded recognition ; it was seen as a merit that individual lives were treated in all their apparently petty but often really significant details, and the utility of these works was emphasized : they did not merely aim at the reader's amusement but might improve him and do him some service, either by way of instruction or of warning.[1]

Edward Gibbon, the famous representative of the great school of English historiography that grew in the eighteenth century out of David Hume's empiricist philosophy, gave similar expression, at the outset of his *Memoirs of his Life and Writings* (c. 1789), to his view of the importance of this branch of literature : " It would not be difficult to produce a long list of ancients and

moderns who, in various forms, have exhibited their own portraits. Such portraits are often the most interesting, and sometimes the only interesting parts of their writings ; and if they
be sincere, we seldom complain of the minuteness or prolixity of
these personal memoirs."

He was aware that a narrative of his own life would subject
him, " and perhaps with justice ", to the imputation of vanity,
and defends his enterprise from that charge :

I may judge from the experience both of past and of the present
times, that the public are always curious to know the men who have
left behind them any image of their minds : the most scanty accounts
of such men are compiled with diligence, and perused with eagerness ;
and the student of every class may derive a lesson, or an example,
from the lives most similar to his own. My name may hereafter be
placed among the thousand articles of a Biographia Britannica ; and
I must be conscious that no one is so well qualified as myself to describe
the series of my thoughts and actions.

Thus there were developed from the spirit of the Enlightenment, for the assessment of the value of autobiography, the points
of view that corresponded to the psychological and moral interest
which predominated in that epoch. Meanwhile in Herder, the
German poet and thinker, a deeper historical view found expression—a view influenced by the idea of the development of human
civilization. Herder induced a number of scholars to collect the
most outstanding autobiographies from different countries and
ages, and in his preface to one of these collections, which began
to appear in Germany about 1790, he suggested that a " Library
of Writers on Themselves " would form an excellent " con-
tribution to the history of mankind ".

Goethe then conceived the idea of a " Collation of the
so-called Confessions of all ages " : light would thus be thrown
upon the great process of the liberation of human personality.

With the renewal of human studies in the nineteenth century,
the scientific interest in autobiography became specialized.
Autobiography then acquired a fixed place among the sources
of psychology and history ; in the collections of autobiographical
works and in the elaboration from them of a historical narrative
the interest in a certain type of social history, usually confined
to the compilers' own nation, predominated. This type was
chiefly concerned with the production of vivid pictures of the
varying conditions of human life in the different ages ; the
material for these pictures was to be found in the autobiographies.

But the individual value of this branch was also more clearly recognized. In this recognition again the historiography and the attitude to civilization of the empiricist (called in France the positive) philosophy led the way ; its exponents regarded the Confessions of unique personalities as one of the finest products of a highly cultivated society. Thus the conception of the *document humain* was given definition by the Goncourts ; Taine set the Confessions of an *homme supérieur*, in which he found the concentrated expression of the nature of an individual, an age, a race, far above the official and documentary material of the historians, alongside great imaginative writing of the type of the Aristophanic comedy ; and Jacob Burckhardt, the eminent Swiss historian, who was filled with the Romance spirit, established, in his standard work *Die Kultur der Renaissance in Italien*, the importance of autobiography for the development and the recognition of individuality.

In the history of literature, too, research was directed in the course of the nineteenth century to autobiographical writings, sometimes with regard to particular works of this branch which had a high place in the literature of nations, such as Dante's *Vita Nuova* and Benvenuto Cellini's *Vita* in Italian literature, Lord Clarendon's *History of the Rebellion* in English, Rousseau's *Confessions* in French, and Goethe's *Dichtung und Wahrheit* in German ; sometimes in connexion with the general problems involved in the development of the psychological and social works of fiction of modern times, problems which may be found alluded to by Balzac, the creator of the modern novel proper, when he declares that " the most moving novels are autobiographical studies, or narratives of events submerged in the ocean of the world ".

If we survey the various efforts we have noted, we may say that in them a comprehensive treatment of the multifarious material was in preparation, however unrelated they may have been in their concurrent or successive appearance. The present book attempts such a treatment. On the lines recommended by Goethe, the autobiographical writings in various European languages are here studied as revealing the ways in which the individual's sense of personality has developed in the Western world. Since the formation of personality depends both on the contemporary social environment and on the self-awareness of the individual, autobiography has two claims to consideration— as a special *genre* in literature, and as an original interpretation of experience. The purpose of this book is to relate the limitless variety of autobiographical writing to the history of the human mind, and to present it in a historical perspective.

Autobiography is unlike any other form of literary composition. Its boundaries are more fluid and less definable in relation to form than those of lyric or epic poetry or of drama, which, in spite of variations from age to age, from nation to nation, and from work to work, have preserved unity of form throughout their development, since their first emergence from the obscure and undifferentiated beginnings of literature. Autobiography is one of the innovations brought by cultural advance, and yet it springs from the most natural source, the joy in self-communication and in enlisting the sympathetic understanding of others ; or the need for self-assertion. In itself it is a representation of life that is committed to no definite form. It abounds in fresh initiatives, drawn from actual life : it adopts the different forms with which different periods provide the individual for his self-revelation and self-portrayal—in inscriptions on monuments, in the public life of the city-state and the law-courts or in the privacy of the confessional, in the spiritual intercourse of religious persons or in the domestic records of a merchant aristocracy. It was only at a late stage of development, in that last epoch of the Greek and Roman world when the classical system had broken down, that autobiography freed itself from all dependence on outward circumstances, and even in that late period, when creative power was failing in other fields, it proved capable of great original works.

Hardly any form is alien to it. Historical record of achievements, imaginary forensic addresses or rhetorical declamations, systematic or epigrammatic description of character, lyrical poetry, prayer, soliloquy, confessions, letters, literary portraiture, family chronicle and court memoirs, narrative whether purely factual or with a purpose, explanatory or fictional, novel and biography in their various styles, epic and even drama—all these forms have been made use of by autobiographers ; and if they were persons of originality they modified the existing types of literary composition or even invented new forms of their own.

This wealth of forms itself shows what life there is in the autobiographical *genre*. It is this that is mainly responsible—paradoxically, almost more than the content of the works—for the peculiar service it renders to the knowledge of what man is. In the epoch of the Enlightenment, when the importance of autobiography was recognized, it was still believed that man's nature was fixed and identical everywhere and at all times, and accessible to purely psychological analysis. In this sense Pope coined the phrase : " The proper study of mankind is man." In the nineteenth century that belief was destroyed by the historical consciousness which was acquired by the educated as " a sixth sense ", as Nietzsche put it. Dilthey, the philosopher of the German historical school, wrote : " Man's type is dissolved in the flow of history." There remained the task of determining the fixed in the fluid, as the banks are reflected in the river or a path is formed by treading it. The man who essays to write a history of autobiography finds himself face to face with this task. For he has before him not only the infinite natural multiplicity of individual life but also the historically determined multiplicity of its forms of presentation ; and he has to seek the point at which those forms come together into a unity—if history is to be more than a gallery hung with pictures of the ever-changing aspects of life.

In point of fact the body of autobiographical writings, when viewed as a whole, reveals at first a Protean character. This genre of literature defies classification even more stubbornly than do the ordinary forms of creative writing. It can be defined only by summarizing what the term " autobiography " implies —the description (*graphia*) of an individual human life (*bios*) by the individual himself (*auto-*).

The term is of recent date. It made its appearance only about the end of the eighteenth century, first, apparently, in German literature, then in English—a word formed artificially, like the technical terms of science, with the aid of the ancient Greek language : who coined it is not known.* But this term of relatively recent formation, with its scholarly association, only raises to the level of clear and distinct consciousness a practice

* The expression is first met with in the title of one of the collections suggested by J. G. Herder—*Selbstbiographieen berühmter Männer* (" Self-biographies of Famous Men "), compiled by Professor Seybold, *I. Thuanus* ; *II. Andreä* (Tübingen, 1796 and 1799).

In his *Grand Dictionnaire Universel du XIX. Siècle* (1864), Pierre Larousse notes under the word " Autobiographie " : " This word, though of Greek origin, is of English manufacture." For this statement he gives no evidence. The great Oxford Dictionary gives as the earliest known use of the term a sentence of Robert Southey in the first volume of the *Quarterly Review* (1809). In his article Southey gives a general sketch of Portuguese literature, and in the course of it he refers to a long-forgotten book by a Portuguese painter on his own life, and describes it as a " very amusing and unique specimen of auto-biography ". The use of the hyphen suggests that the word was not then in common use. It might have been assumed that it was invented by Southey himself, or in any case by one or other of the accomplished that has continued through the literatures of all ages as something natural and human, perhaps all too human. In the literature of various races, not only European but also, for instance, Far Eastern, there appear at a certain stage of development writings of the autobiographical type, and the tendency to self-portrayal which they reveal may be traced farther back to the remote age of recording in which there did not yet exist a " literature " in the sense of written works. This tendency was taken as the characteristic mark of the *genre* by the unknown scholar who coined the word " autobiography ", thereby defining that individual kind of writing as a special class of biography.

It was not the only term. The word came into currency, in the course of the nineteenth century, in place of the earlier customary name of " memoirs ". The traditional name has a deeper meaning, in so far as it has reference to the psychological source of history—and, in the view of the classical Greeks, even of poetry—in the memory, but it was not used in this sense but in a more superficial one, with reference to the peculiarly loose and apparently unregulated method pursued by the writings known as Memoirs. In this application the word of French origin corresponds to the Latin *commentarii*, which in turn served as a reproduction of a Greek conception (*hypomnemata*), as we shall see shortly. This conception includes a definite type of writings irrespective of their content—those only sketched or written without care. Thus the word " memoirs " has no personal connotation, or at least had none originally or until recent times. It can serve as a title for notes of purely factual content, such as official reports of business done or the proceedings of a learned society, just as well as for an autobiographical record. In the latter sense men spoke and probably still speak of *personal*

---

littérateurs and erudite scholars among whom he moved, were it not already to be found ten years earlier in the title of the collection edited by the Tübingen professor of literature.

It was only gradually that the term gained the comprehensive meaning, relating to this whole class of literature, which it has today in all European languages. Seybold's collection, of which only the first two volumes were published, was intended as a " pendant " to another, also suggested by Herder, with the title *Bekenntnisse merkwürdiger Männer von sich selbst* (" Confessions of remarkable men about themselves "). Herder himself, in his preface to this collection, drew a distinction between the " Confessions " (*Confessionen*), whether specifically religious or " humanly philosophical ", and the actual " life-stories " (*Lebensbeschreibungen*) written by remarkable men about themselves. Goethe, who had the whole genre in view, spoke, as we saw, in this broad sense of the " so-called confessions " of all ages.

We shall return to this point when we deal with the development of autobiography in modern times. To this development belongs the process in the course of which the genre was recognized and named as such.

memoirs.   In itself the word simply expresses the unpretentiousness of the writing in question in the matter of literary form, implying that the author has or affects to have no intention at all of coming forward as a literary person.   He proposes only to supply material for a literary work that may be compiled by a future historian, or serve for research in other ways.

The term "autobiography", on the other hand, conveys nothing in regard to the literary form or the standing of this sort of work in relation to great literature ; its main implication is that the person whose life is described is himself the author of the work.

It is on this identity of author and subject that is based the great interest we moderns have in autobiography.   From this point of view this chameleon-like *genre* secures a unity that it does not possess in literary form.   And from this element of unity proceed the substantial merits of the *genre*.   The autobiographer has as a matter of course all the facts of his career in his possession, where the " heterobiographer "—if the term may be permitted—can acquire them only by study and never completely.   Together with the recollection of the facts there will spontaneously awake in the mind of the autobiographer the emotional feelings that were produced by their occurrence, whereas the " heterobiographer " must possess a high degree of sympathy and imagination in order to represent in his narrative the feelings aroused by the events described.   Finally, the man who sets out to write the story of his own life has it in view as a whole, with unity and direction and a significance of its own. In this single whole the facts and feelings, actions and reactions, recalled by the author, the incidents that excited him, the persons he met, and the transactions or movements in which he was concerned, all have their definite place, thanks to their significance in relation to the whole.   He himself knows the significance of his experiences, whether he mentions it or not ; he only understands his life through the significance he attaches to them.   This knowledge, which enables the writer to conceive his life as a single whole, has grown in the course of his life out of his actual experience, whereas we have the life of any other person before us as a whole only *ex post facto* : the man is dead, or at all events it is all past history.

This element in autobiography is a fundamental advantage. It gives it a measure of philosophical dignity.   In the words of W. Dilthey, the German thinker to whom we owe a philosophical basing of human studies on a historical philosophy of life : " Autobiography is the highest and most instructive form in which the understanding of life comes before us." [2] The understanding of " life "—that is, of human life as actually lived by individuals, and of the social and historical " world " in which they live—is the great, inexhaustible task in whose execution philosophers compete with poets and religious thinkers and, on the other hand, find themselves assisted by the detailed work of the various human studies.   Within this boundless realm of human inquiry and meditation, autobiography has its place— it is not merely what its modern name might suggest, a sub-division of biography.   And the special place it takes in the field of human knowledge depends, in the philosopher's view, on the fact that in it " the subject inquiring is also the object inquired into "—" the historian who tells the story is the same who has already lived it and knows it from within in a quite peculiar way ".*

As a manifestation of man's knowledge of himself, auto-biography has its basis in the fundamental—and enigmatical— psychological phenomenon which we call consciousness of self or self-awareness (in German *Selbstbewusstsein*).   Our life in the world does not pass simply as a natural process, a continuity of actions, feelings, and reactions (" *vita motus perpetuus* ") ; we live it con-sciously, consciousness of self and consciousness of the world around us being both primordial, both the products of one and the same mental activity.   In a certain sense the history of autobiography is a history of human self-awareness.

It is true that consciousness is not conterminous with life. There is subconscious as well as conscious life.   Indeed, even the knowledge we have acquired can be " unconscious " in so far as it does not emerge in the spoken word but lies outside the sphere of speech.   Autobiographies in which there is no trace of this hidden, unexpressed knowledge seem to us superficial or intellectually attenuated.

> The human heart has hidden treasures
> In secret kept, in silence sealed ;—
> The thoughts, the hopes, the dreams, the pleasures
> Whose charms were broken if revealed. [3]

But it is of the very essence of human existence that we can raise to the clarity of consciousness that which moves us " deep

---

* Formulations by Professor H. A. Hodges in his *Wilhelm Dilthey : an Introduction* London 1944).

down ". We live in possession of ourselves, after the special manner of a being conscious of itself and capable of saying " I. " To stand as an I, or, more exactly, as an " I "-saying person, over against other persons and living beings and the things around us implies that we are aware of our independent existence, we do not merely impart impulses and perform acts as things of elementary existence, but as living beings we have knowledge of our impulses and actions as our own. Self-awareness gives us the feeling that the impetus of life is a sort of emanation from ourselves. Apart from this knowledge of ourselves it would seem incomprehensible that man should be able to detach himself from the urgency of practical life and come to reflect upon the meaning of his actions.

Growing from this psychological root, the self-revelation of the personality takes on the most various forms according to the epoch and the individual or social situation. In addition to this variation from epoch to epoch, the psychological source from which autobiographies spring ever anew seems itself to vary. When trying to define it we are confronted with different aspects of what may at bottom be one and the same motive. The most universal aspect is a man's need for self-revelation. This, however, is so comprehensive that it is applicable not only to autobiographies of every sort, confessions, apologias, or simple narratives, but also to the works which a creative writer brings forth out of himself as something objective, such as Shakespeare's sonnets, or the lyrics of Goethe, or even Dante's *Divina Commedia*. These works exist independently of the author's person and have no need of reference to his own life in order to be understood, and yet they are self-portrayals in the sense that in them the personality of the poet or thinker is preserved, that his " spirit " is " objectivated " in them. Thus a modern artist may declare with reference to his own creative work : " There is no joy in the world like the expression of oneself, of one's ego, in whatever medium you choose." [4]

A sceptical observer of the world of men will give a different interpretation of the causes of autobiographical writing. He will smile at the way men talk as a matter of course of their " self " or " ego ". He recognizes that it is owing to the self-awareness peculiar to man that the individual with his bodily frame feels himself and is felt by others to be a person ; but he smiles at the naïve idea that places an ego at the back of that psychic phenomenon, as a solid and concrete thing that remains constant

in spite of the changes of life from birth to death.   Against this
he may point to the original meaning of *persona*—a mask, especially
that used by players, being varied according to the different
characters to be represented ;   or, more generally, and transferred beyond the language of drama, the part or character which
anyone sustains in the world or which is imposed upon him by
social or political circumstances.   Thus for the sceptic that joy
in the expression of one's ego is reduced to the joy in the part
we played on the stage of life, a rôle of which, like the actors,
we should like to make the public believe that " we ourselves "
are what we were playing.

Or a biologist may explain the need for self-assertion that
comes into play in the making of autobiographies, manifesting
itself especially in the defence against calumny and the like,
by the instinct for self-preservation, and in general by the struggle
for life, in which victory is rare and frustration the rule.   It is
natural to men to rejoice in victory.   But the urge to talk about
their lives is felt even more when they are smarting under the
frustration of their hopes of accomplishment.   The shipwrecked
want to save from the wreckage an idealized picture of themselves, to show to the world or simply to themselves, either
in order to hide their frustration from themselves or with the
honourable intention of living in accordance with their ideal, our
character being developed through pain and sorrow.   However
they may be conceived, we meet here with natural human
motives, which are strong enough, or at least may be, to overcome the equally natural repugnance which might restrain a
healthy-minded person from " giving himself away ".

Thus, both in regard to its sources in human self-awareness
and in regard to its service to the understanding of life, autobiography appears to be not only a special kind of literature
but also an instrument of knowledge.   When we approach these
entertaining works in the interest of knowledge, the question
arises how much truth there is in them.   This question will need
answering in regard to each of the outstanding autobiographies
on which we shall dwell.   All we will say at the moment is that
in general their truth is to be sought not so much in their elements
as in the whole works, each of which is more than the sum of
its parts.   As regards the various parts of the works, the most
honest autobiographer who is writing a " confession " and not
an apologia, or who writes not for publication but for his own
pleasure or for the entertainment and instruction of his descen-

dants, will be silent on various characteristic details, because probably everybody has a sore spot in his self-awareness which he will not want to touch.   On the other hand, even the cleverest liar, in his fabricated or embroidered stories of himself, will be unable to deceive us as to his character.   He will reveal it through the spirit of his lies.   Thus, in general, the spirit brooding over the recollected material is the truest and most real element in an autobiography.   This spirit is visibly written on the face of the incidents and persons of whom the autobiographer writes ; it is palpable in the way he conceives his life as a whole and builds up his account of it, in his selection of details for emphasis and the weight he places upon the important and the trifling— in short, in what we may call the " style ", in the broadest sense of the word, or, to use a less hackneyed term, the " inner form ",[5] the form imposed or welling up from within, in distinction from such externally, environmentally imposed literary forms as historical record, apologia, letters, soliloquy, confession, and so on. Buffon's famous phrase *Le style c'est l'homme* may be given this wide interpretation.

Behind all creative work in philosophy or poetry, art or religion, behind even the most abstract systems of ideas, our sense of reality detects the man himself.   We love diaries and letters as the most revealing of human documents, seeming to preserve most faithfully the actuality of life by the formless picture of its passing moments—and yet there is nothing truer or more revealing than the inner form.   In autobiography it can be most revealing, because recollection, growing out of the vivid personal experience, and thus eliciting its meaning, in the way we have sketched, performs its creative work in accord with the man's intentions as worked out in his life, and so gives the recollected material form from within.

It is an admitted psychological fact that remembrance does not proceed as mechanical reproduction but tends to creation. Hence autobiographies are not to be regarded as objective narratives.   To regard them as merely sources of special historical information is usually to misconceive the character of this *genre*. The actual events of a life, outward and inward alike, tend, indeed, to lose purely historical value for the very reason that they are recorded as the events of the narrator's own life, and every autobiography can be shown to be deficient in detailed accuracy.   Our most ordinary recollections are impregnated in our own minds by distorting influences, and rarely remain free

from self-deception ; so that the whole body of recollections in
an autobiography, even when it is entirely free from tendencious-
ness, must of necessity be regarded with scepticism. External
facts that interest us as elements of the history of civilization,
and also political events that need no interpretation in order to
reveal their importance, may often be faithfully recorded,* and
are so in periods or societies relying on factual knowledge—for
instance, in such urbane cultures as that of England in the
seventeenth and eighteenth centuries ; but in the reproduction
of inward and especially of religious experiences, autobiography
is a field of auto-delusion. How, indeed, can it possibly bear
witness to anything more than the extent of the self-knowledge
of the individual at the time when, looking back on the past,
he attempts to survey and assess his life as a whole ?

Yet it is just through this welling up from the most intimate
contemporary life of the individual, which includes the past
within itself, that autobiography acquires its own peculiar power,
through which it can attain the truthfulness of poetry without
losing its hold on material facts. Empirical contemplation of
reality affords a comprehensive view only at moments of exaltation : this heightened awareness, shaping its story, while re-living
it, from the present and past seen as a whole, produces a creative
objectivation of the autobiographer's mind that cannot be other
than true. The more style his work has, the farther it is from
mere stylized narrative. The latter breaks in only when the
individual's presentation of himself becomes merely literary or
is no longer taken seriously by him.

Though essentially representations of individual personalities,
autobiographies are bound always to be representative of their
period, within a range that will vary with the intensity of the
authors' participation in contemporary life and with the sphere
in which they moved. In works of inferior quality, which take
their literary form from some other branch of literature, the form
adopted is one of those prevailing at the time, those corresponding
to the average contemporary way or ideal of life. But when an
autobiography is produced independently, out of his own life

---

* Pierre Larousse remarks (1864) that " many errors accepted and facts distorted
even by historians of talent, who are often over-ready to take what they find at its
face value, are rectified at once and given a different aspect by the publication of
some small autobiographical document " (" Nombre d'erreurs accréditées et de faits
dénaturés par les historiens, souvent doués d'autant de complaisance que de talent,
se sont tout d'un coup rectifiés et placés sous un autre point de vue par la publication
d'un petit document autobiographique "). *Grand Dictionnaire Universel*, art. " Autobiographie ".

and by the application of his own gifts, by a person of exceptional calibre, it provides a supreme example of representation—the contemporary intellectual outlook revealed in the style of an eminent person who has himself played a part in the forming of the spirit of his time.

In this exemplary form of autobiography, personality is to be seen and felt not only as the subject of the narrative but as a formative power, just as the personality of the artist is seen and felt—so to say, objectively—in any great work of art. Even in the liberties he takes with the so-called " facts ", or biographical data, the great autobiographer can do creative work that is representative of his time. For in the various ages the historical process leads ever anew, as Dilthey has shown, from factual conditions to the production of spiritual values out of them, and this process of sublimation is reflected in the picture a man gives of the actualities of his life, showing the lasting significance of his life-story through his awareness of what was valuable in it.

Thus the characteristic self-revelations provide us with an objective, indeed, a demonstrable image of the structure of individuality, varying from epoch to epoch. Accordingly a history of autobiography offers an alluring prospect : as men's accounts of their concrete existence follow one another, whether they are merely stereotyped or show a personality in its individual manifestation, there pass vividly before us in a continuous series of self-portrayals the permanence and the changefulness of the values of life. In this way autobiographical works, while to all appearance emerging by chance, and associated only through relations of literary form, make up an intrinsically connected series, which enables autobiography to be comprehended as a kind of organic whole that has developed constantly with the general civilization of the various ages and peoples, down to our own day.

But it is not simply through the continuity of the history of the European mind that autobiographies, those individualistic productions, are brought together into a unity. This linking they share with every section of intellectual life, which in its empirically ascertainable course through the ages acquired its inner consistency through the comprehensive process in which the distinct type of Western Man was formed. Moreover, autobiography possesses structure in itself, because it has various inter-associated functions in life ; owing to these functions its composite unity has grown and found realization in its relation to the ever new awareness and the progressive evaluation of personality in history ; and so has been built up the coherence that unites the autobiographical works of the different epochs and nations and individuals into a historically developing generic whole.

Kein Lebendiges ist eins :
Immer ist's ein Vieles

—" Nothing that lives is single : always it is multiple " (Goethe).

Multiple are the sources from which autobiography proceeds as a manifestation of life. They are not to be reduced to the impulses that lead the individual to the exposition of his own ego, such as vanity, desire for fame or for contemporary notoriety, the joy in story-telling, the love of discussion of human affairs, the urge to self-justification or to confession, and the like. On the whole, autobiography is not of this petty order. Its proper classification arises from the structure of its subject-matter, of life as actually lived. Human life is relationship, its basic relations being those of the individual as a being aware of himself, a " person ", to other persons and to his natural and spiritual surroundings or to the " world " he lives in. In the manifold nature of this relationship the central interest may shift to and fro, and so simple clear-cut points of departure for autobiography may be distinguished—though these distinctions find clear definition only in extreme cases. For the attitudes towards existence which we contrast with one another in the abstract are in reality linked together as a rule by transitional ones.

The most general contrast is formed by the *sinking* of the individual into his own depths and the *spreading* of his interest among outward experiences in the manifold pleasure men find in their own and other men's dealings with the world. We may call this kind of human immersion in the self introspection, or meditation on the self, or self-communion or self-scrutiny or, with special reference to autobiography, " reconsideration of recollections " [6]—to indicate in a phrase the spiritual attitude expressed by the profound German word *Selbstbesinnung*. Among the special relationships in life it is chiefly the self-assertion of the political will and the relation of the author to his work and to the public that show themselves to be normative in the history of autobiography. These main elements have each its own continuity in the evolution of the literary forms used by the autobiographers ; but they are also interassociated, since in surveying his existence a man may proceed from within or from without, and in the latter case especially from his social environment ; and, if he has accomplished anything, either by exerting a formative influence on his contemporaries or by producing works of his own, he concerns himself with this achievement of his.

Man's relation to the world may be conceived actively or passively. From this consideration comes the distinction between autobiographies and " memoirs " (using the latter word with the personal connotation that has become current since the nineteenth century). In memoirs that relation is passive in so far as the writers of memoirs (although like the autobiographers, and even more exclusively, they use the form of the first-personal narrative) introduce themselves in the main as merely observers of the events and activities of which they write, and if they join the active participants it is only in minor parts. What they tell of their own lives serves to explain how it was that they became involved in contemporary happenings or became witnesses of them—how it was that they had opportunities of meeting people of eminence, watching notable persons at close quarters, and gaining confidential information. The autobiographer concerns himself with such things only in so far as is necessary for the understanding of his life-story. This has its significance and its organic nature in itself and centres on the person of the author, even when he portrays himself not as the centre of activities but as the subject of a story of suffering.

Chief among the driving forces of autobiography is meditation on the self and on the world. This kind of meditation, again, has various aspects. In its relation to empirical reality, it appears as reflection on the character and the intercourse of human beings, on destiny and on trends of human life ; and it brings into prominence the sayings and teachings concerning the art of living, derived from shrewdness or from wisdom, which amount among the most different peoples to a beginning, however rudimentary, of human studies ; these reflections promote autobiography as soon as they advance to the stage of a practical philosophy concerned to make explicit the interrelations of human existence. On still more primitive soil there arises reflection upon man in the religious ideas which separate the soul from the mortal part of the individual : the deepening of these transcendental ideas leads to the doctrines of the journeyings of the soul in its search for Reality ; autobiography draws upon these doctrines at its higher spiritual levels. But in the Western world the most direct impulse to the growth of self-scrutiny arose from the formative influence upon life of the consciousness and the evaluation of personality. This consciousness is not part of the general inheritance of peoples ; it has been gradually acquired in the clear light of advancing civilization ; it exists in the most manifold forms and at all sorts of levels, and the other tendencies also, practical philosophy and aspiration toward the eternal, gain this-worldly perfection only through association with the sense of personality. In this way autobiography, through the meditative element in it, co-operates with the great spiritual forces in the freeing and deepening of human life.

All these trends are aspects of this attractive branch of literature, which is as many-sided as life itself. As they make their appearance, in turn or simultaneously, always in different ways and in terms of actual situations and yet intimately associated, now one and now another predominating, or all coming together, they provide our history with a thoroughgoing classification, broad enough to embrace the multiplicity of autobiographical forms and to recognize something regular, even necessary, in the development without impairing the peculiar value of the individual.

The structure we have described provides our history with a standard we need in order to appraise the significance of the first figures that provide us with the autobiographical *genre* in European literature. For here the facts are thinly sown. Barely eight full-length autobiographies, in the strict sense of the term, remain extant in Greek and Roman literature down to the time of Augustine, and the picture that would be gained from studying these alone, without reference to the deeper developments underlying them, would suggest that the ancient world refutes our conception of the nature of European autobiography. It would suggest that this conception is a false generalization based on the state of affairs in modern times.

To illustrate this, if one confined oneself to appearances, one would be led to take as the beginning the earliest work of an autobiographical kind and intention produced in Greek literature, a work by the famous rhetorician, or publicist, Isocrates. This would imply that autobiography arose within what was in the human sense a subordinate department of life, which is all that the Greek rhetorical profession was. And as the rhetorical attitude to the subject-matter was maintained from Isocrates onwards, this would not only seem to be a limitation of Greek historical literature, autobiographical writing being considered an occupation of the rhetorician rather than of the philosopher or poet, but would seem to indicate the very essence of ancient self-portrayal; it would suggest that autobiography did not strike deeper roots until the entry of Christianity into the ancient civilization.

This is the view generally held. The first great specimen of the *genre* is generally considered to be Augustine's *Confessions*. Before Augustine came Paul, and before Paul came the Old Testament poetry of the Psalms and the Prophets. Referred to this tradition, autobiography appears as emerging from religious inwardness, of which the Christian practice of self-examination is characteristic.

Augustine's work gained such immense repute that many other autobiographers emulated it, and their achievement makes a whole class of spiritual autobiography. Its main characteristic is its subjectivity in the contemplation of life, in contrast with the objectivity of earlier literatures including those of Greece and Rome. Those literatures are usually described as objective in the sense that they " reflect the mind as spreading itself out upon external things, instead of exhibiting the mind as introverting itself upon its thoughts and feelings ".[7] Thanks to the predominance of Christianity in the Western hemisphere, the subjective attitude forms a fundamental trait of the modern man ; as Descartes, the cardinal thinker of modern times, formulated the philosophical principle, following Augustine—*Cogito ergo sum* (" I think ; thus I am ") ; or as in the nineteenth century Kierkegaard, the solitary religious thinker who brought renewal to Protestant Christianity, declared : " The subjective is the true —the subjective and not the objective." Thus autobiography ranks in this view as an essentially modern *genre*, modern in the sense in which Augustine (A.D. 354–430) has been described by leading European historians as " the first modern man ". The secular autobiography that has competed with religious autobiography since the Renaissance is thus understood as a secularization of a Christian possession.

Convincing as this picture might seem at a first glance, it does not stand the test of historical research. In reality the channel for all the essential tendencies of autobiography was cut in the ancient world, and Augustine's work is not a beginning but a completion. The poverty of autobiographical writing in the classical epoch of Greek literature is a quite isolated phenomenon in the wider field of European civilization.   It requires explanation since Greece was the matrix of humanism in the Western world.   As we shall see, that peculiar phenomenon does not impair the significance of Greek humanism for the autobiographical attempt : this showed little of importance, but something new was in the making deeper down.

In so envisaging the problem of the Greeks' attitude towards autobiography we are all the more required to assure ourselves, at the outset, of the fact that the " passion for autobiography " which a modern European observer may detect in any " normal " human being is, in a sense, something natural, as the " nature " of man is revealed in history.   It is true that a history of autobiography, since it has to deal with the more complicated phenomena of mental life, cannot reach back to the primitive peoples.   But there is something " primitive " in its subject, in so far as autobiography is not only a department of literature but a method of self-assertion.   Bearing this in mind, we may seek in an early state of society for compositions tending in that direction.

Such compositions are, in fact, to be found in highly-wrought heroic poetry which precedes written literature.   They are, however, accessible to us only in the poetry of the forerunners of the civilized peoples that took over, in the so-called Middle Ages, the heritage of the ancient world, the poetry, for instance, of the Germanic tribes (including the Anglo-Saxons) before their conversion to Christianity, and of the Arab nomads before the appearance of Mohammed.   We shall, therefore, treat of those pre-literary compositions only in the latter part of our history, when the beginnings of autobiographical writing in the modern world come to be studied both in their dependence on the literary traditions of the Christian Middle Ages and in their relation to that genuine kind of self-portrayal of personality which had been produced in the early heroic poetry of those peoples.

As our first concern is with the development of autobiography in the Greek and Roman world, we adopt a different starting-point.   It is to the ancient civilizations of the Near and Middle East, which produced the first literary monuments known to us in our hemisphere, that we look for documents testifying to the existence of autobiography at a time previous to the new achievement of Greece.   However limited this beginning may be, it extends our horizon and makes it possible for us to appreciate the autobiographical achievements of later antiquity.

II

AUTOBIOGRAPHY IN THE ANCIENT CIVILIZATIONS
OF THE MIDDLE EAST

Unexpectedly numerous are the autobiographical documents which we find among the ancient civilized peoples of the Middle East, particularly those of the Egyptian and Babylonian-Assyrian civilizations. So numerous are they that if we could review them in their entirety they would be scarcely fewer than the fruits of this branch of literature among the classical and later peoples, down to the beginning of the massive autobiographical production of the late Renaissance—a roughly comparable period of some two thousand years.

But in all this abundance of material there is an infinite poverty of individual character. In all these documents we scarcely ever find any personal touch. They conform to one settled pattern. Their large measure of uniformity marks them as the product of established usages and of traditional forms of self-presentation.

Thus before the growth of a sense of individuality we meet with a stereotyped or, so to speak, collective kind of autobiography. These examples are the earliest we have, and they extend back into the second and third millenniums B.C. They present themselves to us in an already established form, in fully developed civilizations whose origin is buried in obscurity. Thus we can do no more than accept the fact of their existence, as data that reveal from the most distant antiquity the " passion for autobiography " which in modern minds is regarded as part of our common humanity.

It is indeed a remarkable glimpse that we thus catch of the nature of man in far-off times, when his awareness of his actions was not yet accompanied by a sense of responsibility for them. It reveals to us potentialities of human nature that are in strange contrast with our European attitude toward the individual self, which we owe to Greek philosophy and to the Christian religion. Some of the documents confront us with immoderate, even brutally vigorous, self-glorification, to a degree unique in history, as is also the degree of the majesty and omnipotence, and the courtierly subservience, out of which the oriental despots, along with the heads of their administration, speak to us in these documents. Self-glorification has never since appeared with such naïveté, or with such entire exclusion of all else.

But in all the strangeness there remains something that strikes us as strange only in its form of expression. These oriental documents exhibit a definite type of biographical conception, which is largely characteristic of ancient self-portrayal : in it the writer's review of his life is directed, without any idea of development, entirely to the moments when, in his judgment, he was at his best, and these moments are projected on to a single plane, so that he emphasizes that part of his particular existence which he considers worthy of permanent record, whether a sum-total of power and glory and pleasure or, as in later times, his character. Moreover, some primary and permanent motives for self-portrayal first begin to be discernible. Out of the concern of the living person for his life after death there spread among the Egyptians, in connexion with the religious observances intended to ensure the continued existence of the departed, the custom of autobiographical recording. Then, especially in the Babylonian and Assyrian inscriptions, we meet with the motive which is a special point of departure for historical literature— the great erect lasting monuments to themselves, to proclaim the glory of their name and of their deeds to their contemporaries and to posterity. In both cases the written word usually appears in association with pictorial representation. Finally, we become aware of a very general element of form—the practice of narrative in the first person, the hero of historical and even of fictitious narratives being at the same time their narrator. This method of presentation, which has had such influence in world literature, meets us here as already an ancient and perhaps primeval form.

I. Egyptian Tomb-Inscriptions

Today we see the Egyptian religion in a baffling cross-light: on the one hand there is a traditional attitude of reverence, attributing measureless wisdom and profundity to the intellectual works of that very ancient civilization, and on the other a realistic view, not yet fully developed, that recognizes their practical purpose and justification, but perceives in them even a " childish " self-mystification, in spite of the strangely powerful impression they make on us. This much, however, is quite certain : in the religious notions of the Egyptians, which had a more powerful influence than anything else on their history, the cult of the dead, one of the main roots of all religious life, took the central place in a very remarkable way. Around this central element there then crystallized continuously such impulses toward biography as were fostered among the Egyptians. And yet these biographies have no spiritual or religious content, but are concerned with secular pleasures and occupations and with the glorification of deeds and of careers, until at last the moralistic element enters. It is as though history wished to remind us, with disconcerting directness, of the irrational nature of man : in the habitations of the dead, autobiography begins with the commonplaces of life.

The earth-bound ideas of the ancient Egyptians about the life after death persisted always in the midst of the growth of speculation concerning God and the soul, so that immortality in the next world was conceived as the perpetuation of the individual's this-worldly existence. Among other peoples similar ideas produced a similar care for the supposed existence of the dead, but nowhere was such a cult worked out with such determination through thousands of years, enlisting in its service the instruments of a high civilization, especially writing and the arts. As the life of the upper classes grew easier and brighter, it found representation in pictures of lively funeral feasts and in other decorations in the tombs, so that at the end of the second millennium B.C. the tombs " appear almost as monuments of a glorious life." [1]

Familiar are the vast burial places bult by the Pharaohs and by the mighty of their realm, great landowners and high officials, to whom as a rule the kings granted the means for their erection —as a " dwelling-place for eternity ", in the Egyptians' phrase. If we consider these pyramids, mastabas, rock-hewn tombs, and whole cities of dwellings of the dead, in which the " Lord of the Tomb " received worship from his descendants and even from priests of his own, we obtain an impressive measure of the intensity of the religious belief underlying this custom. All peoples, on attaining a certain cultural level, develop vague fears or hopes with regard to the incomprehensible fact of death, and conceive ideas such as that of a " soul " that outlasts man's mortal element ; but from of old the Egyptians, amid their crowding mass of ideas about the future life, had one fixed assumption—that the actual bodily frame of the dead person had to be preserved. For them the soul, when it entered Heaven, passed into a life like that on earth but permanent and of paradisaical splendour ;

a second soul, a ghostly one, might go to the underworld and rest there, or move among men in one shape or another ; but they hoped also for at least a temporary revivification of the body. Thus they distinguished, in addition to the soul, a special vital force, invisible and entirely indeterminate, which, like the soul, did not pass away for all time at death. They had a name for it—it was the individual's " Ka "—and his portrait-statue was their means of giving tangible existence to the invisible for the purposes of their ritual. It was for the sake of this Ka that the tombs were built and tended ; a tomb was called " The House of the Ka ".

Now, for the very purpose of being able to fulfil its function, and to become united again with the body of the deceased, the Ka was dependent upon the preservation of the body ; thus, for the sake of this union, the body needed nourishment. The cult of the dead started from the concern for this. The mummy was hidden for all time in an inaccessible shaft in the burial-chamber, in a sealed coffin which contained a charm to enable the resuscitated body to emerge from it ; and in the earlier periods of the Egyptian religion everything turned upon the provision of food and drink, upon the " inexhaustible theme of nourishment ". The point of crucial importance for our present purpose is this : where the means for it were available, this service was not carried out in the simple style that contented other peoples, who surrendered to the dead various conventional substitutes for implements and other things that had belonged to the dead person : his whole existence as a member of society and of the working world was to be conserved in a permanent fashion as a real thing.

At this point there was introduced a sort of symbolism that is characteristic of the religious outlook : portrayal in picture and word served to represent the life for which there could be no real reawakening.

The furniture of the tomb was originally meant actually to supply the reality for which it stood ; but through this function it was invested with a dignity which, as time went on and religious interests took another direction, gave it a right to independent existence. In earlier times the Ka was provided with statues— several, to be safe—not only of the dead person but of his household, and pictures showing him with wife and child at a table laden with offerings ; later there were added scenes from household and craft, from official activities and court service, painted from the life, farming and fowling, slaughtering and wine-pressing, with craftsmen and mariners, musicians and dancing girls, and anything else that might seem enjoyable and interesting to a noble Egyptian.[2] Gay pictures of these things covered the walls of the burial chambers, making them into inviting festive rooms. In the course of time the pleasure in detail and anecdote in the life-story outweighed the religious motive of provision for the dead. This tendency reached its culmination in the period of the " New Kingdom " (after 1500 B.C.), which brought the expansion of the empire beyond the national frontiers of Egypt. That expansion resulted in a universalizing of the picture of the world, and this was accompanied by a turning inward of the religious mind. This association, which is typical of the emergence of the sense of individuality, brought about a change in the decoration of the burial-chamber, the past concrete existence and the actual individuality of the dead person coming to form the principal subject-matter, represented, it would seem, for its own sake.

Now, the furnishing of the eternal dwelling also included— not only after this change, but long before it—a biography of the departed, which often was an autobiography. The deceased person told, in the first person, his life-story, or, rather, told of his fame and happiness. One wonders whether these narratives were from the first intimately related to the religious practices which were intended to maintain the departed, throughout his after-life, in possession of all that had made his earthly life valuable and enjoyable. In the earliest stages accessible to us we already see the primitive conceptions of life after death overgrown by the ideas of a blessed immortality conditional upon the purity of the soul, ideas which came from the development of the mysteries of Osiris. This spiritual movement culminated in a monotheistic religion which made its appearance during the period of the New Kingdom ; the union of the soul with the Sun-god, the One God who was considered the source of all life, then became the object of religious practices. These high levels, however, of religious belief did not supplant the lower ones, but fell into place with them by a sort of addition that is characteristic of the spiritual history of this people—so far as we understand it. What had once been a living part of religious belief remained as ritual and magic, while the maintenance of the bodily existence of the individual, with which the cult of the dead had been bound up, became the subject of interests other than religious ; the motives for biographical self-portrayal grew more and more secular with the fading of the original purpose : the aspiration to fame and to continued existence in the thoughts of posterity sprang up on the primitive soil of religion. To bring one's own name " to everlasting existence on the lips of the living " is often the motive expressly stated in Egyptian epitaphs. The purpose of self-glorification underlying these religious works is still more emphatically revealed by the kings who built the gigantic temples to their gods, who were to confer upon them eternal life and victory and fame : from of old every dedicatory inscription, even before it mentioned the temple, began : " He has made this as his monument."

We can trace the biographical inscriptions in the tombs back to about 3000 B.C. From the Old Kingdom of Memphis and even from the so-called " oldest period " we have a few such documents, relating to the great ones of the royal court. They contrast with later productions in their brevity and simplicity. Among the successes, for instance, of a head forester are included his fine house and fine garden ; in the biography of a certain Ptahshepses, after the list of his honours and dignities, it is related that he was brought up at the court of Menkaura, who built the third pyramid of Gizeh.* More numerous and fuller biographical texts then begin to appear in the graves of high officials from the epoch of the twelfth dynasty (about 2000 B.C.), which in the peaceful expansion of its power marked the zenith of the ancient Egyptian civilization ; and finally the New Kingdom, beginning about the middle of the sixteenth century B.C., fully reveals the spread of this custom. A visit to one of our museums will give some idea of the steles and statues of the dead with their autobiographical inscriptions.

What, then, is the relevance of these records to the awareness of individuality which would seem to be implied in that established practice of portraying individual life ? Here again the facts are as remarkable as is everything else connected with ancient Egypt. In one field, that of the fine arts, the representation has a quite personal touch : we find sculpture representing the Ka of the deceased by the portrait of the living man

---

* As to the head forester, named Meten (third dynasty), cf. Erman, *Die äg. Religion*, p. 120. Ptahshepses (2800 B.C.) in E. de Rougé, *Recherches sur les Monuments des Premières Dynasties*, pp. 66–7. The first person is not used here, but instead almost every sentence ends with the name Ptahshepses. In another biography of the same period (*id.*, p. 113), however, the first person appears. A fuller biography in the first person—six pages in translation—is that of the governor Una, of the sixth dynasty (at latest 2600 B.C.), in Sayce, *Records of the Past*, N.S., pp. 4–10.

with his characteristic features. It is worth noting that this tendency belonged to the oldest known period of Egyptian art. Later it was supplanted by adherence to a formalizing canon ; and then in the New Kingdom, just when social life had taken a more personal form, the statue of the deceased, like the other requisites of the service of the dead, became a factory-made product.[3] The statues from the Old Kingdom (the third to the sixth dynasty, *c.* 2700–2400 B.C.) exhibit with complete realism striking portrait-heads, since the dwelling of the Ka then demanded an embodiment of the individual that was as accurate and living as possible ; only the bodies are idealized for the Ka, the man being represented at the height of his physical powers and in a dignified attitude. The biographies, on the other hand, never went so far as to give a full and unreserved account of a man's life-story, though this would seem to be implied in the conception of the Ka. Even when the narrative is in chronological order, it only assembles the details of what was commonly considered to be enjoyable in life, and this view, which was typical of the ordinary man, was even more narrowed in the courtierly outlook of the upper classes. Nothing is told us of the private life, except for the family tree and the pride the Egyptians had in their offspring. The record is concerned with public activities, and especially with relations with the king, from childhood onwards if that could be claimed. The dead man's importance is measured by his success in gaining office and rank. Accordingly the record of his warlike deeds leads up to the tale of his promotions and rewards, the lands given to him, the slaves as spoil of war, and so on ; and his heaped-up decorations in the service of a god or of the king, who was himself accounted a god. The king, in whose enterprises and bounty the dead man had a share, occupies the centre of the stage. In this monotonous narrative the individuals seem scarcely distinguishable from one another except in name and rank. Each stresses his distinctions, but with the result that every man's life is represented as attaining a pinnacle of eminence reached by no other ; and here, too, the relation to the king is the main point. " I was the pride of the king's soul." " I was the only beloved of the king, without a rival." " My praise ascended to the skies."

At a later time the moral qualities of the deceased bulked largely in the funerary inscriptions ; and this seems to have led to the use of a distinct biographical category, that of " conduct ".

But this did not result in the character being seen as giving a unity to the story of the life, as did the corresponding conception in Greece, expressed by the word " *bios* ". And the more personal line which Egyptian thought took in the epoch of the New Kingdom only influenced biography to this extent, that the various dealings of the individual with the world were recorded in detail, in writing and by picture, with reference to typical situations—how he occupied himself, showed his ability, was rewarded by the king, amused himself, and so on. The surroundings of the person have seldom been depicted in autobiography so vividly and so richly as in these funerary inscriptions. In Western autobiographical literature it is only from the later Middle Ages onward, and especially in the Renaissance, that we sometimes meet with this detailed and at the same time crisp kind of narrative, faithfully reproducing the externals of individual life. But in the Western world autobiography had then acquired its modern function of revealing the living man, a function which it performed even if approaching reality objectively. In face of the ancient Egyptian records we may fully appreciate the distance that had had to be covered before this method could become the autobiographer's means of revealing his own personality.

An illustration of this is provided by an elaborate biographical monument from the zenith of the New Kingdom period, placed in the rock-tomb of a magnate called Inni, who bears the usual elaborate titles and attributes, such as wise counsellor of the king, honoured by the king and among men, manager of various building operations, and treasurer. The record is composed in the following way. On one stone there is a narrative of Inni's life during the reigns of the four kings whom he served, and there is another biographical inscription on a second stone. On the ceiling is an inscription in which he speaks of his career, and on the walls are pictures from his life, with fairly long descriptions : Inni receives the king's gifts for the god Ammon, among them negro prisoners of war ; he inspects the treasures of the temple of Ammon and supervises the weighing of the monthly ration of incense for various sanctuaries ; he superintends the reaping of the grain, the bringing home of the cattle, and so on ; he visits his estate in the Delta and inspects his herds of cattle there ; he walks in the orchard he has laid out in imitation of the king on the west bank of the Nile at Thebes. In another monument of this kind we are shown the Lord of the Tomb hunting birds with a throwing-stick, encouraging labourers busy with the new sowing, watching fishing and fowling, and so on.[4] The narrative in the first person begins in these biographies either without any further introduction than the sacrificial formula or a circumstantial record of the date, or with the opening phrase, stereotyped not only in Eastern literature [5]—" N. N. speaks : I . . ." The extent to which the persons dealt with in the inscriptions took part in their composition cannot usually be ascertained. At times we learn that not the Lord of the Tomb but a descendant of his prepared the inscription, or that family documents had been used, or could not be found. This does not matter very much. For the point is that we find here a firmly established usage which, even if the person concerned was unable to comply with it himself, he at least regarded as one of his principal concerns.

The range of moral qualities which the autobiographers claim for themselves is of special interest. These qualities are in part virtues generally recognized as religious or social merits, such as the pious care for the maintenance of ancestral tombs, or the love for parents and for brothers and sisters. Or, for instance, a chief justice praises himself because he " excelled the tongue of the balance in accuracy ", knew what lay concealed in the minds of men, listened carefully and pronounced wisely. This brings us to the other virtues which, by the emphasis laid on them, testify to the high standard of personal and social morality then attained in the Egyptian State. As one of the worthies of the twelfth dynasty declares, " I went forth from the door of my house with benevolent heart, I stood there with bountiful hand . . . Kind was my heart, empty of passionate wrath . . ." Frequently there is self-praise for having been a father to the fatherless, a husband to the widows, a support to the humble ; occasionally quite simply for having borne God in the heart. The great landowners who possessed numberless slaves like to emphasize not only that they never perverted justice, but also that they showed benevolence and gave help to their dependants in time of need. " No minor have I oppressed, no widow afflicted, no peasant or shepherd evicted or driven away ; from no master of five hands have I taken his men for the corvée. No one suffered want in my lifetime, no one went hungry in my day ; for when there was dearth I had all the fields in the region tilled . . . Thus I saved the lives of its inhabitants. I gave away whatever food the region produced, so that there was no one hungry in the land ; I gave the widow as large a portion as the woman who had a husband. I did not prefer the great to the small in aught that I gave. And when the inundations of the Nile were abundant and the farmers rich in all things, I did not impose a new tax upon the fields." [6] This self-praise gives, no doubt, a highly idealized picture, but amid the conventional phrasing of the scribes there is nevertheless at work a conception that regularly makes its appearance in the forms of autobiography determined by social practice : a ruling ideal of morality is accepted and guides the course of the biography.

The emphasis laid on morality had as its background the great change in the religious ideas of the Egyptians that took place in the era of the New Kingdom. This has another special significance for autobiography. For, owing to the belief in Osiris, the hope of a blessed after-life was bound up with an ethical vindication of the dead, however much remained of the material and magical devices of the older cult, which were quite independent of any morality. There also entered into the peculiarly Egyptian practice of the cult of the dead the idea of man's responsibility, and as the outcome of this idea the elaboration of a written form of self-justification. We may describe this form as a confession, if the emphasis be put not on any expression of consciousness of sin but on the general attitude of confession adopted by the individual person toward the deity. We meet here with the Egyptian conception of the Judgment in the under-world—that profound conception which had a great influence also in the spiritual history of Europe. In a great hall, the " Hall of the two Truths ", in which Osiris has his throne and the forty-two judges of the dead sit, the heart of the departed is weighed in a balance, to see if it is lighter than " the truth " ; after being received in the hall by the goddess of truth, and before he gives his heart to be weighed, the departed makes a " confession " of his purity from sin, looking the goddess in the face. This confession has been drawn up beforehand, and placed in the man's grave, so that he may take it with him on his journey to the Beyond. Even before God, man will say nothing but good of himself. This is but one more clear-cut appearance in the religious sphere of the fundamental attitude in ancient times toward self-presentation—there must be no admission of any sort of flaw in one's own character. The idea of giving expression to the sense of sin did not enter men's minds until religion became personal under the New Kingdom. [7] But as part of the religious life the practice of self-justification, as we meet it here for the first time, has a special meaning. To this we must devote further attention, in view of the vigorous branch of autobiography which was to proceed from the religious scrutiny of the self, and which took the form of Confessions, properly so-called.

In this connexion we may try to survey the various forms taken by the practice of confession as it made its appearance among several peoples at different stages of civilization. We find this practice even among some of the so-called primitive peoples whose civilizations have been studied in modern times by anthropologists seeking for the attitude toward life of the " natural " man. With these peoples also confession appears, as in Egypt, to be linked with the dominance of an organized priesthood. Some members of religious orders, who as missionaries met with this practice and recorded it, were so struck by its similarity to certain Roman Catholic observances that they believed it could only be explained by means of the former missionary activity of the Apostle Thomas. Yet these " confessions " were hardly touched by moral ideas. In them the religious exercise was based rather upon judicial procedure or medical practice. Thus among the Polynesians in cases of illness, which were explained as due to possession, confession was applied as a means of influencing the angry deity, together with other more material means of exorcising and expelling the evil spirits. The sick man, together with his whole family, was interrogated, with accompanying religious ceremonies, by the priest, who concerned himself largely with the question whether any infringements of taboo had been committed. " The man confessed quite openly, revoked curses which he had perhaps uttered, and gave the priest the sin-offerings he demanded." [8] In Peru, where (as among the Mexicans and kindred peoples) " confession " had been developed as a formal institution, its direct political purpose is obvious. On particularly suspicious occasions, such as the birth of twins or the wicked behaviour of a son, the priests intervened as inquisitors, in order to elicit the avowal of secret transgressions that might harm the State. The question of absolution was decided by an oracle produced for the occasion. Among the Mexicans appears the more developed form of a voluntary general confession, which was usually made to the god of judgment, but sometimes to the goddess of pleasure. Amid solemn practices— including an assurance of truthfulness corresponding to the oath —the avowal of transgressions was made by enumeration in chronological order, on which the priest determined the appropriate penances and punishments. Just as in early Christian times baptism was often deferred as long as possible, the Mexican made this confession, which could only be undertaken once in a lifetime, when he had reached old age, since relapses were considered inexpiable. Yet here also the practical purpose is particularly plain : the aim was to escape from severe legal penalties through this rite, which thus became equivalent to judicial procedure.[9]

At higher levels of ethical development we find confession in the region of Near and Middle Eastern civilizations, apart from the Egyptians, among the Israelites and the Persians. In one of the parts of the Pentateuch setting forth Mosaic Law we find the following commandment (Numbers v. 5–7, Revised Version) : " And the Lord spake unto Moses, saying, Speak unto the children of Israel, When a man or woman shall commit any sin that men commit, to do a trespass against the Lord, and that soul be guilty ; then they shall confess their sin which they have done : and he shall make restitution for his guilt in full . . ." In the later historical records of the Old Testament we also find the people collectively acknowledging their offences against the Lord when they returned to worship Him. We read, for instance, in the Book of Nehemiah (chap. ix.) : " Now . . . the children of Israel were assembled with fasting, and with sackcloth, and earth upon them. And the seed of Israel separated themselves from all strangers, and stood and confessed their sins, and the iniquities of their fathers." In this sort of " confession " repentance was combined with thanksgiving for God's goodness, a combination which reappears in the famous book of Augustine. As regards the Persians, in the Avesta, the holy scripture of the worshippers of Mazda, in the part dealing with ethics and laws, there is handed down in various texts from about 800 B.C. onward a ritual of confession of sins. Confession, which had to be made on many occasions, especially on the death-bed and at the festival of the departed, is found in many forms. It brought freedom not from judicial punishment, but from requital in the next world for expiable crimes.[10] In these forms, confession is related to the lofty ethical views of Zoroastrianism, with its strict insistence on truthfulness, self-control, industry, uprightness, and reasonableness. But here confession appears, as set forth in a politico-religious context, in general terms, as a formula applicable to every individual ; for this purpose it contains a catalogue of every possible kind of sin. This has its analogy in Christian autobiography, stereotyped confessions being composed in the centuries before and even after the appearance of Augustine's work.

Similarly, among the Egyptians the content of the texts given to the dead for their " confession "—of innocence—before the divine judges consists of a list of forty-two sins in which the simple basic prescriptions of law and of religious and practical morality are developed in many directions. They comprise the generalities of personal and social morality, with an addition of some importance : even useless repentance is considered a sin. These are the texts which are found in their most complete version in chapter 125 of the so-called " Book of the Dead ". But the setting of this enumeration of sins is quite different here. As man is supposed to declare himself innocent of them after his death, the situation is visualized in which the soul finds itself confronted with the deity ; it is visualized as an event that will come to pass in the next world but will be assisted by the confession written down beforehand, in virtue of the magical power of the formula devised—just as the other formulæ used in the cult of the dead prepare the way for his passage " to the West " through their recitation or their simple presentation in writing. In a situation which to our way of thinking excludes every such expedient, where there is no longer anything between man and God, the Egyptian considered a verbal charm quite in keeping.

It is in this connexion that we first find the literary form of soliloquy. On the breast of the corpse, above the heart that is to be weighed, there is placed a stone scarab of sacred design, bearing written words devised to avert self-accusation :

" O heart that I have from my mother ! O heart, part of my being ! Come not forward as witness against me, prepare not resistance to me before the judges, oppose not thyself to me before the master of the weighing. Thou art my spirit, which is in my body . . . ; let not our name stink . . . ; tell no lie against me before the god." [11]

Then comes the confession in the Hall of Truth.[12] It begins with a prayer :

" I am come to Thee, O my Lord, that I may see Thy beauty. I know Thee . . . I come to Thee and bring the truth and banish sin."

The confession concentrates on the protestation of innocence, the moral precepts being taken one by one :

" I have done no sin against men . . . I have done nothing that the gods abhor. I have not injured any man's name in the sight of his superior. I have let no one starve. I have made no one weep. I have done no murder. I have not kept the workman at his daily labour beyond his obligation . . ."

After continuing in this way, on the lines of the self-portrayal found in the biographical inscriptions, the confession ends with the emphatic assurance by the departed of his own purity and of his confidence in acquittal :

I fall not before your sword . . . ye speak the truth concerning me before the Lord of All. For I have done right in Egypt, I have not blasphemed God, and the king of my time had not to concern himself with me . . . See, I come to you, without sin, without evil . . . I live on truth and nourish myself on the truth of my heart . . . Save me, protect me ; ye accuse me not before the great God. I am one with clean lips and clean hands, to whom those who see him say, " Welcome, welcome."

Here we have a method of presenting the spiritual act of confession, that reveals a law of composition operative also in autobiographical writing. The religious act of the individual soul, which in the imagination of the believer has reference to a definite reality in the next world, is conceived as something typical or general, but is given the character of personal experience by the use of the first person. In so proceeding the believer has a practical end in view. The formulæ describing the standard of purity from sin are meant to be effective, when uttered by the departed, in purifying his own heart when he is judged in the Hall of Truth.

There is a parallel instance of this method in the popular Greek mysteries, as illustrated by a curious document from a degenerate Orphic sect.[13] Into the grave of the dead were put initiatory instructions for his entry into the underworld, together with the spells that were to serve as passwords ; and again the formulæ, written on gold plates, are presented as a confession by the soul. In them the deceased, referring to his purity and his kinship with gods, makes known his previous religious life and the claim to sanctification based on it. These formulæ are taken from a larger whole, exhibiting a soul's journey in general terms. The typical course of this journey is thus defined beforehand in the religious text, and is made applicable to the case of any particular individual by the simple form of personal confession.

When considering the way in which religious autobiography took shape we shall be confronted with a similar relation of the general and the particular. For here also the soul's progress appears to be moulded according to rules conceived out of the religious practice of the community, and it is in conformity with these that the autobiographer presents his own life-history. In the case of the Egyptians we can see a first stage in this connexion between religion and autobiography, conditioned by the practical aim of influencing the gods and the destiny of the soul.

Generally speaking, the representation of events in the religious life has a tendency, even when they are not actually personal but collective experiences, to be put into the form of a narrative in the first person singular. This tendency is familiar to us from the " I " of the Psalms in the Old Testament, where the much debated question is whether the speaker is primarily the individual or the community or a corporate personality. The conditions for the creation of religious autobiography arose, however, much later ; they are associated with the development of personal or " subjective " religion, which had not begun when the literary form of confession made its appearance in the Egyptian " Book of the Dead ". But we should add, with special reference to Augustine's Confessions, that the rise of spiritual autobiography cannot be fully explained from the development of subjectivity in religion. This will be illustrated when in a later part of our history we meet with the expression of the inward life in Hebrew religious poetry, which brought personal religion to the maturity it failed to attain in Egypt. The creation of religious autobiography is connected rather with the long and persistent effort of meditation working on the awareness of personality, which it was essentially the function of philosophy to carry out. In following the ways paved in Greek philosophy for the expression of man's self-knowledge we shall gradually be guided to spiritual autobiography.

II. BABYLONIAN AND ASSYRIAN RULERS

A second class of autobiographical writings that have survived from these ancient civilizations is that of the records of rulers' deeds. To satisfy their need of glory by works of art with explanatory inscriptions was a custom of oriental potentates from the time of the earliest remains we have from the great kingdoms of the Middle East. We have already noticed that the Egyptian kings erected of old even temple buildings as monuments to their own glory. The dedicatory inscriptions invariably began with the traditional formula, " He has made this as his monument." On the exterior walls of the temple an expanse was devoted to the representation of its founder's deeds.[14] In Babylonia a similar fixed form of building inscriptions is found. From it the Assyrians developed the long historical inscriptions on which our knowledge of the ancient history of Mesopotamia is largely based. An English expert traces this development : " By elaborating the titles of the king, and giving a more discursive account of the circumstances of the dedication, the scribes were able to give general accounts of the principal events of their time. But in Assyria first came the vital change which converted the building inscriptions into a historical record, namely, the partial suppression of the dedication. Thus arose the general account of a king's exploits." [15] From about 1400 B.C. onward there existed in Assyria a definite form of simple chronicles ; the memorable events of each king's reign, recorded in a bald, artless fashion, were arranged in chronological order, either as annals or according to the sequence of the king's campaigns.[16] We also know that official journals of the ruler's activities were kept at various oriental courts from ancient times.[17] Thus the stage was set for the rise of political autobiography. As the narrative of historical events was centred in the person of the king, it was set forth in his name, by the use of the literary form of the first person.

The rise, or at least the development, of this significant species both of historiography and of autobiographical literature can be assigned to Assyria during the epoch when that military State, expanding in all directions through wars of aggression, became one of the greatest empires of antiquity. It was here, so far as we know, that the recording of the king's deeds came into fashion about the end of the second millennium, in artistically composed chronicles, which, written on clay tablets or on stone, have been brought to light from the ruins of ancient Babylonian cities. Throughout these documents the kings speak themselves, proclaiming their own greatness. Unlike Egyptian funerary biography, this type of autobiographical writing is continuous with Western literature. It continued—with, for us, long inter-ruptions—in monumental form in the Persian Empire, and was taken over and adapted by the Hellenistic princes until it reached its highest perfection in the " Res Gestae " of the Emperor

Augustus. By following the course of this evolution we can reach a conclusion as to the ways in which the rulers envisaged their position in the world.

In the cuneiform chronicles of the Assyrian potentates the subject-matter consists of an elaborate annalistic narration of the king's campaigns and raids, with their attendant devastations, extortions, atrocities, and lootings ; also of his hunts, his ritual performances, the temples and palaces he built—of everything to magnify the impression of his power. Each item is expressed by a pictorial phrase, as grandiloquent as possible and often inspired by a vision of the destructive forces of nature. When we first meet with one of these documents, the effect it produces on us is impressive ; but as the same modes of expression keep recurring we recognize their impersonal character. The historical data are held together by the frequent enumeration of the monarch's titles, introduced with the emphatic repetition typical of the primitive narrative style of all peoples. On the other hand, they are set in a context of appeals to the gods and of prayers, in which later on some personal trait may at times be detected.

The attitude of the kings toward themselves that confronts us here is strange and alien to normal human standards. It appears, however, to be not a personal attitude but a generalized one, intended to express the ruler's power. There existed at the Babylonian court a rigid tradition, fixed in a uniform stylistic rendering, about the way a ruler spoke : he spoke of himself as the gods would speak. It was a part of the fashion of the court, known to the historian as the " court style " (German " Hofstil "). It was only transferred to self-presentation after it had long been developed in the two great kingdoms of Egypt and Babylon ; everyone knows it from the Old Testament, where at times Jehovah speaks like an Assyrian potentate.[18] The elements of which this court style is composed are not only the official titles, exaggerated comparisons, and other bombastic turns of phrase, but also definite political and religious ideas about the status of the king, which appear again and again in the record of his deeds. These concern his descent from the gods, make him out a divinely chosen world-ruler, assert the eternal existence of his house, and explain his deeds as a mission from on high and his reign as the cause of every blessing. It might be supposed that no one at all exists on earth except the king : he is the sole representative of the people he governs, or, what amounts to the same thing here, of mankind. But he assumes this status not because in boundless presumption he regards himself as epitomizing in his own person the character of his nation or of mankind, but in virtue of his unlimited power. As the one man in whose person the entire State is concentrated, he is regarded not only as superior to all other men but as more than man : through his very nature, or at least in virtue of his works, he is lifted into the sphere of the superhuman, the sphere of the gods. According to the original doctrine of the " Old Kingdom ", the ruler was himself divine : that was the case with the Pharaohs. Generation after generation the highest god came down to Pharaoh's queen, in order that an heir to the throne might be begotten of purely divine blood.[19] In the records of the Assyrian potentates another type is displayed : the king's divine origin is traced back through his predecessors, and all that he receives direct from the gods is his power. Enthroned in their place, while dependent on them he is just as powerful as they in comparison with any other creature. Self-glorification here attains a monstrous character, because the glory of the self is neither derived from its divine nature nor related to the nature of men as finite individuals aware of their thoughts, feelings, and actions, but is the outcome of something separative—of the gap opened between man and man by the fact of power.

The religious complexion that is given by the traditional assertion of the king's divine mission is common to all these self-complacent records. For the wars the king wages in order to display his majesty and power, he wages at the same time for the gods, whose power is to be extended over the other nations and their worship imposed on those nations. To the gods belong the buildings whose construction he records with the greatest pride ; and when he praises himself he thereby glorifies his gods.[20] And so his appeals and prayers to them are not simply a pretext for the record of his deeds, but its indispensable basis.

There remains, however, an obvious contradiction within this mental attitude. Based on the alleged proximity of the one man to the gods, his self-aggrandizement may look like a religiously felt relation of the self to that which surpasses our own finite lives ; but it is in fact the outcome not of the consciousness of such a fellowship with the higher and divine reality as is shared by everything human, but of a leap across a gulf—the gulf that separates common men from gods. With this leap the self loses the centre of gravity it has in itself, and the heightened valuation of the self, far from freeing man, leaves him burdened by the imperious power of the gods, which he snatches to himself from without : thus the self-glorification of the Assyrian despots is offset by a slavish self-abasement.   " The enraged gods and wrathful goddesses did I placate by lamentation and penitential psalms"— this phrase occurs in the annals of Assurbanipal.   In order to grasp in its true context the stereotyped representation which these kings give of themselves, or which is given in their name, we must keep in mind the abject self-abasement in the ancient Babylonian penitential psalms, which often have historical situations as their background.[21]   Otherwise we might mistake that type of self-presentation as the expression of a solid, primitive self-assurance.

The confident assurance of the man of action who relies on his strength is an attitude of quite another kind.   It makes its appearance in early heroic poetry, which, as we have noticed, reveals, in a sense, man's " natural " attitude towards existence. In comparison with the poetical self-presentation of the warriors or chieftains of the heroic age, the truculent records of the Assyrian war lords, who were the rulers of great kingdoms, belong not only to a relatively late stage of social existence but also to a less primitive mentality.   We must keep this point in view when trying to appreciate these earliest known specimens of political autobiography.   Though produced by mighty kings, they are not imbued with the naïve self-reliance that primarily distinguishes the man of action.   And because the absolute supremacy and the crushing power displayed in them do not flow from unshaken self-confidence that can face every aspect of life, the mode of presentation of personality in these narratives, in spite of the fullness of imagery that characterizes them, is, in a sense, abstract : it singles out from reality only what is congenial to it, and excludes every disturbing and refractory element.

These documents begin about 1100 B.C. with Tiglath-Pileser I's record of his successful campaigns ; the transcription of this fills fifteen printed pages.[22]   The glorification of his qualities runs through the narrative like a refrain, some seven times repeated, with variations corresponding to the various deeds described : " Tiglath-Pileser, the brave and strong, who opens the mountain paths, throws down the rebellious, sweeps aside all the obstinate . . . the flaming lightning, the mighty storm of battle . . . the brave and strong, who holds a sceptre without equal."

A list of ancestors is one of the regular forms of praise in these monuments.   The one emotion that fills them all is not just delight in battle and victory, but a savage exultation at the unsparing destruction of the enemy. Tiglath-Pileser himself formulates the purpose of his record : " The fame of my mighty power, my victory in battle, the subjection of the enemy who hated Assur, and whom Anu and Ramman had given to me, have I written in my memorial tablet and my foundation-inscription and placed in the temple of Anu and Ramman, the great gods, my Lords, for eternal ages."

With a turn of phrase that recurs regularly in these documents, he bids his successors " for eternal ages in the future for evermore " to care for the preservation of his records ; pronouncing a curse against those who may think of destroying them or even of removing them to a place where they will be out of sight—a curse that had been usual in the ancient Babylonian building inscriptions.

The persistence of this sort of political autobiography is illustrated by the annals of Assurnasirpal, who reigned two and a half centuries later (885–860 B.C.). After an introductory invocation of the gods, whose epithets are modelled on the same ideas of power, he begins :

I am the king, I am the lord, I am the exalted, the great, the strong, I am famous, I am prince, I am the noble, the powerful in war ; I am a lion, I am a hero of youthful strength ; Assurnasirpal, the mighty king, the king of Assur, the chosen of Sin (god of growth), the favourite of Anu, the beloved of Ramman, who is the mightiest of the gods ; I am the unconquerable weapon, which subjugates the land of its enemies, I am the king, strong in battle, who lays waste cities and mountains, the first in conflict, the king of the four quarters of the world, who lays his yoke upon his enemies, and destroys all his adversaries, the king of all kings, of all quarters of the world, of every one of them, the king who suppresses those who rebel against him, who subdues the hosts of the nations all combined. These are the decisions of fate that came for me out of the mouths of the great gods, who established them unchangeably as my destiny. In accordance with the desire of my heart and the uplifting of my hands (in prayer), the lady Ishtar, who loves my priesthood, looked with favour upon me and set her heart to battle and war . . .

To extend the terror of his power over the land, to trample down the enemy in battle like the god of inundation, to rain down ruin, to occupy a town like a flock of birds of prey swooping down on it—these are some of the characteristic phrases also applied to actions which were in fact of little importance.[23] This wallowing in blood is accompanied by expressions of the war lord's delight in the splendour of the booty, which is described in detail—gold and silver, precious timber and ivory,

embroidered garments, light and dark purple cloth. It is, however, chiefly in the technicalities of the slaughter of men that
his imagination revels. " I took them alive and impaled them
on stakes " ; " I dyed the mountains like wool with their blood " ;
" I flayed many of them and covered the walls with their skin " ;
" I built one pile of still living bodies and one pile of heads.
And in the middle I hung their heads on vines near the city." He
also emphasizes with particular satisfaction the care he has taken
for the everlasting fame of his person by means of memorial
tablets, historical inscriptions, and several statues made of him
and erected one in his favourite palace, some others in the
palace and the capital city of a tributary prince, and one by a
spring before which the monuments of two of his ancestors
already stood : " I had a colossus of my royal person made,
and wrote my power and grandeur upon it." Like the gods of
whose favour he boasts, the king says of himself : " Over the
ruins radiates my countenance ; in the service of my wrath I
find my pleasure." [24]

In later times, when the Assyrio-Babylonian empire was
consolidated, the monarch's megalomania satisfied itself with
more peaceful things. Magnificent buildings, works of art such
as the " terrific " lion and bull colossi, public works undertakings,
irrigation schemes on an unprecedented scale, and the like,
provided no less befitting material for historiography than the
military exploits, which had begun to be checked by the internal
troubles of the large centralized State. In this policy the Assyrian
rulers were following the example of the Babylonian kings, who
had long aimed at winning repute as ideal princes of peace.
This tendency may be observed in their inscriptions as far back as
the third millennium B.C. They make no mention of their
warlike deeds, while they take pride in having built magnificent
temples in honour of the gods and presented costly offerings to
them. [25] An example of the adoption of the Babylonians' ideal
type by the Assyrian rulers is offered by the record of the deeds
of Assurbanipal, the most important document of this sort from
the golden age of Assyrian civilization. Sardanapalus, as this
ruler is usually called, reigned for more than forty years (668–626
B.C.)—long enough to witness the beginning of the dissolution
of his empire. It may be that in his case the first-personal
narrative is not mere adherence to convention, and that he
himself wrote his annals. He tells in them of his education,
emphasizing that he was not only instructed in the arts of warfare

but had also acquired the wisdom of Nebo—the priest-god who keeps the Book of Fate—and had thoroughly learnt the art of tablet-writing from all the experts in that subject. It was an art that comprised both literary composition and the technicalities of cuneiform writing.²⁶ Before recording the long series of his campaigns, with the terrible havoc he wrought in the rebellious countries, he praises himself, as was then usual in the court style, for the abundant fruitfulness with which the gods blessed the land on his ascent of the throne : " During my reign abundance descended bountifully, rich blessing was poured down." Grain was five ells high, with ears five-sixths of an ell long— and so forth. Accordingly stress is laid on the virtues of the ruler, such as concern for the welfare of his country, the establishment of peace and good order, and generosity ; he depicts himself thus : " I, the large-hearted, who think not of revenge, and who blot out sins . . ." ²⁷

More intimate and therefore more revealing statements follow. We now find emotion expressed directly, and not merely indicated by the stale traditional metaphors. But the self-revelation is not complete : the typical attitude that allows the man to be seen only at the highest pitch of feeling is still maintained. Assurbanipal displays himself in wrath, in fury, in fear, in radiant joy, and in jubilation. And also in contrition. As he grew old the latent forces of destruction at work in the empire, beneath the outward show of might and luxury, became manifest, while he himself was assailed by a mysterious disease, and he gave expression to the despair that overwhelmed him. Here, amid those " bloody records of cruelty and terror ", we meet with a human document that reveals the state of mind of the Assyrian despot as he resorts to religion without drawing strength from it : ²⁸

The rules for making offerings to the dead and libations to the ghosts of the kings my ancestors, which had not been practised, I reintroduced. I did well unto god and man, to dead and living. Why have sickness, ill-health, misery and misfortune befallen me ? I cannot away with the strife in my country and the dissensions in my family. Disturbing scandals oppress me alway. Misery of mind and of flesh bow me down ; with cries of woe I bring my days to an end. On the day of the city-god, the day of the festival, I am wretched ; death is seizing hold on me and bears me down. With lamentation and mourning I wail day and night. I groan, " O god, grant even to one who is impious that he may see thy light. How long, O god, wilt thou deal thus with me ? Even as one who has not feared god and goddess am I reckoned."

To this document may be added a self-revelation that has come down to us from Nebuchadnezzar (*c.* 600 B.C.). Here, in the prayers which, in accordance with custom, precede and follow the record of deeds, are simpler and genuinely felt expressions of the fear of God, so that it has been possible to say of these passages [29] that in them he " reveals part of his innermost nature ".*

After the rapid fall of the Assyrian empire, when the Medes and the Persians rose to political supremacy in the Middle East, the monumental form of proclamation of the king's glory underwent a significant change. Self-glorification, with its religious correlation, proved capable of being so treated as to convey to us a strong impression of a king's personality. This is shown by the record of the acts of Darius, the great Achaemenid. Here we may see the great revolution in which the consciousness of power was given a moral quality : the ethos of the Persian religion added inner solidity to the feeling of majesty, which was attuned to great words, and a great man could make use of the traditional form to reveal himself in a monumental and yet personal manner.

Soon after the establishment of his power which followed the overthrow of the usurper Gaumata and the suppression of the serious revolts that necessitated a re-founding of the Persian empire (519 B.C.), Darius set up the famous monument on Mount Behistan. On the smoothed rock-face of the mountain, which rose fifteen hundred feet sheer above the old military road from Babylon to the East, in the heart of his realm, he had the long inscription raised three hundred feet above the plain, in his native Persian, with translations in the languages of Susa and Babylon, so that everyone should understand his words. Above it he was himself to be seen as he set his foot on the body of Gaumata, with the captured usurpers in chains before him. The whole monument was crowned by the picture of Ahuramazda, the god from whose grace all the deeds of the king proceeded, the Moral God opposed to the powers of evil and darkness.

" I am Darius, the great king, the king of kings, king in Persia, king of the lands, son of Hystaspes, grandson of Arrames ; the Achaemenid." So he, too, begins, and tells of the nine generations of his ancestors who were rulers. But in place of the pompous phrases of Assyrian historiography there is here the solid archaic simplicity of a language that has not yet attained

* Compare David's last words, 2 Samuel xxiii.

fluency but relates matters of fact in square-cut main clauses, with the regular opening, " And the king Darius speaks." The inscription begins with a list of the lands which Darius had brought back into subjection. Then he epitomizes his reflective consciousness of rulership. With the constructive elements of sovereignty in mind, he declares : " These lands gave me service and tribute . . . Whatever I said to them, day or night, they did . . . In those lands I cherished him who was friendly to me, punished him who was hostile to me. Ahuramazda granted me dominion, gave me help . . ."

The main part of the inscription consists of the record of his deeds. The usurpers whom he has overthrown he brands, characteristically, as " liars "—truth and moral uprightness being almost equivalent for Zoroastrianism. In his account of historical events he concentrates on what was typical, or of regular occurrence, in them, repeating like formulæ the significant terms, such as rebellion and subjugation of rebels ; but by this emphatic use of precise political categories, which set forth the bald facts without figurative paraphrases, he directly conveys to us the impression of the strength of his royal will. Himself he represents as the ruler who by divine grace and help introduces order and prosperity, restoring the security of the country and ruling according to the ways of the ancients. Finally he gives expression to his ethical, religious attitude toward politics, intent on inculcating it on his successors : " These lands that fell away, lying made them disloyal. And so Ahuramazda gave them into my hand. As I wished, so I did to them. Thou who wilt come after, keep thyself from lying ! Punish severely the man who lies, if thy word is : ' My land shall be inviolate.' "

In this spirit he emphasizes the truthfulness of the record of his acts :

Thou art to believe it, and not to hold it for lying. By the previous kings, so long as they lived, was nothing done like this that I have done, in every way, by the grace of Ahuramazda. Believe it to be as I have done . . . For this reason did Ahuramazda bring me help, because I was not evil-minded, nor a liar, nor a doer of violence, neither I nor my family ; according to law did I rule ; neither injustice nor violence did I practise. Him who aided my house did I protect, him who harmed it did I smite. Injustice have I done to no man.

And he adds not only the names of the rebels but also those of the loyal :

These men helped me, until I slew the Magian who said, " I am Bardiya, the son of Cyrus " . . . Thou, who shalt be king after me, protect these men.

The development of factual narrative in the Middle East may be pursued in that period in another direction.   In addition to the rulers there now appear other historic personalities with self-portrayals that exhibit the characteristic association of the political element with a religious attitude.   Witness is borne to this further spread of factual narrative in the historical books of the Old Testament, in the chronicle dealing with the Persian period of Jewish history, which has been handed down under the titles of Ezra and Nehemiah in the canon of the Scriptures. The anonymous chronicler records the rebuilding of the Temple in Jerusalem, the new and exclusive organization of the Jewish community after the return from exile in Babylon, the development of a specifically Jewish public worship, and the rebuilding of the fortifications of the Holy City, whose walls and gates had been destroyed ; and he allows the story to be largely told in the first person by the leading figures, Ezra and Nehemiah, themselves.   For this purpose he was able to make use of personal memoirs of Nehemiah, and perhaps also of Ezra.

Of Ezra, the religious reformer to whom the promulgation of a new " book of the law of Moses " is ascribed, we hear from his own mouth how, through the favour of the Persian ruler, he proceeded from Babylon to Jerusalem with his company of priests and Levites, taking with them gifts of gold and silver for the temple.   The story of these events is accompanied by a thanksgiving :

Blessed be the Lord, the God of our fathers, which hath put such a thing as this in the king's heart, to beautify the house of the Lord which is in Jerusalem ; and hath extended mercy unto me before the king . . . And I was strengthened according to the hand of the Lord my God upon me, and I gathered together out of Israel chief men to go up with me " (Ezra vii. 27, 28).

Another characteristic passage deals with the struggle against the " mingling of the seed " of the Chosen People with the autochthonous pagan population.   This politico-religious matter is presented in personal form as Ezra's astonishment and grief :

I rent my garment and my mantle, and plucked off the hair of my head and of my beard, and sat down astonied.   Then were assembled unto me everyone that trembled at the words of the God of Israel, because of the trespass of them of the captivity ; and I sat astonied until the evening oblation.   And at the evening oblation I arose up from my humiliation, even with my garment and my mantle rent ; and I fell upon my knees, and spread out my hands unto the Lord my God ; and I said, O my God, I am ashamed and blush to lift up my face to thee, my God : for our iniquities are increased over our head, and our guiltiness is grown up unto the heavens " (Ezra ix. 3–6).

There follows a nine-verse prayer of confession on behalf of the guilty community.

Substantial fragments of Nehemiah's memoirs are preserved in the part of the chronicle usually called by his name, the Book of Nehemiah (i–vii, xii, 31, 31, xiii. 4–31). They are mainly of a secular character, corresponding in this with the political standing of their author. Nehemiah, who was of aristocratic Jewish descent, held a high post at the Persian court under Artaxerxes I, and used his position to secure help for the oppressed Jewish community in Palestine. The memoirs begin with a scene at the king's table in the palace of Susa (445 B.C.). Nehemiah had had news of the evil situation of the community ; and, falling on his knee, he begged the king to send him to Jerusalem. He then served there as Governor for twelve years. Most of his report of his administration deals with the restoration of the walls of Jerusalem. This was " what God had put in his heart to do "— a communal task, in which all joined ; he himself organized it in military fashion, in order to ward off the danger from intriguing enemies without and within. Another subject dealt with is what may be described in the words of a Biblical expert as " the national political organization of the Temple community ". Here again the struggle against mixed marriages played an important part, together with the hierarchical ordering of the priesthood and the sanctification of the Sabbath.

Nehemiah also reports on his economic reforms—measures of so radical a nature that they might be compared with the social legislation of Solon, the founder of Attic democracy. He dwells on the complaints of the poor, who had been reduced by the greed of the rich ruling class to a sort of debtors' enslavement.

And I was very angry when I heard their cry and these words. Then I consulted with myself, and contended with the nobles and the rulers, and said unto them, Ye exact usury, every one of his brother. And I held a great assembly against them. And I said unto them, We after our ability have redeemed our brethren the Jews, which were sold unto the heathen ; and would ye even sell your brethren, and should they be sold unto us ? Then held they their peace, and found never a word (Nehemiah v. 6–8).

His appeal to their social and religious conscience had good result. In the assembly a general remission of debts was resolved on.

For himself, he insists on the selflessness and generosity of his administration.

From the time that I was appointed to be their governor in the land of Judah, from the twentieth year even unto the two and thirtieth year of Artaxerxes the king, that is, twelve years, I and my brethren have not eaten the bread of the governor. But the former governors that were before me were chargeable unto the people, and took of them bread and wine, beside forty shekels of silver ; yea, even their servants bare rule over the people : but so did not I, because of the fear of God. Yea, also I continued in the work of this wall, neither bought we any land : and all my servants were gathered thither unto the work. Moreover there were at my table, of the Jews and the rulers an hundred and fifty men, beside those that came unto us from among the heathen that were round about us. Now that which was prepared for one day was one ox and six choice sheep ; also fowls were prepared for me, and once in ten days store of all sorts of wine : yet for all this I demanded not the bread of the governor, because the bondage was heavy upon this people.

This passage (v. 14–18) ends with a prayer : " Remember unto me, O my God, for good, all that I have done for this people." Short prayers and supplications occur repeatedly in Nehemiah's story, which thus sometimes gives the impression rather of a diary than of memoirs concerned with the past. He speaks, for example, out of the existing situation when he appeals to God after telling of the wrath of the enemy, the Ammonites and Arabs, who at the outset had had nothing but scorn for his undertaking, convinced that it would fail :

" Hear, O our God ; for we are despised ; and turn back their reproach upon their own head, and give them up to spoiling in a land of captivity : and cover not their iniquity, and let not their sin be blotted out from before thee : for they have provoked thee to anger before the builders " (iv. 4, 5).

But on the whole the mingling of prayer with a careful detailed narrative of the historic facts corresponds with the definite type of factual report which we have followed as far as Darius' great inscription. The motive of this type of report —the perpetuation of the narrator's name and of the memory of his deeds, performed in the service of the gods and thanks to their grace—appears once more here, though modified, in so far as the specifically Jewish reverence for the law finds expression here, together with the relationship of the human person to the Judge who rewards and punishes. Nehemiah ends his account of his religious reforms with this appeal :

" Remember me, O my God, concerning this, and wipe not out my good deeds that I have done for the house of my God, and for the observances thereof " (xiii. 14, 22, 31).

III. ANCIENT ORIENTAL TALES.

Behind the first person in Darius's inscription there stands the man himself : one feels that these are the king's own words. As a rule, however, the use of the first person in royal inscriptions was merely a traditional literary form : the absoluteness of the ruler would be impaired by an indirect form of speech referring to him objectively.* The case was similar in the Egyptian funerary biographies, though for a different reason : here the use of the first person was prompted by the religious purpose of influencing the fate of the dead. Thus it appears that narrative in the first person does not from the first imply actual autobiography. On the other hand, the memoir-like parts of the historical books of the Old Testament show that the chronicler made free use of narrative in the first person, undeterred by consideration for accuracy.†

Ezra's memoirs, especially, have so been tampered with that a modern critic has declared it to be a pure fiction of the chronicler, who introduced narrative in the first person in deliberate imitation of Nehemiah's work and, in fact, created the character of Ezra.[30] Thus the general problem is raised of the relation between first personal narrative and autobiography on one side and fiction on the other. On this point also ancient Egyptian literature supplies enlightenment.

In pure poetry, when its sole purpose was narrative, the use of the first person had long been adopted. It was such a favourite

---

* In Egypt it was the custom, " out of respect for the king, to speak of him only in the indefinite form (' one '), or to describe him by such expressions as ' palace ', etc." Erman, *Aus d. Papyrus der kgl. Museen*, p. 60, n. 2.

† Thus he follows Nehemiah's description of his sorrow over his fellow-countrymen's state of " affliction and reproach " in Jerusalem with a long prayer (Nehemiah i. 5–11) in which he appeals to Jehovah for mercy for the people. This prayer is obviously a composition of the chronicler's, placing in the mouth of the autobiographer the stock phrases of prayer from Deuteronomy and elsewhere, the confession of sin (that is, of breach of God's law), and the trust in mercy. To take another example, the description, also in the first person, of the solemn procession at the dedication of the walls is so elaborated in the hierarchical style that, in the words of an expert, " Nehemiah's own simple, straightforward story is buried beyond hope of recovery."

in the classical epoch of Egyptian literature that it appears in two out of the six stories that have been preserved from this period of the Middle Kingdom, about 2000 B.C.[31] One is a work of fiction, a poem of courtly style, a specimen of the old Egyptian art of story-telling, called the Life of Sinuhe.[32] In the writing of this story the author was concerned to display his elegant style, particularly in letters and speeches, but in the narrative portions it keeps close to reality, or else adopts the conventional language of fable. It was so famous that throughout the thousand years of the epoch of the Middle Kingdom copies were continually being made. It is of importance to us for its biographical content, though it does not trace its hero's life from youth, but begins with a crisis in his fortunes. At a change of kings Sinuhe, a high official—apparently not a fictitious but a historical person—had gone into exile, through some apprehension connected with the conditions of service in oriental courts. While abroad he had become a powerful chief, and now, when summoned home again, he relates his adventures, his wandering through the desert, his meeting with Beduin, and the prosperity and esteem he won from a sheik in Palestine. As for the biographical character of the poem, it shows the same outlook as the funerary biographies, but it is made more attractive by the setting among the nomads, and by the addition of an impressive description of a duel with the mightiest champion of the country, whom Sinuhe defeats.

Sinuhe's life during exile, though fortunate, became less carefree as he grew older, for he began then to be concerned for his burial. It was for this reason that he obeyed a summons to return to Egypt. This introduces the principal and the most circumstantial part of the poem. He tells of his return, with all the formalities of his summons home and his pardon, and the story ends happily with the construction and the elaborate preparation of his tomb-dwelling, together with his portrait-statue, from means provided by the King.

The use of the first person is here introduced, as in the inscriptions, by a statement of the titles of the hero of the poem, which show him to be a person of very high rank :

" The Prince and Count, royal seal-bearer, the confidential friend, judge, keeper of the gate of the foreigners, the true and beloved royal acquaintance, the royal follower Sinuhe says : ' I was . . .' "

Some modern historians are inclined to take the " Life of

Sinuhe " as genuine memoirs. The illusion of autobiography is kept up not only in this romance, if it is a romance, but also in a famous old piece belonging to another branch of Egyptian literature in which the use of the first person was customary—that of lessons in prudent conduct, which appear among various Eastern peoples as the beginning of a didactic literature. Among the Egyptians these have a specific name, " Instructions ", and a fixed literary form : a famous sage appears and gives his son lessons in conduct. The classical work of this kind (again written in verse), the " Instruction of the wise king Amen-em-het I " [33] (about 2000 B.C.), contains autobiographical sections besides the teaching. In a style that has the charm of a novel, the king describes to his son, whom he has had to take as co-regent, how his own people betrayed him. Further on, in the familiar boasting tone, he describes his exemplary performances—his successes in war, his hunting, his palace-building, his knowledge of literature, and the prosperity and care-free enjoyment of life he bestowed on his people. Here, too, though it is hardly probable, the Wise King may have been the actual author of the work. [34]

There has been preserved from the epoch of the New Kingdom —which lasted about 900 years—a prose narrative in the first person, dating from the middle period of that epoch, about 1100 B.C. Many Egyptologists regard it as a fictitious travel story comparable with the Life of Sinuhe, but it is probably the official report of a diplomatic mission. It is the Story of Wen-Amon. [35] A priest of that name, from the Temple of Amon in Thebes, reports on a mission to the ruler of Byblus, in Syria, undertaken by order of the High Priest Hrihôr, the then ruler of Upper Egypt. The purpose of the mission was to ask, in accordance with long-continued usage, for cedar from the Lebanon for the sacred barge of Amon, which was used for proceeding along the temple lake at Thebes. This unique document is of special historical interest because it gives us a glimpse of the decay of the imperial position of Egypt. Wen-Amon relates that Zakar-Baal, the prince of Byblus, instead of receiving him, ordered him to leave and did not open negotiations until the god Amon, whose statue the envoy had brought, himself intervened. In the course of a sacrificial rite he sent one of the prince's pages of honour into a trance, and made him say while in that state : " Lift up the god's image ! Bring the envoy from Amon who possesses it ! Dismiss him ! Permit him to go his way ! "

Here we have the earliest known example of Palestinian

political prophecy. There follows a diplomatic scene : the envoy describes his audience with the Syrian prince in his coastal fortress. " I found him sitting in the upper hall with his back to the window, while the waves of the great Syrian sea dashed up behind him." Equally vivid is his description of the negotiations, in speech and rejoinder. The prince was ready to carry out " Amon's command ", though not as a command from the Egyptian ruler but only as a business transaction, for a good price. ". . . I, I am not thy servant, nor am I the servant of thy principal. If I roar to the forest of Lebanon, the heavens open and the trees lie here on the seashore . . ." While thus boasting of his power, he recognizes the supremacy of Egyptian civilization and to that extent agrees with the envoy's claim of the greatness of Amon. Zakar-Baal proceeds : " I think that Amon, who established all countries, first established the country of Egypt. Hath not artisanship proceeded from him, and the teaching thereof, to reach my fortress in the end ? But why, then, undertake the long journey hither in the condition in which thou hast been sent ? "

In the agreement then arrived at, the payment for the precious timber plays a greater part than the image of Amon (which is regarded as a divine gift, conferring " life and health "). Wen-Amon gives the precise figures of the sum he paid—so many vessels of gold and silver, so many pieces of fine linen, so many papyrus rolls, ox hides, coils of cordage, so much of lentils, so much fish—and so on. The details recur again and again in the story. Equally precise is the dating of the various stages of the journey. To this extent the document, with its high literary quality, might seem to be the actual report on a mission, and in that case it is the first of its sort ; we shall meet with others in European autobiographies in the early Middle Ages. But we also have here an example of the elementary literary form that is the basis of memoirs ; it may be described as a recording of *memorabilia*. Wen-Amon tells how he sought to win over the prince of Byblus by pointing out the importance of the occasion :

Canst thou not rejoice, and wilt thou not cause a memorial stone to be made ? On it thou wilt say : " Amon-Ra, the king of the gods, sent to me Amon-of-the-Way, his holy messenger, together with Wen-Amon, his human messenger, concerning the beams of the great sacred barge of Amon-Ra, king of the gods. I felled them and placed them on board, I provided him with my ships and my crew, and I enabled him to reach Egypt, in order to pray for ten thousand years of life for me from Amon, beyond my destined end." If then it happens at another time that there comes from the land of Egypt a messenger who is skilled in writing, he will read thy name on the memorial stone, and thou wilt receive the water of life, as do the gods that are here.

This purpose of perpetuating the memorable brings into view the other aspect of the document. The narrator does not merely make his report as an official about his mission, but goes on to tell all sorts of travel adventures. He tells how on his arrival at the Syrian port of Dor he was robbed, how he appealed in vain to the prince of the country for help, and how he then proceeded to help himself by recovering his loss at another port from the treasury of a ship that had come from Dor. Before his departure from Byblus he saw ships from Dor lying in wait for him, in order to take him captive on the high seas. " At this I sat down and wept. The prince's scribe came out to me and asked, ' What is thy trouble ? ' " When the prince learned of the peril, he, too, wept, and tried to comfort Wen-Amon. " He sent me a jug of wine and a dish of roast mutton, and bade an Egyptian singer, who was with him, to come to me, saying to her, ' Sing something to him and let his heart not brood.' "

He made good his escape from the pirates, but on the high seas he came into a storm that drove him to Cyprus (Alasa), where he fell again into mortal danger. He escaped with his life thanks to a shrewd appeal to the sense of justice of the princess of Alasa, to whom he said through an interpreter :

" Tell my lady : we have heard as far away as Thebes, the dwelling-place of Amon, that in all cities injustice is done ; but in Alashiya only justice is done. And now is injustice being done even here ! "

With the success of this appeal the extant fragment of the story of Wen-Amon breaks off.

While in this group of examples the boundaries between truth and fiction appear indefinite, the other old Egyptian story in the first person which has been preserved to us from the classical literature of the Middle Kingdom is simply concerned with marvels. It is one of the naïve popular fables that abounded in Egypt. A returned sailor tells of the enchanted island of the Snake-god, upon which he was cast after shipwreck in the Red Sea, far to the south.[36]

I was going to the mines of Pharaoh, and I went down the Red Sea in a ship 150 cubits long and 40 cubits wide, with 150 sailors of the best of Egypt, who had seen heaven and earth, and whose hearts were stronger than lions . . . As we approached the land the wind arose and threw up waves eight cubits high. As for me, I seized a piece of wood ; but those who were in the vessel perished, without one remaining. A wave threw me on an island . . . I found there figs and grapes, all manner of good herbs, berries, and grain, melons of all kinds, fishes, and birds. And I satisfied myself . . . Suddenly I heard a noise of a thunder, which I thought to be that of a wave of the sea. The trees shook and the earth was moved. I uncovered my face and I saw a serpent drawing near. He was thirty cubits long, and his beard greater than two cubits ; his limbs were overlaid with gold and his eyebrows were of lapis lazuli. He coiled himself before me.

Then he opened his mouth while I lay on my face before him, and he said to me, " What has brought thee, what has brought thee, little one ? If thou sayest not what has brought thee to this isle, I shall make thee know thyself ; as a flame thou shalt vanish."

So he tells the serpent of the shipwreck in the Red Sea, and the serpent tells him in return a story of sad happenings in his life. In the midst of the marvels there comes a reflection expressing the simple human motive of autobiographical narratives of this sort. The Snake-god remarks :

" What a joy it is when someone tells what he has gone through, when the sad events are all over ! "

The adventure itself soon comes to a happy end. The Snake-god is not only kind and generous but wise. He prophesies to the shipwrecked man that in four months' time an Egyptian ship will beach on the island and will take him home to his wife and children. The prophecy is punctually fulfilled. But the island, which had once risen out of the water, would sink again.

Here the narrative started from an ordinary, credible situation. The seafarer began like an official submitting to his superior a report on the discharge of his duty, written in the usual phraseology, and then suddenly he became a fairy-tale hero. This is very reminiscent of the popular legends which Odysseus, cast upon the land of the Phaeacians, tells in the hall of the king as his own adventures. Modern classical scholarship has shown the influence exerted by these Homeric songs upon the later Greek novelists, who took them as a model when writing this type of literature.[37]

We see that the use of narrative in the first person, aimed at making marvels credible, is of ancient origin. It was widespread in the Near and Middle East. In Egyptian literature we find a

further characteristic example of it in a story dating probably
from antiquity, at latest from the epoch of the New Kingdom
(around 1300 B.C.), but first set down much later *—the Tale
of Ahuri, Pharaoh's daughter. [38]

Here the atmosphere of miracle, in which fictional autobiography flourished, is not that of fairy-tale but that of religious
faith. The hero of the story is Ahuri's brother, who in accordance
with old Egyptian custom took his sister to wife. This legendary
prince, named Noferka-Ptah, is introduced as " an accomplished
scribe and a very learned man " ; he penetrated the magical
secrets that were a privilege of the priesthood. Through doing
so he brought disaster upon himself and his wife and child,
and, indeed, brought about the downfall of the dynasty. For he
and Ahuri were the only children of the Pharaoh Mer-neb-Ptah,
who reigned from Memphis over the Old Kingdom at an undeter-
mined time.

He set out to find the book of magic which Thot, the god of
wisdom, had written. The god had sunk it in the Nile, near
Coptos, in a golden casket encased in five other containers of
less precious material—silver, ivory and ebony, sycamore, bronze,
iron—and he had set serpents to guard the treasure. Noferka-
Ptah, thanks to his skill in magic, found the way to the place
of concealment. He overcame the guards and carried off the
book. When he had read it, he understood the language of
birds and fishes and all creatures ; he was able to bend the
heavens and the earth to his will, and he saw with his eyes how it
is that sun and moon rise and set.

The same thing happened to Ahuri when he gave her the book
to read. She and their little son had accompanied him on
the journey by ship from Memphis to Coptos, and there she had
fixed her abiding-place by the river while he made the magic
journey into the waters of the Nile. In her own words,

He gave the book into my hands ; and when I read a page of
the spells in it I also enchanted heaven and earth, the abyss, the
mountains and the sea ; I also knew what the birds of the sky, the
fishes of the deep, and the beasts of the hills all said. I read another
page of the spells, and I saw the sun-god Ra shining in the sky with
all the gods, the moon rising, and the stars in their shapes.

---

* The story takes place in the Middle or even perhaps the Old Kingdom, but
was included in a cycle of legends formed round a son of Rameses the Great, the
high priest Setna Kha-em-uast (nineteenth dynasty, c. 1300) and not written down
until the Hellenistic period, when ancient things came to be in fashion in a sort
of Egyptian Renaissance (about 250 B.C.).

But her brother was able to do even more than she could ; he was able to assimilate the whole content of the divine book, since he could not only read but write. " He called for a piece of virgin papyrus and wrote on it all the words there were in the book ; and he soaked it in beer and let it all dissolve, then he drank it, and thus he knew everything that was in the book."

But the god Thot took revenge for the theft of " his canon and law ". The highest god, the sun-god Ra, gave the intruder " and all that was his " into Thot's power. On the voyage back to Memphis all three were drowned one after another, first the child, then Ahuri, and then Noferka-Ptah himself. His child and then his sister-wife were buried in Coptos ; the prince was buried in Memphis by Pharaoh, and the fatal book of magic was buried with him.

This story is told by Ahuri. It forms the main section of a longer first-personal narrative, complete in itself, in which she tells of her whole life from childhood to death. She tells first of her youth—how as she grew up she fell in love with her brother and wanted him for her husband. Pharaoh, in spite of the ancient custom, was against the union because the two were his only descendants ; but in the end he gave way. She then tells how her happy married life was upset, just after the birth of her child, because Noferka-Ptah gave himself up to magic. " He seemed to have nothing to do but wander amid the graves of Memphis, reading the writings on the tombs of the Pharaohs and on the grave-stones of the scribes." This led to his learning about the book of the god Thot and his making it his life's aim to secure the book. She dwells on their conflict :

" And I said, ' Let me dissuade you, for you are preparing sorrow and you will bring me into trouble in the Thebaid.' And I laid my hand on Noferka-Ptah to keep him from going to Coptos, but he would not listen to me."

Thus we have, as in the story of the shipwrecked sailor, at first a narrative drawn from real life, indeed a love-story, corresponding to the erotic poetry that sprang up in the New Kingdom ; but here, as there, the autobiographical form serves to make credible the tales of marvels with which the narrative is filled. Even stranger than the magic and enchantment must seem the fact that Ahuri tells us not only the story of her life but also that of her death, and even her husband's death after her. The explanation is that it is not Ahuri who speaks but her spirit or double—her *ka*. It speaks because its rest in the grave has been disturbed. The royal tomb in which Noferka-Ptah lay was broken open by a son of the famous Pharaoh Rameses, the high priest Setna Kha-em-uast, himself in search of the divine book of magic. In the cycle of legends that formed round this historic personage the tale of Ahuri is incorporated as a ghost-story. Noferka's ghost in its distress summoned from their graves in Coptos the ghosts of his wife and their son. They appeared and were present when Kha-em-uast broke into Noferka's tomb. Ahuri's ghost tried to prevent the intruder from stealing the book. She told him the unhappy story of her life as a warning to him.

There are also examples of this type of first-personal narrative in Babylonian literature. In the famous Epic of Gilgamesh the tale of the Flood and the Ark is told by the " Noah " himself to his descendant the hero Gilgamesh, who, seeking his advice, made his way to him and found him " far away at the mouth of the rivers ", whither he had been wafted out of sight as a god. In telling the myth Noah even elaborately depicts the councils of the gods who directed the flood, and their emotion, as though he had watched them from his Ark. More remarkable still is an inscription from the library at Nineveh. In this Sargon, the founder of Babylon, whose legendary life is dated before the middle of the fourth millennium B.C., himself relates his mythical origin.[39] Mythological features, to illustrate the doctrine of the divine descent of the kings, also appear sometimes, it is true, in the context of the " court style ", which may have taken them over from a myth of the installation of the first king.[40] But in the Babylonian inscription the king himself relates the complete story of his exposure, a story familiar to us from Moses, Cyrus, and Romulus, and commonly known as a legend concerned with the founders of a religion or a State :

" I am Sargon, the mighty king, the king of Akkad. My mother was of noble stock (? a vestal), my father unknown ; my father's brother dwelt in the mountains. My mother conceived me of noble stock, and bore me in secret. She laid me in a casket of reeds, and closed the lid with bitumen." There follows his exposure in the river, his rescue by a " water-pourer ", his upbringing as a gardener, and his attainment of the kingdom under the protection of the great goddess Ishtar. He ends with the assertion that his dominion was of an extent that would be unequalled by any of his successors.

But the most striking instances of this type of first-personal narrative are found in ancient India. There it can be traced back to the Rig-Veda, the earliest document of Indian religious poetry, and later it appears developed into a widespread literary form, distinguishable to us in the immense mass of Buddhist writings. The fables and tales that here already serve the purpose of illustrating moral teaching are presented in the guise of miracle stories from the pre-temporal existence of Buddha, and Buddha himself relates them as his experiences on his journeying through the cycle of births, through the different forms of existence, animal, human, and divine.*

Different again is the use of the first person in an Egyptian epic in courtly style which Rameses II commanded to be written to celebrate his victory over the Syrians in the battle of Kadesh (c. 1250 B.C.). Seeking to make his story as realistic as possible, the poet narrates the events epically, so that the king is supposed to speak only in prayer and address ; but the first person continually breaks through even in the narrative portions, generally when it is introduced by the insertion of the hero's speeches, so that the progress of the action is described in several places by Rameses himself, and the narrative runs now in the third person and now in the first.[41] This curious procedure is not without parallel in oriental narrative literature. It occurs, for instance, in the Old Testament in the books of Ezra and Nehemiah and in Tobit.[42]

Thus there exists from of old a many-sided connexion between narrative in the first person and imaginative, even fanciful, poetry. It may be tempting to derive this connexion from the influence exerted by autobiography upon fiction. One wonders, however, whether there is any foundation for this view, held by various writers. The use of the first person has a claim to be considered no less authentic in fiction than in autobiography. There is a distinction to be made with regard to its use in poetry, according to the different instances we have described. This use may be a device of the artist, intended to give fiction a semblance of reality. Such narrative in the first person has an artificial, even a sophisticated character ; its instances from ancient Egyptian literature, such as the Life of Sinuhe, may be compared, as they belong to a relatively late stage of literary development, with the late Greek novels in the first person, though these novels have a different content, being concerned with the adventures of parted lovers. Moreover, by allowing

* See below, p. 86.

their heroes themselves to relate their adventures, the writers contrive to make us believe in the authenticity of stories that baffle our imagination. As a device deliberately applied to produce the illusion of actual life, the method is meant to play a trick upon the reader who is inclined to draw a definite distinction between fiction and reality, setting a higher value upon the latter.

But narrative in the first person was also found in the fairytales of the Egyptians. And everyone who is acquainted with the charm of naïve story-telling knows from his own young days, and observes again in children's stories, that the use of the first person is more appropriate to artless fancy than is the objective representation in the third person. Where his imagination revels in thrilling narratives, the story-teller believes in the adventures he has invented just as much as he wants his hearers to, and fills himself as well as his audience with the conviction that he has actually had these incredible experiences. There is something positive at work here : the characteristic activity of creative imagination.

On the higher levels of mental life this activity takes a different shape. Poets feel their creations coming upon them while their imagination appears to them to be in a receptive, even a passive state, " ever new figures, realized with imaginative clearness, crystallizing " [43] out of the first poetical conception. Historians re-experiencing in their own consciousness the lives of other persons, attain in the supreme moments of such reproduction the point at which their own personality is merged in that of their subject. Again, a quite general fact is the peculiar credibility that attaches to the ideas we have ourselves hit on, or have made our own, especially at their first appearance. This causes even an analytical mind to be at first more credulous and less critical than usual at the contrivance or discovery of something new. With these considerations we may tackle the problem of the relation between autobiography and fiction, a problem that confronts us as soon as narratives in the first person begin to appear. As these narratives are of different kinds, we shall be able to say one thing : their appearance is to be explained, so far as they are not of a late, artificial kind, by the psychological conditions of imaginative narration rather than by reference to autobiography ; and thus they are to be regarded as something primitive or natural.

This view is confirmed by curious evidence that shows us the part played by the first-personal method in the narrative art of a primitive people that has hardly developed beyond the stage of totemism. It comes from the Ainu, a white race (proto-Nordic) of hunters and fishers, the aboriginal inhabitants of the Japanese islands, of whom only a small and fast dwindling number live now on the island of Sakhalin. They have preserved by oral tradition a store of old songs and prose stories, which have been collected by European scholars since the later years of the nineteenth century. Of the ordinary tales in prose, short stories of five hundred to five thousand words, only a small selection, twenty-seven in number, has as yet been published [44] ; fifteen of these are told in the first person. The heroes of the stories, whose narrative of their adventures is put into their own mouths, are mostly ordinary mortals. In one, however, the narrator is the legendary first ancestor of the Ainu, in another a god who descended to the earth from the sky, and in three others a god in animal shape, a fox or a bear : this primitive race devoted a special cult to the bear. With two exceptions these stories all start straight off without any introduction— " I lived in my village ", or " I was a god that owned the upper sky ", or " I was a little boy. I lived with my two elder brothers. Every season when they went hunting they killed the deer-creatures. They reared me entirely on the flesh of deer . . ."

Most of the stories in this collection show the type of first-personal narrative represented in ancient Egyptian literature by the story of the Shipwrecked Sailor. They begin with a situation in everyday life—in the village, or in the chase, fishing, and so on—and then describe some wonderful adventure that ends happily and is the foundation of the hero's good fortune, that is to say, his wealth, resulting from continual success in hunting the seal and the bear. The adventure consists in the meeting with a superhuman being, either a goddess whom the hero wins as wife or a demon in the guise of man, animal, or fish, whom the hero or his guardian spirit defeats in battle or outwits. The highest distinction for a man, apart from his wealth, is to be " more artful than a god " or, much the same thing, to be " superior to him in magic power ".

Only one of the Ainu stories is free from the marvellous element ; in it we have the career of a primitive man told by himself. Thus we seem to have here a sort of autobiography. The hero tells how he was brought up in " the ancestors' house " by two uncles and two aunts. He would not go hunting with the rest, until one day they said to him :

" Nephew reared by us, hitherto with difficulty we have brought thee up. Thou reliest only on thyself. Though we would have gone bear-hunting with thee, thou hast refused. And therefore thou shalt go alone." He continues : " So I rose. I took a poor girdle, and girt myself. The ancestors' bow did I take, the ancestors' quiver did I take. I went out, and on the hunting-path went I forth."

He kills a large bear. Returning home with the quarry, he is greeted by his uncles :

" (By our) wish that thou shouldst do this, we have made a man of thee."

They exhort him to look well after the ancestors' house after their death. Thereupon they fall down dead. He raises a fine tomb for them. The story proceeds :

" Afterwards I lived as usual. I was still luckier in hunting than my uncles had been. Having two children, and bringing them up, I taught them."

Little of the fabulous here. But then comes the conclusion :

" Having fallen down on one side, I died. After me, I heard that my children did still better than I."

This conclusion is typical. It comes again in several other of these first-personal stories, but is not so striking in those because they are stories of marvels.

The conclusion to be drawn from this survey for the history of autobiography is that narrative in the first person as an elementary poetical method does not belong to its sphere from the first. The case is different with the realistic novel, which seeks to reproduce reality and tends to do this by means of the use of the first person. There exists here an inner connexion with autobiography, and it will be a task of our history to bring this to light.

THE DEVELOPMENT OF AUTOBIOGRAPHY IN THE POST-HOMERIC AND CLASSICAL EPOCHS IN GREECE

Today we no longer see the Greeks in the romantic light in which their incomparable creations were once revered as the perfect and ultimate revelation of every human potentiality. Historical investigation is everywhere bringing to light the natural conditions that limit human greatness. We are increasingly able to picture the interconnected world of the ancient East, extending from the banks of the Euphrates and the Nile as far west as Hellas, which had given birth to Homer ; we are also learning that the Hellenic spirit did not simply evolve from itself, and the wider panorama opened to us makes it clear that the creative activity of the Greeks, like that of other peoples, was limited by mental characteristics peculiar to them, and by the circumstances of their history. Thus we have reached a position of detachment even toward the culture that has influenced us most deeply, and we are ready to view it critically.

But this modern mood of relativism should not be allowed to destroy our reverence for the classical age of Greece. We must see the historical process as a whole in its true perspective. Stretching back through some thousands of years to the dim horizon of recorded history were the Eastern civilizations of the great river-valleys and plains. Then in the space of a few centuries this relatively tiny Greek people came into prominence and by its own genius reached a new pinnacle of human development, the degree of man's self-knowledge being raised at a bound. Then the tide of civilization turned back to the eastern shores of the Mediterranean ; into this Hellenistic culture Rome forced her way with vast power, underpinning its labile foundations, until in the racial conglomeration of her empire the life of the spirit began to stir and to shift the focus of men's thoughts and emotions, as religion reasserted its claims. Finally there was welded together the powerful all-inclusive spiritual system that was to shelter for several centuries the early development of the modern European mind. Viewed in this light, the history of Western culture seems like the work of some great tragedian, a drama that stirs and purifies the inmost being. It is as an element in this great process that we have to consider the appearance of autobiography in antiquity, necessarily piecing our account together from all too scanty material.

All that the oriental documents we have dealt with had to give us was a general view of the emergence in a highly developed civilization of autobiographical works that did not present the full personal life of their subject. Quite different are the problems offered us by the classical peoples of the Mediterranean. A truly historical consideration of autobiography first becomes possible with the Hellenic world. Here we are no longer confined to an empiricist description of our material, approaching it from without while simply taking note of the opportunities that have occurred for autobiographical writing. Here, in the Greco-Roman world, is enacted the great spectacle of a continuous intellectual evolution. Fragmentary as is our knowledge of long stretches of this evolution, it nevertheless reveals a complete and unified whole, starting from definable beginnings, passing through an incomparable variety of historical periods, and finally coming in the Dark Ages to a visible end, although in the last resort it remains as great a mystery as every beginning and ending of life. If it is to be of any intrinsic human interest, autobiography must be related in its commencement and continuance to the course of this intellectual development. And from the nature of this relationship it should be possible to gain a general insight into the nature of autobiography.

If the relationship were simple, like that prevailing in the modern world from whose different epochs we possess autobiographical documents, then the history of ancient autobiography would be able to provide us with the basis we need ; we should find in Greece a topography, as it were, of the typical forms of autobiography, just as we do in the case of most other branches of literature. The literary forms in which the various methods of men's self-examination are reflected would thus be given in historical sequence, each in its place in the pageant of Greek thought. With this picture before our mind, we should be able to consider the luxuriance of autobiography among the nations of the modern world ; in this later development we should easily recognize, as on a new world-map, the regularity of the appearance and growth of autobiography in modern times and its different character from that of the ancients. This would be of the greater importance since in the Western world

Hellenic culture alone has risen independently to the freedom
of deep human self-knowledge, while it is precisely this ancient
treasure that the later peoples have inherited and then creatively
made their own. But the actual facts of the course of history
are more complicated and have a deeper meaning.

If we take stock of the autobiographies that remain to us
from antiquity, we are struck first of all—as regards the centuries
before the birth of Christ—by a remarkable incongruity. In
the Greek culture, which, as will presently be explained, discovered and freed human personality, and found so many forms
in which to portray it, autobiography has only a restricted place,
as a literary speciality of secondary importance. Apart from
the autobiographies of statesmen and generals, the only type
that is cultivated to any significant extent is that of the literary
man, and as a rule this type only goes deeper for didactic purposes
—the illustration of an ideal of culture, and the like. Even these
autobiographies suffer a good deal from the literary trend that
treated them as mere matter for the display of the art of rhetoric.
Outside the political sphere hardly a single outstanding personality appears among the autobiographers of pre-Christian times.
It was only under the conditions that brought about the collapse
of the ancient type of civilization that autobiography attained
full independence among the ancient peoples, and, as a branch
of literature in the modern sense, undertook the intimate revelation of the whole course of an individual life.

It must be admitted that here we have a limitation of the
Greek spirit. For although the fewness of the survivals, especially
from the Hellenistic period, imposes a cautious reserve in any
general judgment, one thing is plain—that it is not to a mere
chance that we owe our lack of knowledge, but that the reason
for this peculiar feature must somehow lie in the Greek attitude
to the realities of life. Aristotle introduced into his portrayal
of the magnanimous man—his ideal of humanity—as one of his
characteristics the fixed habit in his self-sufficiency of never
discussing either himself or other persons.*

This conception of man is presented to us most clearly in
Greek sculpture—the majestic aloofness of the soul, which will
never entirely reveal and confess its inmost thoughts and feelings,

* Arist., *Nic. Eth.*, IV, 8. Οὐδ' ἀνθρωπολόγος· οὔτε γὰρ περὶ αὑτοῦ ἐρεῖ· οὔτε
περὶ ἑτέρου· οὔτε γὰρ ἵνα ἐπαινῆται μέλει αὐτῷ οὔθ' ὅπως οἱ ἄλλοι ψέγωνται οὐδ' αὖ
ἐπαινετικός ἐστιν· διόπερ οὐδὲ κακόλογος, οὐδὲ τῶν ἐχθρῶν εἰ μὴ δι' ὕβριν. Whether
this is reaction against a prevalence of gossip is beside the point, since here the question
is simply of the position of autobiography in the world of the spirit.

C*

the physical contour and poise of a personality that does not abandon itself to the moment but itself gives form to every situation. Man, who only attains man's dignity in his complete development, has his inner unity not in the historical process of his life, but in the balanced power of a will guided by reason, or, to quote Plato, of " the wise and calm temper which is constantly uniform and unchanging ".[1] Philosophically, this kind of vision is to be found in the Greek idea of life, in the meaning of the word *bios*, which first appears in Euripides. *Bios* means " conduct of life ", the " mode of living " [2] that reflects the man's character. So the whole life is summed up in character, and sculpture, which in its tranquil beauty can seize its subject only in a single pose, is the perfect medium for the full expression of such a conception of man. The sculptor's imagination perceives in every individual aspect of human existence the permanent ethos according to which each man in his own way moves and has his being. It was the sculptor's imagination that provided Herodotus and the Peripatetic historians of the " *bios* " (culture) of Greece with their insight into the individuality of peoples and into the distinct types of civilization. It was at work in the vivacity of the Platonic dialogue, which treats even abstract things " like a piece of sculpture in the round ", handling them and moulding them from every side. Biography, which became a definite literary form among the Greeks, belongs by nature to the same context. Its origins lie in philosophy, with Plato and Aristotle, and its basis was this same conception of *bios*. It did not narrate for the sake of narration, and any question of the development of character lay beyond its horizon. It was essentially concerned with the unchanging ego of the fully matured human being, whose personality, in Aristotle's words, is " first in the order of nature ", even if last to appear in the process of life. So here, too, as in those early oriental documents, man, that complex and variable creature, was treated as a fixed quantity. But here, with deeper insight, it was realized that growth is based on *being*—that is, on something completed—and is not merely the product of elements developing historically. This original reality of a man's character, which in truth gives consistency to his life, should not, however, be separated from the shape life takes : the shaping of life should be considered as a completion that makes a man's beauty. We meet here with the essential connexion of the ethical with the æsthetic that is expressed by the term *kalokagathon*. This Aristotelian or, rather, classical Greek conception of personality was at work not only in the formation of biography but also in other literary forms available for the description of individual life, and may be found epitomized in Pindar's paradox, " Become what thou art " (γενοῖ οἷος ἐσσί), that is to say, achieve what is your real self. Given this deep conception of the character of the individual, we wonder why the classical method of approach, implying the artist's vision of humanity, should, from its nature, preclude the presentation of the true content of an individual personality in biographical form.

The effect, however, of looking at man's experience in this way was that the peculiar task of biography was left on one side and the portrayal of the individual was neglected in favour of some general aspect of his character, as is proved incontestably by the works of Greek and Roman biographers that have come down to us. The ordinary biographer did not proceed inductively from observation of the particular to the discovery of the typical, which does not then lose the features of the individual ; he took as his starting-point the typical forms of life, the philosophical, political, moral, and so on, and then the individual whom he was to depict remained a mere example.[3] There are but few great works of biographical art, including those of modern times, and they are always made possible only by a living relationship between the biographer and his subject, whether resulting from close personal contact or from the historical influence still exerted by the subject and strongly felt by his biographer. Then the writer moulds for himself the literary form he needs. In antiquity the greatest representations of historical personalities, Plato's Socrates, Thucydides' Pericles, Tacitus' Tiberius, are in fact not given in strictly biographical form.

Now, for autobiography that living relationship and sympathetic understanding can, it seems, almost be taken for granted. And, indeed, in modern times autobiography has, for that reason, again and again set a standard for biography in general, which it actually outnumbers in documents of universal human importance. But in Greek literature the writers appear to have neglected the natural basis of the autobiographer's intimate self-knowledge, just as the philosophical impulse associated with the Greek conception of mankind became atrophied in the hands of the rhetoricians. Ancient autobiography did not develop on lines of its own, but remained for the most part dependent on current literary forms, not all of them strictly biographical, and from the outset its highest aim was to depict an ideal standard of culture or a definite type of character, cast into the form of a self-portrait.

In stating this historical fact, however, we must guard against generalizing. We are too inclined to infer from the classical attitude to autobiography that little importance was attached in ancient times to self-portrayal. To assess its importance we must take a wider view, regarding the facts referred to as derivative, and starting from the more deep-seated biographical impulse from which they derived and diverged.

The literary form of biography produced by the Greeks did admit of an all-round portrayal of an individual man. This is generally recognized with regard to the work of Plutarch, and becomes still more evident in the Renaissance. In that epoch, when writers looked to antiquity for their models, we find again in operation the same tendency to present a man's character fully developed rather than in process of development ; yet through their original handling of those literary forms some Renaissance writers mastered one of the crucial problems of biography—that of seeing at the same time, with an artist's eye, the broad conception of the individual, and, more analytically, the characteristics of which it is built up. And it is in the field of autobiography that this achievement is found. There is nothing in the nature of classical art that makes it incompatible with autobiography. Classical art, it is true, does not bow to the particular details of actual life, and it is also true that the objective works created by the imagination or by thought (as, for instance, Plato's dialogues or Dante's *Divina Commedia*) may frame the artist's personality with such truthfulness that on the whole he is seen as his true self and has no further need to speak of himself in his own person : personal matters are first sought by the scientific interest or the human sympathy of a later generation. So long as the imagination can go freely and fully to work, it simply draws from the writer's life the material for the shaping of its story. But autobiography, too, is by no means necessarily bound to the recording of particular details of fact : in it, too, the form of the work and the artistic shaping of the picture of its subject—which, when given, must be true to life—are of more importance than the recording of the actual data of the life of the subject, and as a rule the accuracy of the details remains open to question. Indeed, in face of the formless flow of the narrative of later books of confessions, it must be said that the classical attitude, demanding from the autobiographer both form and style, has permanent validity. Was that not Goethe's own rule? The artistic purpose implicit in Greek literature may have made it more difficult to write great autobiographical works, but it did not stand in their way. The causes lie deeper. They are contained in the very general obedience to historic law which has determined the development of Western autobiography.

What we are concerned with is the manner in which autobiography first became aware of its true object. This object is the revelation of the full content of the life of an individual considered as a characteristic whole, whether that revelation is developed purely from within as the story of a soul or condensed into a portrayal of character or given palpable shape as a record of the outward activity of the inner life, a life grown strong enough to face the outer world without losing itself in it. Other types of literature, which can present human life vividly by setting forth particular situations, problems, emotions, and conflicts, or through a synthesis of different characters, may grow and attain a high degree of perfection without directing their whole attention to the inner life of the individual. For autobiography there is laid down by the very nature of its subject matter a law of development that does not, or at least does not so exclusively, determine the development of poetry or of literature in general. As the scope of the individual's mental life, and therewith his capacity to shape his life (or, in a word, his personality), increases, so also the importance of the autobiographer's attempt grows. But his ability to grasp and then to hold fast to his supreme aim depends on his becoming aware of the significance of that aim : the autobiographer's task must, in the course of the development of the human mind, have been disclosed in its full reality and recognized as a supreme object of human effort. That is the condition for the assessment of autobiography as a thing to be pursued for its own sake, and not merely as a matter of vanity, and for its elevation to the rank of those objectives in whose pursuit the human mind marches forward.

Now, this disclosure of the significance of individual life has been a long historical process. The philosophic spirit of the Greeks traced only the first difficult steps, beginning with the determination of the ethical process on which depends the firmness of character and the trueness to self of the person guided by reason, and proceeding to the Stoic concept of personality.

That concept, fundamental as it remained, was nevertheless formal and, in a sense, abstract—until it came by religious experience to be related to the pantheistic view of the world, so that the individual found himself in his relation to the one universal source of all life, as we shall see in Marcus Aurelius. The full reality of the unique life of the soul was not revealed to the ancients,[4] and devices other than those at the disposal of the sculptor's imagination and the philosopher's reasoning were required in order to give any grasp of that reality with its lack of precise boundaries, its endless expansions, and its elusive changes. But it was from the ancient world itself that these modifications in man's attitude towards existence emerged, to result in Augustine's time in the creative lifting of autobiography above all other types of literature. In this lies the true problem of our history in regard to ancient times. It will have to be shown which literary forms of self-presentation developed in antiquity out of reflection on inner experience, and within what limits they approached autobiography.

In ancient literature, apart from a comparatively large number of political autobiographies, and from the highly sophisticated form of rhetorical biography and romantic self-portrayal, we meet with the more or less embryonic development of that spiritual kind of self-examination which helps man in his task of knowing himself. This creation of personal literary forms of expression in the revelation of self led past Cicero and Seneca to the soliloquies of Marcus Aurelius, and reached its climax in connexion with Hellenistic mysticism in the lyrics of Gregory of Nazianzus and the Confessions of Augustine. It then started afresh and continued steadily in the religious life of the Catholic Middle Ages until it gave the impulse to secular autobiography from the Renaissance onwards. In this sense the foundation of the history of autobiography is to be sought in the ancient Greek and Roman world.

THE DISCOVERY OF INDIVIDUALITY: RELATION OF THAT EVENT TO AUTOBIOGRAPHY

The historic process which, following Jacob Burckhardt,* we describe as the discovery of individuality, may be traced by us at three different points within European civilization. In the glorious spring of the free Hellenic spirit, in those centuries full of promise that followed the age of Homer, between the dissolution of the early orders of society and the consolidation of the Attic civilization of the fifth century B.C. resulting from the victories over Persia, there came the first succession of independent personalities of European stamp, mostly shadowy figures for us but nevertheless unmistakable. They made their first appearance in the enterprising world of the Ionian shores and islands— religious, prophetic figures, the political individuality of the tyrant, lyric poets, thinkers. About the same period, but confined to the religious life, there came the process of the emancipation of the individual, from the seventh century onward, through the spirit of the prophets in Israel—a process that was later to spread through the civilized world. And finally came the new emergence of individuality in the Renaissance, the great day on which man found himself invested with a freedom and scope such as had never before been experienced, at his first awakening to consciousness of self: the inmost soul burst forth out of an eternity of unrealized immanence and found itself awake to this world, so that the individual was able to grasp reality with every organ.

* Burckhardt's famous words about the Discovery of Man may here be quoted from his book *Die Kultur der Renaissance in Italien* :
" In the Middle Ages the two sides of consciousness—regarding the world and regarding the inward man—lay, as it were, dreaming and half awake under a common veil. The veil was woven of faith, childish naïveté, and illusion ; seen through it, the world and history appeared in wonderful colours, but man knew himself only as race, people, party, corporation, family, or in some other generalized form. This veil was first driven off by the breezes of Italy ; with awakening came an objective consideration and treatment of the State and of all things of this world, but at the same time the subjective element developed into full vigour ; man became a spiritual individual, and recognized himself as one."

In so far as these sentences have reference to the historical problem of the Middle Ages and the Renaissance, we shall return to them later, in dealing with the autobiographical literature of the Middle Ages.

The Renaissance became the golden age of autobiography. The religious poetry of the Psalmists had helped autobiography in its great ascent from the expiring ancient world. But its foundation was laid, as we have said, in Greek culture. So the question arises, with what powers did individuality awaken in Hellas, and how far is the beginning to be seen here of the development that led to autobiography?

We have seen that the times before the birth of the European consciousness of personality were not lacking in instances of self-presentation. From the mediæval epoch, too, among the peoples of more modern times, we have relatively numerous autobiographies, not all of them religious, and in these there was at work not merely the association with ancient culture, whether in Christian life or in the traditional forms of Latin literature, but also a primary tendency to satisfy the desire for fame in a way characteristic of the heroic age of those peoples. Eulogistic poems belong to the earliest types of all poetry, and where the epic element expanded in them it was still possible for the song to have reference to a contemporary individual.[1] Epic itself bears witness to such customs among the nobility. The singer told not only of deeds of aforetime but also of the fame of a contemporary, very likely of an actually present hero ; this we find in Homer and among the ancient Teutons, and also among the Arabs of the desert whose early poetry preceded the religious work of Mohammed. Most moving is the way, in the Odyssey, the unknown stranger among the Phæacians hears his own deeds outside Troy praised at the feast by the blind rhapsodist, and then, overcome by his feelings, himself relates his adventures. Odysseus makes his appearance here as the teller of travellers' tales ;[2] but even among primitive peoples the hero is to be found singing his own song of victory.[3] Instances of such songs, celebrating the deeds of the tribe, are familiar in the Old Testament—the Song of Deborah, for instance. Epic poetry also provides us with situations that bring to the hero in his solitude memories of his past life. In a monologue before his death Beowulf recalls his childhood and youth, and the dying Roland recalls his ancestry, his feudal lord, and his victories. We shall enter into this autobiographical tendency of the heroic age in the next volume, when tracing the development of autobiography in modern times in the Western world, and taking account of the pre-literary portrayal of personality produced during the period preceding the Catholic Middle Ages.

It is not a rash conjecture to imagine an autobiography in epic form : in the sixteenth century a Swedish king related his war expeditions in this way in the *Rimkrönikan* or Rhymed Chronicle. But in ancient European literature autobiography did not originate as a sort of hero's self-assertion, but through the individual's reflective awareness of his personality. And the significance it has gained here, in contrast to its position among the oriental peoples, depends on the fact that, however late, it became an organ for the expression of individuality. If we are to build our history on firm foundations, it must proceed from the beginnings of the consciousness of personality, which was a present from the Greeks to the European world.

Personality is not a simple concept ; its method of formation and its structure show similar features, in spite of all individual differences, in the contemporaries of a particular epoch, but vary substantially from epoch to epoch, and there are typical stages of individualization whose formation and order of appearance will gradually reveal themselves to us from the records of lives in the great cultural periods. On the particular type of personality formed in a given age, and not simply on the coming into existence of awareness of the personal life, depends the evolution of autobiography.

The beginning for us is the discovery of individuality in post-Homeric Greece. This discovery was associated with a number of external conditions, not yet peculiar to it but belonging to the common elements of quite different forms of individualization and consequently capable of general description ; [4] these, present among the Ionians, reappear in the further course of our history. There is, to begin with, the growth of material and spiritual culture, as a rule the sudden consequence of the extension of the field of view to previously unknown peoples, with different ways of living. This gives the individual consciousness a more manifold, more comprehensive, and even more heterogeneous content, and the integrating energy must increase if unity is to be conserved. The scope for such integration exists as soon as the traditional social bonds determining men's ends and aims no longer suffice for the individual demand for a field of activity. *Why* man does not rest content with the old but rejects it, exhausting one stable form of social life after another—this ultimate question concerning the reasons for the development and advance of European man can only be answered metaphysically. A regular external feature of these processes that may be discerned is the ebbing of the controlling power by means of which the social and political systems determine the way of life of the individual ; various unrelated stages of the formation of personality show this in different ways—the dissolution of conventional bonds in revolutionary movements and struggles provides a fresh but dangerous soil on which the individual has to establish himself ; the centralizing organization of great States shifts the centre of gravity of the individual's existence from unquestioning association with the nation as a whole to an assertion of personal ideas.   Parallel with this works the destruction of the unsatisfying traditions in religious, moral, and spiritual fields by the widening of the individual's experience of his fellow-men and of the world around him : in the conflict of convictions the individual finds himself thrown upon his own resources, whether for simply making a choice or for new initiatives of his own.

With this picture before our mind we seek the particular feature that reveals itself in the first awakening of individuality among the Greeks, a feature that may explain the relation of that process to autobiography : we seek, as it were, the internal dynamic that raised up and shaped personalities in post-Homeric Greece.   This leads us back to the way in which the fundamental fact of our existence, the inter-reaction of the individual self and the world it lives in, was experienced.

A few elementary distinctions may serve to make the point clear.   We speak of ourselves as " individuals ", in the sense of spiritual and physical living units with such or such a definite make-up ; units aware of their own life—an awareness that is given expression in the little word " I ".   We do not say " It thinks ", or sees or feels or acts, " in me ", but " I think, see, feel, act ".   This is of the very essence of the human manner of existence ; we do not merely impart impulses and undertake actions in our environment (as do many things with a rudimentary physical existence) : as " living " entities we have knowledge of our intentions and actions as our own.   This common awareness of our individual qualities and actions gives us the feeling that the impetus of life is a sort of effluence from ourselves. Thus far, individuals may be considered as the units of which social life is made up.   But this is only one aspect of reality, and a subjective one.

For we do not live on ourselves.   Normal life includes an unquestioning acceptance of the fact that I carry on my life with a content that is not entirely mine, that I live on something and within something which goes beyond myself. I feel myself as emerging from a community whose warmth sustains me. In the words of a modern thinker who was concerned with a historical philosophy of life, Dilthey, " This seemingly independent being, in its self-consciousness so sure of its own unity, as a matter of fact only emerged in connexion with an actual society. . . . The fundamental trends of the will have within the individuals their scene of action, but no sufficient ground of explanation."

Having regard to this, we will set over against the subjective aspect of the bonds that unite individuals in life the objective aspect of those bonds.   Though I myself, from my own particular standpoint, take in the things of the world I live in, enjoying them or putting up with them, acting upon them or being influenced by them, my natural centre of gravity does not lie in myself, as if my gaze and my energies were directed outward from a freely originating centre of my own ; on the contrary, I hang like an apple on the tree of my physical and spiritual heritage, and the roots of my existence go down beyond tracing.   With these distinctions between the individual and the communal, and between the subjective and the objective, we may approach the critical phase in the formation of personality in the epoch of the discovery of individuality.   This phase stands out from the preceding and the following phases of the existence of human society.

The unity between the relations of man to world in religious experience, artistic observation, reasoned decision, and active intervention, exists in an early culture as an objective and stable unity, operating as a matter of course and falling alike upon every individual.   Thus the sharply outlined figures of the Homeric heroes, in spite of all the mobility that gains in the fancy of the supreme poet the naturalness of life itself, have nevertheless a common form : this is not provided by the individual for himself, but extends from the community into the individual as a typical element, in simple motives, feelings, and conceptions generally recognized as binding, connected together not in the individual person but in the moral system of that epic world, even though amid the conventions of aristocratic society the natural force of strong passions breaks through and throws off the conventional restrictions.

To give another example of the objective bond of society, it is characteristic of the Christian Middle Ages that " however independently the individual may act, at all critical moments he submits to fixed forms and views as imposed from without, by accepted tradition ".[5] Moreover, it is perfectly plain how in that epoch the one eternal ideal element in life, founded in God, is commonly considered to be the only real element underlying all man's activities. At a later stage of social development, familiar to us from the modern national States, individualism no doubt spreads under the influence of the thoughtful self-enlightenment of the bourgeois ; but general tendencies of an objective character are also operative ; for in these quasi-bourgeois though still aristocratic societies culture is no longer an undivided whole but is differentiated into intellectual systems independent of one another, such as religion, art, science, government, and so on, which play their separate parts in influencing the individual. He can now develop his personality in specific relation to any one of these.

Different both from that early and from this late type of cultural unity is the situation during the transition period with which we are concerned. To quote a description of Dilthey's relating to the Renaissance, " Every time a culture dies out and a new one is to arise, the world of ideas that proceeded from the older culture fades and dissolves. The individual experience is, as it were, emancipated for a time from the fetters of conceptual thought : it becomes a power in itself over men's minds." [6] Accordingly we may say that at such times individual life—devoid of objective support, as it is no longer merely a part of the community and is not yet developed in relation to well-established cultural influences—may attain a new importance as a single whole. It comes into view, as it were, naked in its fullness ; it is no longer the scene upon which the sources of life lying beyond the individual ego flow together, but it now creates all the content of existence anew and gives to it the only cohesion that lasts.

Through this the totality of the life of the soul must gain a new freedom and creative power ; for power grows through spiritual developments in those aptitudes which have received a new value through the historical or the individual situation. And if such free creative work in the totality of the ego makes up the energy of the personality, the historic fact is that this process does not run its course primarily in the subject itself as a purely internal process, but works itself out in the direct relationship of ego and world that is provided by experience of life. The depths from which such experience came to the Greek personalities of the seventh and sixth centuries B.C., the extent to which in the course of that experience the foundations were laid for the philosophic or religious way of comprehending the unity of life,[7] may here be left in the obscurity that surrounds that period. The essential thing for us to realize is that on the one hand this individualization is not to be understood as a withdrawal into the subject caused by criticism or sceptical negation, but the abundant energy of the personal existence must be considered as the primary and positive datum, in which reflection stands out most plainly as simply the enlightening element ; hence the peculiar mixture of acute rational consciousness and a reformer's mystical, indeed fantastic, faith, faith in the first place of the individual man in himself, which gives a dawning light that in the process of awakening illuminates the personality. And on the other hand we have to realize that this liberation of the person did not proceed from a separation of the inner life, of whose existence we are most certain, from all external things : on the contrary, it is an expansion of the self over the whole experiential world, so that the boundaries between subject and external object, between man and world, become fluid, as man's attitude to the world in thought, feeling, and purpose becomes fluid. The first methods of expression in which the personality raised itself to consciousness of itself must have been determined by this comprehensive dynamic relation between the individual and the world.

We are singling out only the elements that throw light on the method of the formation of personality. The process began in imaginative writing and reached its peak in philosophy : it is in the latter that the actual consciousness of the new is to be sought—in so far as we are able fully to comprehend it and it does not face us, like so many partially or entirely perceived phenomena of this time, as something inaccessible.*

The recognizable beginning is virtually the first narrative in the first person, in Hesiod (about 700 B.C.).[8] Hesiod gives his name at the outset of his work, which applies speculative imagination to the bringing of clarity and coherence into the confused

* We see the tyrants of the seventh and sixth centuries, who were the first political individualities in Greek history, only through the reflection of them in popular fancy, which places on record through traits revealed by anecdote, and through a moralizing attribution of human qualities to the workings of wisdom and of fate, the general impression of the exceptional and eminent quality of their personality. *Cf.* E. Meyer, *Gesch. des Altertums*, II, p. 612, and elsewhere ; he brings into great prominence the phenomena here under consideration.

ideas men had of the world of the gods. He had to speak of himself because the lesson he had to teach, the truth he wanted to set against the lies, as he calls them, of epic song, had not come to him from criticism and understanding but had taken possession of his whole being as he strove after certainty for his very life : he achieved the confidence and courage for personal conviction through the devotion of his whole being, not merely through reflection. For it must be taken as actual reality and no mere poetic form when Hesiod, the shepherd of the mountain village, makes the source of his " Theogony " a revelation, a vision of the Muses of the neighbouring Helicon. Toward the end of the Renaissance, if the comparison may be permitted, the propagation of the most rational religion, deism, by Herbert of Cherbury is similarly pictured quite dramatically as an experience with the personal God : by visible signs God directs the thinker Herbert to publish his work.

In contrast with the unfettered Ionic intellect, the personality emerges in Hesiod with difficulty ; it proceeds not from the restricted circle of cultured persons of social eminence, but from the peasant's existence, bound up with the elementary needs of everyday life. Hesiod's father had come as a peasant to Bœotia from Asia Minor, and Hesiod himself feels that he has been lifted by the Muses' summons out of the ordinary existence of the country-people around him, the " fools and idle gluttons ". The fact that he discovered the moral content of this peasant life, and had the daring to make this everyday material, in a poem on human labour, the theme of the art ennobled by Homer, this joining of self-confidence with the sense of the significance of earthly things, gives us a first full view of the soil out of which personality grew.

In expressing what he has to say, Hesiod keeps to generalities ; only occasionally does he touch on concrete details of his varied life—and he was the first to do this. Thus, in a passage in " Works and Days ", in which in the midst of his rules for peasants he goes over to the subject of navigation, he relates that on one occasion, and on that occasion only, he went across the sea, to a poets' competition at Chalcis, instituted by the sons of the late ruler, Amphidamas, in honour of their father.

> There I was victor in song, and awarded the tripod of honour.
> This my heart bade me consecrate unto Helicon's Muses,
> Who in the past had conferred upon me the gift of the singer.

It is significant that these lines,[9] which in the judgment of scholars contain " the earliest statement by a Greek concerning his life ",[10] have reference to the poet's art, and correspond in this to the procemium of Hesiod's other work, the " Theogony ", to which we referred in connexion with its element of poetic inspiration. Such other references to himself as there are in " Works and Days " have regard less to the course of his life than to its idealist basis. He proclaims the moral and religious sense that helped him over his worst troubles—his brother's duplicity in connexion with their father's property, and the judges' perversion of justice ; he proclaims that only honest work, proceeding from the good ardour that comes from God, brings blessedness ; that right-doing and justice are solid and lasting things ; that the steep and narrow path that leads to moral goodness rises opposite the broad short path of baseness ; and that the bad man is overtaken in the end by divine punishment. Thus his form is moral reflection, which assumes proverbial shape ; and within this a description, inspired by religious ideas, of the evolution of the human race, leading down from the Golden Age step by step to the iron misery of the base present, fits just as well as do the descriptions of the healthy daily operations and the earnings in farming and seafaring and the rules for peasants and seamen.

This is not quite the same thing as reasoned didacticism. As we shall see later, in Marcus Aurelius the apophthegms and rules he lays down for himself lose their abstractness through being practically related to his lively moral sense : here, at the outset of personal poetry, the course is reversed—the individual experience is set down, but it is not narrated for its own sake, so as to produce a literary form of its own, but the practical details lead up to the general reflections. This supplies a basic relationship to autobiography ; so also with the Hebrew prophets—their life with God comes into view only in its result, in the prophesying of divine law and judgment.

More complicated and needing a very cautious approach is the case of poetry, which had existed since the seventh century B.C. in the Hellenic culture that faced the Eastern world, using the forms of iambic and elegiac verse and of the lyric proper. Very significant is the simple fact that it was in such forms as these that the sense of personal life provided itself with its first means of expression. And then came Sappho's songs. Their wonderful art presupposed the play of a secret melody in the soul, creatively echoing its life, so that every stirring of the emotions became a miniature cosmos and formed itself into supreme poetry. Among the new fragments of Sappho yielded to us by the papyri is one in which experts find " some trace of the poem of reflection," in which the audience is, as it were, the writer herself.[11] But the broad fact that at that time individual situations and states of mind had become the subject of poetry is hardly likely to have arisen from such introspection. In Archilochus and especially in Solon we have two quite independent witnesses to the turning of poetry to self-portrayal. In them are contained the actual starting-points of the development of ancient autobiography.

How strikingly hearty and how close to daily life is the self-confidence of Archilochus, who says of himself, " I am the servant of the lord Enyalios "—that is, of the war-god—"yet I am also skilled in the lovely gift of the Muses ". He gives this picture of himself as a warrior : " In the spear is my kneaded bread, in the spear my Ismarian wine ; when I drink I lean on the spear." " Ah me ! " he writes in an elegiac fragment, " lifeless I lie in the toils of Desire, pierced through and through with the intolerable pains the gods have sent me." He attributes his art of song to divinely inspired emotion : " When my heart is stirred by wine I know how to lead the dithyramb, the noble song of the lord Dionysus."[12] His composition springs from the midst of the noisy activities of public life, with all its robust material, persecution, aggression, self-assertion, the grimly practical pursuits of an untamed passion—passion that gave him a keen insight into the neighbour's doings : Archilochus had a tongue to be feared. He talks in the most perfect verses of the concrete facts of his personal existence, of poverty and want, of warlike expeditions and of political struggles for power and of failure in love, of his " mighty talent " of invective, and in general of a life that in enjoyment passes resolutely over misfortune. A member of the knightly estate, but of illegitimate birth, he attacks the pillars of the conventional world into which he was born. He speaks without shame of his flight in battle : " Some Saian (Thracian) is priding himself on my shield, which I abandoned reluctantly near a bush ; but I escaped death. Let that shield go to perdition—I will get another as good." [13] Thus with limitless energy and daring he pursues his egoistic way, careless of the consistency that might create a personality ; for Archilochus had in his art an inexhaustible means for mastery over life. How he contrived to succeed we cannot tell from the extant fragments. What is certain is that he did succeed in making " the petty private affairs of a bastard of Paros, who . . . never made his way in the world, for roughly a thousand years as interesting, first to the whole people and then precisely to those of the finest taste, as the Trojan war." [14] When in the last days of the ancient world autobiography attained a central place in literature, Archilochus became, with Alcaeus, a criterion for the literary valuation of autobiographical material and of the function of imaginative writing in procuring a concrete future existence for the individual. [15]

It required a man of far more profound and far more serious character to make the first effort, through meditation on character and on the purpose of life, to reveal to the individual the moral foundations of his existence. (From this effort came the philosophic self-scrutiny that later produced the highest achievements in autobiography.) That man, in whom the ideal of the Greek art of life was attained with a perfection that ennobled mankind, was Solon, the Athenian law-giver (*c.* 600 B.C.)—one of the Seven Wise Men of popular tradition.

The native Greek legend of the " Seven Wise Men " recorded the emergence in that epoch of a certain type of personality—of men who were revered in the little Greek communities within which they lived, as excelling all others in their public activities and in the spiritual guidance afforded by their sayings. The name of " wise man " was given to one who was shrewd and well-informed, who was, indeed, in full possession of all available knowledge, in making use of which he threw his personality into the scales by intervening with word and deed at critical moments. Revealing his personality through his achievements, he illuminated his acts by the expression of thoughts that linked his personal existence with that of all humanity and gave him, within his own limited sphere, a certain perfection. When Plato once referred to the " Seven Wise Men " with whom it was customary to begin the story of Greek philosophy, this was the character he attributed to them ; he regarded the practical maxims these " philosophers " laid down as expressive of a superior manliness which he considered typical of the Spartan breed and discipline.

Even the commonest sort of Lacedaemonian [he said], whom one may chance to meet, though at first he may seem a poor talker, will yet, when the moment comes, throw some striking observation, brief and pithy, into the discussion, like a mighty archer, so that one suddenly feels as a child in comparison with him. Many have recognized, both now and in former times, that the power of uttering such sayings belongs to the man of perfect culture and to him alone Such were Thales of Miletus, Pittacus of Mitylene, Bias of Priene, our Solon . . .[16]

Solon's elegiacs and iambics, of which rather less than three hundred lines have come down to us, bring him before us in his authentic acts and thoughts as closely as a contemporary ; even Aristotle, who lived but two and a half centuries after him, used these self-portrayals in order to set up Solon's genuine personality against legend and political caricature.[17] From the technical point of view they represent the kind of poetry that was determined by the function of metrical speech in public political life, in the days before prose speech (the *logos*, as it was then called) became general. To quote Aristotle's description of the economic and political crisis in the midst of which Solon came into power :

The many were slaves of the few ; the commons rose against the men of note. The struggle was bitter, and the mutual opposition long, but finally all agreed upon an arbitrator and ruler in the person of Solon, and the reins of government were put into his hands. In the elegy which begins

I know, and pain lies in my heart as I see it,
That the oldest land of Ionia (i.e., Attica) is burning in a fever,

he champions either party alternately and then exhorts both together to make up their quarrel . . . exhorting the rich not to be covetous . . .[18]

Solon's poems recorded his great work of reform, the so-called " shaking off of burdens " (σεισάχθεια), through which he had decided the future of Athens, abolishing the old Attic law of debt, which had permitted loans on the security of the debtor's person, and restoring to freedom those who had thus been enslaved. His poems preface his political work with a declaration of political faith that keeps the social problem firmly in view, and they announce his proud consciousness of his own ability to stand against any assault from the upper or the lower orders : " we shall not permit it " ; they served for the justification and the preservation of his creative achievement, by establishing its principles and its methods of execution and with strong self-confidence summarizing what had been achieved :

I have given to the people (*demos*) just so much privilege as is sufficient for them,
Neither diminishing their rights nor seeking to extend them ;

And such as had power and were admired for their riches,
I provided that they too should not suffer undue wrong.
Nay, I stood with a strong shield thrown before both sorts,
And would have neither to prevail unrighteously over the other.[19]

The reign of law (εὐνόμια, " good rule ")—this was his concern, in word and deed, law and freedom being correlated concepts. For " freedom " meant for the Greeks, in the political sense established by Solon, the subordination of the individual to the local law given by the community to itself. In a lengthy poem on the σεισάχθεια, passed down to us by Aristotle, Solon claims to have been a Liberator :

Many I brought back to their god-built fatherland,
To Athens, many who had been sold, some justly, some unjustly,
And others who had been exiled through urgent penury,
And who had unlearnt the Attic speech ; and those, wandering far, who
    had suffered
Shameful servitude at home, trembling before the whims of their owners,
These I have made free men.

The liberation of the people through the " shaking off of burdens " was regarded also by Solon as a liberation of the earth. The poem opens :

Right good witness shall I have in the court of Time ; to wit,
The great Mother of the Olympian gods,
Dark Earth herself, whose many landmarks piercing her everywhere
I removed, so that she who was once slave is now free.

In this poem too he proceeds from the description of his deeds to the revelation of the political ethic that underlay them :

By fitting close together Right and Might
I made these things prevail, and accomplished them, even as I had said
    that I would.
And ordinances I wrote, that made straightforward justice
For each man, good and bad alike.
Had another than I taken the goad in hand,
An unwise man and a covetous,
He had not restrained the people ; for, had I been willing
To do now what pleased this party and now what pleased that,
This city had been bereft of many men.
Wherefore, mingling for myself strength from many quarters,
I stood at bay like a wolf surrounded by a pack of hounds.

Thus he humorously pictures his defensive attitude above the parties—exposed to attack from both sides, from friend and foe. He strikes a similar note where he speaks of the great temptation that would have assailed a man of less integrity, invested with such absolute power as the Athenians had temporarily entrusted to him—the temptation to make himself a despot or " tyrannos ". He tells of the way he was derided by the general run of politicians, who interpreted his selflessness as weakness :

> Solon has no horse-sense, he's a timid soul :
> Renouncing the good fortune that Heaven offered !
> He had the quarry in the net, but feared
> To draw it in, as though he had lost his nerve.

His comment is :

Even had I the power, I should not care
First to have boundless wealth and be dictator
And then to be flayed for a wineskin and to have my posterity wiped out.

To this irony he adds the positive expression of the moral sense that inspired him, the sense of the duty of observing due measure, incumbent in an aristocratic society on a personality of worth :

> If I have spared my country
> And have not engaged in tyranny and in ruthless violence,
> Befouling and disgracing my good name,
> I am not ashamed of that ; for in that I think
> I shall instead surpass all other men.

Thus far we have in this an example from the archaic period of the specifically Greek type of self-presentation of the political personality :   an active life in the highest sense, such as was possible only through passionate energy and determination, penetrated with good sense, so that the man of action was displayed in the simple ethical ideals, religiously inspired, of justice, of restrained virility, and of submission to the divine ordering of the world—a consistent set of principles on which to base his activities.

But that is only one aspect of the statesman's attitude towards existence, which urged him to portray himself to the world, using his art to reduce the tensions between men.   The expression of his personality is rounded off in his other elegiacs, in which the same principle of harmonious moderation in living reveals itself as cheerful and vigorous enjoyment of the good things of this world of ours.   Here again the general character of the message is preserved :   the personality secures and maintains its independence not, as in the later sophisticated ideals of freedom, by means of aloofness from the outward life of the world, but just by accepting the abundance of the good things of life and by preserving into old age the capacity for enjoyment together with the readiness for a continually advancing experience of life.

" As I grow old I learn ever more and more." Thus the picture we get here of an individual life is not shaped from the writer's ideology, but his figure emerges from his story through the reflections accompanying it. The finest of these poems, no. 12, which we possess in full, gives direct expression to Solon's mental attitude through a process of self-examination that takes the form of a prayer. It begins with the exposition of the values that enrich the personal existence, values of which Solon himself would wish to feel assured :

> Grant me prosperity at the hand of the blessed gods,
> And good fame ever at the hands of men ;
> Make me sweet to my friends and sour to my foes,
> To these a man reverend to behold, to those a man terrible.
> Wealth I desire to possess, but would not have it
> Unrighteously ; retribution comes afterwards alway.

Then his contemplation is directed deeper, to the ideal basis of his own existence, which for the philosopher-statesman becomes the basis of all life—human responsibility and the divine justice that permits no ill-gotten gains to thrive and in manifold ways sooner or later overtakes the evil-doer. Then it turns to a typical field of reflective poetry, that of the manifold activities of man, the various occupations in which each man works and strives after his own fashion. To all these activities the principle applies that there is no aim where there is no sense of proportion, since everything depends on the operation of the divine rules in the world.

With this moral reflection, by which he himself was guided in his actions, the poem comes to its end. In essence a monologue, in form this elegy is a religious act : at the outset Solon invokes the Muses, daughters of Zeus : " Hear my prayer." The artistic rule that demanded for the elegy the form of an address fitted in with the simple piety of a man who, though steadfast and conscientious, was aware of human limitations.

Solon's elegiacs were handed down as his poems " to himself." This title has a history illustrating the development of spiritual autobiography in Greek literature. The Meditations of the Emperor Marcus Antoninus (second century of our era) were given the same title, *Tὰ εἰς ἑαυτόν*—(treatise) " to himself ". This superscription is again borne by the book of Gregory of Nazianzus, containing his subjective lyrics, which developed into autobiography. Augustine, on the other hand, writing in Latin, found for his monologues, which aimed primarily at the goal reached along new paths in " confessions ", the " new and perhaps hard name ", as he called it,* of Soliloquies.

Poetic contemplation of the self, in which the religious attitude was united with that of the wise man, was only one form among others for giving expression to the personal existence of which man had been made conscious by the intellectual movement of these post-Homeric and pre-classic centuries. But the whole of that creative period is before us only in fragments, and it would be vain to try to determine the shares that belonged to poetry, religion, and philosophy in the formation of individuality. We also have no answer to the essential question what estimate we ought to place on the pessimistic moods that appear already in archaic Ionian poetry ; they are certainly not to be attributed simply to the increase of culture, or to the loss of political freedom through the Lydian conquest, with the resulting ebbing of the joy of life, but have a deeper, a problematic significance. This difficult problem, the solution of which would be of great importance for the understanding of the history of the Greek and also of the European mind, offers one more task for a history of autobiography. For the realization of the uncertainty of the meaning of life tends, when combined with a pantheistic outlook, to give the individual a deeper sense of the universal human content of his thoughts and feelings. This is illustrated in later antiquity by neo-Platonic mysticism, and then in the Middle Ages and again in the Romantic movement of modern times : in all these instances that tendency developed in poetic forms of autobiography of a metaphysical character. As regards the Greek religious, poetical, and philosophical movement of the sixth century B.C., we know in general that in that great spiritual movement, in which the monistic religions of the Middle East were operative, the same influences first made their appearance in European culture from which spiritual autobiography drew strength in its relatively rapid rise under the changed conditions of the centuries after Christ. But we are in search of tangible realities that will make possible a confident decision as to the extent to which the men of that distant period applied themselves to the forms of literary expression of their own experience. And into this it is only possible for us to gain a scanty insight.

To start from the religious life, it may confidently be gathered

---

* Augustine, *Soliloq.*, II, c. 7, 14. " Soliloquy " hardly corresponds to the cynical expression αὐτοφωνία.

that in the mystical school of the Greeks which flourished in the sixth century B.C., forms of self-representation were developed in which the religious personalities introduced their doctrines of salvation to their followers, or to wider circles, as divine revelations, and based their mission on their own experience of divine grace ; modern scholarship has observed the varied later use of these forms in general and especially in philosophical Greek literature.[20] So far as we can see, their content was mainly determined by the religious imagination, which represented the fate of souls after death, and their processes of penitence and purification, in pictorial descriptions of the underworld and of Heaven, whether the writers contented themselves with simple representation as in a vision or carried their report of their experiences further as in journeys through Hades. Revelations of the future, with a political purpose, are also given with introductions in this form of visions, as in Epimenides. These types have their analogy within the more clearly discernible development among peoples of more modern times, and this enables us to assess their significance. In the Christian Middle Ages the expression of their religious inner life by the mystics, both monks and nuns, appears first only incidentally, alongside the essential revelations, which have as their subject the soul's journeys of discovery into the other world, sometimes with prophetic appeals to public opinion with reference to ecclesiastical, social, or political unrest.

So far we may illustrate the scanty fragments of the archaic religious poetry of the Greeks by mediæval literature that appeared about two thousand years later. But on the way the mystical life then shut itself off more and more from the outer world, while self-portrayal developed out of other types of revelation and the inner life freed itself from pictorial visions—on this advance toward spiritual autobiography such as is found in the Christian Middle Ages and also in the first four centuries after Christ, no light is shown by that remoter period.

Only in a last echo of the prophetic poetry of the sixth century B.C., in the transition period when the age of a different conception of man had already dawned, do we find the self-portrayal of the religious teacher in a vivid and even a strangely powerful form—in a poem of the philosopher Empedocles of Agrigentum (c. 450), called " Purifications ". This poem, of which several fragments are extant,[21] is one of the two principal works of the famous Sicilian thinker. The other, also in the Homeric metre,

" On Nature ", attempts a rational explanation of the universe
on the lines of the early Greek philosophy of Ionian origin.
The religious teaching. of the Purifications, which was only a
part of the work of this famous man, was concerned with the
dogma of transmigration of souls, or metempsychosis, a dogma
of the new religion of the Pythagoreans and also of the popular
movement of the Orphic Mysteries. Journeying through the
country as a prophet, Empedocles publicly recited his verses to
the people, in the robes of a priest and " purifier ", concerned
for man's salvation from " the wheel of births ". In " Purifications " men's life on earth and all individual organic life is interpreted as a series of penitential stations for the soul, which by its
nature is a divinity. The individual soul has fallen into a state
of misery from the original blessedness of all-pervading union
in love and harmony, when " there was no discord nor unseemly
strife between the members " of the living body called the
Universe. The causes assigned to the fall of the soul-dæmon
are hatred and strife or " perjury " and " murder ", which last
includes the consumption of flesh and blood ; all living beings
being ákin to one another, so that it is parricide to lay hands
on the animals.

The penance is a 30,000-year-long pilgrimage through the
manifold forms of living beings, plant, animal, child, until the
highest stage of individual existence is reached, the stage that
brings souls back into the neighbourhood of the gods, " as singers,
physicians, and leaders of men "—Empedocles himself was all
these, and thus was at that stage of the purification of souls
from which " they spring up as gods highest in honour, sharing
the hearth of the other gods, free from human sorrows, safe
from destiny and from all harm."

The means of success, which makes the dæmon once more
pure and free, is asceticism, abstinence from earthly stains and
especially from meat-eating. This preaching is introduced by
and interspersed with a self-portrayal in which Empedocles proclaims his atonement and his deification. Thus, after words of
greeting to the people, he opens with this striking passage :

I come among you as an immortal god, no longer a mortal ; as
such I am honoured everywhere, as is my due, crowned with woven
fillets or with wreaths of blossom about my head. When with my
train of followers, men and women, I enter into prosperous cities, I
am worshipped, and thousands follow me in order to learn the way
that leads to salvation. Some ask for an oracle, others inquire about

manifold sicknesses, to hear one little word that may bring recovery
. . . But why do I speak at length of this, as though I were achieving
some great thing ? I am more than they, the mortal men, doomed
to manifold corruption !

From this picture of his mission Empedocles proceeds to the
revelation of his doctrine of faith, and here again he describes
himself as one who has himself experienced what makes up the
content of his doctrine. In him as in all other men came into
effect the " resolve of the gods from all eternity " concerning the
fall of each individual soul and the transmigration of souls.

" To these did I, too, belong, one cast out by God, a wanderer,
when I placed faith in the furious strife . . . I was in the past a
boy, a girl, a shrub, a bird, and a dumb fish emerging from
the stream."

He describes the misery of this world as an imagined experience personal to himself :

" I lifted up my voice, I wept and wailed, when I saw the
unfamiliar place. A hideous shore, on which dwell murder,
envy, and the troop of baleful destinies, wasting corruption, and
disease."

Returning to the dogma of the fall of the soul, he exclaims :

" From what glory, from what abundance of bliss have I
fallen here upon earth, to consort now with mortals . . . Woe
is me, that a merciless day did not earlier destroy me, before I
wrought evil deeds, devouring food with my lips " (Diels' edition,
115–18).

One wonders how far Empedocles means here to represent
himself, telling the history of his own fall, and how far he is
playing a part, representing perhaps the fall of man, and interpreting the process of salvation, in a sort of theatrical performance
corresponding to the cult of the Mysteries. There is something
of both, and probably an acquaintance with earlier religious
literature would show that in the passages that strike us as
peculiar, especially " I come as an immortal god, no longer a
mortal," the predicate has the character of a formula expressing
a dogma familiar to believers. By the use of religious formulæ
the poet traces back his own spiritual history, of which he tells
in the first person, to that of mankind, as whose representative
he speaks.* In any case, these passages must not be regarded,
as modern ways of thought would lead us to do, as purely personal

* This corresponds to the use of the " I " form in the ancient Oriental inscriptions, which we studied in the innocence-confessions of the Egyptian Book of the
Dead. *Cf.* above, p. 31.

utterances—as though it were a free poetic development of
Empedocles' own soul's experiences in imaginative pictures
when he depicts " the destinies of the ego, felt to be immortal,
as a soul's wanderings ".[22]

The narrative in the first person, by a founder of a religion,
of his rebirths preceding his contemporary emergence in this
world, that strange transposition of things imagined under the
influence of a faith into the key of personal experience, is found
as a stylistic form in the religious literature of India, the classic
land of the belief in the transmigration of souls. In the sacred
writings of Buddhism there is a collection called " Birth Stories "
(stories from former births) * which professes to be a record of
some 550 births of the Buddha. The " holy men " or ascetics
were credited with such spiritual power as to be able to remember
their former births, and in these legends Gautama the Buddha,
whose earthly existence came to an end, according to the prevailing historical tradition, about 480 B.C., appears as the narrator
of his many incarnations, and recalls his actions and experiences
in various forms of existence as animal, bird, man, or god. Here,
for instance, is the opening of one of these stories :

" And again in another life I was a young hare, living in
a mountain forest ; I ate grass and herbs, leaves and fruits,
and did evil to no being. A monkey, a jackal, a young otter,
and I lived together . . . but I instructed them in duties and
taught them what is good and what is evil . . ."

In India this setting of religious dogma serves for moral
teaching by fable and fairy-tale. The collection of the stories
from Buddha's former births is arranged according to the various
cardinal virtues—beneficence, abstinence, long-suffering, friendship, and so forth. These the future Buddha had exhibited one
by one in the course of his incarnations, while now in his lofty
perfection he exhibits them all, and points their moral for his
disciples. Empedocles, on the contrary, concentrates upon his
own self the regular course of man's spiritual history from the fall
of the soul to its purification, and makes impressive emotional
use of the belief in metempsychosis for the heightening of his

---

* *The Jataka*, English translation, ed. by E. B. Cowell (1895–1913). *Cf.* Rhys
Davids, *Buddhist India* (1903), chap. 11. Herm. Oldenberg, *Buddha* (4 ed., 1903)
makes the comparison with Empedocles, writing : " The difference between the
Greek and the Buddhist conception is merely that the latter raises the marvellous
to the uttermost extreme of the marvellous." It is not impossible that Empedocles
was influenced by Indian conceptions. Yet the difference between the Greek and
the Indian attitude to personality is particularly clear in regard to the doctrine of
the transmigration of souls.

personality. Here we meet with the contrast between Greek humanism, which accepts the assignment of value to individuality, and Indian mysticism, which denies the value of individuality and its very existence.

The Greek thinker's self-exaltation shows its most dangerous extreme when he proclaims himself a god ; even among the ancients that was felt to be charlatanry. Reflected in the " austere harmony " of his verses, the figure of Empedocles presents a romantic appearance. Philosopher and prophet, politician and priest, even " purifier " and enchanter ; poet and physician, one of the founders of the Italian school of medicine, he shows a versatility that confronts us with opposite extremes in one and the same person. Though himself a noble, he played a leading part in the democratic revolution of his Sicilian mother-city. In his didactic poem of natural philosophy, which has rich scientific content—it contains the doctrine of the Four Elements —he adopts the attitude of the empiric, declaring that we must make the best use we can of our senses, checking one by another ; conscious of the limitations of human knowledge, he addresses his pupil, " Thou shalt learn no more than mortal mind has power to learn " ; but he ends his instruction like a magician, professing to have superhuman powers ; he promises to give his pupil power over wind and rain, over age and sickness ; " thou shalt bring back from Hades the life of a dead man ". As an enlightened thinker he accepted the results of contemporary philosophic speculation, but he also accepted the doctrines of the Mysteries, in order to have a reforming influence over the masses, to reveal to them the secret of life and the interconnexion of all things in the world, and to bring them salvation. Envisaged with regard to man's self-knowledge, this striking figure, in spite of the bizarre exaggeration of certain traits, again reveals the typical structure of personality in that epoch of the first discovery of individuality in the Western world. Behind the apparent vainglorious assumption implicit in Empedocles' claim to divinity, we recognize a characteristic type of self-confidence, a creative man's belief in himself, which we might today describe as a sense of genius.

The greatly extended and even contradictory elements of civilization that surge round the individual in an epoch of transition, battled with one another in Empedocles to an exceptional degree ; and thanks to his personality he embraced and reconciled them all : the strength of his personal influence over men and women was incontestable. But he could not explain to himself the mystery of his creative power, of which he was in some way conscious, from his own empirical, even mechanistic, views of man and of nature ; instead he associated his supreme self-confidence with divinity, an attitude favoured by popular conceptions of the supernatural. In the Renaissance we shall find an analogous attitude. There again the conception of man born of the natural sciences stopped short of the highest functions of the soul, while mysticism provided an explanation of these gifts in the ideas of " brilliance " and " inspiration ", making credible a direct illumination by God of a peculiarly gifted individual, lifted above ordinary human nature. In Empedocles, in place of that psychological explanation of the highest intellectual gifts, we find the story of the wanderings of the banished soul ; these end with the return to God, but before that end, which implies the dissolution of the individual in the unity of the universe, the elect attains the highest stage of human spiritual activity, represented in the seers and poets, statesmen and physicians. In this way Empedocles drew from the doctrines of the Mysteries a warrant for the assumption of the style of deity.

Yet philosophical thinking had already completed the decisive step in advance that was to provide a deeper basis for the contemplation of the self. Jacob Burckhardt formulated the law that the development of personality is bound up with its discernment by the self and by others.[23] The early Greek thinkers who had raised mankind to the new level of lucid philosophical reflection were concerned with the unitary comprehension of the " nature "—that is, both the essence and the growth—of all things in the world, man included. They did not start from the question, " What am I ? " (as did the Indian metaphysicians who introduced the method of introspection), but came to the problem of man from the explanation of the natural world. But this " objective " method of philosophical approach was in them the feeling of its way by the self into the whole of reality, which was itself considered to be a living, even a psychic, being. " Psyche ", the Greek word for " soul ", meant both the individual soul and life pervading the universe. Accordingly the sayings of the early Greek philosophers reveal at once the personality of the thinker as well as the thought uttered : they were not impersonal statements as in modern scientific speech. This form of communication is found again among the philosophers of the Renaissance, as an appendage to autobiographies. It is not to be regarded as a point of departure for autobiography, as a modern interpreter viewed it ;[24] the process, however, that prepared the way for the self-revelation of personality had been started : Heraclitus bears witness to this.

Heraclitus of Ephesus, who lived about 500 B.C., was an author, a stylist—a writer of whom it might be said that *le style c'est l'homme*. His style, proverbially obscure—he was nicknamed " the Obscure "—shows the enigmatic lucidity characteristic of the early metaphysicians. Plato, who discovered the greatness of this archaic thinker, formulated his root-principle in a plain sentence repeated again and again, " All things pass, nothing abides ". Heraclitus himself did not say this, nor did he refer in plain language to the universal flux : he said, " Entering the same river, other and still other waters flow toward you." This antithetical mode of expression has an objective significance. It does not merely show wilful individuality. Nor did Heraclitus simply adopt as a literary mannerism the oracular speech fashionable in his time. His style reflects his abiding consciousness of his metaphysical task. Aware of the hidden meaning of the world to be found in every part of it, he disclosed through the combination of seemingly contradictory sayings what may be called the " dialectical " character of reality. " Strife is the father of all things, even king over all " (fr. 53).* In transferring to Strife the predicates which in the traditional religion were the attributes of Zeus, he laid down the central conception that the flame of life is lit when opposite forces meet.

More than a hundred sayings of Heraclitus have come down to us, quoted by thinkers of later times. These extracts prove consistent, though there is no outwardly visible order, the book being lost. Their consistency is to be found in the dynamic character of his thought. He formulated the pantheistic principle of the one-and-all dynamically—" One from all, and all from one." This formula also holds of his style.

If we could have had his book before us as a whole, we should have been able to gain a demonstrable insight into the structure of this powerful personality, which was the first to live in the full confidence of solitary creative originality. This self-confidence was based on the consciousness of having originated a newly achieved advance in philosophic thought, and revealed itself aggressively in contemptuous expressions of his

* The figures give the numbers of the sayings in *Die Fragmente der Vorsokratiker*, ed. by H. Diels.

own superiority. " Of all whose sayings I have heard, no one advances so far as to recognize this : that Wisdom is something apart from all other things " (fr. 108). The fragments we have of his work are not fragments in the sense of detached pieces that need to be placed in their context in order to be understood and appreciated. Each is a whole, like an epigram, excellent both in brevity and in weightiness ; each gives us a separate glimpse of the whole of his thought. It would be tempting to regard them, following modern analogies, as aphorisms, and to see in this form of aphorism the appropriate expression for soliloquy as a method of philosophizing.[25]

The unity and consistency of the thought, clearly shown by the fragments, suggests at all events that Heraclitus shaped his intuitions as a whole ; but it may be assumed that the form he devised was not purely logical and abstractly systematic, but perhaps consisted only in an artistic adjustment of the aphorisms to a comprehensive unity. He himself formulated his whole attitude of mind in the significant declaration " I have searched myself ". This " metaphysical reflectiveness ", [26] which has nothing but contempt for learned empiricism, for imaginative invention, or for the self-satisfied living from day to day of the average sensual man, discloses the real depth of his thought.

Heraclitus' conception of the value of the outstanding personality is attested not only by his own self-confident utterances but by this generalization : " One is ten thousand to me if he be the best " (fr. 49). Then there is his valuation of fame, which lifts the " Few " out of the stupid mass : " The best men choose one thing above all others : they choose everlasting fame above all things mortal " (fr. 29). He himself, of princely birth, but taking part in the political affairs of his community as a spectator rather than an actor, appears within the petty conditions of Greek political life as an arbiter of " fame ", assessing men as though he were charged with the destinies of humanity. A good many sayings show this concern. A master of invective comparable with Archilochus, and sparing in praise, he set himself to correct public opinion about illustrious leaders in Greek spiritual life, from Homer and Hesiod to Pythagoras and other representatives of the intellectual and religious movement of his age. Anything but impartial, his judgments are imbued with the critical passion of one whose thought is moved by the desire for reform. He denounced Hesiod and Pythagoras as men of learning without the faculty of reasoning ; he even spoke of some famous men as impostors or liars. The value of these denunciations may be estimated from his conviction that " even Justice is strife ". Like the Seven Wise Men, he threw his brief and pithy sayings into the present. The Seven represented to the Greeks that distinct type of the independent personality of the individual in which, as Plato depicted it, wisdom was at one with superior manliness. Heraclitus also judged knowledge not only with regard to its content but as the test of a man's character. Free from the odour of sanctity and, on the other hand, not yet reduced to a matter of science, wisdom formed a unity with the esteem in which a man was held. In this sense " fame " was almost equivalent to ἀρετή, " virtue " or " inner power ". Since there did not then exist the conception of what we call conscience, fame was the means of ascertaining one's own achievement. When the propounder of the doctrine of flux spoke, in an apparent contradiction of that doctrine, of immortal fame, he had in mind the moral worth of the personality, a quality that does not disappear with death.

At this point we find his aristocratic attitude in harmony with the religious ideas of the representative of humanism in modern Western thought. Goethe, who no longer accepted the Christian idea that everyone has a divine, immortal soul, of equal value and conferring an equal right to personal salvation, expressed his belief in the individual immortality of the best men. Nature, he argued, would not dissipate her treasure and destroy in death the mightiest minds. These he regarded as active units lasting beyond death and taking their place within the gradational order of divine forces operative in all Creation. In this way he combined his belief in the immortality of some of the elect with the organic, pantheistic view of Nature. Now, just as Goethe refused to admit the passing of a fully developed individuality at death, so Heraclitus seems to have claimed for the pure, the elect, not only the reward of fame but also the continued existence of their individual soul after death, in such a way that these souls, as " wakeful guardians of the living and the dead ", comparable with the heroes and dæmons of the old faith, remain in contact with the life on earth, though the nature of that contact lies in mystical obscurity.[27]

On the other hand, the psychological profundity of the philosophy of Heraclitus lies in the very fact that by his insight into the unceasing flow of life he destroyed the static idea of man's person. Stability and rest being mere appearances, the common notion of substances lost its basis. Substance, however one may interpret it, means something immutable, and immutability was regarded, from the conception of substance, as characteristic of true reality, the " essence " of reality being then separated from " becoming ". What we are wont, from our traditional Aristotelian logic, to distinguish by these abstract terms was assumed as one in the conception of " nature " or " physis ", which underlay the explanation of the universe offered by the early Greek thinkers. While depending on this conception, Heraclitus pursued with it a course of his own, dissolving individual life into a continuity of transitions and so denying personal identity in man—so far as one's person is commonly regarded as secure, stabilized by a permanent element in the living being. In freeing us from this idea he discovered in all vital processes the continuous happening, becoming, and disappearing, oppositeness and the co-existence of opposites, so that the only constant thing was the law of change. The nature of psychic life, in which all is occurrence, was illuminated by this realistic outlook, which was extended from the soul over the whole world, considered as itself a living being. This conception received support in the physiological view of the soul as an emanation of the divine universal fire, regarded as basis of the universal flux, while, on the other hand, all becoming is " steered " by the Reason that pervades the universe. If, then, we go on to observe how the progress not only through the various stages in a man's life but from day to day is conceived by Heraclitus as a becoming new and different, described in terms of living and dying, we have the impression of a dictum from the present day, when the emphasis on the eternal instability underlying psychical processes has dissipated the idea of a fixed personality.[28] Taking this together with the valuation of individuality already mentioned, we may well ask how far Heraclitus saw the problems that face us here.

His answer is the affirmation of his pantheism ; it also gives his definition of the purpose of life—that the divine Reason which is at the bottom of the life-process of the universe, " steering all things through all things ", shall become conscious of itself in man. Our part is deliberately to realize the soul's relationship to all-pervading Reason, through the intelligence, by reflection (*phronesis*), so that with insight into the divine forces operative in us we may live our lives as specimens of universal life. " It is a duty to follow that which is general " ; " wisdom is the speaking of the truth and the doing it, in accordance with nature, whilst listening to it " (fr. 113, 112). He thus defined, as by self-description, the philosopher's activity. The influence of word and deed was characteristic of wise men such as were the Seven. Heraclitus retained from that definite type of personality the union of theory and practice, but based this effective union upon objective knowledge, truth in speech and action being bound up with the understanding of the nature of things. Aware of the inherent dignity and responsibility of the new type of wisdom he embodied, he distinguished philosophy, speaking in the name of Reason, from what we may call mere " science ", and what he called " polymathy " ; that is, the intellectual attitude of men content with wide but unrelated knowledge. " Much learning does not teach a man understanding " (fr. 40). To " listen to nature " is the attitude of one who, while intent on objective knowledge, does not abandon himself to the objects but from his own centre extends his self over all the world. In so basing both wisdom and true action upon reflection, Heraclitus reduced what is reliable and valuable in man to something rational and of general validity. Accordingly he decried, for instance, the poet Archilochus. But if in the description of his attitude the emphasis is laid not on the basic conception that the element of value in the human person is something universal, but on the denial of personal independence, is it a complete expression of the thought of Heraclitus ? And is his consciousness of individuality only to be conceived empirically as the self-confidence of the thinker who has recognized the truth that remains beyond the comprehension of other men ? [29]

No doubt the reason, that most impersonal element in man, is the first organ to provide clarity concerning and consciousness of the individual self, and at the very first outburst of the energy of the mind the valuation of that energy increases, as Heraclitus declares—" The thinking activity is common to all men " ; " thought is the greatest power " ($\dot{\alpha}\varrho\varepsilon\tau\acute{\eta}$). But the essential thing for us is still that which is behind the consciousness of reason and gives it its personal quality. Here the realization of the dynamics of the life of the soul is the essential thing : through it the boundary, not sharply fixed from the outset, between the physiological and the psychical processes was made completely fluid, and the Logos, which is the uniform divine element in man, remained nevertheless, as the element governing psychical changes, united with them, thus preserving room for some sort of incorporation of the consciousness of personality. There is ambiguity in the saying that the ethos is man's dæmon, ἦθος ἀνθρώπῳ δαίμων, " man's character is his fate ", as we may interpret it, without fully conveying its profound meaning ; for a concrete reference was intended in the term " dæmon " used by Heraclitus and later by the tragedians. We refer " character " both to moral strength and to individual peculiarity. Heraclitus conceived it as something general, as he did personality. He contrasted the human with the divine " character ", declaring insight to be " an element not of the human but of the divine ethos " (fr. 78). While thus attaching man's limited condition to his ethos, with reference to the religious idea of the inferiority of human wisdom, he credited it with the most decisive function, our fate depending on it.

The Greek word translated by " fate " is " dæmon ". In this word lies the entirely practical concern with the religious faith that claimed knowledge of what the dæmon is—with the theological conception of the soul as a divine individual being, housed in man's physical frame but with its own separate exist- ence ; or with the widespread primitive conceptions of a personal dæmonic familiar, a special tutelary spirit associated with the individual from birth, to rule over him through his life and to guide his soul as he departed for Hades. Concerned with the problem of self, Heraclitus opposed this belief from the same point of view from which he adopted the no less primitive idea of the warrior-heroes destined to be " guardians of the quick and the dead ". The belief in tutelary spirits represented a primitive view of individual life. As a personal partner in his life, the man's dæmon accounted for his dealings with the world, his good or ill fortune, and his actions. Individual life, though regarded as a single whole, was not credited with a centre of its own, but derived its unity, in that primitive view, from a special superhuman being. In the Homeric poems we meet with a similar view, a god intervening at critical moments to make the choice for the hero or to increase his strength. The idea did not yet exist that men are autonomous beings capable of making decisions of their own and acting on them.[30] But the Greeks created the great dramatic poetry (" drama " means " action "). In the poetical and philosophic movement following the epic period, when the individual aspect of man was disclosed, as well as the unitary nature of all things, " dæmon " came to be an expression for " fate ". Heraclitus employed the world in this sense. Declaring the ethos of man to be his fate, he asserted man's moral autonomy in opposition to the religious belief in a tutelary spirit.

Another fragment (fr. 85) points to the moral process through which the formation of personality then began under Socrates and his successors : " It is hard to fight against the desire of the heart ; for what it wants it buys with the soul." Democritus added, in place of this second, explanatory clause, " but victory reveals the man who has taken thought (*nous*) " (fr. 236, Diels). And if the identity of substance of the person was discredited by Heraclitus and the unceasing renewal and change of the soul seemed to dissolve the identity of the individual into a continuity of transitions or " deaths ", it was now seen how in the process of " dying and becoming " the self existed continuously in the progress of life : " Such is the logos of the soul : it increases itself " (fr. 115). According to archaic usage the quantitative expression signified improvement rather than accumulation, and did not merely refer to organic growth. Heraclitus stood by the moral experience of self-fulfilment through self-control. Read against this background, the meaning of the saying can hardly be mistaken. In speaking of the self-improvement of the logos or rational energy, while confining such improvement to the human soul, he distinguishes life as individuated in men from the other life-processes in the world by its capacity for heightening its own status.

Finally comes his deepest intuition, probably including once more a revulsion against the Mysteries and their established doctrine of the course of the soul, and determining the metaphysical foundation of the life of the soul, the god in us, as the Unfathomable, a forecast of Augustine's *internum æternum* : " The bounds of the soul thou wilt not find, though thou traverse every path—so deep is its logos." * It is because its rational element is inscrutably profound that he who attempts to see into the soul finds himself drawn to the unfathomable. In this sense Heraclitus, while despising the theologians' notion of the soul as a spaceless substance within the body, the vehicle of man's immortality, was brought by his cosmological view of both Life and Reason to the mysterious point at which the soul, linking man's existence with the vital process of the world, yet raises him above Nature as the being " searching himself ".

---

* Ψυχῆ πείρατα ἰὼν οὐκ ἂν ἐξεύροιο, πᾶσαν ἐπιπορευόμενος ὁδόν· οὕτω βαθὺν λόγον ἔχει.

AUTOBIOGRAPHY IN CLASSICAL ATTIC LITERATURE

The flowering of Attic culture in the century and a half from the Persian wars to Aristotle and Alexander has a direct importance, in its characteristic formation of personality and the corresponding presentation of character, in two respects for our history. The type of autobiography that proceeds from inward experience now gains, from the Socratic examination of the self, the guiding line for its future development. And, on the other hand, toward the end of the period—in Isocrates— autobiography makes its first appearance as a branch of literature. In addition to this there is a special problem for us, a famous document, in letter form, defending Plato's Sicilian policy. This is attributed to the great philosopher himself, and if genuine it precedes the rhetorician's work as an autobiographical document.

I. THE SOCRATIC SHAPING OF PERSONALITY AND THE PLATONIC HISTORY OF THE SOUL

If we consider the relation of these developments to the general course of the evolution of personality in this period, we find more plainly revealed the material situation we sought to grasp in our introduction. So far as that course reveals itself in great art, it may be given the following general description : A start with an idealization of man, and then the progress of individualization shown by the character-drawing in Euripides and in the Socratic dialogues, and in sculpture by the character portraits of the fourth century. This ideal representation both of men and of gods, practised also in the honouring of a famous contemporary, for instance, a victor in the arena, derived its enduring significance from the relation of the individual to the national whole, embodied in the *polis*, the city-state. In this characteristic type of State the community was considered to contain not only its human members but also the gods worshipped as its founders. Religiously seen as a moral institution existing to further the higher or the " good " life among its members, the *polis* thus, like an intellectual cosmos, kept alive the association of the idea of the State with belief in the divine ordering of the world, and so kept alive also the inviolable authority of justice and of the moral law : an ideal order that, in the words of a modern historian, was to the citizens " as real as any experience of the senses ".[1] In it, indeed, reality itself was absorbed, so that the artistic creation which conceived man in his perfection, that is in moral command over himself, invested him with a majestic self-confidence, assembling the national ideals in form and unity in his person through the ethically inspired imagination.[2] This material content gave its fullness and completeness to the classic conception of man, and so determined the new type of personality, the formation of which began with Socrates, in contrast with the form of individual existence offered by the earlier Hellenic epoch.

If we seek the point at which autobiography struck root on this soil, we find that its first independent appearance, in Isocrates, dates from the middle of the fourth century, and so from the midst of the full blossoming of the Greek art of characterization ; yet there is no sign in it of any posing of problems of the individual character : on the contrary, it is built up from the ideal of civic virtue which was then that of the average Athenian. Consequently this autobiography of Isocrates can claim no more than a limited validity as a specimen of man's self-presentation. It is connected with the contemporaneous development of personality not through its specific value but only in so far as it was that development that made its appearance possible. The course of our history would be misrepresented if we were to regard that contemporary development toward the conception of men as individuals as other than contrasting with the autobiography of Isocrates.

The growing interest of society in its outstanding men, and in their character and their private lives,[3] forming a fresh current in the general development, also supplies a background for auto-biography, though not its definite starting-point. Various cases may be observed here in which things that happened would have produced autobiographical works had they happened among peoples of more recent times ; in this Attic culture the general rule was that the corresponding methods of conception and representation were first worked out in other forms than that of autobiography.

The first memoirs appeared in the last third of the fifth century, about 430 B.C., in highly-cultured Ionia ; in them a versatile writer of the second rank, Ion of Chios, wrote about the great contemporaries with whom he had been personally acquainted. A few fragments of what might be called Ion's " Travel Pictures " are extant, recollections of Pericles, Sophocles, and Kimon, and also of Aeschylus ; they exhibit clearly a way of looking upon personality which we shall find typical of a social method of characterization. The impression made by the individual in society is placed on record, so that his qualities as a man are caught, as it were, from without, independently of any moral or intellectual assessment, with the modest charm of the simple joy in observation. Such traits are sketched as a self-confident, challenging approach, or the conversational gift, and with them the physical appearance is noted ; or a characteristic scene is reproduced, with witty and charming and vivid touches ; Sophocles, for example, is introduced as one of the guests at a meal, with all his natural unassuming kindliness and yet spreading illumination with his great mind. These pictures are the work, of course, of an Ionian, and " no Athenian or Western Hellene could have done them so well ".[4]

Ion's remained in that epoch the only work of its kind : " Athenian society's sense of the need to portray itself "[5] did not produce a successor to Ion, though its outcome was seen in philosophical literature, the dialogue taking over this function as an incidental element, and introducing even more regularly, as we know from Plato, characters and picturesque contemporary detail.[6] But there are further clear instances of the mingling of the description of contemporary events with character-sketches of persons of eminence.* While the great historical art of Thucydides rose to the conception of natural law which recognizes that the course of history is determined by the interplay of political forces and of concrete interests, and which fits individuals into their place amid these objective circumstances, the independent treatment of personalities was continued in the political memoirs of soldiers, and in the following Hellenistic epoch the personal became the central element in political and military historiography. As regards the classical epoch we have Xenophon's *Anabasis*, written under a pseudonym as a political

---

* Compare also the political polemic of Stesimbrotos, contemporary with Ion. It is clear that this was largely made up of irresponsible political anecdote, but a fragment describing Cimon's personality speaks of his distinguished and upright character and his reserve, in contrast with Attic smartness and chatter, and sums him up as " more in harmony with the Peloponnesian cast of mind ". *Cf.* I. Bruns, *Das literar. Porträt der Griechen* (1896), pp. 49-50.

CLASSICAL ATTIC LITERATURE

apologia. In it Xenophon uses the third person in order to give his account of himself the appearance of historical objectivity. His biographical epilogues to the work contain finished literary portraits that are masterpieces—concise assessments of character, based on an ethical standard, with notes of individual traits, enlivened by anecdotes. This technique will accompany us throughout ancient times ; the moment it is applied to the development of autobiography it becomes our concern, self-portrayals proper then appearing ; but nothing of that sort is known in Attic literature. We find in Athens discussion of the conditions for the appearance of a historic personality like that of Themistocles, and, in particular, discussion of the question whether such eminent qualities as his are the outcome of natural gifts or of education.[7] Similar problems were also approached in the eighteenth century ; then they appear in the background of autobiography, and a special analogy is offered in democratic England by the corresponding discussions in the circle of Gibbon and Johnson, where the influence of these critics on the art of biography may be gauged. No such influence is to be found in the biographical literature of the Attic Enlightenment.

To these negative instances may be added the accounts, not unworthy of credit, of two or three sculptured self-portraits of the sixth and fifth centuries B.C., independent statues in bronze or marble ; and the famous group by Pheidias on the outer face of the golden shield of his Athene Parthenos. Here, in the midst of idealized figures of Athenians in battle with Amazons, there stands out a bald elderly man in his working garb, with a block of stone in his raised hands : tradition identified him with the artist himself, and the man next him, in full armour, throwing down an Amazon, with Pericles.* In that case plastic self-portraiture (of which the resemblance remains problematical, and which is of the greatest rarity in antiquity, not occurring even on coins)[8] would have preceded autobiography by a century and more.

The concrete conditions under which autobiography then at

* On his bronze statue of Theodoros of Samos (sixth century), famed for its reputed likeness, see Pliny, " Nat. Hist.", XXXIV, 83. On a marble portrait statue of Cheirisophos (probably sixth century), Pausanias VIII, 53, 8 ; C. Roberts, in art. " Cheirisophos " in Pauly-Wissowa's *Real-Enzyklopädie*, considers it not improbable that this statue was from the artist's own hand. Interpretation of the figure on Pheidias' shield in Plutarch, " Pericles ", 31 ; Furtwängler calls this a guides' invention ; Julius Lange interprets the figure as the artist's signature and as a mark of originality—*Die Darstellung des Menschen in der älteren griech. Kunst*, pp. 34, 166 *sqq.*

last appeared will reveal themselves to us later in detail. But
what was the essential significance which the great process of
formation of personality must have had in this field? This
central question brings us to the development of inward experience
in Greek philosophy and to the influence exerted by this philosophical tendency on the conception of the personality of the
individual. It is in the emergence of self-scrutiny, not in particular autobiographical writings, that the essential factor is to
be seen.

The first condition is here the great redirection of intellectual
interests brought about by the change of social life in democracy, with its urgent practical problems and with the upheavals
it suffered, especially after the Peloponnesian war. That redirection is first seen in the movement of the so-called Sophists—an
intellectual revolution often described as the discovery of man,
or as the shifting of the intellectual interest from heaven to earth,
but requiring a more accurate definition in view of the preceding
epoch of the " discovery of individuality ", as we termed it.*
The mental phenomena which in that epoch had been conceived
as part of the natural world came to be seen in the Sophistic
movement as distinct from the physical universe in which they
had been included by the interpenetration of psychic and cosmic
life which we have described, and were distinguished as an
intellectual cosmos. In the study of language and thought, in
reflection on the State and on morality, the subjects of the human
studies had now come into the foreground of philosophical
enlightenment. Furthermore, the spirit of scepticism had proceeded from the recognition of the contradictions of the early
Greek attempts at a natural explanation of the universe to the
declaration that the nature of things was unknowable, and so had
furthered the same advance which had been promoted by the
social situation : the individual, who now had to decide for
himself, became aware, through observation of himself, of the
principles of human action and thought. Thus a new stage was
reached in the conception of individuality : individual action
was no longer the direct expression of the personality that was
a function of the whole community, but was based on reflection,
producing rules, where rules were possible, which were to give the
individual a firm basis and a fixed standard for his conduct in
life.

The great movement of inquiry of the Sophists, in which

* See above, pp. 67 *sqq.*

the problems of human life were raised, can count here only as a preparation and opening of the path. Its tendency is epitomized in the dictum of Protagoras, " Man is the measure of all things." But this famous and often discussed phrase, even if given the widest permissible interpretation, does not provide the theoretical foundation for the value set upon individuality, as a distinguished modern historian suggested, declaring that it amounted to the " recognition of each and every personality and its world of ideas " as the only reality that matters.[9] For in order to attain to such a valuation of individuality we must have become aware of the inner productive power of the individual's personality, and there is no sign of this awareness in the sceptical attitude maintained by the famous Greek Sophist ; it was fully reached only in the Renaissance. Under the positivist view first advanced by Protagoras, the human personality has no permanent form, every man is at all times a complete variable, and only through the processes of recollection and recognition does something constant enter in. Indeed, it may be that it is from Protagoras himself that the positivist doctrine comes that dissolves the unity of the self into an aggregate of partial consciousnesses : [10] Heraclitus' conception of individual life without the *logos* that gave it its profundity. For the Sophists' conception of the individual, rejecting the limitations placed upon the individual by the traditional contents of communal life, there remained only the φύσις, in the new sense this concept acquired as opposed to convention (νόμος)—a conception of the natural man that is rather ambiguous. That conception refers to fundamental characteristics of outstanding men, such as vitality and unrestrained self-assertion, or the gift of genius, considered as an abundance of inborn power that only needs a free outlet in order to be productive ; but it also covers an abstract idea of humanity regarded as one and the same in all individuals and in all ages, thus contrasting " nature " with conventional values. It will be seen that the problem of individuality was simply left aside here when a philosophic historian like Thucydides, in the only passage in which he pronounces his valuation of the man of genius in a subjective assessment, has no other explanation to offer of this phenomenon of the outstanding historic personality—he was writing of Themistocles—than that which he puts at the beginning and end of his character sketch, that the greatness of Themistocles came from " the strength of his nature." [11]

Personality is not a natural endowment but a product of

living. In the process in the course of which it comes into
existence there is at work, together with the unconsciously formative forces, the inner activity which goes on in the intercourse
with men and things, and which produces from a man's individual
nature, and from the many potentialities that each individual
possesses, the characteristic form of existence of the man who
has a centre of his own within himself. The first steps that lead
to insight into the nature or essence of personality and to its
independent cultivation are made not with the coming into view
of unconscious " nature " or growth, but with the disclosure of
the work men must do for their own development.

Since the renewal of philosophy along the path of man's
reflection about himself was the work of Socrates, all the fore-
going considerations lead us to the work of that unique man.
It is the custom today to dwell with regard to Socrates on the
destructive effect of his realization of the responsible existence of
one's self, a realization that constitutes a break with primitive
simplicity. Thus Nietzsche decried Socrates as the great sinner
responsible for the degeneration of Hellenic culture. The general
question for us is, from what sources did there come to men the
certainty about life which is at all times the characteristic of a
ripened personality ? Are there epochs in history in which the
individual, without having the support of settled conventional
systems and traditions (which cradle him in the pleasant simplicity
of a sense of fitness accepted by the whole community, and so
relieve him of individual decision, the customary being accepted
as the obviously right), grows into a full man as though by a
natural process, simply through the uninfluenced working of
formative nature within him ? And is the demand for steady
criteria, more or less universally acknowledged, a prima facie
sign of diminishing vitality or of increasing difficulty in finding
the way in a life grown more complicated ; or can moral reflection confer strength, and is the moral way of living explained
only through a consciousness of what is reasonable, a consciousness strong enough to yield the clear guidance of reason ? Differences between man and man and between age and age play
their part here, and autobiography among other types of literature, especially from the Renaissance onward, will be able to
throw much light on the questions each man answers according
to his experience.

In Socrates it is clear, and is even more powerfully demonstrated by his death than by his life, that the type of reflection

he introduced among men was an outcome of the authentic power of the ethical, a power which he released and disclosed. The purpose of that reflection was to draw the individual man away from a life of unthinking acceptance of the current ideas, conventions, and usages of his community, an attitude that had already been attacked by the criticism of the Sophists, and to make him the master-builder of his own existence within the community. The fruitfulness and the eternal significance for all mankind of the message Socrates set out to convey lay in the fact that he openly stood for all the joys and the good things of life which Athens offered in exquisite multiplicity ; he did not merely oppose an academic ideal to reality, but addressed his appeal to the moral consciousness that works upon all conduct in men's lives, alike in the ordinary striving after happiness and desire for enjoyment and in just dealing, bravery, friendship, and all that inspires us to the highest aims. With his inquiry into the character, value, and significance of all things in life he brought men, while still going about their ordinary activities, to watch themselves and reflect upon those activities. That reflection was an application both of the intelligence and of the ethical sense, and directed the energy of the investigating mind to the discovery of the things that are truly of vital importance, a discovery that must make possible a rationale of human activity.

This honest self-questioning, this sense of reality, this never-ceasing effort to bring conduct within the control of clear ethical notions, entered into history as part of the mentality of the classical age, a mentality that now revealed itself once more with both its limitations and its strength. Inward experience, as we are wont to call our knowledge of ourselves as opposed to that of the world around us, was not yet regarded as the primary means of access to reality. We may speak of the " inner man " with reference to that psychic reality which is directly and immediately apprehended by us as the reality that it is, not as a mere phenomenon or aspect of reality, such as may be the multiplicity of external things, but as something self-evident beyond which it is impossible to reach anything more real. Socrates did not rely on that kind of immediate experience, though he started from it. Superior to it was, in his judgment, the logical system of all the values of life, in which the empirical had its place and was thus raised to the status of true knowledge, the lower value being duly subordinated to the higher. Thus the intellect, in its comprehending and controlling power identical with ethics, seemed to be like the overlord from whom the actual derived its claim to validity. Consequently the Socratic reflection on self, in the course of which the person becomes aware of his independence from external conditions such as inherited traditions or ready-made beliefs, proceeded by an intellectual method which resulted in the individual being reduced to the general and rational. The " know thyself " with which the oracle of Apollo had warned men of the limits of the human condition, was directed to the individual man not as an individual, but as man, citizen, bearer of the communal consciousness, so that he might raise into the sphere of reasoned knowledge the manifold and heterogeneous values of life that moved him uniformly with other individuals. In this way he might formally stamp his existence, as it were, with the value of the personal, by giving his activities the sound basis of universally valid principles, to be deduced from a single supreme aim, the final aim of " *eudaimonia* ". The irrational element which we perceive in the lives and characters of individuals had no place among the moral facts which, conceptually explained and arranged in logical order, should give existence its shape and its independence. This Socratic attitude remained the criterion for the forms of self-examination that developed in ancient literature.

Socrates himself, by the unique power of his personality, aroused the creative imagination of his disciples so that it should bring into view this unfathomable life, and he must have had a feeling of it. His " daimonion ", as he called it after the old religious conception of a " dæmon ", is evidence of his consciousness of an inscrutable element which he possessed in the depth of his person. Antisthenes, after Plato the most outstanding figure among the disciples of Socrates, and founder of the school of the Cynics, spoke of " Socratic power " ; this, in his judgment, was all that was " needed by the virtue that suffices for itself " ; the individual's sureness of himself was bound up with the discipline of " work " and of " abstinence ". His picture of the sage as the fighter, the true Herakles, lasted many centuries, passing ultimately into that of the saint. Then in the Renaissance Cardano, who was the chief investigator of the problem of individuality in that age, sought to comprehend the phenomenon of his own genius by means of the Socratic *daimonion*. But Socrates himself allowed that profundity to remain unexplored within the sphere of traditional religion, from which he emancipated morality : the *daimonion* was not in his conception a constructive, creative force, but acted only as a warning voice, which he heard within him like a direction of divine origin, and so he did not bring the irrational types of experience into his system of personal morality. His belief in the exclusive power of universally valid knowledge to build up both political life and the individual existence was in keeping with the constructive, not destructive, character of his reasoning, directed always to positive conclusions, to objective determination of the content of *eudaimonia* ; consequently his teaching attained its goal at least in so far as the foundation of moral education was laid once for all : Man is challenged to use his reflective activity (*phronesis*) and to apprehend, as latent in our natural human impulses, the true values in their hierarchical order in relation to the highest aim of life ; only by so doing can he become free and take into his own hands the shaping of his life. It was the " formal " traits, so to speak, of the moral consciousness that were here brought to light as constituting the personality : the movement toward clarity concerning the aim in life—leaving nothing in the obscurity of the unrealized—and the consistency in holding to the good when it was once discovered : to remain true to oneself, *se tueri*. The limitation of this first form of self-guidance, by means of which it does its work in the pure intellect, was centred on the conviction that the knowledge of what is good necessarily involves its performance. We may wonder at this conviction, which contradicts our common experience. *Video meliora, deteriora sequor*—" I see the good, but do the bad." But at the bottom of that conviction was no illusion but the strong belief in the capacity of the reason-guided will to do that which is good. And this belief was not that of Socrates alone, but was characteristic of the enlightened thinkers who had founded a personal morality. There is a saying attributed by tradition to Confucius, " To see that which is good and not to do it is to lack courage." From Socrates we hear the maxim : δεινὸν γὰρ ἐπιστήμης ἐνούσης ἄλλο τι κρατεῖν καὶ περιέλκειν αὐτὸν ὥσπερ ἀνδράποδον—" It is appalling to possess understanding but to allow something else to prevail over us and drag us away from it like a slave." To that extent the paradoxical identification of virtue, or inner power, and knowledge—ἀρετή and ἐπιστήμη— meant an imperishable reinforcement of our moral energy, thanks to the man who could think so highly of man and his freedom. Under the influence of Socrates the ancient self-scouting grew out of this faith in the adequate force of the reason-guided will.

To this idea of the foundation of personality corresponds a conception of the course of a man's life in which, for the first time, we find biographical material treated from an evolutionary point of view. To single out this or that period of a life-span and treat it as a typical form of human expeiience, so that instead of one continuous life-story we have a succession of quite distinct phases considered as stages in a person's development—this systematic way of regarding a human life is characteristic of the mentality and outlook of periods of enlightenment, and is in principle the same as Kant's definition of character in terms of practical reason and moral law. Here Plato led the way. He systematically surveyed the evolution of philosophy from the Ionian beginnings down to his own time ; and at one time he gave in biographical form a description of the essential progress made in that development. In the *Phædo* he makes Socrates tell the story of his career. In this autobiographical narrative Socrates starts from his youthful belief that the solution to the riddle of the world was to be found by research into nature ; then came perplexing questions, typical of the stage of doubt. The mechanistic view of the world was counteracted by the conviction, prompted by the moral consciousness, that it is not physical causes but the aims he pursues that determine a man's action in a given situation. Hence the thinker searched for an explanation of the world satisfying that moral conviction. There appeared to be a prospect of the fulfilment of this quest by a teleology complementing the mechanistic view. In this sense Socrates refers to the work on *nous* by Anaxagoras, the Ionian philosopher who became the friend of the Athenian statesman Pericles ; he refers to it in order to show how he was impressed by the conception of the divine *nous* or reason ordering the universe according to its ends and aims, a teleological conception of God as the world-orderer that seemed to provide an explanation of those phenomena which were beyond explanation mechanically. But this, too, failed to bring conviction. And now the crucial turn—away from the material world to the truth in the realm of thought, from *pragmata* to *logoi* ! The explanation of this fundamental Socratic, or rather Platonic, insight into the primacy of *logoi* is one of the main themes of the *Phædo* ; Socrates' autobiographical narrative intervenes in the discussion in this dialogue at the point at which that insight is about to be reached, and so paves the way to it biographically, showing how Socrates was led to it stage by stage by his " desire for knowledge ".

We have several self-descriptions of this sort dating from the last few centuries of antiquity. In these documents scepticism also represents a typical stage of intellectual development, but takes a different form : the student goes round the various opposing schools of thought, sampling them all ; ultimately he reaches conviction based either logically on mathematics or religiously on Christian teaching or scientifically on the method of empiricism. That is the intellectual counterpart of the history of the soul that emerged from the emotional experiences in Christian mysticism ; among the peoples of more modern times both appear together in the Middle Ages, and in a sketch by Leibnitz of his own development the typical traits of the description given in the *Phædo* reappear.

The emphasis placed on the " conversion " that comes with the gaining of the first sure knowledge, a conversion from which a new epoch of positive work dates, as recorded in Plato's " Apology of Socrates ", became an effective element later in autobiographical literature. Just as in the Apology " conversion " is associated with an oracular pronouncement, which is given as the first cause of Socrates' public activity, so it is in one of the first extant stories of conversion among the ancients, that of Dio Chrysostom.

Plato's constructive conception of the stages of spiritual development gained immensely deeper significance for autobiography when he made use of it in order to develop his philosophical feeling for reality, which contained within itself the relation of the soul to the divine order, or the realm of Ideas. We must not enlarge further, however, on the subject of Platonic idealism. Spiritual autobiography, as soon as it set itself higher tasks, was bound to be continually affected by that idealism, as all high intellectual effort so truly has its source in Plato, even though for fifteen hundred years, from the very moment when self-presentation began to rise to a higher level among the ancients, he lived on only in Neoplatonism. Here, in the last resort, lies the origin of the whole type of interpretation of life that conceives the events of the individual existence as a process of striving after an end, finding in them a twofold nature, both earthly and divine, and explaining the empirical course of a man's life in terms of the higher or other-worldly reality into which

108   AUTOBIOGRAPHY IN GREECE

our human life extends. This might be described as the counter-part in the history of thought of the static division of man into an empirical and a truly vital, spiritual personality.

It was, however, rather in a dynamic sense that Plato himself conceived the relation between the human soul and the super-sensible or noumenal or spiritual world—however we may prefer to indicate what he meant by the myth of the Realm of Ideas beyond the universe. It is the dynamic relation of what is below to what is above, a relation familiar to us from the phrase *sursum corda*. In this sense the influence of Platonic idealism in the biographical field may be seen first of all in the fact that the religious conceptions that directly affect man in his highest concerns—that of man's kinship with God and the paths of the soul toward deification—are now raised to the stage at which they become the fundamental reason for an independent effort of the individual to cultivate the divine within him. This highest education of man, which leads the soul back into the spiritual world to which it belongs, is not a development in the sense of following the temporal course of the life-story ; what matters is the ultimate destiny of my soul, not what happens to me in this life ; this latter is something accidental, whereas the other is the essential, that is to say the vision of reality, of the Ideas in which the soul attains its true life. In this vision there is reflected the metaphysical consciousness that is present in the philosopher as continual experience, as well as longing, as the philosophic mood that turns away from the colour and splendour of appearances to the essential content of truth and beauty and of the good : thus does the true philosopher become immortal even on earth and divine, living in the Islands of the Blessed :* βάκχοι δ᾽ εἰσίν οὐκ ἄλλοι ἢ οἱ πεφιλοσοφηκότες ὀρθῶς.†

From this attraction of the philosophical mind toward the ultimately real, all other aspects of human life are given sense and significance, to form a unified whole that serves the attain-ment of the highest good. The longing that sends man on the search for truth, or, to give Plato's phrase, on " the pursuit of that which is ", is satisfied when his mind takes the turn from things actually seen or experienced to the order of ideas under-lying them, ideas grasped solely by the intellect ; with this turn to the unseen as the truly real the soul's divine power of percep-

* *Rep.*, 600D, 519C, 540B. *Symp.*, 212A. *Cf.* Rohde, *Psyche* (2nd ed.), II, 285.
† " As they say in the Mysteries, ' The thyrsus-bearers are many, but the mystics few ' ; and these mystics (literally ' Bacchants ') are, I think, those who have been true philosophers "—*Phædo*, 69D.

tion is purified from all clouding by the world of the senses in which it is captive.

Thus, here too knowledge is the royal road that leads to perfection. In the vision of the Ideas—conceptual entities that proceed from no experience of the senses—and in their inter-relations, is reflected the connected whole of the spiritual world, and dialectic is the method of proceeding through the hierarchical order of this sublime realm, in stern labour of analytical thought. As a method of reasoning, however, Platonic dialectic is a means of transcending the limits of the intellect by its own intuitive power —" *Ascende per te ipsum supra te ipsum.*" At the end of the toil-some methodical ascent through the realm of ideas the god-related nature of the soul breaks out in a full experience and, leaving dialectic far behind it, in a sudden act of revelation gets into direct contact with the highest Idea, the idea of the Good as Plato called it, from which the spiritual realm (and with it life and the world) derives its unity. This enthusiasm, which is the vital source of Plato's dialectic as of all higher human activity, now announces itself as the directing energy of the progress of the soul, while Plato develops the way that leads to the vision of God in the emotional attitude of man.

The love that reveals itself again and again in mysticism, with continually renewed content, alike as reality and as a symbol for the union of man with that which he regards as the highest, is concentrated here as the philosophic Eros in the relation of the soul to the eternal order of things. So in Plato's *Symposium* Diotima reveals the mysteries of Eros. The love for an individual human being, for a figure lovely to see, becomes the birth of desire, which in constantly higher unity seeks its object and with the increasing elevation of the object brings a growth of creative power. There are various sorts and degrees of love : its char-acter and quality are measured by the loved object. The higher the object of love, the higher is the rank of the love itself.

Once more the stages are distinguished by the degree of their universality and their distance from sensuality. First love may turn from the beautiful individual to beauty as manifested in this or that outward form ; then comes the turn from the sensual to the spiritual, first in the love for the individual and then in the love for beauty as manifested in the action and the behaviour of the beloved individual ; from here the way upwards leads to the love of wisdom—that is, philosophy,—and the creative power of this highest earthly love reveals itself in the productive working of philosophic thought. To go beyond this means transcending all human limitations. To the divine philosopher life at its best is love, centring round the Absolute. This transcendental goal appears to be attainable through the union of the individual with the deity, the so-called mystical union that consists in the beatific vision of the inexpressible divine fullness of reality, embodying the highest values, such as truth and goodness and beauty.

This Platonic type of spiritual history [12] had the lasting effect of a prototype for the didactic representation of religious experience in mysticism. It entered autobiographical literature from Neoplatonism ; when dealing with this event we shall try to make clear how far the form of all religious autobiography was dictated by that Platonic path of love. We shall find its most perfect exposition in Dante's *Vita Nuova*, a work equal to that of Plato in picture and symbol, and also comparable with Plato through the two-sided aspect of the empirical world that resulted from its relation to the realm of Ideas. For this world, which loses all significance when contrasted with that eternal realm, regains it as a sort of mirror in which the heavenly light is dimly to be seen by the human spirit, which is thereby incited to its upward voyage. Conceived in this way, terrestrial beauty and love, however transitory, reveal the eternal in the temporal— a Platonic conception, Dante's realization of which heralded the dawn of the Renaissance.

II. PLATO'S SEVENTH EPISTLE

Plato speaks to us through his work as though he were a contemporary, but he never speaks to us in his own person, and never lifts the veil from his own life and thought. The life he presents in his dialogues is that of Philosophy itself, as it unfolds and continually creates itself anew in the interplay of question and answer. The character sketches he makes as an artist belong essentially to the type of his method of expounding philosophy ; through them he attaches the line of thought in the themes he discusses in each dialogue to the reality of human life : only the person actually concerned in the subject is allowed to speak on it, or rather to answer the questions concerning that subject. Then questioning aims at raising to the level of distinct consciousness the subject in which the questioned person is concerned. Thus, throughout the various dialogues, Plato brings before our eyes the figure of the philosophizing person, together with the various characters sketched at the outset of each dialogue ; but the philosophizer is not Plato himself but Socrates, with whom he has identified himself in a wonderful way, no less artistic than profound. He makes Socrates direct the course of the conversation and utter the crucial questions and pronouncements, while Plato himself, holding the threads in his hand and systematically opening up the course of the discussion and each seemingly chance turn in it, remains in the background. He gives of his own without revealing himself or even showing himself reflected in any of the others. In the unique figure of Socrates he incorporated his own philosophical individuality in a mysterious way, showing both his constant proximity to the unceasing questioner and the growing distance of his own visionary thought from the Socratic irony ; until finally, in his old age, when the gap became too wide, he invented new figures in place of Socrates to give utterance to what he had discovered.

In view of this self-suppression, this sublimely objective manner of approach, the idea of any autobiographical writing of Plato's might seem absurd. And yet there has come down to us a document attributed to Plato and written in the first person, in which we meet the " divine philosopher " as a man among men, and see him in speech and action. It is one of the thirteen epistles that have been handed down with the dialogues in our Platonic MSS.

This so-called Seventh Epistle has withstood the criticism of modern classical philologists * who have shown at least half of the epistles attributed to Plato to be forgeries. It is distinguished if only by its length from the other epistles of the famous old man that have come down to us ; some of these others may also be genuine. This letter is almost a book, longer than some of Plato's early dialogues, and longer than the Apology of Socrates. To some extent it may be compared with that incomparable work ; for the " great letter " itself contains the philosopher's defence against charges concerning his influence over young people and, consequently, the political effect of his teaching. But this comparison shows up only the more strongly the gulf that separates this direct self-disclosure of Plato's from the great

* This epistle is now regarded by the leading experts as genuine. Von Wilamowitz pronounced it genuine in his *Plato*, II (1920), pp. 282 *sqq*. A. E. Taylor, in *Plato* (1926), p. 7, agreed with the general view. Forty years ago the opposite view predominated, so that the author then saw no reason to include the epistle in a history of autobiography. This section has been added to make good the omission.

works of his creative art. This gulf exists although the letter treats of a great historical subject. For Plato's sake we will deal with it at some length.

The epistle is concerned with Plato's much-discussed political "adventure" in Syracuse, which in truth was much more than an episode in the thinker's long life. He himself speaks of his "unhappy Sicilian vagary", and closes with that judgment his narrative of the "astonishing and almost inconceivable things" that happened at the court of the Sicilian despot Dionysius the Younger. But this judgment expresses only his ultimate feeling, in retrospect, in view of the unfortunate issue of the bold enterprise ; and it also refers only to the personal side of the affair, which could be judged from the common human consideration of good and ill fortune. The thing that mattered for him, as it does for us, was the high intention, under the guidance of his philosophy, that led him into the Sicilian enterprise. This makes his "vagary" one of the memorable historic events by which we measure the greatness of human endeavours and the limits of human achievement.

Late in his life, when he was over sixty, Plato left his own realm in the Academy at Athens, in order to labour in Sicily, then the most powerful State in the Greek civilized world, for the realization of his ideal of the State—though in his mother-city he had abstained all through his life from any sort of political activity. Dionysius the Elder, founder and "tyrant" of the Sicilian military State, had suddenly died (367 B.C.), and the prospect had opened for Plato of carrying out, in collaboration with his friend and disciple Dion, the most eminent member of the Sicilian ruling house, the practical mission of philosophy in reforming man's existence in society.

Dion counted on the teachability and the readiness to take advice of the young ruler, who was his nephew and also his brother-in-law ; the ruling power had descended to the young man from his father as in a monarchy. The younger Dionysius was then not quite twenty years old, a youth with little self-reliance and no experience in political affairs, but accessible to spiritual influence and unstained by the violent deeds of the founder of the realm. The two friends' intention, as Plato himself expresses it, was that he should train the young man and "rear him up to be a king worthy of the throne" (333b). But they had miscalculated. Dionysius, concerned to safeguard his position, became antagonistic to Dion and got rid of that eminent would-be guardian as a dangerous rival : in the presence of Plato he ordered Dion's exile from the country. Thus the high adventure began with an ordinary political quarrel.

It might have been tempting to see at once in this setback the radical difference between ideal and reality. Plato did not view it so. He tried to bring about a reconciliation between the brothers-in-law, and in spite of Dion's exile he held for a time to his function of tutor to the young despot. Six years later (361–360), with both intentions still in his mind, he returned to Syracuse in order to exert his influence over the ruler, who meanwhile had secured his independence of the various party leaders. Plato approached Dionysius in the guise of an embodied philosophic conscience ; but he failed to gain any sort of moral influence over him. After this disappointment he confined himself to the effort to end the unhappy dissension between Dionysius and Dion. Here, too, he failed. Instead of a reconciliation between the two there came a struggle for power. In this struggle Dion gained the victory. His victory brought within reach the great aim of building a true State on Plato's principles.

Thus far the course of events resembles that of a dramatic work in which the hero makes his way past an illusion and its dissipation to reach his goal. But this Sicilian drama of actual history ended in tragedy. Scarcely had Dion established himself as ruler in Syracuse (353 B.C.) when he was assassinated, being suspected of himself aiming at autocracy.

It was under the shock of Dion's end that the epistle was written. As Plato says in its epilogue, " When he had attained the summit of his mastery over his enemies he fell . . . and, so brought down, he lies, enveloping Sicily in immeasurable woe " (351d).

This picture of the fallen hero opens a quite different perspective from that of an adventure of a philosopher who had strayed from his path. And yet Dion, as pictured in the letter, is at one with Plato ; indeed, he completed Plato's work by forming, as it were, the active element in the Platonic philosophy which failed to materialize in Plato's own life. One of the main purposes of the document is to represent Dion as an exemplar for the active politician. In the friendship between Plato and Dion is disclosed the lasting and more than personal importance of the events which, so far as they affected Plato personally, were but a transient affair in his life. In the passages in the epistle that touch on Dion's assassination, we detect a sense of more than personal tragedy, as in those words in the epilogue. But this feeling does not govern Plato's conception of his experiences, as we might have expected, so as to give the unhappy course of events something of tragic proportions—using the attribute " tragic " in its precise sense, which is not at all equivalent to " unhappy ". For us the true tragedy in the philosopher's political enterprise is symbolized in Dion's fate. We see a necessity rooted in the nature of the historic process in the fact that Plato, in association with the statesman striving after the right, was involved in the struggles for power in the political world by his effort to transfer his ethical conceptions of political action from the realm of thought to contemporary reality ; and we seek to explain his failure by this historic necessity.

Plato himself tries in his letter to explain his failure, but he sees in it only a temporary setback, and not the outcome of a tragic conflict. In accordance with this view he tries to resist fate, which nevertheless took its irresistible course after Dion's assassination. He states the reasons why his and Dion's action did not succeed, in order to defend the idealistic policy they had pursued and so, by exhorting Dion's party to maintain that policy, once more to intervene, at the last moment, in the progress of events. This practical political purpose determines the outward form of the document. It has the form of an open letter, addressed " To Dion's Associates and Companions ", and begins with the urgent advice to them to hold fast to the political programme of their dead leader, as against the policy of partisan violence that was gaining ground in Syracuse. Plato uses this literary form, however, mainly in order to defend himself and Dion from calumnies—a use of the epistolary form with which we shall meet again in the autobiographical literature of the Hellenistic period. This frame for an apologia may have appealed more to the famous thinker than, for example, that of a fictitious defence in court. But this personal aim also produced an extroversion. The philosopher who found himself compelled to justify his action before public opinion seems mainly con-cerned for his own reputation and for that of his school, which had suffered from his political ill-success. To that extent he adopts in the document an attitude that is fundamentally different from that of a man suffering from a blow from fate.

The great aim Plato was pursuing when he embarked on the Sicilian enterprise may be judged in various ways. Those who see in the *Republic* the foundation of political wisdom will credit

Plato with the intention of bringing into existence in this world in his own day the State he had built up in thought, the State truly based on the idea of justice. Those who proceed from the realistic picture of the epoch of Sicilian history which has been drawn by modern research may offer the version devised by an eminent interpreter of Plato : " Plato's object was not, as had been fancied, the ridiculous one of setting up in the most luxurious of Greek cities a pinchbeck imitation of the imaginary city of the *Republic*. It was the practical and statesmanlike object of trying to fit the young Dionysius for the immediate practical duty of checking the Carthaginians and, if possible, expelling them from Sicily, by making Syracuse the centre of a strong constitutional monarchy to embrace the whole body of Greek communities in the west of the island." *

Both views can claim support from the letter. The practical political purpose is mentioned by Plato in his account of his first efforts in the training of Dionysius. He and Dion, he says (Ep., VII, 333a), represented to the young ruler the task that had fallen to him as heir to the realm—the removal of the menace from the " barbarians " which his father had only staved off. Plato went to work as tutor and counsellor by bringing Dionysius' ambition into play, in order to induce him to abandon the " Sicilian life " of indulgence to which he clung, and to adjust his mode of life to the moral requirements (especially the need for self-control), the fulfilment of which he represented to him as the necessary condition for his growth into a personality equal to his great task. In this connexion the solution of the special problem presented by the historic situation appears as the true aim and the philosophical education only as a road, the royal road, to that aim, which itself followed the traditional path of the power politics pursued since the days of Gelon by the Sicilian " tyrants ".

Matters appear in another light when Plato proceeds from the idealistic purpose by which he and Dion were inspired. Here the educative task was confined to raising the legitimate wielder of power to the spiritual and moral elevation of the philosophic life. That purpose had all the nobility the man of action can evince in this world, and the great act of statesmanship that would be the logical outcome of the union of power with the philosophic spirit would work for the good of all men, " barbarians " and Hellenes alike (335d, 326e).

* A. E. Taylor, *Plato* (London, 1926), p. 7.

This twofold aim accounts for the ambiguous situation into which Plato was brought by the Sicilian enterprise. We can see here the conflict within him between the philosopher and the politician. This conflict, which he had resolved in his youth by placing loyalty to philosophic truth above practical politics, had faced him again in his old age, as his later dialogues show. In these we see his effort to reconcile philosophical ethics with political practice. In the epistle, which reveals to us the Plato of this late period, the relation between philosophy and practical politics accordingly forms one of the main themes ; it is treated here directly,—in contrast with the impersonal presentation in, for instance, the dialogue *Gorgias*,—as the vital problem that it was for Plato.

In the epistle he refers to the original emergence of the conflict in his youth and to the solution he then found. Thus we have a piece of Platonic autobiography : we shall occupy ourselves with it shortly. But the clearness about his position that he reveals in this retrospect gives way to inward uncertainty as soon as he shows himself in the midst of the action that is the subject of the epistle. In telling of his Sicilian journeys, and even of the motives that inspired his decision to embark on the enterprise, he adopts successively or even simultaneously the different positions of philosopher and politician, without showing signs of any effort to unite them from within, as if, indeed, he did not notice the essential difference—a very astonishing thing in a thinker of his calibre.

This incongruity cannot be explained by the defensive character of the document or by its practical purpose, but it has the same effect as those features : the philosopher's presentation of his personality, as revealed in the epistle, is just as much impaired by the lack of inner unity as is the presentation of his great action by the superficial explanation of its failure—a double deficiency that is characteristic of the picture of Plato given by the epistle : it shows alongside great and strong traits the petty and all-too-human vanities which regularly make their appearance when a personality is endeavouring to impose itself on its environment. It seems evident that the self-presentation here given was prompted by the actual circumstances and not by any intention of portraying the whole man. This is consistent with the inferior position of autobiography in classical Greek literature. In this respect the document becomes an important one for us, even though it should be not Plato's own work but that of one of his disciples. But the problem of its genuineness, with which Platonic research is concerned, also gains special importance in connexion with our history. A disciple who set out to defend the head of the Academy against attacks might bring the externals of the personality, in which the person appears in his dependence on the circumstances of his life, into the forefront without doing any great harm. If Plato himself revealed himself in this way, he did more for the dimming of the lustre of his genius than we should wish.

In view of this alternative it seems of importance to examine the document more closely. We will follow the course of the self-portrayal without deciding in advance as to its genuineness : in what follows we speak only tentatively of Plato as its author.

(1)

The document is not a self-contained whole, but is made up of three different sections, held together only superficially by the epistolary form. The first and third sections are mainly narrative, the middle one didactic—an unmistakable difference but one that affects form rather than content. For in the didactic section Plato treats of the same happenings as in the other two ; in this section he brings them together from a systematizing standpoint that is the outcome of the doctrine laid down in this middle section. On the other hand, the two narrative sections, treating of Plato's two Sicilian journeys, widely separated in time from each other, are not purely narrative : each has a special theme that determines the selection of material.

In the first section the philosopher's attitude to practical politics is the main theme, and the point of departure is the grand conception of Plato's philosophy of the State, familiar to all his readers from the famous passage in the *Republic*, " Unless either the philosophers become kings in our States or those people who are now called kings and potentates take genuinely and thoroughly to philosophy, and political power and philosophy come to be one and the same . . . there can be no cessation of evils for our States, and, in my opinion, none for mankind " (*Rep.*, 473*d*).

Plato quotes this passage near the outset of his letter (326*b*), where he tells of the events that led up to the moving story he has to relate. In this self-contained passage (324*b*–327*d*), which forms a psychological and historical introduction to the whole document, he shows that " the beginning of all " that had happened was to be sought in his first meeting with Dion, twenty years before the death of Dionysius the Elder. Plato had reached Syracuse (388 B.C.) in the course of the journey he made through the Greek civilized world before the founding of the Academy, some time after the death of Socrates. At the court of the Sicilian despot he met the young Dion, then about twenty years old, and so began the friendship, based on the philosophic Eros, that lasted through his life. Genuine friendship depends, in Plato's view, on a community of the loftiest convictions, and this community proceeds from the " love " between men through the younger man forming himself on the model of the older man who loves him. In the epistle Plato makes no mention of his love for Dion, but the Platonic conception of friendship and of its soul-shaping power underlies the whole narrative. In accordance with this conception he treats as the principal outcome of that meeting the fact that it determined Dion's views and aims once for all, and to describe this final way of thinking adopted by his friend he sets forth the fundamental ethico-political conviction at which he himself had arrived at the time of his life when he first met Dion. In this context he makes use of the famous passage from the *Republic* to formulate this mutual conviction.

It is strangely moving to find this passage, which is quoted in every book on Plato as the classic formula of his philosophy of the State, quoted in this way by Plato himself. There is a substantial difference between the statements an artist or other productive person may make in the course of his production in explanation of his purpose—statements that have the character of revelations, evoking that which moves him to undertake the work or holds him to it, and describing, or, rather, revealing *the matter itself*—and statements that represent a judgment *concerning* the work. These latter, in contrast to the statement revealing the matter itself, are theoretical disquisitions *concerning* it, which can equally be produced by the author of the work or by other persons. Plato's self-presentations in the seventh epistle are largely of the latter type. The philosopher speaks of his own doctrine in the way another person, familiar with it, might speak about it. This accords with what we might call the academic treatment in the epistle of that striking passage. In the *Republic*, when Plato's Socrates utters that passage, the words are spoken in the consciousness of their dangerous and paradoxical nature. Derision and contempt, says Socrates emphatically, must be expected by anyone who ventures to express so radical a view. In the epistle Plato treats the passage as one currently accepted, and makes the view psychologically intelligible by showing how he arrived at it. In this connexion we are given the fragment of autobiography already mentioned. It runs as follows (324*b*–326*b*) : [13]

When I was young I was in the same state as many others : I intended, directly I became my own master, to enter into public life. But it so happened, I found, that the following changes occurred in the political situation.

In the government then existing, reviled as it was by many, a revolution took place ; and the revolution was headed by fifty-one leaders, of whom eleven were in the City and ten in the Piræus—each of these sections dealing with the market and with all municipal matters requiring management—and Thirty were established as irresponsible rulers of all. Now of these some were actually connexions and acquaintances of mine ; and indeed they invited me at once to join their administration, thinking that to be due to me. The feelings I then experienced, owing to my youth, were in no way surprising : for I imagined that they would administer the State by leading it out of an unjust way of life into a just way, and consequently I gave my mind to them very diligently, to see what they would do.

And indeed I saw how these men within a short time caused men to look back on the former government as a golden age ; and above all how they treated my aged friend Socrates, whom I would hardly scruple to call the most just of men then living, when they tried to send him, along with others, after one of the citizens, to fetch him by force that he might be put to death—their object being that Socrates, whether he wished or no, might be made to share in their political actions ; he, however, refused to obey and risked the uttermost penalties rather than be a partaker in their unholy deeds. So when I beheld all these actions and others of a similar grave kind, I was indignant, and I withdrew myself from the evil practices then going on.

But in no long time the power of the Thirty was overthrown together with the whole of the government which then existed. Then once again I was really, though less urgently, impelled with a desire to take part in public and political affairs. Many deplorable events, however, were still happening in those times, troublous as they were, and it was not surprising that in some instances, during these revolutions, men were avenging themselves on their foes too fiercely ; yet, notwithstanding, the exiles who then returned exercised no little moderation. But, as ill-luck would have it, certain men of authority summoned our comrade Socrates before the law-courts, bringing against him a criminal charge of the gravest nature, and one which Socrates of all men least deserved ; for it was on the charge of impiety that those men summoned him and the rest condemned and slew him—the very man who on the former occasion, when they themselves had the misfortune to be in exile, had refused to take part in the unholy arrest of one of the friends of the men then exiled.

When, therefore, I considered all this, and the type of men who were administering the affairs of State, with their laws too and their customs, the more I considered them and the more I advanced in years myself, the more difficult appeared to me the task of managing affairs of State rightly.   For it was impossible to take action without friends and trusted companions, and these it was not easy to find ready to hand, since our State was no longer managed according to the principles and institutions of our forefathers ; while to acquire other new friends with any facility was a thing impossible.   Moreover, both the written laws and the customs were being corrupted, and that with surprising rapidity.   Consequently, although I was filled with an ardent desire to engage in public affairs, when I considered all this and saw how things were shifting about anyhow in all directions, I finally became dizzy ; and although I continued to consider by what means some betterment could be brought about not only in these matters but also in the government as a whole, yet as regards political action I kept constantly waiting for an opportune moment ; until, finally, looking at all the States which now exist, I perceived that one and all they are badly governed ; for the state of their laws is such as to be almost incurable without some marvellous overhauling and good luck to boot.   So I was led to the praise of the right philosophy and to the declaration that by it alone is one enabled to discern all forms of justice, both political and individual.   Wherefore the classes of mankind (I said) will have no cessation from evils until either the class of those who are right and true philosophers attains political supremacy, or else the class of those who hold power in the State becomes, by some dispensation of Heaven, really philosophic.   This was the view I held when I came to Italy and Sicily, at the time of my first arrival.

We dwell on this autobiographical document, precious as it is to every friend of Plato, less on account of its content than of its style of self-revelation.   In regard to this we observe in the first place that Plato has here in view only one side of his development, the side that is relevant to the subject of the epistle.   He selects from his early days, full of youthful genius, at the time when he was making his way to the attainment of his aims, his emergence from politics to philosophy.   This aspect is a counterpart of the description of intellectual development which he gives in the *Phædo* (96 *sqq.*), also in the first person, but as the story of the youth of Socrates : we met with it when we were seeking the prototype of a narrative treatment of a career in Plato's dialogues.*   There Socrates makes much the same point in the opening passage :

* See above, p. 106.

" When I was young, I was tremendously eager for that road to wisdom which they call investigation into nature."

In that account Plato's Socrates worked out the stages of intellectual advance, but explained the advance itself as resulting from the opposition of the moral consciousness to the prevalent mechanistic explanation of nature. Similarly here, when Plato brings into the foreground his " urge to political activity ", he proceeds from the traditional definition of the purpose of life, offered at that time to a scion of any of the leading noble families in the Athenian democracy, and explains his steady alienation from that normal way of life by his moral antipathy to the dissolution of laws and customs that had spread in that time of political chaos, following the unhappy outcome of the Peloponnesian war (421–406). But while the autobiographical passage shows the same inner development as the narrative in the *Phædo*, we see at once how far, in depth of self-realization, it lags behind the description of a process of development in the philosophical dialogue. This concerns the moral consciousness itself. Morality, or, what amounts to the same thing, " just dealing ", is scarcely distinguished in the epistle from the traditional standard the decay of which made it seem hopeless to the young aristocrat to attempt to gain the connexions necessary for a political career. Thus, too, the friendship based on community of ideas is here conceived in a political sense that diverges widely from the philosophical tendency of that life-relationship between men which is revealed to us in Plato's youth, thanks to his friendship with Socrates.

Here, too, it is true, Plato ascribes crucial importance to his association with Socrates. He mentions Socrates alone by name, and calls him the " most righteous ", the morally pre-eminent man of his time. But the main concern seems here to be with the injury his friend suffered, and nothing is said of the philosophical activity of that unique man, though Plato himself saw that activity as the essential thing when he described Socrates' life in the *Apology*. As he there depicts him, there is embodied in him the directing of thought to the Absolute, which speaks to us in the moral consciousness ; Socrates—and here that also means Plato—turns away from political life for the sake of the absolute desideratum that even politically comes foremost— to care for the nature of the State or " the State itself " instead of political deals, and similarly for the true self instead of personal interests (*Apol.*, 36). Here, on the contrary, Plato says of the philosophical efforts of his youth only that he " continued to consider by what means some betterment could be brought about in those matters and indeed in the whole government " (325e). Those who are unacquainted with Plato's youthful labours can scarcely have any notion of the immense pioneering energy of thought at play in those " considerations ", and may see in them only the typical attitude of a thoughtful young aristocrat hampered in the application of his own powers. Thus we feel that a leap has been made when Plato ultimately, as the outcome of his political experience, declares his decision to embrace philosophy ; suddenly this man born to action and biding his time for it, has turned into the philosopher who pronounces a devastating judgment on all existing States, and gives expression to his sense of the importance of the " right " or true philosophy, and his vision of the salvation of mankind, in the paradoxical pronouncement that the philosophers must rule or the rulers must become philosophers.

It should be clear that this autobiographical fragment is not of the sort that could properly be made the basis of a biography of the philosopher, as some eminent classical philologists would have it. In order to assess its value as a source we must keep in view the purpose it serves. Plato tells the story of his youth not for its own sake, its purely biographical interest, but with a view to the central thought with which it concludes, and the fate of which in the world forms the great theme of this apologia. He propounds this theme in the introduction to the document. After making the idea of the kingship of the philosopher emerge into prominence from his own life, in the next section of his historical introduction he treats of the converse course, along which philosophic thought, transcending all experience, grew to be a power in political life, as happened through his friendship with Dion. Both sections are parts of a single whole. The story of Dion's youth which follows is attuned to that of Plato's youth.

Dion was inspired with his aims by his meeting with Plato, who instilled into him the philosophic outlook on life. But as a statesman by birth and not, like Plato, a philosopher, he was led straight into the application of the philosophic spirit to politics. In accordance with this difference the ethical and intellectual directives of his development vary from those attributed to Plato's youth, though on the whole they correspond with them. Of Dion's " views and aims " Plato says that he was able to speak " not merely from conjecture but from precise knowledge " (324a). He was able to say this because of their community of spirit—the result of the talks in which, as he puts it, he instructed the young man " in his views on the highest good of mankind and urged him to act in accordance with them " (327a). What he tells of these talks has reference to the philosophic life, which forms the soul of man. But here again Plato is not speaking of the soul and the fulfilment of its longings in the beatific contemplation of Ideas, but stressing the empirical, practical side of his teaching : in the context of the epistle, " philosophy " means moral living, in accordance with philosophical principles.

Dion, says Plato in summarizing the result of his intercourse with him, turned away from the customary " Sicilian life ". Personal morality or " virtue " was the simple formula for this. This ethical directive covered the political one ; for in Plato's judgment the cultivation of personal uprightness must precede the reform of the State. Here, however, Plato only hints at this fundamental thought, to which he gives full expression in other passages in the epistle ; here he is merely speaking of his influence over the young Dion. This influence, as he emphasizes, was purely spiritual and moral, and free from political aims. He declares expressly that at that time he had not the remotest idea that (as proved later) by his intercourse with Dion he " was, in a way, unwittingly contriving the future overthrow of the tyranny " (327a). In thinking of Dion's end he was inclined to attribute what he himself had done, without knowing or intending it, to the fatal working of higher powers : " it looks as if one of the superior powers was contriving at that time to lay the foundation of the events which have now taken place in regard to Dion and to Syracuse " (326e). He asks, was it chance or destiny that led him, in his years of travel, to Sicily, and he prefers to accept the religious interpretation.

But while he records the unintentional and the incalculable element in the initiation of the whole affair, he gives a rational account of the course of events that led to his intervention in the world of politics, and in this way he dissolves the dark association of human will and destiny to which he referred. He surveys from Dion's standpoint the long period between the " beginning " and the critical turn produced by the death of Dionysius the Elder, but he does so in such a way as to give Dion's life in those twenty years the appearance of a foil to his own course from politics to philosophy. In this short sketch he proceeds from the moral attitude Dion had acquired under the influence of the " right teaching ". The way of thinking and the way of living that Plato's disciple pursued as he stood at first alone at the Sicilian court, an offence to all who followed the " tyrants' usage " of sensual indulgence, found emulators—so Plato relates— in the course of time ; a circle was formed of like-minded persons such as Plato had lacked in his political youth ; Dion noted this development and built upon it the hope that the young heir to the throne might be won over. Success in this—the sketch closes with the mention of that aspiration—would be " an un- speakable blessing " for the whole country : the rule of sanguin- ary violence would give place to " true, happy life " (327*c, d*).

Thus does Plato represent his friend as he sent back to Plato, full of confidence, the thought he had received from him. The call to action which Dion sent out to Plato after the sudden death of the tyrant seemed the closing stage of a natural process in which the influence of Plato's spirit had gradually spread from the one person whom he had filled with it and had finally reached the heir to the throne. Plato was to come to complete the process. The parallel was perfect. There was going to be repeated in the young Dionysius, Dion was sure, what had happened to himself at his meeting with Plato when the philo- sopher aroused in him " the aspiration after the complete, the good, and the beautiful life." But this time it was the legitimate ruler who was, in question. In this situation there came from Dion in his summons to Plato the great formula from the *Republic*, like an echo of those last words in Plato's story of his youth—" Now, if ever, all our hopes will be fulfilled of seeing the same persons at once philosophers and rulers of mighty States " (328*a*). Thus did the development produced by Dion coincide with the political line laid down at the end of the autobiographical section. In his old age there opened out before the philosopher the prospect that that directive conceived in his youth would after all attain its goal. Plato quotes a sentence from Dion's letter to him—" What better opportunity are we to await than is now afforded by divine dispensation ? " (327*e*).

At this stage, in view of this closely thought-out and artistic- ally constructed biographical introduction, it might have been thought that the author was preparing the way for a full-scale record of the fragment of Sicilian history which is memorable for Plato's sake. The time was ripe ; the great project, inspired by the highest earthly aims, could be carried into operation. But the document does not take this course. At the stage on which we should have been glad to dwell, the narrative passes on at once, and in its flow submerges the fact that the writer is changing his attitude. Plato proceeds to explain the motives that induced him to respond to Dion's summons ; and this explanation of his motives reveals the unsureness of a man dependent on the circumstances of this world, and concerned to justify before the world his part in an enterprise that had failed.

In this full account (328a–329b) he first refers to the reasons Dion put forward in his letter in order to induce him to make the journey—reasons that came from beyond Plato's domain. For they no longer echoed his own philosophical purpose but were the arguments of a statesman concerned with giving effect to considerations of power, judging the chances of the enterprise from his knowledge of the persons at court, and taking into account—and exaggerating—his own position of influence. " And ", writes Plato, after quoting the sentence mentioned above from Dion's letter, " he dealt in detail with the extent of the empire in Italy and Sicily and his own power therein, and mentioned the youth of Dionysius and the great desire he had for philosophy and education " (328a). He then reconstructs the line of thought resulting from Dion's arguments, and tells how he considered long and deeply what should be his decision. There could, he said to himself, be no counting on the young son of the dead ruler ; " for the desires of youth change quickly, and frequently in a contrary direction ". It was different with Dion : " His character was, I knew, stable by nature, and also fortified since he had now reached middle age." That settled it. " If anyone were ever to set himself to bring to realization my thoughts on legislation and government, now was the time to undertake it ; for by thoroughly convincing one single person I should have achieved all manner of good " (328c).

But Plato was not moved solely by that practical consideration ; a motive that weighed equally with it was that of loyalty to his friend. In order to throw light on that aspect, he makes use of a rhetorical device. He refers to the later situation at the Sicilian court when Dion had been brought down and exiled from the country, and introduces into the considerations that influenced his original decision a foreboding of that danger. How ashamed he would feel—such was the reflection that decided his course—if he had left his friend in the lurch ! What answer could he give if Dion came to him as an exile and threw on him the responsibility for his ill-fortune ? He elaborates that aspect in words he puts into Dion's mouth. He shows his friend accusing him of desire for ease and lack of courage. The consideration of the point of honour is reinforced by that of the moral and religious obligation toward Dion as his friend and visitor, under the protection of Zeus Xenios, guardian of hosts and guests.

In this imaginary talk, attuned to the sense of public morality, Plato also brings forward his own qualities, especially as teacher. " I come to you ", we hear Dion say, " as an exile, because you have left me destitute of those persuasive arguments whereby you above all, as I know, are able to convert young men to goodness and righteousness, and thereby to bring them always into friendship and good fellowship with one another." This self-praise indicates the obligation laid upon him by his public position as a representative of philosophy. Dion proceeds : " But my condition is not the worst reproach to you. It is to Philosophy, whose praise you are always singing, while declaring her to be ignobly treated by the rest of mankind, that you have proved traitor, as far as lay with you, as well as to me."

In view of that attitude we can scarcely be surprised that Plato's first and certainly predominant motive, his desire to see his political conceptions, worked out in the course of long-continued mental labour, at last put into practice, is not expressed here with the full sense of freedom and strength of the man of creative spirit, but is once more brought forward as the reaction to another consideration: "I was not guided by the motives which some have supposed, but chiefly by concern for my own self-respect, lest I should seem to myself to be nothing more than a mere theorist (literally ' mere *logos* '), a man who would never willingly take action." This concession to the despisers of philosophy who opposed to its *logos* their own desideratum of " sound practical thinking ", is made, however, only half-heartedly, and is at once withdrawn at least in part, by Plato's reference to his work in the Academy. After this statement of his motives he resumes : " Therefore I interrupted my own pursuits, not indecorous though they were, and submitted to a tyranny unbecoming, as it seemed, both to my teaching and to myself " (329*b*). This statement again is no self-revelation. In this way even a mere spectator, unconcerned with the conflict in Plato's mind, might envisage the situation, regretting the famous philosopher's venture into a world alien to him.

Then comes the story of his experiences at the Sicilian court

(329*c*–330*b*). Although this covers a period of more than a year, it takes up less space than the analysis of the motives for the journey. It is cut short because the facts are selected from a particular point of view—the point of view that prevailed in the philosopher's account of his motives for following Dion's summons and hampered him, as we have seen, in the free affirmation of his great political and philosophic purpose. Plato makes no mention here of his efforts in the first months after his arrival, when he had Dion at his side, to make cautious approaches to the young ruler as an educator ; of these we learn only in the next, the didactic, section of the epistle. He deals instead with the political situation at the court at Syracuse. The relative position of the opposing elements was quite different from what had been conveyed by Dion's report. Plato gives the facts very briefly : dissension and intrigues against Dion, who was suspected of plotting against his nephew ; Dion's fall, and his ignominious banishment. These bare facts form the framework for the picture Plato draws of his relations with Dionysius under these circumstances.

In this picture he sets out the outline of the figure of the autocrat, which he fills in in the last section of the epistle ; for the moment he contents himself with the traits needed for his own justification. At the outset, after the arbitrary stroke against Dion, there was general fear of the despot. Plato shared this fear with the other friends of the exiled man. He tells of a rumour that went round Syracuse that he himself " had been put to death by Dionysius as responsible for the whole course of events ". But there followed at once a rumour contradicting this : " Dionysius is marvellously devoted to Plato " (330*a*). This he denies. " What were the facts ? for the truth must be told." In his first horror he had thought of leaving Sicily at once, but he had to remain because Dionysius desired it. He saw through the tyrant : Dionysius came to him begging him to stay, his motive being the fear that Plato's flight would damage the ruler's reputation ; but " we know that a tyrant's wish contains an element of coercion " (329*d*).

Dionysius showered attentions on him, insisted on having him in his immediate entourage, and provided him with a dwelling in the citadel, outside the city. All this, as Plato shows in detail, was simply a cunning way of making flight impossible for him. During many months he lived in these conditions, in daily contact with the despot, and there naturally resulted a closer understanding between the two. Plato writes of this : " Dionysius grew to like me more and more as time went on and he became acquainted with my way of life and my outlook on life ". But there was a qualification to add. The autocrat sought to win him over out of selfish motives incompatible with true friendship. " He wanted me to show more admiration for him than for Dion, and to regard him rather than Dion as my special friend." The teacher in Plato adds his comment : " He shirked the best way of attaining his object, if it was to be attained —that is, by occupying himself in learning and in listening to philosophical discourses and by associating with me." He explains the ruler's unwillingness by " his dread of the talk of the slanderers, lest he might somehow be entangled and Dion might accomplish all his designs " (330b). Dionysius was not yet a pure autocrat, and his character was not yet the explanation of his resistance.

From a later passage in the epistle we learn that the rapprochement was not entirely one-sided. Plato made use of the personal association with the ruler that had been accorded him to induce him to recall Dion, and the two arrived at an agreement on this point. Plato had to promise before his departure that he would return, and Dionysius in turn promised that he would recall the exile at the same time as Plato. In this passage we read further that before his departure Plato brought about a friendly alliance between Dionysius and Plato's friend, the statesman and thinker Archytas of Tarentum, through whom the Pythagoreans had regained power in Lower Italy, so that Plato had also been politically active in the interest of his host (338a, c). All this he passes over in the earlier section. It does not fit in with the theme he is pursuing in that section of the narrative—how the idealist purpose with which he entered the political world came into conflict with the opposing forces at the tyrant's court. The story, which started with the ideal of the philosopher-king, ends with the unresolved tension in the personal relations between the philosopher, out to train the ruler, and the young despot, out to evade all pedagogy. Plato sums up : " I waited patiently through all that, holding fast to the original purpose with which I had come, in the hope that he might possibly gain the desire for the philosophic life ; but he won the day with his resistance " (330b).

(2)

In the next section (330c–337e) we find ourselves in a different situation, indeed, transferred to a different world. As if he were tired of story-telling, which is not a philosopher's business, Plato breaks off the narrative of his Sicilian journeys at the very point where the personal matters that interest the biographer had come into the foreground, declaring that he is in danger of " giving the first place to matters of secondary importance ". Proceeding to " the principal matter ", he takes up once more the main theme of the epistle, the political task of the philosopher. But he does so from another point of departure and in a different way. He starts now no longer from the task of a ruler's tutor, but from the function of the philosopher as adviser on the constitution of a State, a function his Academy had fulfilled in many cases and on which he was himself, at the time when the epistle was written, about to complete a fundamental book in his last great dialogue, known as " The Laws ".* He had introduced himself as political adviser in the first sentences of the epistle, where, in the epistolary style, he addressed himself to Dion's supporters and urged them to hold fast to the policy the assassinated man had pursued. But this introduction was no more than an outward form ; the main emphasis was laid on the fact that his friend's policy had been inspired by Plato himself. He then proceeded at once to the biographical narrative we have been following. Now, however, he takes up the attitude of the counsellor, and speaks definitely as an instructor, with the introductory formula of an educational work—" This is what I have to say . . ." (λέγω δὲ τάδε).

He speaks in general terms of the reform of the State. It must not—this is his first point—be conducted by means of force. Force is appropriate for recalcitrant slaves, not in relation to free men. These must seek advice of their own accord, but must be prepared to follow the adviser when he calls on them to alter their way of life. With this simple fundamental principle Plato gives expression to the reforming purpose of his thought, based on the personal moral consciousness. The reform of the life of a State demands personal morality as its basis, and, like that, is a matter of personal decision, such as must not be forced upon a responsible human being.

To throw light on this negative side of his position, where

* A. E. Taylor, *Plato*, p. 464.

freedom means freedom from compulsion, he makes use of a familiar analogy from his dialogues and compares, as in the *Republic* (426*b*), the task of the political adviser with the healing of a sick person who is leading an unhealthy life. Like the physician in dealing with the patient, the philosopher, who has realized the evils of the constitution of the State in which he lives, will avoid all interference, although he is well aware of the facts, if he finds the rulers of the State unprepared to alter their way of living. A further point has reference to the constitution. The "right" constitution is the ordering of the laws on the principle of justice, in contrast with despotism, but also in contrast with party dominance, which undermines the equality of all before the law (334*c*). Here we find the positive conception of political freedom, which Solon, the founder of the Athenian democracy, had laid down—freedom as the binding of the citizen by the laws which the community has given itself. In their content these doctrines are an excerpt from Plato's political dialogues, especially from the "Laws", in which the speaker is a philosopher-statesman, called "The Athenian". In the epistle, in which Plato advances the doctrines as his own, he recommends them to the politicians who had approached him for advice, for observance in the given situation, but at the same time he mentions them in connexion with the past events narrated in the document, as the convictions that guided him in his political attitude. Thus this part of the epistle also serves his self-justification.

In the first of these two principles lies the justification for the aloofness from the political life of his mother-city for which the "unpractical philosopher" had been so widely criticized. This detachment, which in the story of his youth he had explained on the psychological ground of his revulsion against the lack of moral principles in political practice, and which then, in explaining the motives of his Sicilian journey, he had regarded with the eyes of the world as a weak flight from active life into the realm of thought, now receives its true explanation as the wise man's attitude, based on principle, to the world into which he was born : " If his own State appears to him to be badly governed, he should speak, provided that his speaking is not likely to prove fruitless or to cause his death ; but he must not apply violence to his fatherland by revolutionary methods . . . but should keep quiet and pray for the best both for himself and for his city " (331*d*).

The wise man is no hero. But in those teachings there is also a preliminary indication of the determination to act, as he did, boldly enough, in the Sicilian enterprise. That determination stands in the foreground, and it is evident throughout the period of his life dealt with in the epistle. He infers it here from those principles, by following each of the two main principles of his teaching with the corresponding biographical facts in the various years and situations—his first meeting with Dion (388 B.C.), his efforts for the education of the young Dionysius twenty years later (367), and his last Sicilian journey, of which he has still to tell (361). He sets these down not as stages in a progressive operation but as examples for the rule of action he has laid down in general terms for the political adviser, the rule he now shows in the consistent application he made of it under the changing conditions.

In this connexion he brings forward one after another the various objectives he pursued in the Sicilian enterprise as time passed and as the complexities of the political task revealed themselves. Here we find the formulation, already mentioned as characteristic, of the philosopher's educative task in relation to the heir to the throne—" to train and rear him up to be a king worthy to rule " (333b). Here, on the other hand, we learn that Plato and Dion, in their joint effort to induce the young despot, with his addiction to sensual pleasures, to alter his way of living, united their educative effort to strengthen his personality with a practical political intention determined by the historic situation. They wanted to bring him to see that he stood in need of moral training in order to maintain his rule in the State that had been conquered by force, and that it was only through the harmonizing and associative force of just laws that the State could become so strong that it would be able to withstand the onset of the barbarians (332d–333a). We also see here how Plato, in view of the dissension within the ruling house, conceived his task as one of reconciliation ; here he emphasizes the political influence he brought from his mother-city, the city with the great democratic tradition—" I, a citizen of Athens, a friend of Dion, an ally of his own, went to the tyrant in order that I might bring about friendship instead of war " (333d). These various intentions appear here as consequences of a single principle, a principle of which only the applications differ, and which communicates to every application the moral worth implicit in it.

In regard to the moral aspect Plato seems to have been

compelled by the attacks upon him and Dion to lay emphasis on the obvious fact that in his political action he had no self-regarding motives. The element of apologia runs through this section as through the others. He represents even Dion's resort to force in order to end the differences between himself and his nephew as a moral disciplining ; he says of Dion's victorious armed campaign against the tyrant : " He took practical steps to bring Dionysius to reason " (333*b*). But the self-justification comes here, when he speaks as a teacher, in a different and a worthier way than in the narrative parts. He takes up his stand on the super-personal plane appropriate to the thinker and observer, and thus deprives of all basis the suspicions directed against him personally, and he gives these suspicions a positive answer by bringing the facts that had given rise to them—facts capable of various interpretations—within the unambiguous content of his teaching.

To this extent we have here a philosophical type of self-defence. But we are also brought up here against the limits of self-portrayal determined by the practical purpose of the document. Thus arranged, the biographical facts make up a connected story by proceeding not from the centre of the personality but from the part Plato played as a political adviser. And as that rôle was bound up with that of the academic teacher, the personality of the philosopher appears under a special and all-too-narrow aspect : his self-assurance rests on the possession of firm principles which he consistently upholds and brings forward at every opportunity.

This intellectual attitude corresponds to the way Plato explains the frustration, or, rather, the ill-success as he considers it (as we have already mentioned), of his political action. This explanation is to be found in the didactic section of the epistle. In attaching so much importance to the rebuttal of the charges made against Dion and himself, he is moved not merely by considerations of his friend's memory and his own reputation, but by his opinion that his and Dion's failure was to be attributed to the misinterpretation of their intentions by their opponents and to the intrigues of calumniators. He disposes of his own failure by saying : " I . : . went to the tyrant in order that I might bring about friendship instead of war ; but in my struggle with the slanderers I was defeated " (333*d*). He uses this explanation to cover the various events from Dion's banishment to his assassination, and again proceeds by treating the individual facts as instances of the obedience of events to a general law. Thus he associates his experiences with Dionysius with the later happenings in Syracuse, which led to Dion, after he had driven out the autocrat, being removed by assassination. Contemplating that terrible experience, with the passionate emotion that takes possession of him and threatens to overcome him as he recalls it, he yet holds fast to the line of thought concerned with the identical significance of the various events. If, he declares, the Syracusans turned away from Dion in suspicion of the man who had set them free, they did, or rather " suffered ", " the same thing " that Dionysius had done when he eluded the educative influence of philosophy " from dread of the talk of the slanderers " (333*b*).

We find here a thoroughly rational, pragmatic conception of the historic events ; but, as expressed in this apologia, in order to explain Plato's and Dion's ill-success, it does not exhaust the philosopher's thoughts in his reflection upon those events. With these thoughts went the very different emotional view of the fateful character of what had happened. This brings us back to the point we advanced when we confronted the view of Plato's Sicilian " adventure " dominant in the epistle with the picture of Dion's death that emerges at the end of the document, representing him as the conquering hero brought down by evil devices at the moment of victory. The significance of that picture is illustrated by an epitaph on Dion in verses written, if we may place faith in the tradition,[14] by Plato :

The fates decreed tears for Hecuba and the Trojan women even at the hour
    of their birth ;
And after thou, Dion, hadst triumphed in the accomplishment of noble deeds,
    the dæmons spoilt all thy far-reaching hopes.
But thou liest in thy spacious city, honoured by thy fellow-countrymen, Dion,
    who didst madden my soul with love.

Whatever significance may be attached to this witness to Plato's love of Dion, the verses show the characteristic association of conceptions of heroism and fate that comes from the tragic poetry of the Greeks. That world of the poets comes into the foreground in the epilogue to the epistle as the spiritual medium from which the lament for the dead draws its expression. But in the epistle this tragic-heroic motive does not find undiluted expression ; as we shall see, it appears there among political considerations, ethical and rational, which also serve the exaltation of Dion, and in this combined movement the intelligence is given the last word and the highest prize.

While thus the tragic moment is only rising on the horizon, the thought of destiny, or, more generally, of divine dispensation, returns again and again, where Plato regards his Sicilian experience as a whole : he has there in view the consideration that this part of his life was at the same time a part of the political history of his time. In the biographical introduction to the epistle he said of his friendship with Dion, with reference to its historic consequences, that it began through a fateful chance, or, as he prefers to put it, that higher powers were at work in this " beginning of it all ". In the narrative sections he pursues this thought no further ; in them he treats of his experiences with the tyrant, closing with the outbreak of the conflict, so that Dion's victory and fall are not described. But in the didactical section, in connexion with his political advice to the friends of the murdered man, he deals with that horrifying event, and these few pages (333c–334e) are for us, in our search for utterances of the philosopher's that directly reveal his mind, the most important in the whole document.

When Plato comes to speak of Dion's assassination, he stops. Something " wicked and shameful " (334a) has happened. He has no intention of suppressing the facts, but he does not want to dwell on them, " for there are many others who make it their care to tell the story again and again, and will continue to do so in time to come ". He gives expression to the thing that moves him, though not in a single great outburst of his feelings, but treating it objectively in a consideration which, proceeding from changing standpoints, grows profounder step by step.

At first, here again, the defensive element predominates. The crime had compromised Plato's school.* The instigators of the murder, a certain Kallippos and his brother, were Athenian citizens and belonged to the Academy. Dion had been a friend of theirs ; Kallippos had placed his house in Athens at the exile's disposal. They had taken part in his expedition against Syracuse, with many other members of the Academy ; and then they had betrayed him. Plato enters into these particulars in order to clear his school and his mother-city from the shameful deed. So far as the Academy was concerned, he points out that these men's friendship with Dion " was not derived from philosophy", as might have been assumed, " but from that ordinary companionship which is current among most friends,

---

* Von Wilamowitz sees in this one of the main considerations that induced Plato to take up the pen. *Plato*, II, p. 299 ; I, p. 644.

and which comes from mutual entertaining and initiation into the different mystic ceremonies ". What a contrast was his own friendship with Dion ! He points to that for the honour of Athens ; his loyalty to Dion outweighs the treachery of those two Athenians, who " had never been men of any account " : " I assert that it was also an Athenian who refused to betray that very man when, through Dionysius, he could have gained both wealth and numerous honours " (333*e*, 334*b*, *c*.) Thus he throws the public repute of his own person into the scales, places himself alongside the traitors, and even finds it not beneath his dignity to point out that he had not permitted himself to be bribed by Dionysius. As though he felt it painful to advance that argument, he speaks of himself in the third person. The praise of the true friendship that has its sole source in intellectual life, is one of the great Platonic themes of the epistle. We saw how he sharply distinguished his friendship with Dion and his friendship with Dionysius from this standpoint. But what he says here of his relationship with Dion has a touch of the morality of the Academic school : " He had become his friend not in the bonds of vulgar friendship but owing to mutual participation in liberal education, in which alone a wise man should put his trust, rather than in kinship of soul or of body " (334*b*). Thus he removes the veil from his friendship with Dion—in the same breath in which he summons the poets to sing the praises of the fallen hero.

In his further remarks Plato himself, in his sorrow for his friend, strikes a heroic note, not in order to give voice to his deep emotion but to make an end of lamenting. " He died nobly ; for whatever suffering a man undergoes when striving after that which is noblest both for himself and for his State, is always right and noble." In these words Plato returns to that early Greek view of heroism which, preceding the tragic view of it in the great Greek creation of the drama, simply saw in a glorious death the completion of a happy life. He associates this harmonious-heroic view with religious thoughts of comfort, thoughts of the immortality of the soul and of reward in the other world, the credibility of which he bases on ancient and respected tradition. To this extent the philosopher takes up an attitude not substantially different from that of the unphilosophical man who holds to positive articles of faith when blows of destiny, such as the death of those who are near to us, destroy the normal security of his life.

But Plato dwells no more than a moment on that standpoint of common humanity. For him the appalling element in his friend's death lies not at all in the fate of an individual, but beyond the whole sphere of life in which the significance of events is determined through the personal relations of human beings, in happiness and in suffering. It lies for him in the task Dion had been destined to accomplish. In this sense he associates the vile assassination of his friend with the resistance he had himself met with when he was trying to accomplish his great task by training the young Dionysius to be a true king. By a surprising turn of speech he expresses the identical significance of these two experiences, combining passion and paradox—" I have every right to be angry with the men who slew Dion, in a sense in the same way as with Dionysius ; for both they and he have done the utmost harm both to me and, it may fairly be said, to the rest of mankind—they by destroying the man who intended to practise justice, and he by utterly refusing to practise justice, though he had supreme power throughout his empire."

Eloquently he describes what might have been. A true State, formed on the principle of justice, such as, in Plato's view, must necessarily proceed from the union in the same person of philosophy and power, would have worked, wherever it was set up, on all men, Hellenes and barbarians alike, as a revelation of that moral principle, and thus " the true view " of the highest good would have become the common property of all mankind —the view he had argued and elaborated in his philosophical work (335*d*, 336*b*).

Let us pause over this self-disclosure of the philosopher's. Once more it seems strange to us to hear Plato speak of himself in this way—" to me and to the rest of mankind "—as though he had personally to bear the injury inflicted on all men. It is not the content but the form of the utterance that startles us. For the mood here expressed is characteristic of the philosopher, as of the prophet or poet, who may say with Faust : " Der Menschheit ganzer Jammer fasst mich an " (" All the misery of mankind is upon me "). For he himself is convulsed by the grief he suffers with other men, in a super-personal, disinterested way : the suffering affects not only him or the community to which he belongs, but all human existence, since he has taken men's destinies upon his own shoulders. But when Plato expresses this super-personal feeling in that personal way, we feel something approaching an inner inconsistency. It is much the same when, in connexion with the idea of the beneficent effect of setting up the true State, he expresses a hope for the spread of the conceptions of political ethics at which he has arrived, as of a sort of orthodoxy. The philosopher's disclosure of his self-assessment is made here as in an impulsive reaction of his whole being to a wounding attack, and yet what he says about himself is virtually what any assessor of the importance of the Platonic philosophy of the State might say.

Alongside the passion that speaks out of accusation and aspiration, the thinker's reasoning proceeds to find a virtually identical element in apparently quite different events. He expresses the paradox thus : Dion's murderers, without knowing it, " have done the same harm as Dionysius ", whose other acts of violence scarcely count in comparison with that one crime (335e). The only difference is that they did not know what they were doing. Led astray by the suspicion that Dion was aiming at tyranny, they imagined that they were serving the cause of freedom, and in Dion they struck at the cause they were trying to serve.

In reality the charges against Dion were not so baseless as Plato represents. In order to maintain his position in the internal political struggles that followed his victory, Dion had had to proceed to such violent measures as the execution of one of his opponents, against his own philosophical principles. Plato passes over this. He represents his friend as the ideal statesman who united his task in practical politics with his ethical attitude, and he testifies to the purity of his intentions—" as far as it is possible for a man to speak with assurance about other men " (335e). Indeed, he lauds him as the incorporation of all the virtues. Thus he averts his gaze from the hard fact that the attempt to give effect to the political ideal was bound up with the armed struggle which, from the nature of things in this life, involved the fighter in guilt. The tragic element in this entanglement, which led to the fateful assassination, is watered down in the paradox that the instigators of the deed achieved the opposite of what they intended—an intellectual analogy to the irony of fate.

In this statement there remains, however, an element of the unexplained. " Some deity," Plato concludes, " or some avenging spirit broke in with lawlessness, with ungodliness, and, worst of all, with the boldness of folly " (336b). This is the same idea as in his poem on Dion's death. But in the epistle this religious thought leads back to the rational principle of explanation of historical events. The evil dæmon embodies the dark power of Unreason, which works through calumny, suspicion, and misconception, through lack of understanding or of knowledge. The passage quoted ends : " The ignorance which is the root whence all evils spring for all men, and which will later produce most bitter fruit for those who sowed it, this it is that for the second time has wrecked and ruined all " (336*b*). A basic idea of Platonic as of all metaphysics underlies this charge of lack of knowledge. But here Plato does not oppose, as in his dialogues, the philosopher to the unseeing crowd, but conversely sees something abnormal in the rule of folly in the world. That there should be such failure to appreciate the noblest of men as to produce the assassination shows an abyss of stupidity only to be explained as the work of a superhuman power intervening in the rational course of events.

Since, in Plato's view, the collapse of the enterprise was not implicit in its nature but was determined from without, the possibility remains that after two failures a fresh effort may still bring success. With this possibility in view he brings forward in the epistle his political teaching, which includes an indication of the right course of action. Self-defence thus passes into self-assertion. He lays great emphasis on the contention that it was for the same fundamental ideas which he had expounded in the past to Dion that he then sought to arouse the enthusiasm of Dionysius, and now, " for the third time ", sought the allegiance of Dion's friends. This consistently urged advice he accompanies with the same promise which was associated with the appearance of the philosopher-king : " If the victors prove themselves more completely subject to the laws than the vanquished, then all things will abound in safety and all evils will disappear " (337*d*). The unity of the teaching and the unswerving faith of the teacher in its rightness and efficacy give to the special picture of Plato's personality which we gain in this part of the epistle a consistency which the philosopher's self-portrayal as a whole does not possess and at which it does not aim.

(3)

The third and much the longest section (337*e*–350*e*) is still less uniform than the first. Plato now takes up the thread of his story again with an account of his last Sicilian journey, on which he started in 361 B.C., when he was nearly seventy years old. He made the journey although Dionysius had not kept his promise to recall Dion at the same time from Athens, where he had spent the years of his exile. Once more there is a change in Plato's attitude. The story of this journey is a story of suffering, not only in its content but in the way Plato puts forward his defence, which is in strong contrast to the active pursuit of it in the didactic section.

We find this at once in the motive given for his decision to make the journey ; the motive is once more expounded at length (338*b*–340*a*). It is a typical example of the all-too-human tendency to shift on to other shoulders as far as possible the responsibility for a decision one regrets. He begins by mentioning that he had twice declined Dionysius' invitation, although Dion had urged him to accept it ; Plato seems annoyed with his friend for doing so : " I deemed it safer, at least for the moment, to give a wide berth to Dion and Dionysius " (338*c*). But they gave him no peace, and his Pythagorean friends pulled the same string. He describes how he was urged from all sides : " Those in Sicily and Italy were pulling me in, and those at Athens were, so to say, by their entreaties actually pushing me out " (339*d*). He quotes from Dionysius' letter of invitation a passage showing the pressure the ruler was putting on him, making reconciliation with Dion dependent on Plato's coming. Dionysius employed yet another device to take away any possibility of an excuse from the hesitant guest—" for, in fact, he sent a trireme to fetch me, in order to make the journey easy for me ". Under such circumstances Plato could only give way.

He had a reason for dwelling on the pressure put upon him. Plato had still hoped at that time to make Dionysius into a philosopher king, and he was not ready to admit that he had been under an illusion. The last Sicilian journey brought final disillusionment. Now that he has to tell of this journey, he brings forward again that main motive, but with all reserve, and he reconstructs his motives accordingly. He does this in an embarrassed way that betrays his wounded pride and also his effort to conceal the wound.

He starts from the information that had reached him about the situation at the Sicilian court. According to this, in the years that had passed the ruler's attitude to philosophy had entirely changed ; he had returned to the position which he had taken up before the quarrel with Dion and on which the whole enterprise had originally been built up. " Dionysius ", so Plato was assured, " was now once more marvellously devoted to philosophy " ; he had even " made marvellous progress in philosophy " ; he now prided himself on having been a disciple of the famous philosopher who for months had been his guest (338*b*, 339*b*). Plato, we must assume from his account, received this news with scepticism. It is true that he does not directly say so, but he allows us to gain the impression that he had no belief in any change in Dionysius' outlook. Before his account of the motives that induced him to make the new journey and so brought him once more into the midst of the Sicilian empire's affairs, he explains how the supposed change in Dionysius' views had come about, and in this explanation he proceeds from the opinion of Dionysius at which he had arrived in the course of his last Sicilian journey. He had studied the autocrat. He wants to show that he had seen through him. Accordingly he now proceeds along the line he had laid down in his earlier narrative.

Dionysius' apparent return to philosophy was—or so he preferred to assume—a delayed result of his first intercourse with him, determined entirely by external circumstances. That intercourse with Plato had given the ruler the reputation at his court of being a philosopher, and, ambitious as he was, he sought to make all the capital he could out of the part this enabled him to play. There had come to the Sicilian court, as we know from other sources, representatives of various schools of philosophy ; one of the most eminent of these was Aristippus, the disciple of Socrates who is famed as the founder of Hedonism. The historian of philosophy would gladly have learned something of the meeting between Plato and this antagonist of his, but Plato speaks only in general terms of " some others " whom he describes as " men stuffed with some second-hand knowledge of philosophy. These men ", he adds, " tried, I believe, to discuss those subjects with Dionysius, on the assumption that he was thoroughly instructed in all my thought " (338*d*). Dionysius sunned himself in this false radiance, and now, says Plato in his analysis, regretted that he had wriggled out of all philosophical discussion with him ; he was afraid that he would lose caste if this became known, and wanted to make up for the lost opportunities ; but above all he was afraid of being disavowed by Plato—" lest any should suppose that it was owing to my poor opinion of his nature and disposition, together with my experience of his mode of life, that I was now in my anger no longer willing to come to his court "

(338*e*). Hence the urgency of his invitation and his persistency in pressing it.

After this preparation Plato enters into his own motives. He had not permitted himself to come in the slightest degree under the influence of Dionysius' wiles, as some might think. He rejects any such suggestion with just as much emphasis as he had earlier denied the rumour that he and Dionysius had become friends. " Now I am bound to tell the truth and put up with the possibility that someone, when hearing what took place, may despise my philosophy and regard the tyrant as a wise man" (339*a*). He grows sarcastic at the suggestion that he had taken a foolish step. He does not deny that it was unwise to yield to the pressure ; in the end his " many fears and misgivings " proved to be only too well founded, though he did ultimately " get safely back again ". He is able to show that he was in an awkward position when he accepted the invitation, and to do so without making any admission, as he had to deal with an autocrat. But it would have been incompatible with his dignity to allow himself to be guided by an illusion, still less by vanity, instead of by rational considerations. These were his reasons : " I felt that there would be nothing surprising in a young man, who was apt at learning, attaining to the love of the best life when hearing lectures on essential subjects ; that I must, there-fore, make a definite test of how the matter stood, and on no account expose myself to the grave reproach I should deserve if there were any truth in the reports I had received." This sense of his responsibility justified him, even though, as he adds, he risked life and limb, " blindfolded with that argumentation ", and incurred the suspicion of egregious folly.

Such are the motives advanced for the course described in the narrative that follows. Plato first tells how he proceeded in order to secure information concerning Dionysius' attitude to philosophy (340*b*–341*b*). From this account we are able to gather a good deal that fills in our picture of Plato the pedagogue and must fascinate anyone interested in philosophic education.

He began this time by giving the ruler regular lessons in philosophy. In these he showed, as he puts it, " what the subject is as a whole, and what is its character, and what preliminary studies and how much hard work it will require ". It might be called a sort of introduction to philosophy, or, as the ancients would have called it, an exhortation to philosophy, such as is familiar to us from later philosophical literature. A famous work

of this sort was Cicero's *Hortensius* ; in Augustine we shall see
how the reading of that work, a product of the Platonic tradition,
awoke the young rhetorician to the higher spiritual life.* Plato
gives this description of the effect which a lecture of the sort he
gave to Dionysius can have :

> The hearer, if he is truly philosophic, in sympathy with the subject
> and worthy of it, as a man akin to God, realizes that he has been shown
> a marvellous path which he must at once brace himself to follow, life
> being not worth living if he does otherwise. After this he braces both
> himself and his guide on the path, and does not desist until either he
> has reached the goal of all his efforts or has acquired the capacity of
> directing his steps himself without the aid of him who has shown him
> the way (340c).

We may assume that Plato did his best to work upon Dionysius
in this way, and that he thus entered upon the essential task he
had wanted to pursue from the first. The passage quoted ends as
follows : " Throughout his life such a man, whatever may be the
occupation in which he is engaged, always holds fast beyond
all else to philosophy, and to that mode of daily life which will
best make him apt to learn, and of retentive mind, and able
to reason soberly by himself ; but the mode of life which is the
contrary of this he shuns to the end."

These sentences, in which he expresses his experiences as a
teacher in general, appear to have been written with reference
to the special case of Dionysius. But according to his account
he gave his lectures not as a teacher of philosophy but, as a diplomat might, with the secret purpose of studying his hearer's
reaction, and of drawing from that reaction his conclusions as
to the attitude he would have to take up toward the tyrant.
He insists that in this he was going methodically to work. He
had elaborated a plan for making certain whether or not the
ruler's interest in philosophy could be regarded as genuine. The
lecture was a means to this end. As an old and experienced
teacher, he knew that when philosophy was placed in this way
before young men in its whole significance, but also in all its
difficulty, they reacted to its appeal in very different ways :
enthusiasm might be kindled in them, but it was also possible
for them to be frightened by the size of the task, which they felt
to be beyond them ; or conversely they might fail through over-
confidence : " they persuade themselves that they have been
sufficiently informed on the whole subject and have no need of
further efforts " (341a).

* See below, Part III (Vol. II), Chap. III.

This last was the case with Dionysius. His reaction was such that Plato abandoned the attempt to give him any further instruction. This decision does not seem to have been the result of a disappointment, but, as Plato himself indicates, the end of a mistaken course on which Plato had only embarked in order to make quite sure of the young man's selfish intention.

He now confined himself to the special purpose of his journey, the achievement of a reconciliation between Dionysius and Dion. The things that happened then between him and the autocrat, and the treatment he had to put up with at his hands, were the " unexpected and incalculable " element, not Dionysius' failure in philosophy. The story of these happenings fills the last section of the epistle, giving it the character of a tale of misfortunes.

The great disappointment Plato had, in fact, suffered in being compelled to give up all hope of the materialization of his political ideal finds expression, however, in the epistle, though only indirectly. Before entering into that personal matter he dwells on the principal aspect of his experience with this false pupil, in a section that seems a digression but is relevant in so far as he treats in it of the relation between the teacher of philosophy and his pupil. While dealing mainly with this relation, he expands his pedagogical theme and goes more deeply into it. To what he has said about the imbibing of philosophic instruction by the pupil, he adds from the standpoint of the productive thinker to whom the communication of philosophy is a problem, and here he reaches the deepest question, that of the nature of philosophic knowledge (341b). The lighthearted way in which Dionysius was obviously treating philosophy was reason enough for Plato to contrast the right and wrong attitudes to philosophy.

But he also had a special ground for entering upon this subject in his apologia. Dionysius had come forward as a philosophical author. His book was concerned with " the highest principles of nature " (344d), as Plato calls what has since become traditionally known as metaphysics. Plato regarded the book as an attack upon him, although, or even because, in it Dionysius described him as " leader and master ". Plato writes : " He wrote on those subjects of which he had heard at that time as if he was producing knowledge of his own different from what he had heard " (341b, 344e). There is nothing unusual in the history of philosophy in a pupil writing an attack on his teacher. So far as Plato is concerned, historical research into his work has shown that in the figures of his dialogues he not only introduced opposing views but dealt with opposition that had actually been offered in his own school. In the epistle we have an undisguised case of polemic of this sort, so that we have a picture of the great thinker from this angle. His polemic is not directed against the self-styled disciple. With a lofty gesture he refuses to deal with Dionysius' work : " I hear that he has since written . . . I know nothing of it " (342b). He concerns himself with the whole class of philosophical writings of which that of Dionysius is but a specimen of minor importance, and exposes the fundamental misunderstanding of his philosophy, or rather of philosophy in general, that underlies that class of works. They treat the fundamental knowledge as something that can be objectively established and conveyed as a doctrine by means of books, so that anyone can gain possession of it. To this he opposes his insight into the super-rational and dynamic character of the original metaphysical knowledge, as we may call it. He, the originator of our metaphysical tradition, speaks unassumingly of " that with which I am earnestly concerned " (341c), and declares with regard to it that " it is not expressible, like other studies ; but, as a result of long application to the subject itself and communion therewith it comes to birth in the soul on a sudden, as light that is kindled by a leaping spark, and thence it nourishes itself " (341c).

Anyone who is familiar with Plato's writings will think of the magnificent passages in the *Symposium* and the *Phædrus*, which are among the high peaks of these dialogues—Diotima's description of the metaphysical experience in which the reason is lifted above itself by the sudden act of spiritual vision, and the prophecy of the pharaoh Thamus in the *Phædrus* about the dangerous effect of the invention of writing in crippling the faculty of productive thought. It is the same central concern as this that he has in the epistle. We met with it when we dealt with the type of soul-pilgrimage of which Plato writes.* But again, how different is the way he brings forward his view here and in those philosophical dialogues. Here, where he speaks in his own person, he does not speak as there out of the fullness of experience, but treats the matter theoretically. He speaks as the teacher who has discovered the limits of the literary presentation of philosophy, and watches over the observance of those limits. Moreover, he offers his own practice as a model ; that sentence about the inexpressible is preceded by a statement about his own writings

* See above, p. 109.

which the sentence is intended to confirm—" There does not exist, nor will there ever exist, any writing of mine dealing therewith."
This extreme statement is surprising. Some interpreters are tempted to regard it as ironical. We are more inclined to think of the mystics for whom silence is the soul's answer to illumination. But has ever a thinker made the power of the word more fruitful for the representation of the true life of philosophy, or done more to communicate the knowledge of the inscrutable to the thought of a period governed by the enlightenment of the understanding, than the philosopher-artist Plato ? We should be compelled to doubt whether Plato was aware of the magnitude of his work if we had not other witnesses on the subject. In the *Phædrus*, in which he made Socrates convey in the form of a divine oracle the paradoxical assertion of the disadvantage of writing in life, he set limits to the radical negation of the value of that which is set down in writing, by recognizing, or making his Socrates recognize, in opposition to the oracle, a certain genuine function of writing—as, for example, an aid to memory, or, in allusion to his own dialogue, as a " game ".

Philosophical writings may, Socrates admits, retain some importance if they are accompanied by the consciousness that the thought enshrined in writing is only an image " of the living and besouled word of him who knows ", the word " which with intelligence is written in the mind of the learner " (*Ph.*, 276a). The productive unfolding of thought through the direct relation between teacher and disciple is the actual means through which philosophy has its being ; it is a life-relationship, the guidance by the philosopher of his pupil's soul. In contrast with this " serious " character of the philosophical life, which is ever renewing itself, writings are only a " game ", yielding something accomplished. But they are a festal, glorious game (*Ph.*, 276c–e), which through its beauty also has a share in truth ; is, indeed, united with it in the " divine madness " that " is the source of the chiefest blessings coming to us " (*Ph.*, 244a).

In the *Phædrus* we have a witness to the fact that Plato recognized the enthusiasm that filled his philosophical mind and was, indeed, in his judgment, the source of all higher life, as the vitalizing basis also of his writing activity. So far that dialogue marks the height he reached in understanding himself, though he let his Socrates express his discovery. In comparison with this indirect self-revelation, the express statement about his

writings in the epistle loses its weight. The renunciation, polemical in purpose, of every past and future attempt to touch on
" that with which he was earnestly concerned ", in writing and
even in the spoken word, sounds like an orthodox manifesto of
the academic school, then tending toward scepticism, through
the mouth of its head. The same impression is created by the
talk in the epistle of the " inexpressible ", which for us is surrounded by an atmosphere of mysticism. In its technical character that talk is sharply distinguished from the words with which
Plato refers in a famous passage of the *Republic* to the unfathomable basis : " It is the source of knowledge and of truth, and
yet itself surpasses them in beauty . . . It is not essence but
still transcends essence in dignity and power " (*Rep.*, 509a, b).
To the phrase in the epistle about the inexpressible Plato adds,
as if to safeguard the authority of the head of the school : " This,
however, I know, that if it was to be reduced to the spoken or
written word, it would be best conveyed by myself " (341d).

In the main section of these general remarks, which now
follows, Plato appears entirely as the representative of the philosophy of the school. In order to give the reasons for his rejection
of the false metaphysics that are put forward as a theory to be
grasped purely by the intellect, and also to make plausible the
claim, not easily to be credited, that his writings offer no access
at all to that which was the subject of his as of all serious philosophic effort, he reverts to the theory of cognition and inserts a
closely reasoned didactic passage that might have come from
an academic lecture on the theory of Ideas. We are given here
a systematic analysis of the factors and the stages of cognition,
which lead up from the name and the perceptible form of things
to the contemplation of their inexpressible essence. All who
hold Plato in honour will be grateful to the writer of the epistle
for this inserted passage. But in the context of the epistle it
serves to support the thesis that " no man of reason will ever
venture to commit to language the conceptions of his reason,
especially when it is unalterable—as is the case with what is laid
down in writing " (343a). This thesis is even more extreme
than that of the *Phædrus*, as it has reference also to the spoken
word ; but it gives an entirely different sense to the original
profound thought of the dangerousness of writing. Plato declares
that the philosopher who communicates to the public in speech or
in writing his cognition of the essence of things exposes philosophy
and himself to the danger of being laughed to scorn by men

(343*d*, 344*c*). This follows from his exposition of the theory of cognition. For ordinary people, who are unconcerned with cognition, but cling to that which is perceptible to the senses, which has a name and is familiar, cannot understand what the person with cognition, who lives in the contemplation of the eternal, means by his words, and he is helpless against the twisting of his words : for he cannot show the ideal subjects of thought, of which he speaks, to those who have not learnt to turn away from the empirical world in which we live and act, and to direct their gaze to the realm of the spirit, in which the soul has its home.

Thus does Plato expound the antagonism between the philosopher and the unphilosophical person who glances through his dialogues. He does not treat this antagonism, however, from the reforming standpoint of the ethos that underlay his political action, but purely in the interest of cognition ; and here, too, the consciousness of the philosopher's mission " to make men see " (344*a*) cuts across the academic claim of the esoteric character of philosophy. To gain insight into the invisible essences which can be contemplated only by the intellect, and which underlie the things that are known and have names—this, he declares, is done only by few. For it requires not only a long and strenuous schooling of the faculty of thought, in the course of which the intellectual energies grow, but a special gift of such a sort that the demand for something eternally whole, good, true, beautiful, which the philosopher awakens in his disciples, is met in them by a " natural connexion or affinity " with the object of their desire (343*e*–344*a*).

Is Plato referring here to the difficulties he generally experienced with his pupils ? [15] Surely not. He has in mind the special case of Dionysius, whom he had tried to gain as a disciple, but who had not followed him and whom he now disavowed before all the world. He sets in motion all the machinery of the theory of knowledge in order to show that philosophy is the affair of a few elect, to whom Dionysius did not belong—and that through his own fault ; for access to the sanctuary had been open to him. His presumption had barred the way for him. Vanity had led him to profane the holy place as a writer on philosophy. The general verdict against philosophical authorship which Plato had built up on that systematic analysis of the factors of cognition had this personal objective—to show that Dionysius, by coming before the public with his manuscript, had shown that he did not know what philosophy is and means. Since true philosophy was embodied in Plato, that ignorance proved that the ruler, in spite of his intercourse with Plato, had gained no access to the philosopher's world of ideas.

Plato burdens his account of his Sicilian journey with this four-page argument, as though it were not enough to establish the fact that Dionysius' relationship with him was not that of disciple to master. But it is that fact that bothers him. Plato repeats untiringly, with reference to that lecture on philosophy to the young ruler, in which he showed him the goal and the path —" I instructed him on that one sole occasion, and never again after it." And he insists : " I did not, however, expound the matter fully, nor did Dionysius ask me to do so " (345a, 341a). That was the sore point. He is trying to explain why he then got no further. And as he tries to do so he reveals the disappointment Dionysius inflicted on him. Once more he enumerates the possible reasons why young fellows, to judge by his own experience in teaching, fail to keep up with their teacher of philosophy —discouraged by their feeling of inability to follow him, or unimpressed because they imagine they know all about it already. But to that alternative he now adds : " Or does Dionysius regard my teaching as worthless ? " And he feels it necessary to give an answer to that rhetorical question : " If he does, he will be in conflict with many witnesses who maintain the opposite, men who should be vastly more competent judges of such matters than Dionysius." He closes with the bitter reproach : " If he considers it valuable for the education of the mind of a free man, how, unless he is a most extraordinary person, could he possibly have treated the ' Leader and Master ' with such ready disrespect ? "

After this outbreak he continues the narrative : " How he showed his disrespect I will now relate." By this transition, a sort of heading for the next section, he bridges over the gap between the things of philosophical importance he has mentioned and the description of his further experiences with the autocrat (345c–350b). These have reference to the dissension between Dionysius and Dion. The story first follows the same lines as during the earlier visit. Dionysius had no thought at all of reconciliation, and resorted to a new act of violence against Dion. Plato wanted to depart, but had to give up the idea. He remained for a further year. But this time he remained, he says, " to expose Dionysius' devices to actual test " (347*b*). This test brought a crisis that ended with a breach.

With the change of content, the story takes on a changed character : it takes on something of the style of court and political memoirs, and sometimes borders on the rhetorical. Plato portrays himself in the unhappy rôle of the mediator between his host and his friend. Dramatically, in the form of a monologue, he presents the reflections that determined him to enter into negotiations with the despot in Dion's interest. As the intention to make use of his personal standing in approaching Dionysius for this practical purpose took the place of the spiritual influence which the philosopher was called to exercise as the guide to a high aim, so the interests he represented as Dion's friend now had their centre of gravity in material things. The negotiations were long drawn out over Dion's possessions, which were great, dangerously great, so that Dionysius planned to confiscate them and finally, after all sorts of intrigues, did confiscate them in defiance of Plato. Plato tried to save at least something, in order to avert a complete fiasco (347*b*). The decisions he had to make in this situation are again described with their reasons ; but the reasons were simply considerations of what was the best that could be done in the circumstances.

With the bringing down of the human relations to an everyday level comes a picture of the moods in which the attitude of the persons involved found expression in their dispute. Plato represents himself as annoyed, angry, filled with suppressed rage, and finally disgusted, in an ascending scale of feelings in which his growing antipathy to the ruler and at the same time his impotent struggle against the ruler's arbitrary proceedings are revealed. The super-personal point of view does not entirely disappear, but is reduced to Plato's identification of the material interests he represented on Dion's behalf with the cause of philosophy. He sums up his efforts as follows : " Up to this point I had been assisting in that way both philosophy and my friends " (347*e*). He describes the ultimate situation—he and Dionysius entirely estranged, but preserving the outward appearance of friendship ; and gives this description of his own state of mind : " I was gazing out of my cage, like a bird that is longing to fly up and away " (348*a*).

This pretty picture gives the impression of being a genuine expression of feeling ; but it is borrowed—from the *Phædrus*, from the splendid myth of the soul and its original attachment to the divine foundation of existence owing to the contemplation of Ideas in the supermundane regions. In the *Phædrus* Plato used that picture to describe the situation of the philosopher in the world, as that of the perfected man who " separates himself from human interests and turns his attention to the divine. When he sees the beauty on earth, remembering the true beauty, he feels his wings growing and longs to stretch them for an upward flight, but cannot do so, and, like a bird, gazes upward and neglects the things below " (*Ph.*, 249*d*). A disciple of Plato, painting the picture of the philosopher as the prisoner of Dionysius in the citadel of Syracuse, might give his description a point hardly in the best of taste by this literary borrowing. But can we credit Plato with such a profanation of philosophy ? *

The story goes on like a historical novel—the Philosopher and the Autocrat. It comes to the stage of open conflict. The break came from Dionysius. It arose out of Plato's association with a supporter of Dion among the Syracusan notables, an influential army commander and politician named Herakleides. The narrator now describes the exciting happenings with rhetorical vividness. One scene may serve as an instance. There had been a rising in the camp of the mercenaries ; Herakleides came under suspicion of having instigated it, and in view of this rumour he fled. A connexion of his, Theodotos by name, undertook to bring him before Dionysius to enable him to clear himself, if the ruler would promise not to use arbitrary violence against Herakleides. Dionysius gave this promise in Plato's presence, but broke his word and sent out his spies to capture the fugitive. Plato learned of this through Herakleides' friends, who asked him to go with them to see the ruler.

So we set off and entered the presence of Dionysius ; and while they stood in silence weeping, I said to him : " These men are

---

* Classical philologists who claim the letter to be genuine may offer the explanation, in order to remove this objection, that the picture of the captive bird who " is longing to fly up and away but cannot " may not have been invented by Plato but may have been a commonplace in the literature of the time, so that he made use of it in different ways in the two places—philosophically in the *Phædrus* as a simile for man's situation in the world and for the enthusiasm that inspires him (" *sursum corda* ") ; and in the seventh epistle in a simple empirical way to illustrate the situation of a prisoner. But this explanation can hardly suffice. For, once Plato had made use of this imagery in a philosophical connexion in the *Phædrus*, it involved the distinction between " below " and " above ", between the life on earth and the supermundane sphere in which the soul has its home. Thus it has the effect of a parody of the philosopher's " disregard of the things below " when he makes use of the picture in the seventh epistle, where it has reference to his unsuccessful struggle with Dionysius over entirely mundane things : " I was gazing out of my cage like a bird longing to fly up and away, while he schemed how he might shoo me back without paying away any of Dion's money."

alarmed lest you should take some step in regard to Herakleides, contrary to the agreement of yesterday ; for I think he has been seen making his way in this direction." On hearing this he blazed up and went all colours, just as an angry man would do. Theodotos fell at his knees and, grasping his hands, burst into tears and besought him to do no such thing. I broke in to encourage him, saying : " Cheer up, Theodotos ; for Dionysius will never dare to act otherwise, contrary to yesterday's agreement." Then Dionysius gave me a highly tyrannical look, and said : " With you I made no agreement, great or small." " By the gods," I replied, " you did—not to do what this man is now begging you not to do." And when I had said this I turned my back and went out (349a, b).

In this style Plato brings his unhappy story to its end. He describes how Dionysius now regarded him as an enemy, and how he found a pretext for dismissing him from his entourage, finally ordering him to stay outside the citadel among the mercenaries. Plato mentions rumours that the mercenaries " threatened to make an end of him if ever they caught him ". In his distress he turned for help to his Pythagorean friends at Tarentum. They sent a ship to Syracuse, under the pretext of an embassy from the State, in order to persuade Dionysius to allow him to depart. Under this pressure from abroad Dionysius gave way.

The picture Plato here paints of the autocrat does not fit in well with what he says at the beginning of this section about his fortunate rescue : " For this I have to thank Dionysius next to God, because, whilst many planned to destroy me, he prevented them and gave some place to reverence in his dealings with me." The inconsistency is characteristic of the different attitudes taken up in the different parts of the epistle, according to their subject.

At the end he changes his attitude once more. The story closes with a scene in Olympia, where Plato, on his homeward journey, meets Dion and reports to him. Dion swears to take revenge for himself and his friend : Dionysius has committed a sin against the sacred law of hospitality. And Plato ? He does not attempt to restrain the avenger ; he even holds out the prospect of the support of the Academy in the campaign against the autocrat. Yet he claims for himself the position of a mediator, standing above the parties, with " ties with both of them ", and as the adviser who now becomes arbiter. He even saddles Dion with the same guilt as Dionysius, whom he seeks to excuse : " It was you yourself,"—such is his record of what he said at the time to Dion—" who, with the others, practically forced me to become a guest at the table and the hearth of Dionysius, and a partaker in sacred rites with him ; and he, though he probably thought that I, as many slanderers asserted, was conspiring with you against him, yet refrained from killing me and showed a feeling of respect " (350c). This utterance, as he himself says, was the outcome of his " loathing " of " the unfortunate Sicilian journey " (350d). But the judgment he delivers in retrospect also hits at Dion and Dionysius equally, as though both were adversaries of his : " By their disobedience and their refusal to heed my attempts at reconciliation they have themselves brought upon themselves all the evils which have now happened." It might have been possible to end the dispute, " but as things are they rushed one against the other and so have flooded the world with evils " (350e).

But that is not his last word. He withdraws his blame of his friend at once. In a sort of epilogue, devoted to Dion, he glorifies him, with his heroic death in mind, thus completing the general purpose of the epistle, to represent Dion as a model for politicians. It is as if he saw in Dion his other self when, in the passage quoted, after a pause, he continues : " And yet Dion had the same designs as I myself ought, I should say, to have had, or anyone else whose purpose regarding his own power and his friends in his city was the decent one of conferring the greatest benefits when reaching the height of power and privilege " (351a).

These greatest benefits consisted, he repeats once more, in " the ordering of the State by the justest and best laws, without the least resort to executions and banishments ". According to Plato's teaching, the political purpose described in that phrase is only the second-best, in comparison with the ideal of the philosopher-king ; in the didactic section he refers to that distinction, put forward in the *Republic*, between the ideal solution and the second-best way. But this view did not prevent him from idealizing the man in whom he saw the practical pursuit of philosophy embodied. The tribute to Dion proceeds further, indeed to the limit of ethical commendation ; but with a surprising turn. Plato—or whoever may have been the author of the epistle—once more pictures the avenger who has issued the call to arms, and then turns to his glorification, which culminated in the picture of the fallen hero. Now, this picture, which we placed at the outset of our analysis as a token of the Sicilian tragedy, and which we then saw used in reference to Plato's

expression of his grief in the ode to Dion, appears in the epilogue
of the epistle at the end of a passage that runs as follows : " Now
while Dion was pursuing that course, having chosen to suffer
rather than to do wrong—although taking precautions against
so suffering—none the less he fell at the very peak of his mastery
over his foes . . ." (351c). Here we have a surprising, indeed
an inconsistent, transition. After depicting his hero in the
passion of revenge he resorts to the Socratic principle of morality,
which opposes violent reactions such as revenge, and uses
Socrates' famous formula that to suffer wrong is better than to
do it, in order to define Dion's true character. Then he passes
over to the heroic view of the events, contrasting the noble
intention of the true statesman with his tragic fate. Once more
we ask whether such blindness to the contrast between different
ethical planes can legitimately be imputed to Plato.

The tragic note, however, fades away at once. For the
passage quoted does not end with the picture of the fallen hero,
but continues without a break—" nor is there anything extraordinary in what happened to him ". There had happened to
Dion what usually happens to a noble and thoughtful man who
has to do with evil men and succumbs to them : he is under no
illusion as to the character of his antagonist, but does not dream
of the full extent of his evilness—" as a good pilot, though he
would not fail to notice the approach of a storm, yet might fail
to realize its extraordinary and unexpected violence, and so
might be forcibly overwhelmed. It was this that caused Dion to
fall." He could not foresee such vileness, or, what amounts to
the same thing, such a " pitch of folly ". Plato himself found this
incomprehensible, and ascribed it, as we have seen,* to a
" dæmon ", that the " folly " that underlay the fatal misconception of Dion's character had been humanly possible. By
returning at the end to this consideration, Plato defends his
friend from the charge that lay against his statesmanship, of
having shown lack of judgment. Dion remains the good pilot,
even in disaster. Intelligence and character are one and the
same thing.

Thus from beginning to end of the document we meet with
significant and familiar ideas from the Platonic philosophy, which
are made use of in the shaping of the biographical material.
And this material, although the story covers only a few years of
Plato's life, is so rich that it might have yielded a general picture

* See above, pp. 138 sqq.,

of his personality. But that intention was far from the mind of the writer of the epistle. To a modern reader who supposes himself to be closest to the realities of life when he sees a man with all his inconsistencies, it may seem true to life when Plato does not attempt to show himself in the formal character of a philosopher as he shows Dionysius in that of an autocrat and Dion in that of the ideal statesman. But to approach the apologia with this positivist conception of reality means turning its literary character into its opposite, and destroying its connexion with the Platonic world of Ideas. As our analysis has shown, the material, though consciously shaped, has not been shaped from the whole man but bit by bit, according to the attitudes in which Plato comes forward or to the part he plays. What we are given is only disconnected fragments of a picture of the philosopher, and no means of grasping the whole ; nowhere, except where he speaks as a teacher or quotes famous sayings of his own, do we feel the breath of the great man, still less the secret foundation of human greatness. Instead he measures himself—or the author of the epistle measures him—mainly by the common measure that yields ordinary morality. Everything goes to show that the self-portrayal here has a different function from that familiar to us ; it has in it nothing of the autobiographical intention that gives philosophic dignity in our eyes to self-portrayal—the intention of making life intelligible through life itself.

Thus the question of the genuineness of the epistle is scarcely to be settled purely from internal considerations, because in the classical attitude to autobiography it makes no substantial difference whether an author is presenting his own life or that of another person. But the literary borrowings scattered through the document in the form of quotations from the writer's own works, and above all that from the *Phædrus*, should suffice to show that the view of Plato from without that we get here is in reality the view of a member of the Academy. And so we have no need to allow our conception of Plato as a man to be lowered by this letter attributed to him—the conception expressed by Goethe when he wrote of him as one whose relation to the world is that of " a blessed spirit that deigned to dwell in it for a while ".

III. ISOCRATES' AUTOBIOGRAPHICAL ORATION

We turn now to the one completed autobiographical work written in this epoch, the *Antidosis*, or, rendering the traditional

Greek title approximately, the " Challenge ", of Isocrates (436–338). This, as the first conscious and deliberate literary auto-biography, is the earliest explicit example of our subject matter in ancient times. The famous Athenian publicist, ten years older than his fellow-countryman Plato, outlived Plato ten years. He published his autobiography at an advanced age, in 353, in a form corresponding to his profession—as a speech in court for the defence in a lawsuit concerning his interests as a citizen. There is no direct connexion, as we have pointed out already, between the great spiritual movement of that age, represented by Plato and Socrates, and this autobiographical work, which reveals its rhetorical character in form and title, and no artistic transition can bridge the gap separating the representative of rhetorical education from philosophy. But coming, as we do, from Plato's Seventh Epistle, we are struck by various elements of similarity between these two heterogeneous works, and it is difficult to avoid the assumption that one of them was influenced by the other. In addition to this there is the relation in time : Isocrates published his autobiography in the same year in which Dion's death fell. Here is a fixed point from which the genuineness of Plato's epistle may be re-investigated. We are faced with two alternatives : either that epistle preceded the rhetorician's work, in which case it certainly comes from Plato, or the opposite is the case. Now, it is quite conceivable that Isocrates, who had always regarded the considerably younger philosopher as a rival, had Plato's political missive in view and sought to overtrump it. But in that case Plato must not only have drafted but published the epistle so soon after Dion's death that Isocrates could place an equally comprehensive work alongside it in the same year, and that is considered most unlikely even by those who regard the epistle as genuine.[16] It seems more probable that the rhetorician, who was inventive in matters of literary form, came first with his autobiography, and that this rhetorical work of art led a disciple of Plato to elaborate the stories of the Master's " Sicilian adventure " that were current in the Academy into a political apologia of the head of the school—a work that was also a publication of a programme.

However that may be, the very possibility of comparing the rhetorician's work with the philosopher's is of considerable importance. The two are comparable because both are con-troversial works. Autobiography first set foot in Greece in the field of political authorship, which was a field of intellectual life that was occupied by rhetoric. The motives at work in this process lead back to more general considerations.

As a rule the appearance of autobiography is bound up with the fact that in social life certain habits and practices obtain which provide a legitimate opportunity and objective for self-portrayal ; and it is in this connexion that autobiography takes its rise. Among the Athenians it was the democratic conventions of the city-state that favoured such conditions. In the publicity of political and forensic affairs rhetoric gained an importance hardly imaginable to us. Eloquence in speech and energy in action were generally regarded by the Greeks as together constituting the personality of the wise man, and as the most effective forces in the citizen's struggle for existence ; " orator " became the term for the practical statesman.

The remarkable literary status won by forensic advocacy in Athens, so that works of literature originated in this sphere, so remote in our view from cultural issues, had the result that self-portrayal in the speech in court is here particularly deserving of attention.[17] The parties in a hearing had to conduct their case in person ; even in an ordinary hearing the accused was permitted in his defence to discuss his own personality, and, as is expressed in one of these orations, " to bring to the fore his own virtues and to praise the services rendered by his forefathers ". When the charge had reference to political views there resulted a full account of the defendant's own public life. And the democratic procedure of the δοκιμασία or scrutiny, under which a newly-elected official was subjected, before entry into office, to an inquiry into his fitness, and, if an objection was raised to him, to a formal hearing before the council or a court designated by it, provided continual occasions that made it actually incumbent on the person attacked to give evidence in self-defence as to his career and his character.

These self-characterizations could not as a rule be devoted to full individual self-portrayal ; at most they would give data concerning the career, and they would deal mainly with the ἠθοποιία, the delineation of character so far as concerned the subject's civic honour : this was their practical purpose. The parties to an action usually ordered the needed orations from their advocate, with the intention of learning them by heart, so that they themselves usually functioned simply as mouthpieces. But if an advocate came forward in a case of his own, the possibility was presented of a direct self-portrayal—which, in view of the growth here and there of the custom of publishing the pleadings for political or literary purposes, was capable of developing into a literary work.

One of the first documents thus published of which we have knowledge is the speech in his own defence of Antiphon, praised by Thucydides (8, 68). Antiphon, an eminent orator who had been the intellectual leader of the Athenian oligarchy, was charged with treason on the restoration of the democracy in 411 B.C., and was sentenced to death. We also have from the end of the fifth century speeches in which a crucial event in the speaker's life arising out of his struggle for a livelihood is dealt with in the course of prosecution or defence. From that point of view the author deals in a narrative section with his circumstances as a citizen, his honour, and his services to the State, or with his past.*

The connexion between the usages of practical life and autobiography may be traced a step further in the State oration. Since the time of Pericles eloquence had become a weapon to be wielded by the statesman, as the Ionic weapons of elegiac and iambic had been wielded by Solon ; an oration thus fulfilled its purpose in the same way as an act, through its effectiveness. Only at the height of the display of political eloquence in Athens, so strangely bound up with the corruption of democracy and the decay of the State, did the increased interest in prose speech and the artistic work done in it promote the development of literary style. Then Demosthenes (384–322) made the State oration a work of literature ; he was the first, since the fifties of that fourth century B.C., to publish in the service of his policy writings that were orations only in form and were not bound to the actual conditions of the orations *coram populo*.[18] Thus, too, the masterpiece in which he gave an independent description of his activities as a statesman and their motives, the oration " On the Crown ", is not to be understood as an actual pleading. It is represented as having been spoken by Demosthenes in his defence in court, when Aeschines, leader of the opposing party, sought to obstruct the public honouring of the eminent man by bringing a charge against him of infringing the Constitution (336 B.C.). The forensic style is only an incidental, and in the perfected form in

* Lysias, in his twelfth speech, as prosecutor against Eratosthenes, one of the Thirty Tyrants, whom he arraigns as the murderer of Polemarchus, brother of Lysias (403 B.C.). Andocides " On his Return " (before the popular assembly), and " On the Mysteries ", as defendant, 399.

which Demosthenes published the work [19] it is in any case a literary document so conceived from the outset, a powerful statement from the leading Athenian statesman, positive, active, and not merely the product of an enforced defensive. In the decisive battle for his political purpose, the last great struggle in furtherance of the national policy of Athens, a policy that had already been doomed to failure by the defeat of Chaeronea, Demosthenes here summons up the dæmonic power of his eloquence in order to bear witness concerning his work for the mother city and concerning his whole life—" not before the sovereign populace of the Pnyx, but before the nation of the Athenians at their best, before their great forefathers and before posterity ".[20]   Writing with passion, with impetuosity, even with lack of discernment, under the spell of his art, he has converted the emotional power of his speech into will power, intent on annihilating his opponent in measureless hatred, regardless even of actual truth in the urge to self-assertion. In this way he represents himself with imaginative force as the man in whom is embodied all that still exists of the national traditions of the democracy, the greatness, the liberty, and the honour of Athens.   Thus the oration " On the Crown " is a work of a biographical nature and, in a sense, the first and for a long time the only autobiographical work that gained a place in world literature.

But autobiography in the finer sense of the term did not proceed from the pursuit of political power. The idea of an autobiography as a literary task entered upon for its own sake, independently of the competitive existence of the city-dweller, had been adopted in the preceding generation, two decades before the oration " On the Crown ", by a writer who was a man of letters or an artist rather than a politician. Isocrates had held aloof throughout his life, like Plato, from active politics and even from the public life of the courts. Unlike Plato, however, he had found his true calling as a writer. His writings had been the instrument through which he sought to exercise influence from his study upon contemporary public opinion. He had outstanding success as a political writer or publicist, and still more as a teacher of oratory and of the art of writing.   Toward the end of his long life, in 353 B.C., when he was eighty-two years old, while fully aware of his success, he felt that it was necessary to establish his standing in competition with the new prestige acquired by philosophy through Plato and the Academy ; and in that year he wrote that new kind of work which, in the form of a defence pleading before a court of justice, contained his self-portrayal. He described its purpose as [21] " to reveal to those who had mistaken ideas about me, and to posterity, my character, my life, and the sort of education to which I was devoted ". He intended to " make known the truth " about himself—the work was to provide " a true image of my thought (*dianoia*) and my whole life ". " I hoped ", he wrote, " that this would serve as a monument, after my death, more noble than statues of bronze."*

This new and express setting of the subject-matter was the result of a comprehensive literary movement in which Isocrates played an important part—a movement which also included the other general element that contributed to the emergence of autobiography in the classical epoch. That element was the enterprise of rhetoric in taking the life of an individual as a subject worthy of study for its own sake. The idea of regarding man as an end in himself came from philosophy, which by then had so raised the general intellectual level in Athens that that fundamental idea, after developing in the context of the theory of knowledge or of ethics, could bear literary fruit. Isocrates was a pioneer in this, as he was in his work as a publicist : thanks to his close touch with current trends he ventured to deal with outstanding problems such as biography and public affairs,[22] which gave factual importance to his formal art.

As the son of a well-to-do man, amid the incomparable cultural wealth of the Athens of that time, he had been prepared for his literary work by his intellectual training. He had sat at the feet of the so-called Sophists, especially Gorgias, and had even been in the company of Socrates. Plato bears witness to this in the *Phædrus* (the many-sided dialogue to which we referred when treating of the philosopher's attitude to his own writings). Plato here developed his philosophical conception of rhetoric, which Aristotle took over from him and systematized. Plato seems to have intended for Isocrates the task which Aristotle carried through ; for at the end of the *Phædrus* he puts into the mouth of his Socrates a " prophecy " about the future of Isocrates. Isocrates was then a young man of about twenty-five, and had

---

* This phrase is echoed in Horace's famous line, " Exegi monumentum aere perennius ". In Isocrates' case the phrase had a special point : a bronze statue to him had actually been erected in a temple of Eleusis by the statesman and army commander Timotheus, his favourite pupil, " in token of his affection for the man and of his respect for his wisdom ".

made his mark only in the writing of court pleadings.*   Socrates says of him :

" I should not be surprised if, as he grows older, he should so excel in the speeches he is now setting to work at that all who have ever dealt with rhetoric shall seem less than children ; and I think this profession will not satisfy him but a divine impulse will lead him to greater things ; for something of philosophy is inborn in his mind."

Isocrates did not pursue that path.   He gave up the writing of pleadings in the course of time, about 390, in order to found a school of rhetoric—this may have been the occasion for Plato's expression of good wishes in the form of that " prophecy ".   But Isocrates held firmly to the popular conception of that art, defined by Gorgias, its founder, when he separated it from philosophy and confined it to playing a part in practical life as an instrument for political or other everyday ends.   As Plato put it when he introduced Socrates in conversation with the famous rhetorician : [23]   " Now come, Gorgias, and tell us what is that thing that you say is the greatest good for men, and that you claim to produce " . . . " I call it the ability to persuade with speeches either judges in the law courts or statesmen in the council-chamber or the commons in the Assembly or an audience at any other meeting that may be held on public affairs . . ."

Isocrates brought to perfection the instrument Gorgias had devised for this art of persuasion, the so-called artistic prose. This was a musical prose style, emulating poetry in rhythm and tone.   It was marked by the conscious art of the building up of periods of greater or lesser length, thus both pleasing the ear and flattering the intelligence.   His fame rests on this æsthetic achievement.   Through it he exerted an influence that lasted beyond his day and spread beyond the Greek-speaking world. Cicero adopted this " florid " or " ornate " style of prose writing, and through Cicero's works it influenced political and even Christian pulpit eloquence of later times.   Yet his great success cannot conceal the fact that he did not attain the heights to which he was summoned by Plato's judgment.   At one point in his autobiography he touches on the essence of the matter.   He complains that his critics refuse—out of envy, he supposes—to recognize that in his speeches things were " well " said :   they

---

* *Phædrus*, p. 279. The action in this dialogue takes place about 410 B.C. The work was probably published about 388, when Plato founded his own philosophical school.

were credited only with being " charmingly " said.* To put things " well "—that is to say, to find the *mot juste*—was, it is true, in the opinion of Plato and Aristotle, the achievement of the genuine philosopher.

From the characteristic line he took we may understand the part Isocrates played in the development of biography. When a rhetorician of this type and of such rank undertook the task of writing a man's life, he could not trouble about giving a faithful portrait of an individual : all that would interest him would be the new material for his art of effective conferment of praise and blame, or in the present case, since invective was out of the question, of giving form to the praise of a man's virtues. But the results of this attempt were, after all, first essays in biography ; for there remained operative, as an element of the artistic attitude of the classical Greeks, the fundamental direction of the biographer's attention † to the fully developed nature of man, as revealed in his career, and this could not be entirely stultified in the rhetorical treatment of the material.

Soon after 374 B.C., in an obituary notice of Euagoras, king of Salamis in Cyprus, ordered by the king's son, Isocrates published the first biographical panegyric, or *enkomion*, as a type of literary work of his own invention,[24] and through his practical and theoretical elaboration of the *enkomion* it became one of the most widespread forms of biographical literature. In the introduction to this work he gave for the Athenian public a general formulation of the task of eulogizing in prose the deeds of eminent contemporaries. The obituary itself is a specimen of court flattery, but if it was not a true portrayal, at least it contained a plan for depicting the character of an individual,[25] and it was in this connexion that Isocrates founded the autobiographical *genre*, whose mere appearance, and especially its first emergence, would seem to be the sign of an author's consciousness of individuality.

Thus in Isocrates we first have autobiography moulded by a literary form settled beforehand, and so the rhetorician's *enkomion* acquires importance for our history. It maintained this importance ; even in the Middle Ages we shall meet in autobiography with traces of the rhetorical tradition still persisting. Rhetoric was, after all, not a dead thing, especially among the ancients with their keen appreciation of words and of form. When it did

---

* *Antidosis*, 62 : οἱ χαριέντως μὲν εἰρῆσθαι ταῦτα φήσουσι (τὸ γὰρ εὖ φθονήσουσιν εἰπεῖν).

† See above, pp. 62 *sqq.*

not degenerate into mere virtuosity, it responded to the feeling of the ordinary man who dislikes anything that disturbs his code or habits of life. Such is the inner relationship between the *enkomion* of Isocrates and his autobiographical *Antidosis*. In this, as we shall see, he portrayed the *ethos* of the patriotic citizen. Similarly, when writing his *Euagoras* he was started on his course [26] by a practice of extolling a man's virtues which was indigenous in the aristocratic society of Greece, as well as in the Roman republic, where we shall find still more prevalent this source of biographical literature—the public praise of a dead person in the funeral oration. In classical Athens this custom had led to so exalted a moment as that of Pericles' oration on behalf of the council of state at the memorial festival in honour of men who had well served the State.[27]

Isocrates expressly associated the new *genre* of the *enkomion* with this custom : in his prologue to the *Euagoras* (§ 11), he compared the *enkomion* with the traditional poetic form of the lament for the dead, the *threnos* ; he had set out, he said, to supply an example of the way the prose oration, which, indeed, he regarded as something of higher rank than poetry, could take over this function of the poems familiar through Pindar's *threnoi* —and in Pindar the *threnos* was inspired by an aristocratic conception, deeply religious, of the unity of the family in the march of destiny.[28] This type of work, Isocrates held, should become an independent class of prose writing, in accordance with the then new interest in biography, a class that should be concerned with the praise of the great men of the day, freed from elements of heroic myth.

With this literary form Isocrates claims to have been the first to invent the appreciation in prose of eminent contemporaries,[29] and he turns against " the philosophers " (a term that meant, as it did in the eighteenth century, all writers or other intellectuals who were representatives of enlightenment) with the charge that in spite of their many activities they had " never yet ventured to write on such a subject ". In this polemic, which ignored the portrayals of individuals in the Platonic dialogues, it was probably vanity, which limits a man's outlook, that spoke loudest ; but there spoke also the enlightened mind of the Athenian of good family, who was out to employ in a modernized form the traditional means of satisfying the desire for fame. As an exponent of enlightenment and of the civic virtues, in introducing the *enkomion* into literature he placed in the foreground the pedagogical consideration that the young should be spurred on to the emulation of virtue by the spectacle of its celebration. The object Isocrates had in view in the *enkomion* [30] was to help people to understand what is permanent in the nature of man. We can soon realize why he succeeded. For rhetoric takes no trouble to give a picture of the individual existence based on realistic observation : its abstract postulates are based on an ideal picture of the type of life it envisages, and these postulates are vindicated if we can find them fulfilled in an actual person. But by means of this abstract process, which simply ignores the very refractory material of the particular reality, it is able quickly to present an ideal (not an actual) literary character as soon as it is known what kind of ideal is sought.

This technique of Isocrates' *enkomion* consists in the conceptual selection of the qualities or virtues of the hero in the course of, or at the very outset of, the various sections of the life-story ; this is heightened in the middle of the eulogy, where the account has reached the fully developed personality, and thus becomes an exhaustive description of the character, the outlining of which suggests a Socratic reminiscence. Euagoras, who has to be shown in the incomparable glory and virtuousness of his king-ship, is presented as a philosophical ruler ; the alleged greatness of his rule is attributed not only to natural gifts but to deliberate intellectual self-education ; the moral ideas of the philosophers, having been assimilated by the enlightened citizens, are repre-sented as maxims of the ruler's, and as proof of their observance the general characteristics of a ruler's ideal conduct in life are displayed as those of Euagoras—in his imposing presence, in his intercourse with good and bad men, in his official duties as king, statesman, army commander, all as traits of the *bios*, introduced by the words, " Throughout his whole life he conducted himself in such a way that he . . ."

Among the typical features of this *genre*, which make their appearance in this work of Isocrates, is the introduction of stories of childhood with omens of the hero's future greatness, leading up to a conclusion in which his praises are sung. (In ancient biography the date of birth is sometimes given, but usually not in autobiographies.) This feature will be met with again in ancient autobiographical literature, and also in the Middle Ages, as constantly as the general tendency to glorification.

Of importance to the permanent shaping of the encomiastic portrayal of a human life—which presents the deeds not in their objective significance but as manifestations of the moral and intellectual character of the individual—was the next advance of this type of work, which followed the publication of the *Euagoras* ; we have an example of it in Xenophon's *enkomion* of King Agesilaus, who had just died (360). Here an independent series of chapters is devoted to the description of the hero's qualities, following, as the second main section, the chronological account of his deeds, which is only interspersed with reminders of his virtues. This second section is actually arranged in accordance with character-categories—piety, righteousness, abstemiousness, and so on ; here and there the individual traits catalogued emerge from vagueness. In the final chapter Xenophon describes his hero's nature as a whole, portraying his conduct in life through the enumeration of general qualities, habits, views, while celebrating his moral qualities even more than Isocrates did.

Isocrates' autobiography is to be understood as a development of the *enkomion*. It is similarly introduced by a prologue that stresses the " novelty and originality " [31] of the enterprise. The exposition of character, views, and way of life is here formulated, as we see, expressly as the purpose of the self-portrayal. To this formulation is added another showing the relationship between life and work ; as he sums up later (50) : " Now you have heard the whole truth about my capacity ($\delta \acute{v} \nu a \mu \iota \varsigma$), my philosophy, my profession—whatever you care to call it." He also adds the pedagogical element that is to make his life-story a splendid example : " There is also in it matter which it would be well for young men to hear before they set out to gain instruction and training." There was no need for him to carry over the tendency to elaborate glorification from the *enkomion* for his own benefit ; in his epideictic orations he had always satisfied his craving to talk of himself, mostly using the mask of an affected modesty ; self-praise and the abuse of enemies and of the envious, which is so boring in his works, was a customary propaganda method in the professional work of the rhetoricians, who had to maintain their position against strong competition. Yet the matter-of-course way in which he united the idea of autobiography with encomiastic portrayal is astonishing. He tells how he prepared himself for the task : " I reviewed my life and my actions, dwelling longest on those for which I thought I deserved praise " (§§140-1).

The ideal which Isocrates claimed to represent was the Sophistical ideal, with a Socratic veneer, of culture and civic virtue, an ideal to be attained by means of training in the art of speaking impressively on all subjects and of carrying every case through to victory in the battle of words, which was what decided the issue. He unmasks when emphasizing his superiority to other philosophical teachers of his day (84) :

> I maintain also that if you compare me with those who profess to turn men to a life of temperance (σωφροσύνη) and justice, you will find that my teaching is more profitable than theirs. For they exhort their followers to a kind of virtue and wisdom which is ignored by the rest of the world and is disputed among themselves ; I, to a kind which is recognized by all.

His only problem in his autobiography was the technical means of carrying out this conception. For a simple borrowing of the form of the *enkomion* could not be permitted ; to begin with, as he himself points out (4), because account had to be taken of its public nature, which made that direct type of eulogy out of the question, and because the considerable quantity of the autobiographical material could not be compressed into that form : the autobiography is much longer than his other works. It consists of 323 paragraphs averaging ten lines in length, and in addition the excerpts, running to about a hundred paragraphs, quoted from his other writings to illustrate his achievement.

Of still more importance was the unspoken intention to give the new subject-matter of the autobiography (which in his case took shape not from any inner urge but in all probability owing to hostile criticisms of his work) at least superficial plausibility by associating it with the existing conditions of life. Thus Isocrates used the outward form of the pleading in court, and invented an action that offered occasion for an exhaustive autobiography and, indeed, also gave it actuality : having been charged with misguiding youth, he must defend himself in public. His accuser, the fiction ran,* alleged that he, Isocrates, was able " to make the weaker case appear the stronger " and so taught his pupils to win their advantage contrary to justice.

It is the same charge that was brought against Socrates, the stock charge against the " Sophists ". Isocrates does not shrink from representing himself to the public in a situation similar to that of Socrates facing the judges who condemned him to death. But to forestall any misconception he gives his apologia a preface in which he expressly declares that in his case the dishonouring charge is a pure fiction. He did indeed, he says, have one

* *Antidosis*, 15, 30, 56.

lawsuit, but on a different issue—on money matters. He had been called upon to discharge a most onerous public duty for which only men of the wealthiest class were drawn upon in Athens. He declined the office, was prosecuted, and lost his case. In this lawsuit,[32] he declares, " my eyes were opened ". For he came to realize that the lay public not only " indulged in extravagant nonsense about my wealth and the number of my pupils " but was also " disposed toward me otherwise than I had thought " : misled by his detractors, it held mistaken opinions both about his pursuits and about his character. This he wanted to set right, and so he had come to the idea of publishing " a true image of my thought and of my whole life ". In order to do this " without arousing the displeasure or even the envy of my hearers ", he adopted the fiction, he writes, " of a trial and of a suit brought against me " (4, 5, 8).

In reality the motives for the work lay deeper. As we have already remarked, he was moved partly by the urge to self-glorification and partly by the attacks from his critics, who had opposed the political course he had been advocating and also the type of rhetoric for which he stood. These latter charges, too, which came from Plato's Academy and so were prompted by philosophical considerations, he placed, by the fiction of a capital charge, on the plane of civic morality.

The fiction was not so far-fetched as it may seem to us. In Attic literature fictitious pleadings associated with a case that had actually been heard had long been a favourite form of narrative, adopted as early as the beginning of the fourth century.[33] They took up afresh in the field of literature cases that had been fought out in court, or altered the situation by turning a person only incidentally involved in the case into the actual defendant. The first brisk controversy concerning the standing of a great contemporary, the controversy over Socrates, and also that over Alcibiades, had been thus carried on in literary form, in orations for defence and for prosecution. A literary lampoon provided invective as defence in an action brought by the person it defamed. A rhetorical school exercise in the representation of a particular type of character was put in the form of an oration, a comical old man coming forward in the part of the defendant, to give an account of his life. Isocrates himself had taken advantage of the defence pleading in the proceedings concerning Alcibiades to give an encomiastic picture of him ; this had been written before the *Euagoras* and did not yet reveal the biographical trend of that work. The whole background of autobiographical orations which we have indicated must be kept in mind in order that the form of the defence pleading, which seems to us so artificial in Isocrates' autobiography, may be accepted as the merely incidental feature, in no way remarkable, that it was— as merely connected with the general rhetorical culture and the popularity of polemical orations.

There remains, however, something characteristic of him in the setting of his fictitious pleading in court : Isocrates took the proceedings against Socrates as his model.[34] The celebrated rhetorician purposely elaborated in detail this association of his autobiography with Plato's *Apology of Socrates*. For behind the literary assimilation there stood the human contrast : Isocrates had the effrontery to set up his idealized version of his own life as a pendant to the great exemplar Socrates. In the judgment of the common herd among his contemporaries, which paid honour, as the crowd does, to the achievements of pushing smartness, that might pass for justified self-confidence ; but the autobiographer spoiled the effect of his work by this perverted moral assessment, so that the relative historical importance of the autobiography can only be recognized after overcoming this painful impression and forgetting the great spirit whom the rhetorician has called up. For the form of a defence pleading remained a merely superficial device. And a comparison [35] with Plato's creative genius is out of the question : Plato made artistic use of the dramatic situation to develop the character of his Socrates through the events of Socrates' own life " as through an artistic analysis " ; Isocrates had no dramatic self-portrayal to offer, but applied the technique of the *enkomion* to his autobiography and tried to make it plausible by means of a fiction that was a pilfered reality. For the technique of autobiography this stagecraft had only the secondary effect of plastering the whole work with a network of polemic and self-justification and of outbursts of injured vanity against rivals and opponents and the envious, and especially, it would appear, against Aristotle, who taught rhetoric as a disciple of Plato.

The method of this autobiographical oration is systematically descriptive, or, rather, eulogistic, characterization. The various elements of Isocrates' career, his activity as publicist and as teacher, his relations with his pupils, his domestic arrangements, are dealt with one after another, with emphasis on the virtues revealed. In the second main section he gives a general account of the cultural ideal he embodied. All with a garrulousness that does not give facts but talks about them—but with a stylistic ability that impels to admiration and, as an element of form, became of lasting importance.

In the initial extolling of his literary achievement he adopts the method of presenting lengthy extracts from his principal works, the epideictic orations, which fill here the rôle of the deeds quoted in the praise of heroes ; and the novelty of this method of treatment may be seen from the reason he feels bound to give for it, that for the purpose of self-characterization he is producing old passages and not new ones (20).

The passages chosen for this purpose are taken from only three out of the thirty or so writings of his that are extant. Two of these three are political speeches ; the third is an essay, disguised as a letter, on the principal elements of personal morality. He does not mention the court pleadings with the composition of which he had begun his career ; these he had long left behind. He gives this description of the nature of the discourses which he had chosen to write, in contrast with court pleadings :

> They deal with the world of Hellas, with affairs of state, and are appropriate to be delivered at the Pan-Hellenic assemblies—discourses which, as everyone will agree, are more akin to works composed in rhythm and set to music than to the speeches which are made in court. For they set forth facts in a style more imaginative and more ornate ; they employ thoughts which are loftier and more original ; and, besides, they continually use figures of speech in greater number and of more striking character (47).

Here he speaks of himself as technically a writer, or rather an artist ; and he further boasts of the high moral plane on which he moves, in contrast to other professors of rhetoric :

> They are satisfied if through the prestige of their names they can draw a number of pupils into their society : I, you will find, have never invited any person to follow me, but endeavour to persuade the whole State to pursue a policy from which the Athenians will become prosperous themselves, and at the same time deliver the rest of the Hellenes from their present ills (85).

Yet more—he claims for his " art of discourse " what Plato had said of the " divine frenzy " of the philosophic Eros, that " of all the faculties which belong to the nature of man, it is the source of most of our blessings " (253).

Of the two political writings, from each of which he makes a quotation extending to some forty paragraphs, one is his *Panegyricus*, the famous work written in 380 B.C. to prepare the way for the new Athenian policy inaugurated by Timotheus ; it was this work that made him the leading Greek publicist.[36] In it he defended the programme of foreign policy which Gorgias had set forth some decades earlier, and which was now being advocated by many patriots : let the Greek States at last give up their internecine struggles and unite voluntarily under a single leadership in order to fight the common enemy, the Persian Empire—" the only war that is better than peace : more like a sacred mission than a military expedition ". In a commentary with which he prefaces the extract from the *Panegyricus* he emphasizes what is less evident in the actual work, that he had urged the leadership of Athens in the " expedition against the barbarians ", and that at a time when it called for courage to do so ; for " then the Lacedæmonians were the first power in Hellas, while our fortunes were at a low ebb " (57).

The other political writing from which he gives an extract is a discourse *On the peace*, which he had published only a few years earlier, in 355, and which had reference to the internal affairs of the Athenian Naval League. Here he again advocated the Pan-Hellenic idea of a confederation of free states with a chosen leadership, and he pictured the misfortune which the imperialist policy had brought down upon Athens and upon the whole Greek world. In his own words : " I attack our dominion over the Hellenes and our sea-power, showing that it is no whit different, either in its conduct or in its results, from tyranny " (64). He goes on to say that he chose this quotation to show that he could not only compose speeches that " recount ancient history " but also those " which denounce our present mistakes and counsel what we ought to do " (62).

In the " moral and philosophical " essay from which the last extract is taken, he treats at length of the then much discussed subject of guidance by reason and " care for thyself " as the path of virtue (69–70). This work had been addressed to the young King Nicocles of Cyprus, son and successor to Euagoras, in order to expound to him the duty of a monarch to his subjects ; but in his comment here on his letter to Nicocles he states that he drew it up with the incidental purpose of exhibiting his own moral principles. Similarly the motive he alleges in explanation of his decision to present that letter in his apologia was that it should rob of its force the charge that had been brought against him of holding anti-democratic views.   In his own words :

Through it you will best see in what spirit I am wont to deal with princes as well as with private persons ; for you will see that I have expressed myself to Nicocles as a free man and an Athenian should, not paying court to his wealth nor to his power, but pleading the cause of his subjects, and striving with all my strength to secure for them the mildest rule possible.   And since in addressing a king I have spoken for his subjects, surely I would urge upon men who live under a democracy to pay court to the people (70).

In his remarks on this work Isocrates also touches on style, so that we have evidence here of the artist's self-criticism.   He says of the letter :

It is not composed in the same manner as the other extracts which have been read.   For in those each part is always in accord and in logical connexion with that which goes before ;   but in this, on the contrary, I detach one part from another, and breaking up the discourse, as it were, into what we call general heads, I strive to express in a few words each bit of counsel which I have to offer (68).

On the whole, however, we scarcely find in Isocrates' apologia a literary assessment, such as, when we pass to later writers' autobiographies, we shall find in Cicero's *Brutus* ;   the main emphasis is on the moral aspect, on praise of the moral and patriotic qualities of his writings.   His main contention is that his artistic and patriotic activity stands high above the common profession of advocacy, as high as Pheidias above a turner. In a concluding chapter he sums up these virtues—justice, piety, candour, devotion to the most universal, the highest, the most sacred interests of the Hellenes ;   and in his rhetorical comparison he goes so far as to set his speeches, in view of their greater weight and more general utility, above the works of lawgivers and philosophers.   Here again he has the Platonic Academy and Plato himself in view.   We touched on Plato's *Laws* above (p. 129), when dealing with the Seventh Epistle.

After this extensive section, in which he speaks of his works and lets them speak or rather intone for themselves, comes a shorter section dealing with his pupils.   Here the fiction that he has to defend himself from the charge of corrupting youth has a particularly facile and unconvincing character.   For that stock charge referred, as we have mentioned, to the intellectual activities of the philosophers or " Sophists ", Socrates included, dialectical enlightenment being regarded by the ordinary Athenians as corrupting the character. But the things Isocrates tells about his pupils refer not to the intellectual or æsthetic education they received from him, but purely to the moral element, and this in relation to civic virtue. He gives the names of a number of his first pupils, young Athenians, and writes : " All these men were crowned in Athens with chaplets of gold . . . because they were honourable men and had spent large sums out of their private fortunes upon the city " (94). In their civic virtue was reflected his own morality, in accordance with the rule which he singled out as " the basis of judgment "—that men " are esteemed on account of the manner of their lives and also of the character of their associates " (97). He had reason to be proud of his success as a teacher, and he grows warm when he speaks of his pupils' devotion, of " the affection " he had had " from men who had received rewards in recognition of excellence " (96). But once more he spoils the effect by the inordinate vanity with which he sets himself on a level with Socrates and Plato. He borrows from the Apology of Socrates the proud phrase which Plato puts into the mouth of the condemned man, that, rather than that verdict, he had merited the highest honour, that of feeding in the Prytaneum, the (sacred) town hall, in which foreign ambassadors, and Athenians who had especially well deserved of the State, were entertained as public guests. When the rhetorician takes over this phrase it becomes flat, and, indeed, rings false : " I should deserve from you greater gratitude than those who are maintained in the Prytaneum in recognition of excellence ; for each of the latter has furnished to the city his own high qualities alone, whereas I have furnished those of all whom I have just now named to you " (95).

From the mass of pupils whom he does not treat individually he singles out the one man with whom he had been specially united by friendship, Timotheus, the statesman and commander of the Attic naval league. To him he devotes (107–131) a veritable *enkomion*,[37] and here he rings true and speaks with courage. Timotheus had recently died, after experiencing the ingratitude of the populace : he had suffered a naval defeat, and for this had been deprived of his office, charged with treason, and sentenced to a heavy fine (354 B.C.). Isocrates declares, rejecting the charges against his friend and, under the fiction, against himelf as well : " I should have thought that even if I were proved guilty beyond a doubt, yet because of my friendship with him I should be entitled to go free " (102). Indeed, in the picture he draws of his relations with Timotheus there is an element of realism that stands out from the torrent of words. He describes how he sought to persuade the proud Timotheus, who, as an aristocrat both by birth and in outlook, " was by nature as inept in courting the favour of men as he was gifted in handling affairs ", to overcome his feelings and to accept the services of the orators who controlled public affairs (131–8).

" You observe ", I would say to him, " the nature of the multitude, how susceptible they are to flattery ; how they like those who cultivate their favour better than those who seek their good . . . You have paid no attention to these things, but are of the opinion that if you attend honestly to your enterprise abroad, the people at home also will think well of you . . . And yet I wonder if you realize how many men have either come to grief or failed of honour because of the misrepresentations of those orators ; how many in the generations that are past have left no name, although they were far better and worthier men than those who are celebrated in song and on the tragic stage. But the latter, you see, found their poets and historians, while the others secured no one to hymn their praises. Therefore, if you will only heed me and be sensible, you will not despise these men whom the multitude are wont to believe . . . but will in some measure show attention and pay court to them in order that you may be held in honour both because of your own deeds and because of their words." When I would speak to him in this wise, he would admit that I was right, but he would not change his nature . . .

But once more, even in this human and pleasing picture of friendship, one is unable to escape from the feeling that Isocrates in his praise of Timotheus was trying to outdo Plato's alliance with Dion.

This section of the rhetorician's self-portrayal ends with a survey of his further excellences, artistically clothed in the form of a conversation with a young pupil whose part is to sing the praises of his master (140–166). Aristotle was struck by this method of indirect self-praise in the *Antidosis*, and describes it as exemplary : one should let " a third person speak " of oneself. Among the things discussed in this way is the author's material situation. Isocrates makes the pupil bear witness : " Though you have held aloof from public offices and the emoluments that go with them, and from all other privileges of the commonwealth as well, you have enrolled not only yourself but your son among the twelve hundred who pay the war-taxes and undertake the liturgies " (145). So Isocrates tells in broad outline of his property and its good administration and patriotic application, boasts of the honour conferred on him, and makes much of the fact that the highest of them came from abroad. This is a typical feature of the autobiographies of writers. We shall find similar details in the humanists, especially in England, where they are placed at the end of the self-characterization.

In the second main section (180–290) Isocrates treats of his profession in general terms, praising it as the highest sort of *bios* and commending it as sound practical philosophy, in contrast with pure learning and with the purely mechanical argumentation of the Sophists. On the strength of this section it is customary to classify the *Antidosis* as an essay on education, in apparent conflict with our characterization of the work as autobiographical. The conflict is resolved in this way : when the classical Greeks made one of the characteristic forms of intellectual life, such as philosophy, rhetoric, or politics, the subject of inquiry, they did not do it in our abstract way by inquiring, for instance, into the " nature " of philosophy ; they had the philosopher, the rhetorician, the statesman before their eyes—the type of person who embodied the subject. Thus Isocrates, when he treats of the ideal of general culture, represents himself as the ideal man of culture and teacher of culture. Regarded from the rhetorician's standpoint, this section is characteristic of a particular form of literary autobiography ; we shall meet with such portrayals in various forms in the Middle Ages and in the Renaissance. A plan had here been supplied for carrying self-characterization beyond the analysis of the writer's nature to the concrete presentation of the objective content and purpose of his work, so rounding off the summary of his nature as a thinking person and bringing into view his whole personality.

In this first autobiography in European literature, the ancient self-glorification made its appearance in a petty form. Nevertheless, it ranged from vain boasting to the proud consciousness of personality that dwells with pleasure on mundane achievement, in the fine ordering of the world or of the State, in the exertion of will-power and the acquisition of honour and immortal fame. Already in ancient times, in those late periods in which men lived less in the present than in the past, that decent sort of pride was alluded to as a characteristic feature of the way a free man spoke of himself. Plutarch (*c.* A.D. 100), in one of his essays in moral philosophy, wrote at length on self-praise, under the significant title, " On the manner in which we may praise ourselves without exciting envy in others." [38] In that essay he quotes a number of instances from Greek literature from Homer onwards, and from these he builds up an investigation of the forms of self-glorification, dealing with the tact required, the situations involved, the purposes served, and the precautions necessary in order to remove offensiveness from self-praise. With a similar collection of classical quotations the rhetorician Aristides (*c.* A.D. 170) wrote of the justification for self-confidence.[39] He arranges his passages according to social groups and shows how the heroes in Homer, the victors of the musical or the gymnastic contest in the poets, the statesmen and military commanders in the historians or in their own songs and speeches, and writers of all sorts, uniformly speak with pride of themselves. He thus comes to the conclusion that it was " a very old custom and a genuinely Hellenic one " to think proudly of oneself, and that without such a frame of mind nothing great was achieved in deed or word. In this " virtually inborn " " kind of mentality " he finds a characteristic that united all Hellenism and distinguished it from the " barbarians ", who might have other merits, but had no share in this greatness of soul.

The *ethos* for whose expression self-portrayal served in Demosthenes as in Isocrates, was provided by the morality developed in Athenian democracy. A relation of this sort between self-disclosure and a socially universal element is to be found everywhere in the autobiography that proceeds from practical life, not only at the outset and later in ancient times, but also in the burghers' chronicles of the Middle Ages or in the self-portraits of the *honnêtes gens* of the seventeenth century. Through Isocrates' method of self-idealization, carried further in ancient times, literary autobiography remained, in contrast with its modern development, at a far lower level than the characterization achieved in the portrayal of other persons. On the other hand, here, too, the elaboration of definite forms continued to make progress. And since idealization was united with the rhetoricians' pedagogical trend, from Isocrates onwards autobiography was assigned the function of exhibiting a cultural ideal as embodied in an individual man.

Of similarly general significance for the autobiography that came not out of self-communion but out of contact with public life, was the formal attitude to one's own life as a material, not differing greatly from other objects, for the application of stylistic and oratorical arts. The high degree of formal education in the men of ancient times, to whom mere sketches without artistic style were a literary monstrosity, was bound to work against the free and vigorous development of the autobiographical *genre*. In ancient times the rhetoricians and the statesmen monopolized autobiography. And this remained so until Augustine's *Confessions*, which were not meant for quiet reading but for declamation. In ancient autobiography the rhetorical element favoured the dubious blend of sincerity and posing which we find in the *Confessions* of Rousseau ; this is true alike of Augustine and of Seneca. The idea of spiritual autobiography as a solitary, inward labour was first fully attained in the Christian Middle Ages. The beginnings of this process bring us to the Hellenistic age.

PART II

AUTOBIOGRAPHY IN THE HELLENISTIC AND GRECO-ROMAN WORLD

A new stage in human development in the Mediterranean world began with the age of Hellenism. One name, that of Alexander the Great, symbolizes the whole dynamic of events of pre-eminent historic importance which introduced a new epoch, or paved the way for it and hastened its arrival. The centuries that followed the death of Alexander saw profound changes in every sphere of civilized life, including political organization and intellectual and literary activity. The influence of these changes extended to certain epochs of Western history down to the present day, and though they were diverse even to the point of including mutually opposed developments, they were the product of a single long-continued intellectual movement. Taken as a whole, this movement embraced not only the Hellenized East but also the imperial republic of Rome and the rise of the Roman Empire with its Greco-Roman civilization, and it continued as far as the very different period of Diocletian and Constantine and of the early Christian State church. In the course of these centuries the autobiographical *genre* was given a turn toward " subjectivity " which it has again, and more definitely, followed in modern times.*

One of the famous achievements of the later nineteenth century was the recognition of the importance of the Hellenistic epoch to the history of the Western world. It was the epoch of the actual formation of the widespread civilization of the Mediterranean peoples, out of which grew our European civilization. As the discovery of the Middle Ages widened the vision of the stages of civilization for the evolutionary schools which since the end of the eighteenth century had come into prominence in German philosophy and in French Positivism, so research in Hellenism is capable of closing the most serious gap in our picture of the continuity and the obedience to law of the history of the human mind in the Western hemisphere. For in the six centuries between the flourishing of Attic culture and the spread

* See Introduction, pp. 17 *sqq.*

of Christianity in the Greco-Roman world there gradually took place the changes which, considered simply with regard to their result, create the illusion of a breach in later antiquity in the progress of Western civilization—the breach indicated by the contrast between the Catholic Middle Ages and classic antiquity ; the breach of which the closing may be attributed to the epoch of the Renaissance.   One still hears it frequently stated that in the Renaissance the peoples of modern Europe started again at the point at which progress had broken off in the second century B.C.   This applies in particular to the Greek achievement in philosophy and science, which was revived in the Renaissance. As the supreme intellectual possession of the Western world, that Greek heritage rivalled the Christian faith in its claim to be considered the leading spiritual force in society.   Now, in the twentieth century, we no longer share the belief spread in the Western world since the Renaissance, that science is equal to the task of guiding man's conduct in his personal and social life. The developments that took place in the Hellenistic epoch have reference both to that belief in science and to its overthrow by revealed religion, and to this extent have relevance to the questions which our own age has to put to history in order to gain clarity in regard to the relation of science to life.

At the outset of the Hellenistic era the scientific spirit distinctive of Greek thought was still predominant.   In that era it made itself independent of the philosophical speculation by which it had been nurtured.   This emancipation of mathematics and the inductive sciences—mechanics, astronomy, zoology, anatomy —and also of human studies such as literature and rhetoric, furthered by the foundation of great libraries in Alexandria and other capitals of the successor States, was one of the most remarkable features of the intellectual development in the Hellenic civilization from Aristotle onwards.   The significance of that feature is unmistakable.   For it is in accord with the so-called " law " of the development of human thought in three " stages ", the theological, the metaphysical, and the scientific or " positivist ", enunciated in the early nineteenth century by Auguste Comte, the systematizer of *la philosophie positive*.   In the Hellenistic age we have an instance of progress from the second to the third of these stages ; but we also meet with the problems involved in that historical " law ".   Establishing itself in the study of nature, the scientific spirit made the conviction of the universality of the interrelation between cause and effect an accepted element in the outlook of educated people. But at the same time there came a fulfilment of the Socratic mission to evoke self-knowledge. For as reason now attempted to take control over human life in order to shape it, in the Stoic school of thought the idea of the " free man ", and with it the concept of the freedom of the human will, worked its way out of the determinist conception of Nature as the controller of all.

While philosophy was thus engaged in turning back from the natural world to human life with its distinctive awareness of the self—a process promoting the recognition and appreciation of personality—there took place also the transition to a new religious situation, a transition culminating in the spread of Christianity over the Greco-Roman world. This change might give the impression of having been even more revolutionary than the previous emancipation of the different branches of knowledge from the control of the philosophical systems ; but it, too, can be regarded as conforming to law. For if we consider that situation quite generally, instead of envisaging its specifically religious aspect and its historical matrix, we see it as the result of tendencies immanent in the development of the human mind, tendencies that urged the intellect toward profounder and more intimate experiences through which man could discover the hidden unity of all experience. This discovery can be achieved through philosophy as well as religion, but must always be unattainable by means of natural science. We can, therefore, foresee that the positivist phase must ultimately come to an end. Laws of this sort are seen, indeed, to operate in the development of the human mind, viewed historically ; but it is only by the concrete, particular form in which they impose themselves at a given stage of history that their actual effect on the general development of the human mind is determined. In ancient times philosophical thought probing that hidden unity of experience took a religious turn, marked by the revival of Pythagorean doctrines since the last century B.C., and later by the so-called Neoplatonism ; but specifically religious experience, or rather revelation, also occupied the scene in the Hellenistic world from the first centuries of the Christian era, and this development had its lamentable side, as the event showed : in gaining its independence religion swallowed up all other interests, so that its triumph in the deepening of the inner life was purchased at the cost of the destruction of the ancient culture, the enslavement of philosophy and learning beneath theological authority, the loss of the sense of the life of this world, and the incursion of religious conceptions and practices that usually belong to the lowest cultural levels.

Since these developments were already germinating within Hellenism, the crucial question we have to ask with regard to this epoch is how all this could have grown out of the soil of Greek culture. It cannot have been a simple matter of historical fact, of ecstasy, magic, and the like being foisted upon the highly cultured peoples of the Mediterranean by the incursion of religious influences from the Near and Middle East : the narrowing of their intellectual horizon, which came about through a fundamental craving for reality, must have been imposed upon them for the moment by the need of the mind to acquire composure in troubled times ; and if this turning of the mind inward ruled out important elements of cultural life, there must have been essential reasons for this in Greco-Roman culture itself as it had developed in the Hellenistic epoch.

Autobiography, still with but a modest share in cultural life, was closely linked with these movements : the problems arising from them directly affect the history of this *genre*, as its central concern is with the awareness of personality. As has been shown above, autobiography, though virtually based on the unfolding of individuality, was not from the outset directly related to this historical process. If we are to find a historical explanation for the high pitch of achievement attained by autobiography in the time of St. Augustine, we must suppose that it was the work of the preceding Hellenistic epoch to establish that direct relation. Now, autobiography is a many-headed creature. In Hellenism it first showed its complexity, and among its diverse aims that of making personality explicit eventually gained the upper hand. From now on, therefore, its development is more closely linked with the progress of its age, of which both the greatness and the limitations are reflected in it.

Individual life freely developing in various ways is one of the outstanding features of this epoch.[1] A glance at the historic changes that separate Hellenism from Attic culture shows the extent to which the conditions had been created for a personality to become aware of itself. For in the Hellenistic epoch the individual's conventionally imposed participation in the life of the city-state—which, though limiting him, had been satisfactory because it had given his life the character of an integral part of a whole—was ended, and the bureaucratic State took shape, making political tasks no longer the centre of the citizen's public-spirited activities, and concentrating those tasks instead in the hands of a single person or a small number of persons. Here the private existence of the individual emerged for the first time, over against the rulers, the men filled with lust for power, and the throng of intriguers at court. Moreover, there had taken place since Alexander the Great an immeasurably pregnant event : the Greeks had mingled with the Orientals in the Hellenic universal States ; Hellenic culture spread westward and eastward until it became a world culture, held together at first by the power of Greek philosophy and learning. Accordingly men's horizon widened to embrace the different modes of living of individuals and peoples, their minds being the meeting-place of the various contents both of national pasts and of the greatly broadened present. In this period of flux we see the energy of educated people directed to establishing a *modus vivendi* in this new world, and philosophy helping them to do this, while the inductive sciences, now liberated from philosophy, concurred with it in securing for reason a position centred in this life. These and other factors in a change that extended to every sphere of life were all intimately related to the emancipation of the individual ; and they resulted in the formation of a definite type of personality wherever they or their like operated later on, whether during the growth of the Roman Empire or in the national States of more modern times.

At this stage the individual, if he wanted to become a full man, had to acquire fullness out of separate elements, determined by the differentiation of social life into the various spheres of activity. He was active in politics or literature or in some other function in society, but the multiplicity of activities was without the unity of the conventional existence that had been associated with the city-state ; thus the formation of personality could now proceed entirely from within, the citadel of the man's soul becoming his true refuge, as the political and personal security of the individual had been destroyed through the destruction of the communal cohesion. With this inwardness there came a universalization of the bases of existence : the individual provided himself with a free relationship with the world through personally acquired convictions, by virtue of which he became more than a separate individual ego because his reasoned attitude to life gave him a confidence and assurance which in turn could influence others.

Here Hellenism struck out a new path. It had inherited

from Attic culture the strong equipment of humaneness that enabled men to make a firm stand against any oppression of the individual such as that of oriental despotisms. Now a free sphere of his own in the community had been secured to the individual for the first time. To fill this sphere there were the systematic notions derived from the philosophic schools, which now effectively fulfilled the function of providing individual human beings, as they emerged from the mass, with some firm basis for the conduct of life, and of thus endowing them with inner freedom. These philosophical notions were no longer the expression of a national culture, but proceeded from the various possible methods of rational living afforded by thought itself. In accordance with these various methods the idea of the individual existence was now differentiated into various types of deliberate conduct of life ; the creation of these different types, the Platonist, the Stoic, the Cynic, the Epicurean, the Sceptic, and the Peripatetic scholar, was one of the greatest achievements of the Greek spirit. The idea of " schools of philosophy " gained here a wider meaning : their original purpose of establishing in philosophy the interconnexion between all labours of learning was outweighed by their effect on conduct in life as centres for instilling community of outlook between individuals who no longer derived it from their social setting.

The power of a superior personality was felt in these philosophical communities, in much the same way as in the sphere of political activity, which had now become extraneous to personal life ; and parallel with the oriental worship of deified kings in the successor States there developed among the devoted followers of the founders and inspirers of schools of thought a new feeling— the mark of a historical epoch—of spiritual, even religious, allegiance and loyalty, based, in contrast to political dependence, on free contact between men. Adoration of this sort had not been paid to Socrates in his time ; this intensification of the personal feeling for the pre-eminent power of a man who represented an ideal of living issued, in the changed intellectual environment, from the immediate disciples of Plato and especially of Epicurus.[2] The Stoic ideal of the god-like sage is, as it were, the logical completion of this way of feeling. In so far as it was an expression of the conception of philosophy as a means of shaping personality, that ideal was common to the Stoics, the school of Epicurus, and the Sceptics. But only in the Stoa was there the formative power of the will, the courage that appreciates the seriousness of life, accepts the hard battle, and does not take refuge in seclusion ; the heroism which, though excelling the life of ordinary men, nevertheless recognizes the responsible individual's community with humanity as a whole. In the words of a modern thinker, in Stoicism the idea was conceived of a personality that is autonomous and complete in itself.[3]

A further element in individualization lay in the consideration of the differences between peoples, of whose peculiarities the all-perceiving Greeks were acutely aware. In this epoch choices between widely varying alternative ways of living opened out before men as never before, and the State left ample room for free activity until, from the third century of the Christian era, the despotic rulers and the Church authoritatively stereotyped the culture that had accumulated.

In the midst of this multiplicity of ways of living, freedom itself, as the form of personal life, attained in the Stoic philosophy (which most completely represents the consciousness of the age, even in its transformations) clearer and clearer recognition and demarcation from nature and the external world ; the concepts of conscience and consciousness of the moral personality, of duty and of self-training with a view to the autonomy of the moral will, were now gained for all time, and in this way we see operative in the cultural movement the self-scrutiny, the fundamental significance of which for the enterprise of autobiography we have followed from Socrates onward.

Plastic art took full account of the growing appreciation of that which is individual, and furthered the growing development from the fourth century onward of the realistic portrait in the original art of human portrayal. Of Hellenistic literature we know too little to be able broadly to assess the importance of the realistic vision and the individualizing characterization in it. As for autobiography, its connexion with general literature comes into view only piecemeal and can only be laid bare step by step ; the contact and mutual influencing took place in many different ways. In these processes the course now establishing itself for the first time has to be identified—the course in which critical reflection upon the self paved the way for the deepening of the autobiographical *genre* ; and the general question arises of the extent to which autobiography came to fulfil the function of interpreting the individual's experience of life, a function that fell to it in those ages in which the individual, who had to direct his existence on his own initiative, found an essential means for the formation of personality in introspection.

When approaching the autobiographical literature of the Hellenistic epoch with this question in our minds, we are confronted with the difficulty that the quantity of autobiographical writings handed down to us from that epoch is in no way proportional to the significance for the development of the *genre* of the historical processes we have sketched. Only in one field, that of political life, is a continuous, though fragmentary, series of autobiographies or statements concerning them extant, so that this branch can be steadily followed from Alexander far into the Roman imperial epoch. Apart from this, for three centuries after the autobiography of Isocrates we have no knowledge of any autobiographical work. Only from the time of Cicero do the sources gradually begin to well up in growing profusion. There can, however, be no doubt that this means only a delayed emergence, and that a good part of this autobiographical production reflects the work of earlier centuries, which saw either the actual appearance of autobiographies that served as models or a development of literary forms that explain its existence.

If we proceed from this view, we meet with a general phenomenon that corresponds to the character of Hellenistic individualization. Sporadically though the traces make their appearance, they nevertheless bear witness to a differentiation of autobiographies into a relative wealth of developed or still embryonic types, determined by the various environments and types of experience. First there is the self-portrayal of the political man, itself of many sorts, embracing reports of activities, factual reminiscences, court memoirs, and historical romance. Then, certainly reaching back to the early Hellenistic epoch, there are the autobiographies of writers and poets, again differentiated into biography in a definite form, works playing with this form, and records of the author's education or of his writings. Finally there came the most fruitful process of all, the production of literary forms based on enlightened self-scrutiny ; this is accompanied by a tendency to realistic description of life which, in drawing upon experience of life or calling upon the imagination, is intimately associated with autobiography ; it entered into Augustine's Confessions, and even before that work there may have existed autobiographies in the form of realistic fiction. On the other hand, with the transition from philosophic self-examination to religious experience there were multiplied once more the experiments in forms of self-disclosure, and various types of spiritual autobiography emerge.

Thus a cross-section from the second century after Christ will offer, without detailing every path of development, a picture of differentiation. We find appearing in close succession the Emperor Hadrian's political autobiography, Galen's writings concerning his own books, the Meditations ("To Himself") of the Emperor Marcus Aurelius Antoninus, the famous romance of Apuleius, commonly called "The Golden Ass", with its final autobiographical section concerning the author's initiation into mysteries ; Lucian's first-personal narrative entitled "The Dream" or "Lucian's Career" ; the "Sacred Discourses" of Aelius Aristides, concerned with his daily intercourse with the god Aesculapius during illness ; and the visions of the martyr Perpetua, alongside Hellenized stories of conversion such as those of Justin the Apologist or of Cyprian, Bishop of Carthage.

In surveying this heterogeneous series of autobiographical writings, we notice that a special feature which belongs to auto-biography in the more modern sense frequently makes its appear-ance, in consonance with a basic tendency of Hellenistic literature —the reporting of actual everyday life with its trivialities. This is found alike in court memoirs and emperors' autobiographies and in the self-portrayals of rhetoricians. Of an entirely intimate nature is the character-sketch which the Emperor Marcus Aurelius Antoninus gives of Antoninus Pius, his adoptive father, in his "Meditations", a sketch ranking with the masterpieces of literary portraiture.

Considering that we have only a remnant of all that was written in the Hellenistic epoch, we may certainly infer from the obvious facts of the case that autobiography enjoyed wide recog-nition at that time.* We shall, in fact, see how Cicero and Tacitus drew attention to the ethical value of the autobiographies

---

* We have only nine complete works, and not all of them are autobiographies in the strict sense ; mostly we have only small fragments or mere reports that something existed, sometimes with no certainty that it was an autobiography.

The extant works of autobiographical nature are, in chronological order : that of Cicero in *Brutus* (46 B.C.) ; Nicolaus Damascenus "On his own Life and Educa-tion" (about A.D. 10) ; Ovid, *Tristia*, IV, 10 (A.D. 10) ; the *Res Gestae Divi Augusti* (before A.D. 14) ; Josephus, "Life" (about A.D. 90) ; Lucian's "Dream" or "Career" (about A.D. 165) ; the book "To Himself" of the Emperor Marcus Aurelius Antoninus (before A.D. 180) ; the "Sacred Discourses" of Aelius Aristides (about A.D. 190) ; Gregorius Thaumaturgus in his address returning thanks to Origenes (A.D. 239).

For other elements of tradition and the extant self-portrayals that may throw light on development, see the relevant chapters in this book.

Possibly autobiographical : P. Valerius Cato (about 70 B.C.), of whose work

of Romans of the Republic. The use of the word *hypomnema* should also permit conclusions to be drawn. The word in itself simply means that something has been " noted down as an aid to the memory "—a conception indefinite in itself, simply expressing the absence of artistic elaboration ; * it served, as did its Latin equivalent *commentarii*, to indicate all the manifold documents in which the writers were concerned only with the contents, and not with any use of the rhetorical style ; [4] it was the usual name for autobiographical works, in addition to *bios* in the sense of " way of life " or " career ". It seems that through its use for anything in the nature of memoirs the word *hypomnema* acquired a connotation relating rather to the person concerned than to the material of his recollections, portraits being described as " hypomnema of the body " and writings as " hypomnema of the mind " of a man.† But the essential witness is Plutarch (about A.D. 100). He read and used the existing literature of memoirs with an eye not to the contents but to the personality of the writers ; his biographies owe their intimate charm largely to this method, which has only been re-learnt by modern historians.

In view of this position of autobiography it is of the more significance that it was not recognized as a literary *genre* which, in spite of its variety, has qualities that are entirely its own. This epoch still did not realize what is for us a commonplace, that there is a special value in a man's life being recorded by himself. As late as the third century after Christ, self-portrayal based on diaries that dealt mainly with neurotic states of mind was judged purely as a work of rhetorical art.‡ And where, as in Cicero, we come upon theoretical observations on a type of

* See Introduction, p. 6.
† In Aelius Aristides or. sacr. V, 63 (ed. Keil, II, 466) we find : τοὺς μὲν νεὼς τοῖς θεοῖς προσήκει καθιεροῦν, τοὺς δὲ ἄνδρας τοὺς ἐλλογίμους τῇ τῶν βιβλίων ἀναθέσει τιμᾶν, ... ὡς δὴ τοὺς μὲν ἀνδριάντας καὶ τὰ ἀγάλματα τῶν σωμάτων ὄντα ὑπομνήματα, τὰ δὲ βιβλία τῶν λόγων. (" Just as men dedicate temples to the gods, so it is fitting that eminent men should be honoured by the ceremonial setting up in public of their books, . . . for the books are *hypomnemata* of the mind, as statues and pictures are *hypomnemata* of the body.") Cicero describes as a *hypomnema* one of his volumes of memoirs, in which he was concerned with demonstrating his rhetorical art (see below, chap. I, where there are other examples).
‡ Philostratus, in his " Lives of the Sophists ", Book II, 9, on the *Sacred Discourses* of Aelius Aristides ; see below, chap. III, IV.

Indignatio (Sueton. de gram. 11) we know nothing, not even whether it was in prose or verse. Also Thrasyllus, court philosopher to Tiberius (see below, chapter III).
    The fragments of Greek autobiography, so far as they belong to historical literature, have now been collected in the comprehensive work published in 1929 and 1930 by Felix Jacoby, *Die Fragmente der griechischen Historiker*, Part 2, " Zeitgeschichte ", nos. 227-38, " Autobiographien, Memoiren, Memoirenhaftes ".

autobiography, it can be clearly seen that the writing of one's own life-story is regarded as an evil to be avoided rather than as anything of value : the literary form in which the career of a historic individual was to be described suffered and lost influence and convincingness if the author was the person concerned. We meet here once more with the tendency to glorification which we described when dealing with Isocrates. Cicero spoke from the standpoint of the Roman aristocracy when he declared publicly that " Ambition (*studium laudis*) moves all of us, and the nobler a man is the more he is led by the idea of fame. We should not disclaim this undeniable fact but rather admit it unabashed." [5] This aspiration could be satisfied through the labours of some other person just as well, and, indeed, better than by those of the person concerned himself. Thus in those observations on autobiographical writings Cicero [6] mentions only " the defects of this type "—" he who writes about himself must show great reserve where there is anything to be praised and must pass over the blameworthy ; thus (he concludes) trust-worthiness and authority suffer, and many disparage " any singing of one's own praise instead of leaving that to others.

In reality autobiography did not suffer any such loss of credit ; the self-praise characteristic of it could not be restrained by any sort of diffidence even if theoretically it ought to be ; and according to a statement * by Pliny the younger (about A.D. 100) it was, on the contrary, a happy combination when the two elements existed together, deeds of fame and their narration by their hero. It remains, nevertheless, a fact, to be observed particularly among political writers, that in this society, in which there were available for the perpetuation of a man's memory the various resources of the plastic and literary arts, from the portrait statue to the medallion and from the epic poem or the rhetorical history to the epigram carved in stone,† and in which a representa-

---

* See below, p. 211.

† A relatively early example showing that monumental self-glorification was common in the Hellenistic world not only among the kings with their quasi-divinity but also among ordinary mortals, has been discovered in Thera, the southernmost island of the Sporades. In that island a certain Artemidorus, who had come from Egypt and had rendered such services to the city's peace that he was rewarded with its freedom, set up a strange sanctuary in which he was priest (about 250 B.C.). It was hewn out of a cliff, and contained a number of altars with sacramental inscriptions and reliefs, including a portrait in relief of Artemidorus, crowned with laurel. In the inscriptions he makes several mentions of his civic services and his titles. On the altar of Tyche he placed an inscription averring that that memorial would proclaim his name " so long as heaven and earth continue ". The scholar who worked on these inscriptions was able to reconstruct the career of Artemidorus. *Corp. Inscr. Gr.*, XII, fasc. iii, suppl., pp. 294 *sqq.* (1904).

tive like Cicero of the aristocratic tradition could publicly describe the satisfaction of the desire for fame in all such forms as the goal of all and especially of the best,[7] instead of autobiography the indirect approach through a historian or poet was chosen in preference, and tales of a man's own career were generally regarded as not literary works and were sometimes issued under an assumed name.

In our days, if a man writes of his own experiences we feel some reassurance, but the ancients did not, and personal experience was not regarded as sufficient ground for taking up the *stilus*. The reason lay not simply in the confident assumption that practical ends were being served in the writing of any autobiography, but in a depreciation of the actual facts of a career as the subject of a literary work, a depreciation that is found again in the attitude taken up toward historical persons in general. There seemed to be no clear dividing line between the actual and the invented, so long as the latter was kept within the limits of the possible. Aristotle had clearly distinguished the two. " The distinction between the historian and the poet," he wrote in his " Poetics ", " is not that the one speaks prose, the other verse, . . . but the point is that the one deals with what has happened, the other with what may have happened." But in drawing this distinction he was guided by the attitude of Greek thought toward historical reality, an attitude that made impossible any full appreciation of individuality ; for he continued : " Hence poetry is a thing more philosophical and of greater import than history ; for poetry tends to reveal the universal, history the particular."[8] He regarded any actual historical happening as something merely particular, since it has dates and persons and places of its own, in contrast with the essential and universal (while intrinsically possible or inevitable) represented by the typical figures whose creation is the work of the poet. Thus he separated in principle things which in our conception of history are fundamentally connected, as they are in poetry also. As to the latter, we may refer to Goethe's famous dictum that true poetry, while concerned with the particular, sees the universal as inherent in it.* As regards history we rely

---

* Goethe, *Maximen und Reflexionen* : " It makes a great difference whether the poet seeks the particular with the general before his mind or regards the general in the particular. The former type yields allegory, in which the particular has importance only as an example of the universal ; but the latter is of the true nature of poesy : it gives expression to the particular without thinking of the universal or indicating it. Yet he who has a lively realization of this particular receives at the same time the universal with it, without becoming aware of so doing—or becoming aware of it only later."

on the fact, set forth by Goethe's follower the philosopher Dilthey, that in its living reality (as distinguished from historiography) we nowhere find mere singularity but always the singular interwoven with the general, a connexion the disclosure of which invests the historian with philosophic standing. In denying him this standing, Aristotle appears to us to be biased owing to a limitation of Greek thought which even that great thinker could not overcome. For the ancient Greeks had not the sense of period and the full feeling for historical reality with which we are imbued.[9] It was owing to this deficiency that the notion of autobiography as both an original interpretation of experience and a special *genre* of literature remained beyond the horizon of the Hellenistic age, a man's life-story being regarded as material like any other : only with the beginning of philosophic self-examination did a change come, in this very period.

If this material remained without rhetorical elaboration, the work was unliterary, an example of the *hypomnemata* or " commentaries ". If it was put into literary shape, the form was adopted from general literature without any substantial change through its use by an autobiographer. Of these forms the principal was biography, which, rooted in the scientific spirit, was now elaborated into a definite *genre*. Its counterpart was the type of Hellenistic historiography which " set out to rival exalted poetry, epic, and drama," [10] and which could take as subject for a narrative appealing to the emotions in this way the life of a historic personality or a dramatic excerpt from it, without being tied to historical accuracy.[11] Among the fragments of autobiographical literature that have come down to us from the Hellenistic epoch there is only one instance—a vainglorious work of Cicero—of which we have certain knowledge, in which an autobiographer has used that romanticized writing of history.* But what a light it throws upon this period that it was permissible in this way to extract the passions from an individual life and to make use of that style for the historical presentation of one's own person !

From this mixture of history and fiction a definite type of treatment of human affairs spread in prose literature. Its chief characteristics are the rhetorical art of appeal through the intellect to the emotions, the liveliness of imagination that makes everything credible, and the technique of direct description of

---

* See below, Section I, 3. Probably, however, other hypomnemata, especially that of Sulla, should be included in this category.

feeling in first-personal narratives, with soliloquies. This type established itself in European literature through various intermediate elements, particularly through the so-called late Greek romance, which derived from Hellenistic historiography about the beginning of the Christian era, and through the rhetoric concentrated in Ovid's love poetry. From general literature it entered autobiography in various ways. In more modern times we have a most instructive instance of the effective connexion which confronts us here, in the baroque European literature of the seventeenth century. In that period tragedy, history-writing, and romantic story-telling once more came together in a complex whole, in virtue of a predominance, through deliberate exaggeration, of passion and fancy in the artists' picture of human life ; and from this complex whole there emerged both autobiography and the psychological novel. In a similar way there grew toward the end of the ancient world a heterogeneous literary milieu for self-portrayal. The period in which Augustine's " Confessions " were written must be thought of as inundated with this sort of rhetorical picture of emotional states. In contrast with this is the association between autobiography and genuine imaginative writing that was effected in the fourth century after Christ, showing itself most clearly in Augustine, but perhaps in even more unqualified fashion in Gregory of Nazianzus. This association came from profound religious and metaphysical experience.

The principal autobiographical works belonging to the Hellenistic epoch are directly associated with philosophical trends prevalent in that epoch. From Aristotle came the conception both of man's development and of the relation between character and career that underlay the appearance of a literary species which may be termed " Autobiographies of writers ". On the other hand, the self-portrayal of the political personage, at its supreme stage in the Roman aristocracy, was based on the Stoic doctrine of personality ; it was clearly influenced by Posidonius, the last universal thinker. But, above all, self-portrayal did not now appear exclusively as a by-product of culture reflected in it here and there, but played a part in the progress of intellectual life. A thing of essential importance happened to it : out of self-examination there developed new forms of representation of an individual's spiritual life. These, too, had their roots in the Stoa ; for the Stoic moralists worked out the fundamental ethical process in which the divine reason in man asserts itself over restless passions through the recognition of the necessities of our existence, and thereby enables him to ensure his freedom.   In practising self-examination with this aim in view they deepened man's moral consciousness itself, and this development led in the *Meditations* of Marcus Aurelius Antoninus to the breaking of the fetters implicit in the Socratic and Stoic conception of personality.

For, modern as the Hellenistic period may seem on account of its " individualism ", which it is tempting to compare with that of the Renaissance, its limitations are shown in its very conception of individuality.   What did the individual find in himself, after he had been liberated from communal systems and thrown upon himself ?   We have already seen that men were not yet fully conscious of the importance and the formative power of the experiences of personal life ;   accordingly the constructions of thought and imagination were able, as the quotation on page 188 from Aristotle's Poetics showed, to outweigh in men's minds the realities of life as actually lived by them.   The same fact may also be observed from the way in which the definite types of human conduct came to be differentiated, as we have noticed,* in accordance with the tenets of the prevailing schools of thought. For in all cases the personality of the individual, although recognized as the matrix of freedom and happiness, was built up not so much out of his relations to other men and his own struggle with destiny as through reliance upon the dogmas formulated by one of those established systems of philosophy ;   these served almost like a creed, accepted by men in place of convictions hammered out by their own efforts.   This shows at once that the importance of differentiation, a principle inherent in all organic life, was by no means appreciated ;   on the contrary, versatility in man and the inevitable difference between one individual and another only became an argument for scepticism. In refuting this argument, dogmatism defended itself by claiming that individuality was something inessential in comparison with the reasoning faculty common to all men, which was the basis of morality.

The most effective attack upon the general notions that were held to be the principles of knowledge and action had been made by Antisthenes, the other great disciple of Socrates ;   his influence upon Western thought is comparable, indeed, with that of Plato, for it was Antisthenes who inspired the extreme individualism of the Cynics, out of which grew the Stoic idea of

* See p. 182.

the individual's personality and moral freedom. Platonism was, in a sense, the answer to a political situation, and so, in a different way, was Antisthenes' denial of the universal validity of know-ledge : as the forerunner of Diogenes he turned away from communal and social relations, education and culture included. Wisdom he treated as no more than practical knowledge identical with moral will-power, giving this interpretation to Socrates' famous dictum that virtue and knowledge are one and the same. All this certainly indicated a profound personal experience. But the question arises, where did the isolated individual, declared by Antisthenes to be " self-sufficient ", possess a field of activity in which to live the " natural life " in contrast with the great artifice of civilization ? This very thing had first to be found, and after a long struggle led by scepticism it was revealed in the formless reality of the inner life.

Our concern is with this disclosure, as it paved the way for the appearance of spiritual autobiography. In this context the practice of self-scrutiny played an essential part, illustrated by the writings of the later Stoics. Now, to appreciate what took place in the course of these writings we must be aware of the limitations of the Hellenic sense of reality, limitations that reappear in the outlook characteristic of that school of thought. The reference is here to the pantheistic view of the universe, derived from Heraclitus, which formed the other distinct aspect of the Stoic system whose Socratic tendency to ethical idealism we have outlined. Finding himself to be a member of the organism of the universe, the individual was liberated from isolation ; he had firm supports for his existence in the recogniz-able necessities of this divine whole, and in the reason he possessed a directly divine element. But in so taking naturalistic pantheism as the basis of their ethical system, the Stoics availed themselves of the conceptions of the physical world elaborated by the natural science of the Hellenistic age. These conceptions provided the philosophers with an idea of life the chief characteristic of which was the identification of mental activity with the active principle of " force " permeating all matter. Accordingly the Greek con-viction of man's kinship with God changed its character, turning from a religious idea into intellectual acceptance of an established objective fact. The idea of deity itself revealed among the later representatives of the Stoa a mixture, scarcely comprehensible by us now, of the material and the spiritual.[12]

As a naturalistic type of pantheism the Stoic view of the world may be described by Spinoza's formula, *Deus sive Natura*. Thus their own principal formula, advising men to " live in accordance with Nature ", may be religiously interpreted as the enlightened acceptance of the divine order or " will ", in everything and every event. But this sublime religion was impaired, at least in our judgment, by the " materialistic " view of reality that derived its compelling force not from metaphysical or religious vision but from the natural science of the period. Difficult as this conception of reality, midway between objective natural life and subjective immaterialization, is to grasp clearly, because it remains alien to us, its workings are visible, and we shall come many times upon experiences that make this plain. Not only the Stoic moralists but Paul and Augustine had to do battle with it.

The limitations of the outlook of the ancient Greeks, apparent to us in regard to the formless reality of man's inner life, also affected their attitude to the historical world with the awareness of which the development of autobiography is closely connected.

The Greeks [declares von Wilamowitz] [13] did not produce a true science of history ; their thought was directed to deriving abstract rules from observation and working with these abstractions, and so they regarded the types developed among them in the course of history as in fact conceptually pre-existent ; anyone who made a tragedy did not invent it but " was the first to find it " . . . From the moment when the type had " attained its true nature," tragedies could only be made in that form through all eternity.

The history of the intellect and of civilization consists of such discovery, which is the achievement of the great men, the benefactors of mankind. The case is similar with the philosophic idea of the universal State, conceived by Antisthenes some time before Alexander's conquests, and developed by Zeno, the founder of the Stoic school, whence it entered the world-empire of Rome to become its inspiration. Seen from this cosmopolitan standpoint, the nature of the State, considered to be essentially the same at all times and in all places, was to be uniform, all differences of nationality, standing, education, or occupation being merged in it ; the commitment to a political community thus appeared the firmer and " truer " the more universal was the system of the community.[14]

This is the context in which we have to interpret the characteristic attitude of the various schools of thought toward historical personalities. The veneration of great men, of rulers and of heroes of the intellect, developed in Hellenism as the controlling and essential element in the religious feeling of that secularistic epoch.[15] But intelligible to us as is the fundamental belief in the manifestation of a divine element in the power of great men, there is still something missing here. For veneration was literally a religious cult, and to attach the predicate " god " to a man and to accord him divine honours was not merely an expression of the experience that his eminent achievements or the ideal he represented were present in the minds of grateful men and were continuously effective, but meant an objective lifting into the region of the superior powers alongside the similarly deified natural conditions of our existence or the powers of destiny such as the goddess Tyche. Here, in so far as the cult was genuine and not a mere convention, there was a religion, but a natural religion, in contrast to the veneration of heroes evolved by Carlyle from German transcendentalism.

The personality of the great ruler or philosopher, and soon also of the founder of a religion, was not only the individual man of genius, but embodied historical or intellectual developments of wide influence, and their achievement in the struggle with the problems of life or with the political powers had a palpable and a beneficent effect on the life of various groups, small and large, and, indeed, of the whole Roman empire. In the concept of the representative personality our historical consciousness is able to offer a psychological explanation of this. Ancient thought had not the means for doing so, and associated that powerful continuous influence with an enduring and objectively divine element. The drawback of this deification of historical persons was inevitably the underestimation of the individual human element and of the full historic reality. As though Plato became something more by appearing as Apollo Soter, and Augustus did not lose his best qualities by being regarded as Hermes descending from heaven, and Christ was more deeply understood if He was a god on earth. Marcus Aurelius, who lived so entirely in the truth, freed himself from any obsession with immortal fame by recalling how quickly the greatest men became a " myth ".* The historical personality, in the view of Seneca, is divine in the same way as the human soul, which, if contemplated in its purity, would compel adoration.†

Thus the idea of personality as the highest happiness and aim

---

* *Meditations*, 4.33, 8.25, 12.27.
† *Cf.* Seneca, ep. ad Luc., 66.6 *sqq.*, 115.3 *sqq.*, 102.1 and 21 *sqq.* See below, chap. III, 3.

of life on earth was not originally concerned with the particular, but was virtually identical with the conception of practical reason, of the universal and uniform moral law. That in his moral sense man possesses something divine, was not for the ancient Stoa a mysterious fact revealed inwardly to the individual : reason was divine because it was more than a moral force of which men automatically had experience in their working lives —it was regarded as an objective entity governing the various stages of the life of the organism of the world, man included, in correspondingly varied degrees of activity or (to use the Stoic term) tonicity ; an entity that has to be deliberately created in its full force in the free man, who in recognizing it becomes equal to God. Epicurus, too, only takes incidental account of individual peculiarities, though his conception of personal life would seem to further their realization. For, in contrast with the Stoic reliance on strength of will, he exhorted his followers to appreciate the many good things furnished by Nature to the individual, including the happiness that comes from the intimate relations between human beings. The differences between individuals counted for so little in the judgment of the Epicureans that they were only considered in their negative aspect, as not preventing the sage from living a happy life " as a god among men ".[16]

Thus far the ideal of the sage, in which the various schools of philosophy sought the visible model of the conception of the complete personality, could only be the personification of a thought. But after the middle of the second century B.C. there came in the Stoa, as a result of its contact with the Roman aristocracy, the great change [17] that allied self-sufficing thought with the forces of a concrete reality, forces that could not but be recognized in the course of practical observation. Accordingly the conception of personality was also adjusted to reality. Panætius, the friend of the younger Scipio, allowed scope to individual differences in his ethical teaching, and no longer based the aim of the life according to nature simply on the general nature of reason considered as the same for all, but took into account the personal character, the rational development of which was the duty of every individual.[18] It is true that in this the fundamental notion persisted that what matters is not individuality as such, but the reason which, in various workings, is common to all men in contra-distinction to the animals ; the perfection attainable by men, with the characteristics innate in them, was regarded only as the second best in comparison with absolute perfection resulting from wisdom in its highest sense.[19] No attempt seems to have been made to gain a more thorough grasp of the relation of individual characteristics to those common to all humanity ; it was only declared that there are, " so to speak, two rôles (*personæ*) assigned to us by Nature ".

This attention to character is found in the historical work of Posidonius, who was a pupil of Panætius. It was the intellectual atmosphere in which, at the beginning of the last years of the Republic, the first autobiographies of Roman statesmen were written. In Cicero, who gives the doctrine of Panætius, there appears the idea of the manifold differences, the *varietates*, in mental make-up, differences which are even greater than in the bodily frame, " countless differences of nature and character ".* He opposes the view that these are defects and blameworthy ; on the contrary, " each one must cling to that which is his own ", and follow his own nature even if others are more important and better ; to remain true to oneself throughout life and in every act, that old demand of Greek ethics, is impossible if one " imitates the nature of others and abandons one's own " ; " fittest for each one is that which is most his own ".† In the choice of his vocation in life each one will find guidance as a rule in the example set by his ancestors.‡

This turn to individual realities was associated in the Stoa with a weakening of the objective view of reality that proceeded from the Greek philosophical tradition. In the Roman view of

---

* Cicero, *De Officiis*, I, 30, 107 and 109. *Cf.*, among others, Quintilian, *Instit.*, Or. II, 8 : " Notare discrimina ingeniorum et quo quemque natura maxime ferat, scire. Nam est in hoc incredibilis quaedam varietas nec pauciores animorum paene quam corporum formae." (" Note must be taken of the differences in men's minds, and knowledge must be sought of that with which Nature mainly endows each person. For in this there is an incredible variety ; and the spiritual forms are no fewer, or scarcely fewer, than the corporeal.") And especially Sextus Empiricus (*Pyrrhon. hyp.* 14, 85), where attention is drawn to physiognomy in connexion with the " probability " that men differ just as much in soul as in body.

† Cicero, *op. cit.*, 31, 110–11, 113–14. ·The demand that each one should develop that which is characteristic of him had appeared in the radical Sophist individualism. Socrates countered it with the question what this characteristic element is, and answered only so far as he himself diffused the particular in the universal (see p. 105). The Stoic thinkers whom Cicero follows were also not in possession of the full principle of the ethical value of individuality, with which Socrates' question could be answered ; this is confirmed by the line, described above, which the Stoics took later, proceeding again in their contemplation of the self from the concept of reason common to all men : the process of individualization took place through this abstract concept of reason becoming concrete and actual in the course of the inward turning of the mind, and not through a direct experience of the, inner life, resulting in the meditators becoming aware of its individual character and assigning to it a value of its own (see below, chap, III).

‡ *Ibid.*, 32, 116.

life there were no such inhibitions in the way of the perception of individuality, for the Roman outlook was based on the purposeful will and so was naturally open for the acceptance of the facts of the contemporary world and of the past. With the rise of the Roman Republic to world power, this characteristic " attitude of will " entered as a new and independent force into the history of the European mind [20] and fructified philosophic thought ; but in this epoch of the " fusion of Greek philosophy with the Roman outlook on life " [21] we find at the same time, so far as the problem of individuality is concerned, a development contained in philosophic thought itself, which was promoted by the fight of the Sceptics against the belief in reason as the guiding principle of the universe, human life included.[22]   The two came together in the critical reaction which may be described as the turning back of philosophy to man as a living person endowed with will.

Here begin, after the first century of the Christian era, the documents of self-scrutiny which allow us to observe the ways in which thought penetrates into inner experience.   These, where they appeared in the Roman Empire, started once more from the stern general conception of personality prevailing in the old Stoa. In the great days of the Roman Republic to which we referred,* a man's right to his own individuality had been virtually recognized in practice and yet only relatively by philosophy ; at that time the men born to action were to be found in a national community in which the person was fully represented outwardly, and philosophic thought fulfilled the function of penetrating the manifold reality of this political activity with the Idea.   When after the constitutional upheaval under the Emperor Augustus, social and political conditions arrived in Rome—as they had done earlier in the Hellenic universal States—in which the individual man began to be dependent on himself, he could only hold once more to the general principles of reason, making them the guiding principles of his dealings with the world ; through their application and his personal experience of them he succeeded eventually in transcending the sphere of pure reason.   So far inwardness was closely bound up with uniformity.   It was only in the later stage of religious excitement that the consciousness of personality lagged behind the reason, which had proved insufficient to make the inner life comprehensible—but here again individuality, however much it was now sublimated, was felt only

* See p. 195.

as belonging to the world of mere appearances and did not yet merge as an entity with the personality, which sought its secret inner union with the eternal and divine. That individuality is there for its own sake, that Nature, in Goethe's words, " seems in all her work to be concerned for individuality ",[23] and that the individual is moral for the very reason that he develops the common nature in the characteristic way innate in him in the actual relations of life—this pregnant idea of personality was not realized in the ancient world.

We have now to try to grasp as a whole the development of autobiography during these five centuries in the middle of which came the life of Jesus. The stock of traditions, which is wanting for the first productive generations of individual men in the period from about 300 B.C. onward, does not permit any comprehensive arrangement of the material in order of time, any thorough classification of it by periods. The main types of autobiographies may, however, be distinguished. Starting from this classification we shall treat of each type separately in the following three sections. In thus pursuing in turn the various species of the *genre* we shall gain a picture of the consistent development of the whole, unfolding more or less chronologically. For political autobiography reached its highest point in the last century before Christ and in Augustus, whereas the existence of autobiographies of writers becomes evident at various points from Cicero to the second century after Christ. And the autobiographical expression of inward experience leads then into the philosophico-religious movements of the Christian era. In all three sections we take together the typical Hellenistic productions and the characteristic Roman ones, and we seek in this connexion to assess the originality of the Roman literature, which particularly impresses the impartial observer in the field of autobiography, especially political autobiography.

CHAPTER I

AUTOBIOGRAPHY IN POLITICAL LIFE

There have been self-portrayals of kings since the oriental rulers had their works recorded in formal court style in the first person. In the Attic democracy the state oration in the agora had become a literary form in which a statesman could display his personality in the context of the national ideals. The situation created by Alexander, and his own shining example, brought with the new development of the power of the monarch, such as had only been known in the East, a reinforcement of his sense of power by the Greek idea of personality, which raised political force to the level of responsible and creative activity : the self-reliant personality of the ruler became the constituent principle of the splendour of power.[1] The newly emerged political individuality of the Hellenistic age, however, was just as multiform as was political life itself in that age. The very conceptions that helped to form it are different from one another —the natural right to power of the man of genius or the strong man, displayed both by the doctrine of the Sophists such as Thrasymachus and by the Euripidean drama ; the authority of the ethical activity, as conceived by Plato and accepted by Aristotle, of the ruler exempt from the coercion of traditional laws ; the sovereignty of the strong will in perfect kings as the Cynics proclaimed it ; and now in addition the conceptions of oriental absolutism, especially the idea of the god-king, an idea which, foreign as it was to Greek humanism, lost something of its extra-human quality owing to the Hellenistic experience we have sketched * of the individuality of the great ruler, embodying widespread historical developments.

There was not here, as there had been in the Middle East, any single established style for the self-portrayal of princes and statesmen. The existing forms were continued, with modifications ; it was possible to adopt the forms that had come into existence in the East, while on the other hand the power which literature exerted over Greek public life gained increased significance ; particular methods of political biography were

* See above, pp. 194 *sqq.*

199

introduced from general literature, and new types emerged from political life. We can still observe this multiplicity of forms (which in itself is expressive of individuation), though most of the works are no longer extant, so that as a rule we have no means of discovering how far they served the expression of personality.

1. HELLENISTIC POLITICAL MEMOIRS

Both the continuity with the East and the new development are conspicuous in the history of the monumental record of deeds that continued down to the *res gestæ* of the emperor Augustus. But half a millennium separates that Roman " queen of inscriptions " from the last and most important example of this custom in an oriental ruler, the great rock inscription of Darius. Of the Hellenistic princes who served as a connecting link in the tradition, laudatory inscriptions containing some biographical data are extant only in isolated examples ; in addition to the usual self-glorification on the strength of divine origin and divine ancestry they show in a few instances, of later date, the significant introduction of the ruler's victorious achievements by the phrase, " I first and alone among the kings hitherto".[2]   How usual, however, the appearance of the ruler's record of deeds was in the earlier period of the Hellenistic epoch may be seen from the fact that at the outset of the third century B.C. a rationalistic compiler of Egyptian history, Hecataeus, gives the inscribed *res gestæ* of Isis and Osiris,[3] whom he regards as primeval deified kings. And the imposing funerary monument which King Antiochus of Commagene erected (about A.D. 38) on the Nemrud-Dagh, a Taurus peak visible far around, gives an impression of the way plastic art together with the device of inscriptions perpetuated the divine glory of a Hellenistic prince.

The king, half Syrian and half Persian in origin, and living amid the interplay of Persian, Chaldæan, and Greek beliefs, introduces himself in the pompous rhythms of his inscription, which begins with an " I " (it is a festal proclamation, not a report of deeds), as the " just god made manifest ",* and declares that not only the hero-company of his ancestors but " all the gods " would be enthroned in portraits in his sanctuary, and among them would be placed his own picture, so that " the ancient honour of the great gods " should become " contemporary

---

* θεὸς ἐπιφανής is a title familiar since the Seleucids—*cf.* Wendland, *Zeitschr. f. neutestam. Wiss.*, V, pp. 338–9.

with a new Tyche ". " All " these gods—three in number—
were set up, in statues eight metres high, each in mixed Greek
and Persian style, in front of the gigantic stone tomb, which was
itself surrounded with portraits of ancestors—reaching back to
Darius. In their midst were the statues of the king himself and of
Tyche, the guardian goddess of his kingdom and " all-nourishing
fatherland ". This row of five colossal statues, among which
stood out, highest of all, that of Mithras-Zeus, was conceived as
an integral expression of the auto-apotheosis of Antiochus, in
whom this Commagenic pantheon had been resuscitated as a
whole. Separate reliefs with representations of his sanctification
and elevation to equality with each of the gods brought in the
apotheosis once more as an actual proceeding ; astrological
evidence of it was added in the king's horoscope, which was also
shown in relief.[4]

Of an altogether different sort was a memorial erected to
himself by Hannibal, toward the end of the Second Punic War
(218–201 B.C.), when he could scarcely fail to see that his
ambitious plans for the destruction of the Roman rule over Italy
were doomed to failure, and he had instead to defend his own
country against the Romans, who under Scipio had taken to the
offensive in Africa (in 203 B.C.). Before he finally left Italy,
after fifteen years' invasion, he set up in the land of the enemy,
at a spot visible from afar, an altar with an inscription concerning
his campaign. This memorial stood near the temple of Hera on
the promontory of Lacinium, the easternmost point of Calabria,
which had been his basis of operations since the battle of Cannæ.
Considering its author and its subject, it must have been one of
the most important documents of its sort, but there is no record
of its contents. We know of it only through the ancient historians
who refer to it. Livy mentions it as Hannibal's " immense
inscription " recording his exploits.* We learn more from
Polybius, the great Greek historian, who described the " Han-
nibalic war " as the beginning of the vast process in which
" almost the whole inhabited world "—that is, the Mediterranean
world—" was conquered and brought under the dominion of the
single city of Rome ".[5] Among his sources he mentions this

---

* Livy, *Ab Urbe Condita*, Book XXVIII, chap. 46 : *Praeter Iunonis Laciniae templum
aestatem Hannibal egit ; ibique aram condidit dedicavitque, cum ingenti rerum ab se gestarum
titulo, Punicis Graecisque literis insculptis.* (" Hannibal spent the summer by the temple
of Juno Lacinia ; and there he built and dedicated an altar, with an immense summary of the things he had done, inscribed in Phœnician and Greek characters.")
According to Livy this was in A.U.C. 547, i.e. 205 B.C.

inscription of Hannibal's ; he relies on it in the characteristic way of the genuinely scientific historian for exact details of the figures he includes in his account of Hannibal's invasion of Italy ; for instance : [6]

" The whole march from New Carthage * had taken him five months, and he had spent fifteen days in crossing the Alps, and now, when he thus boldly descended into the plain of the Po and the territory of the Insubres, his surviving forces numbered 12,000 African and 8,000 Iberian foot, and not more than 6,000 horse in all."

Still more detailed are the figures of the strength of the troops he left behind for the defence of Carthage and Spain—a main consideration of the war policy pursued in Carthage : [7]

In Spain he left with his brother Hasdrubal 50 quinqueremes, two tetraremes, and five triremes, 32 of the quinqueremes and all the triremes being fully manned. He also gave him as cavalry Libyo-Phœnicians and Libyans to the number of 450, with 300 Ilergetes, and 1800 Numidians drawn from the Masylii, Masæsylii, Maccœi, and Maurusi, who dwell by the Ocean ; and as infantry 11,850 Libyans, 300 Ligurians, and 500 Balearians, as well as twenty-one elephants.

On these figures Polybius offers this remark :

No one need be surprised at the accuracy of the information I give here . . . an accuracy which even the actual organizer of the details would have had some difficulty in attaining, and I need not be condemned offhand under the idea that I am acting like those authors who try to make their misstatements plausible. The fact is that I found on the Lacinian promontory a bronze tablet on which Hannibal himself had made out these lists while he was in Italy, and thinking this an absolutely first-rate authority I decided to follow the document.

This is the first instance we have of the assessment of a document of autobiographical nature as a source of historical information. Polybius, from whom the assessment comes, re-presents for us, as a genuine successor to Thucydides, the influence of the Greek scientific spirit on the writing of political history, which flourished in Rome, the centre of high politics. Thus in the inscription itself the accuracy of detail on account of which he valued the document so highly was certainly due not only to the matter-of-fact routine of the army commander, but also to Hannibal's Greek education. Hannibal knew Greek, he was versed in Greek literature, particularly, perhaps, in the literature of the art of war ; on his campaigns he took with him several

* Cartagena, in southern Spain, founded by Hamilcar Barcas, Hannibal's father.

Greek scribes, to write as eye-witnesses the story of his deeds ; [8] thus the inscription at Lacinium was bi-lingual, written in Greek and Phœnician.

This brings us to the Hellenistic type of political memoirs, which, in contrast to the ancient oriental tradition of self-glorification by the despot, corresponded to the age in which the positive sciences began to develop. Its actual form and mental attitude entered into literature from Alexander's military entourage [9]—the factual and unrhetorical report, depending on original sources. One of the Diadochi, King Ptolemy I, gave the history of Alexander's campaigns from the records of the General Staff, probably incorporating in it experiences of his own. The memoirs of King Pyrrhus (c. 275 B.C.) were probably no less factual : in the view of Wilamowitz [10] they must be regarded as " the publication of the royal *hypomnemata*, and so as documents ". To record the facts of history day by day in diaries, to preserve these records in archives, and to leave their literary elaboration to a professional writer—in some cases one of their own choosing—this seems to have been, following Alexander's example, the practice of the Hellenistic princes ; like him, they had their court historiographers. Cicero himself regarded Alexander's method as the pattern of the way the indispensable task of providing for literary glorification of one's famous deeds should be performed : " How many scribes recording his deeds Alexander the Great is said to have had about him ! And yet, when he stood at the grave of Achilles he exclaimed : ' Thou fortunate youth, who didst find a Homer to proclaim thy greatness ! ' How right he was ! " [11]

The Hellenistic statesmen and army commanders, however, were also capable of being their own trumpeters, and while they did not mingle with the rhetoricians they intervened at all events in public controversy with apologias of their own. An example from the third century B.C. is offered by the political auto-biography written by Aratus of Sicyon (271–213). Sicyon, a small city in the Peloponnese, near Corinth, played a prominent part in the Greece of that day, which was torn by controversies on home and foreign politics. As a young man of twenty, Aratus had liberated his city from the tyranny to which his father had fallen victim, and had restored the city's democratic constitution. Through him Sicyon became the leading member of the Achæan League, a confederation of some ten cities, and an organization in harmony with its time, since the days of the city states were over and those of the great powers had still to come. Aratus himself became the head of the League and remained so throughout his life ; he was elected its *strategos* (army commander), and was re-elected as often as the constitution of the League or the circumstances permitted, sixteen times in all. His warlike enterprises were directed against Sparta, which was aiming at hegemony over the Peloponnese. In these he was less successful than as statesman and diplomat. But his policy also was not permanently successful. He sought and obtained the help of the king of Macedonia against Sparta, but the result was Macedonian domination over the Peloponnese, for the prevention of which the League had been founded in the fourth century. He personally was sometimes trusted, sometimes distrusted by the king, until in the end there came an open breach. It is said that the king had him poisoned. On the other hand, we have knowledge of attacks on his Macedonian policy by a contemporary historian, Phylarchus, in a work compiled in the rhetorical and dramatic style then current. Clearly Aratus had good reason to publish his memoirs in self-defence. They formed a substantial work of more than thirty " books ",[12] each of some ten thousand words. He wrote them about 215, when he was over fifty years of age. Polybius did them the honour of mentioning them at the outset of his great History of the World. He states there that his work begins where Aratus' memoirs end, that is to say at the end of the war against Sparta (299–222 B.C.)—the so-called Cleomenic war.

To judge from the remarks of Polybius and Plutarch, the work was one—and for us the first *—of the unliterary, " hypomnematic " narratives, apparently carelessly and aimlessly thrown together, with no attempt at choice of words ; Aratus had no further purpose than to state his case,[13] and it is evident that he missed the opportunity afforded by one scene that could have been artistically worked up.[14] But the outstanding element in the fragments is a genuine motive of memoirs in general—self-exculpation, on the plea of necessity or of *force majeure*, attribution of treachery or breach of faith to other persons, trumpeting of his own services, and malevolent abuse of his

* For the rest we know only that Demetrius of Phalerum wrote after his downfall a history of his ten years' activities as governor of Athens : περὶ τῆς δεκαετίας. Diog. V, 80. *Cf.* F. Jacoby, *loc. cit.*, no. 228.—The " Hypomnemata " of Antigonus Gonatas are to be regarded as " diaries ", not as memoirs.—Köpke wrote on hypomnemata : " De hypomnematis Graecis ", I (1842) ; II (1863). (Progr. der Brandenbg. Ritterakademie.)

enemies ; silence in regard to weak points, and explicit defence not only against calumnies but against justified attacks. One senses the atmosphere of subtle diplomacy and intrigue in the account which Polybius, obviously following Aratus, gives of the latter's fatal decision to turn to the Macedonian king Antigonus, when he saw that the war against the Spartans under their king Cleomenes was taking a turn unfavourable to the League. Here he writes in regard to Aratus : [15]

He perceived that Antigonus was a man of energy and sound sense, and that he claimed to be a man of honour, but he knew that kings do not regard anyone as their natural foe or friend, but measure enmity and friendship by the standard of expediency. He therefore decided to approach that monarch and put himself on confidential terms with him, pointing out to him the probable outcome of the existing state of affairs. Now, for several reasons he did not think it expedient to do this overtly. In the first place he would thus expose himself to being outbidden in his project by Cleomenes and the Ætolians, and next he would damage the spirit of the Achæan troops by thus appealing to an enemy and appearing to have entirely abandoned the hopes he had placed in them—this being the very last thing he wished them to think. Therefore, having formed his plan, he decided to carry it out by covert means. He was consequently compelled in public both to do and to say many things quite contrary to his real intention, so as to keep his design concealed by creating the exactly opposite impression.

And now it appears that the specific type which from the seventeenth century onward we have known as political memoirs, the type that grows in the atmosphere of courts, comes from Hellenism. The practice of keeping a diary (in the third person), [16] introduced by Alexander (probably in continuation of oriental traditions at the courts of the Persian kings) and kept up until the Roman emperors, and of summarizing in it the events occurring within the sphere of the ruler, provided room not only for affairs of state but for details of the prince's private life ; and there were certainly court journals, [17] for happenings in the royal house and for festivities and the like, at least from the time of the emperors. The public interest in anecdotes and disasters in court history is revealed only too clearly in the Roman tradition, especially in the imperial biographies based partly on the " diaries " : [18] is it likely that the literature of Hellenistic memoirs would fail to be influenced by it ?

It may be surmised that there was something of this sort in a remarkable work of Ptolemy Euergetes II, which is quoted under the innocent title of *hypomnemata* and described by authoritative philologists as a collection of note-books of the Egyptian king on his travels and his studies. Its general character can no longer be determined, but Euergetes was at all events no innocent observer or patron of learned studies. His life was full of adventure and of scandalous episodes such as we find later in the biographies and, indeed, in some of the autobiographies of the Roman emperors. He ascended the Egyptian throne in 169 B.C., when his elder brother Ptolemy VI (181–145) had fallen into captivity in Syria. He owed his throne to his popularity with the native population of Alexandria ; but after five years of joint rule with his brother he had to make way for him and to content himself with the crown of Cyrene and Cyprus. After the death of Ptolemy VI the infant son of his marriage with his sister Cleopatra was proclaimed king by the Alexandrians, but Euergetes seized the kingdom and held it for thirty years until his death ; only once was he driven out for a short time. He had married the regent Cleopatra, his brother's widow, who was thus both his sister and his sister-in-law. The Alexandrians gave him the nickname Physcon (" Pot-belly ") ; his corpulence was enormous even for a Ptolemy. Following Shakespeare, we might infer a certain good nature. But according to the Greek historians he was just as cruel as he was fat. After his marriage with Cleopatra he made away with her son by her marriage with their brother ; he then got rid of her in order to marry her daughter Cleopatra, a sister of the murdered child. Thus there were both " Queen Cleopatra the Sister " and " Queen Cleopatra the Wife ". But he seems to have had the humour of the fat. His memoirs were considered so amusing that three hundred years later they were still much read, or at least much talked about. And the few passages of his voluminous work that have been preserved [19] show that he had an eye for the oddities of other people and could laugh at his fellow-kings.

In these fragments there is a biographical thread that suggests personal memoirs. Incidental notes, of Lucullian interest rather than of any value as natural history, are made during journeys and campaigns, recording some particularly cold spring water, sea-wolves, artichokes, and other things which he or his soldiers enjoyed ; he tells of his banquets and his all-excelling lavishness, of the amorous adventures of one of his predecessors, of things noted abroad and at foreign courts, such as the service at table and the magnificent dinner service of Massinissa, king of Numidia, and of that king's pleasure in small children ; or of the expensive indulgence of King Eumenes of Pergamum in the breeding and fattening of snow-white pigs. The study of gluttony must have been a characteristic feature of the work ; for Athenæus, the antiquarian writer to whom we owe our knowledge of it, not only made extracts from it, as from many hundred other works, for the enormous compilation to which he gave the title *Deipnosophistai* or " Table Talk of Learned Men ", but made a direct reference to that feature in order to crack a cheap joke :

King Ptolemy, in the twelfth book of his *Commentaries*, speaking of the royal palace at Alexandria and the animals kept in it, says : " Also the kind of pheasants which they call *tetaroi* ; not only did he procure them from Media, but by mating Numidian birds with them he produced quantities of them for food ; for it is asserted that they make a very rich delicacy." Here you have the word of that most illustrious king, who has admitted that he had never even so much as tasted a pheasant, but kept the very birds we have here as a treasure to be carefully stored. But if he had seen that each one of us today has a whole pheasant served to him besides the food already consumed, he would have filled another book to add to the famous stories in his *Commentaries*.[20]

But there is a passage in the memoirs that is almost reminiscent of *Trimalchio's Feast*, that very famous fragment of Petronius' satirical romance, with which we shall deal presently.* In this passage the king of Syria, Antiochus Epiphanes, an uncle of this Ptolemy, is shown throwing among the crowd in the street the money left over from his orgies, or in the public baths throwing a bucket of precious ointment over an intrusive plebeian, and then himself slipping in the puddle with a loud laugh.[21] This story is also found in Polybius,[22] but without the amusement which the writer of the memoirs found in the incident.

There were also memoirs of Herod,[23] in which he is said to have touched not only on the many petty intrigues and scandals but also on the tragedy of Mariamne ; he told, in any case, of his meeting with Cleopatra. And Olympus, the physician and confidant of Cleopatra, published a story of her last days [24] from which the masterly comedy of Cleopatra played before Augustus, of which Plutarch tells,[25] is said to have been taken. Thus it is certainly permissible to trace this very pregnant form of memoirs to the Hellenistic courts.

All that is extant, however, of the Hellenistic autobiographies is a few isolated outlines. Only from Rome do we obtain a fuller view, and there there are certain new forces at work.

* See below, pp. 224–5.

II. ARISTOCRATIC FAMILIES OF THE ROMAN REPUBLIC

Politics and political history, those great elements, with jurisprudence, of Roman national literature, form also the principal field of Roman autobiography. The reminiscences of statesmen and army commanders, and then of emperors, are crowded here as they had not been since the records of the deeds of the oriental despots. With the revolutionary period, from the last century of the Republic, there appears this branch of our *genre* among the Romans, to continue in varied style and with many interruptions until the end of the third century after Christ and into the fourth. In the period following the failure of the reforming efforts of the Gracchi and before the appearance of the dictators, leading members of the Senate (that is to say, the aristocratic body which for centuries had had the government of the Roman commonwealth in its hands) opened the series— Æmilius Scaurus and Rutilius Rufus, with their books *de sua vita*, " concerning their own lives ". Contemporary with or earlier than these express autobiographies is a work by Q. Lutatius Catulus " concerning his consulate and his deeds " ; he was Consul in 102 B.C. with Marius, the famous tribune of the people, and shared with him the supreme command in the campaign against the Cimbri and the Teutons, who had invaded Italy. Then came Sulla, the dictator ; he left behind him a substantial work of memoirs. In the next generation came Cæsar's Commentaries and Cicero's voluminous efforts at literary glorification of his own statesmanship ; and M. Terentius Varro, antiquarian and a most voluminous writer, whom Cæsar had designed as head of the great public library he planned, found time in his old age for a work *de sua vita*. There existed a full autobiography by the emperor Augustus, which he had published in his middle life, immediately after his restoration of peace in the empire, forty years before the brilliant report on his *res gestæ*, which we have in the so-called Monumentum Ancyranum.* Agrippa, son-in-law and lifelong friend of Augustus, and probably also Mæcenas, his other loyal collaborator, to both of whom he dedicated his autobiography, also wrote their memoirs. To these should probably be added the famous republican orator Messalla Corvinus, who had fought against Augustus alongside

---

* This current designation is due to the fact that the great inscription first became known through a copy (in Latin and Greek) discovered in the sixteenth century on the walls of the temple of Augustus at Ancyra, in Galatia.

the assassins of Julius Cæsar and then went over to Augustus. Messalla became so attached to the emperor that it was he who later (2 B.C.) proposed for Augustus the honorific title of *pater patriæ*.

There is also a trace of war memoirs of a more or less ephemeral nature dating from the time of the triumvirate.* Then there is the post-Augustan period. Tiberius, Claudius, perhaps also Vespasian,† then Hadrian, and Septimius Severus, that is to say half of the emperors who come into consideration owing to the length of their reign, continued this series of autobiographical works. Even an empress-mother, Agrippina, who ruled for a time jointly with her son Nero, until he drove her away, followed the custom ; and then there is mention of the reminiscences [26] of Constantine the Great (306–322).

This heterogeneous series of princely names, with which may be contrasted that of the emperor Marcus Aurelius Antoninus with his " Meditations ", can be studied only in a general way in regard to the varied treatment of the common material, since only small remnants, mostly isolated sentences or mere titles, have been preserved. It cannot even be said with certainty whether the books were all written in Latin and not some of them in Greek,‡ or whether the use of the first person was general. But the very production of this voluminous material is significant : in political life, where the desire for power finds its most intense expression and the maintenance of a man's position in the public eye is one of the most constant concerns, autobiography, which appeared only rarely among the ancients in other spheres, was widely resorted to, and life in Rome, which aimed at individual leadership and responsible activity, in short, at the development of practical common sense and thus at consistent pursuit of a definite purpose, supplies the bulk of the self-portrayals from ancient times.

Here autobiography was clearly regarded as a recognized type of literary work. The first expressions of opinion of ancient writers on autobiography mention this fact, and it then became

* Q. Dellius, who on account of his many changes of party was called by Messalla *desultor bellorum*, " changer of horses in mid-war ", wrote on Antony's campaigns against Parthia, at which he had been present as *legatus*. *Cf.* Strabo, XI, 523.

† But Vespasian's *Commentaries* were probably only official records compiled by the commander or his staff office, and published as documents. The same applies probably to those of Titus. *Cf.* W. Weber, *Josephus und Vespasian* (1927).

‡ It is possible that Rutilius Rufus, Catulus, and Sulla wrote in Greek. *Cf.* Peter, *Hist. Rom. Reliq.*, pp. cclxvi, cclxxii, cclxxviii. Cicero's *hypomnemata*, written in Greek, included Latin comments and a Latin poem with the same content.

the point of departure, from the humanists onward, for the theoretical consideration of this *genre*.*

Of the earliest of these autobiographies, from the Republican period, the books of Scaurus and Rufus, we have a reflection in the assessments by Cicero and Tacitus. They appear there as authentic national products, which give evidence of the true moral greatness of the Romans of old. Scaurus, a senator who had risen from narrow circumstances, is described by Cicero as an admirable personality of innate dignity and irreproachable character ; he sets Scaurus' *Vita* alongside the *Cyropædia*, of which he relates elsewhere [27] that Scipio Africanus had that book always beside him, and with good reason, as a book for rulers. Scaurus' autobiography, he declares, is " very well worth reading, though no one reads it. Men prefer nowadays the story of the life and training of Cyrus—a splendid book, no doubt, but not so suited to our conditions and not deserving to be preferred to Scaurus' encomium of himself." [28] And Tacitus, in the biography he dutifully compiled of his father-in-law Agricola, writes emphatically at the outset that such a celebration of a deceased contemporary is a national tradition, which ensures the effectual permanence of his *virtus* ; for Tacitus the old autobiographies support that view, since they established a man's true fame, even if he broadcast it himself.[29]

To hand down to posterity the work and ways of famous men was our fathers' custom : our age has not yet abandoned it even now, indifferent though it be to its own children, whenever, at least, some great and notable virtue has dominated and overpowered the vice common alike to small states and great—misapprehension of integrity (*ignorantia recti*) and jealousy. But in our fathers' times, just as the doing of deeds worth recording was natural and more obvious, so also there was inducement then to the brightest spirits to publish such records of virtue. Partisanship was not the motive, or ambition ; a good conscience was its own reward ; nay, many men even counted it not presumption, but self-respect, to narrate their own lives. A Rutilius, a Scaurus, could do so without overdrawing his credit or

* Ag. Mascardi, *Dell' Arte Historica* (Venice, 1655), tratt. III, c. 1 : *Se dell' uomo politica sia propria cura lo scriver historia* (" Whether the writing of history is a concern proper to the politician "), gives an almost complete list of these autobiographies from Scaurus to Hadrian (together with Philo's *Legatio ad Gaium* and Josephus' *Vita*, and thus, apparently, the first historical consideration of autobiography. Then, still in connexion with the great generation of philologists, comes D. Huet, in his *Commentarii de Vita Sua* (1719), p. 420. A modern special account was given by Vittorio Rossi in *Le Autobiografie e gli Epistolare Italiane*, chap. 1, " La Roma Pagana ". The work is a part of the *Storia dei Generi Letterarii Italiani*, which began to be published in 1907, at the same time as the German edition of this book : only five parts, however, were issued.

provoking a sneer ; so true is it that virtues are best appreciated in those ages which most readily give them birth.*

These sentences from Tacitus became in the Renaissance a lasting " peg " for autobiographers, who drew justification for their enterprise from the example of the Romans. The passage was taken as a motto by the humanists in the French and English aristocracies, first by de Thou, and with it the statement in Pliny's Epistles that happiness consists in the achievement or the description of memorable deeds, and the highest happiness in the combination of the two. Then Alfieri, the famous Italian dramatist of the eighteenth century, once more placed the words of the great Roman historian in front of his *Vita*, and Goethe read it there and took a copy of it.

The fostering of one's own fame, or, rather, reputation, in accordance with the Roman tradition that had grown out of an established national custom—this element, which Cicero and Tacitus found operative in the autobiographical literature of their day, differs essentially from the tendency to self-glorification with which we met in the earlier documents of political autobiography. It led to a new typical method of autobiography : this was found first in the Roman aristocracy, and its soil proved fruitful for the independent growth of the *genre*. This was the solid earth of family life from which a strong growth of biography and auto-biography proceeded. In the prominent families who were the supports of a republican order, there developed through the relations between father and son fixed traditional forms that assured the continuance of domestic, professional, and political labours through the generations ; a store of domestic traditions that provided the individual with the moral and practical bases of his existence, and gave him self-confidence. It made him familiar, too, with the whole body of family circumstances—the property and business leadership acquired by tenacious industry, the family authority and the distinction of public office, the political influence of the family and its share in the national history. Thus he was endowed early with a sense of historic continuity.

The process of development of autobiography that here set in will have to be shown clearly in detail among the civic aristoc-racies of the Italian and German cities in the Middle Ages ; it will have to be shown how informal diary entries of all sorts,

---

* Tacitus, *Agricola*, opening.   Translated by Maurice Hutton, in the Loeb Classical Library.

household books, family trees, and family papers led ultimately to family chronicles and history, and in connexion therewith to self-portrayal. Among the Romans the development in this as in other fields of their literature did not proceed so organically. But the underlying feeling for life found expression in original forms and customs, which, though not leading straight to the Roman autobiographies we know, show nevertheless on a specially large scale the obedience to law of a development which under other historical conditions was able to pursue its course to the logical end.

Here again we find one of the roots of biography reaching far down into religion. The Romans' ancestor-worship, which remained one of the most real elements of their piety, was redolent of the soil, a quality long preserved by the religion of that peasant people, with their mythless cult of the many divine powers operative in the world.[30] Their beliefs did not soar creatively in thought and imagination, but kept close to practical life and its healthy interests. As the German classical scholar Usener has shown, the formation of Roman religion is to be understood as typical of an early stage of development when the world of experience, inner and outer, gave such an overpowering impression of living reality that at every point, in every important action or situation, something independent of man's will was encountered ; it seemed to be working deliberately, for good or evil, and had therefore to be deliberately influenced through religious observances. These superhuman powers, to which no human or animal shape was attributed, were believed to work each in its own closely defined sphere of activity, within which it had to receive a definite form of worship and to achieve something positive in return ; this sphere was implied in its conceptually formed name—names such as Janus (doorway), Vesta (hearth), or Terminus (the boundaries so important to the farmer).

Accordingly the ancestors themselves had a fixed position and function in the contemporary life, politically highly developed, of the noble family, whose name, together with those of the other great houses (*gentes*) with which the family was connected, the Fabii, Julii, and so on, was in itself a symbol of the State. In the *atrium*, the great hall of the house, stood in small temple-like receptacles the busts of the ancestors with portrait-masks of painted wax—a privilege of the patricians. Below the busts were inscriptions, *elogia*, with the name in the nominative, proclaiming the dignities and deeds of each one and showing in due alignment, linked by brackets, the family tree.[31] In the patrician city of Nuremberg, at the time of the Reformation, the humanist Pirckheimer threw light in his " Mirror of Honours " on the moral content of this custom : the busts and titles of the ancestors were intended to arouse emulation through the constant contemplation of their *virtus*.[32] Even the untruthfulness associated with the tendency to glorification, familiar and indeed almost to be expected in family genealogies, which gave the Greek word *eulogia* the meaning [33] which it has received in the biographical term " éloges ", and still more the crowding of august forefathers, is accounted for by a Roman scholar of the first century A.D. by the love for *virtus*.*

The individual's awareness of himself had its basis in this relation to the ancestors as the representatives of the national ideals. Thus once more personality was conceived, as among the classical Greeks, as something static and general, but its general character differed from that implied in the Greek basing of personality on the principle of objective reason immanent in the universe. We have here an impressive instance of that definite type of self-awareness which Burckhardt, in his chapter on " The discovery of man " in the Italian Renaissance, described as characteristic of earlier times : " Man knew himself only as race, people, party, corporation, family, or in some other generalized form." † The Roman association of the personality with a family life which was the embodiment of practical common sense, and in which morality was at one with the national traditions, a unity described as the *mos maiorum*, the way of the ancestors, permitted to the ruling nobility the primitive portraiture that is so different a species from the classic Greek type, which aimed at no actual portraiture even of a Pericles but at the ideal figure of the generalized human being. That attitude to individuality seems to us moderns to distinguish the Romans from the Greeks, but as it was rooted in primitive religion it did not surpass but fell short of the high plane of thought on which the classical Greeks moved with their theoretical or æsthetic treatment of the reality of human life. There is therefore no contradiction to be found, as has been imagined,[34] in the co-existence of the traditional Roman ancestor-worship with the suppression in principle of individuality, strictly carried out in his History of

---

* Pliny, "*Nat. Hist.*," XXV, 8 : *Etiam mentiri clarorum imagines erat aliquis virtutum amor* (" Even falsehood in representations of illustrious persons was a sort of love of the virtues ").

† See the quotation above, Part I, p. 67, note.

H

Italy by Marcus Porcius Cato, most Roman of Romans, the father of Roman history (about 200 B.C.), in his deliberate opposition [35] to the cult of personality among the Hellenistic historians. In Cato's work the great individuals appear only as servants of the State, and their names are consistently suppressed. But the " Consul ", as he called himself, inserted his own speeches in the history of his time, verbatim, in defiance of the standards of the Greek historians, whose influence he fought though he was in fact influenced by them. He could quote his speeches in formal style as he had delivered them in the Senate because in them his individual personality and the *mos maiorum* were at one.

In his public self-presentation a high official liked to interpret his career in accordance with the traditions distinctive of Roman political life, starting from the speaker's own ancestors. This was not, as in the Athenian democracy, by way of defence in a public inquiry into his integrity,* which the positive character of the Romans took for granted in the absence of any notorious evidence to the contrary,[36] but as a magistrate's right after taking office, at the first address of the new Consul to the citizens, or at the annual edict of the prætor : the speaker, in presenting his political programme and principles of administration, produced also the guarantee of his nobility and the record of his past achievements.[37]   Cicero, in the dialogue on the theory of Ethics, one of the imaginary dialogues in which he comes forward as principal speaker, brings forward as a trump card against the Epicurean philosophy a historico-political argument : the Epicurean theory, he says, that pleasure is the only good cannot appeal to the great names of history, and is incompatible with the attitude required of a servant of the State.   In this way he places before his interlocutor, a Roman aristocrat whom he introduces as a spokesman of Epicureanism, this aristocrat's situation if he had to answer for his views and activities when he ascended the *rostra* and had to declare before a public audience the object of his actions, aims, and endeavours : " For you will have to announce the rules that you propose to observe in administering justice, and very likely also, if you think good, you will follow the ancient custom of making some reference to your ancestors and to yourself." [38]   And Suetonius mentions as characteristic in Tiberius his praise of a prætor because he had " once more followed the ancient custom of telling of his own ancestors before the assembled citizens ".[39]

* See above, p. 156.

The living power of the illustrious dead, and with it the *ethos* of the Roman family, was visibly displayed in a most impressive manner when a member of the aristocracy was called to his fathers. The whole succession of forefathers, sometimes more than a hundred, was crudely represented by men, mostly actors, who wore the painted portrait-masks and the whole stock of official robes and decorations, and who, seated on high cars, conducted the dead man in solemn procession from the house of mourning. The dead man lay uncovered on a bed of state borne by his sons ; or he appeared standing in his robes like a living person, represented by a clothed wooden figure with a waxen mask, preceded by records of his deeds as in a triumphal procession.[40] Then, when the procession had reached the Forum, the dead man entered into the historic past that represented the continuity of life. This was the natural climax in the function of the ancestors. It was this celebration that Polybius (6, 53) described, from the powerful impression it made on him, as the source of the strength that made the Roman youths into men. In front of the *rostra*, facing the dead man, sat the ancestors on the ivory seats ; the followers stood round in a circle, and a son or the nearest relative of the dead delivered the funeral oration, the *laudatio*, turning not to the relatives but to the Roman citizens, the Quirites. He began with the fame of the house, then recalled the life of the deceased from youth up, his deeds and offices and honours and, especially, his virtues, and finally proceeded to the forefathers seated there before him, one after another, beginning with the remotest, praising their deeds.[41]

This display of the enduring life of the family at the funeral of one of its eminent members might seem to us to be a counterpart of the other ancient custom, also religious in origin, celebrating the living at the height of his success—the triumphal procession of the victorious army commander. The word " triumph ", and the conception, are Roman. The Roman conquerors regarded the process of history as a national struggle for power, and in their view the highest honour a man could achieve was that earned by a victory over a foreign enemy which extended the boundaries of the State. A primitive national festival of thanksgiving to the gods thus turned into a ceremony of tribute to a single man. In the solemn procession headed by the magistrates and the senate, the tokens of victory were first conveyed—booty and captives and pictorial representations of battles and conquests ; then came the *triumphator*, the conquering general, at the head of his soldiers, in a car drawn by four horses ; he appeared like a god in robes of purple and gold, with a laurel wreath and carrying a sceptre, while the golden crown of Jupiter was held over his head by a slave.

The triumphal processions [wrote a modern historian in the heyday of Liberalism],[42] were not spectacles for the curious, and not only an expression of joy at national victories, but served more especially to exalt the *triumphator* before the people, to flatter his vanity and that of his family, and to mark him as a great man. The eagerness with which Roman statesmen longed for the distinction of a triumph became an uncontrollable passion. Whoever had a shadow of a pretension to such an honour importuned the senate with his claims, laboured to place his exploits in the most favourable light, to extol and exaggerate his successes . . . At length the senate endeavoured to guard against unsubstantial claims by resolving that a triumph should not be accorded to any commander who had not slain at least five thousand enemies. The only result of this restriction was that the mendacious reports were swelled to the required proportion.

This custom had, however, like the festival of the dead, a certain grandeur. The thing that concerns us here is that it worked in a monumental style in the building up of the life-story. The triumphal arches are familiar to us, with their sculptured panels in which the ruler's victories, his acts of government, and other scenes from his life, are represented. In the Renaissance the emperor Maximilian, called " the last of the knights ", took the Roman triumph as the model for the series of pictures, seventy-five metres long, which he had painted in his honour by such masters as Albrecht Dürer.

The ancient Roman custom of the *laudatio funebris*, the laudatory speech at the funeral, had similarly lasting consequences. In many cases the speeches were preserved in writing in the family archives, and later—so far as we know, from the third century B.C.—they were published as books [43] ; thus a permanent concern with biography was started, providing, before the beginning of the literary or philosophical treatment of an individual life, a historical centre of biography in the family. In Rome as in Athens the spoken oration was the successor of the funeral hymn, the *nænia* sung in praise of the dead person, which remained alongside it as the mere rudiment of a cult.[44] To that extent there is a repetition here of the development we followed in Greek literature in connexion with Isocrates, in regard both to the *enkomion* and to the ideal type of citizen. In Rome, however, this development took place within the family, and the celebration of a representative of the ruling families meant, in Cicero's words, " adding great glory to the name of the Roman people ".[45] Since families, and not individuals, were recognized as the original units on which social and political life was built up, it is reasonable to proceed from the fundamental family relationships of father and son, and husband and wife, in order to comprehend the peculiar Roman variation of the typical development.

A picture of a true Roman of the great old days of the Republic, drawn by his son, has come down to us at least in outline, that of the *pontifex* Lucius Cæcilius Metellus, who died at an advanced age in 222 B.C., shortly before the outbreak of the second Punic war.   An excerpt from the funeral oration spoken by the son has been preserved in a work written three centuries later by a most learned Latin writer of the early imperial age— Pliny's " Natural History ".   In the section of this work that deals with Man there is a passage in which Pliny discusses the old question, Who is the happiest of mankind ? As one of the exceptional instances of human happiness he quotes the life of Lucius Metellus, as described by his son.   This passage begins : *Gentium in toto orbe praestantissima una omnium virtute haud dubia Romana exstitit* (" The one race of outstanding eminence in virtue among all the races in the whole world is undoubtedly the Roman ").

Pliny starts the excerpt from the funeral oration with the list of the offices and dignities of the deceased : " He had been Consul twice, Dictator, Master of the Horse, and Land Commissioner, and "—this comes next—" he was the first person who led a procession of elephants in a triumph, having captured them in the first Punic War."   Then comes the reward of his virtues :

He had achieved the ten greatest and highest objects in the pursuit of which wise men pass their lives : for he had made it his aim to be a first-class warrior, a supreme orator, and a very brave commander, to have the direction of operations of the highest importance, to hold the most honourable office, to attain the summit of wisdom, to be deemed the most eminent member of the senate, to obtain great wealth by honourable means, to leave many children, and to achieve supreme distinction in the state.[46]

Such achievement in all ten points, the speaker emphasized,

was unique ; the honour of it had fallen to his father and to no one else since the foundation of Rome. And his father gained yet another unique honour in his old age : " As he had lost his sight in a fire when saving the statue of Pallas from the temple of Vesta, the nation bestowed on him a privilege given to no one else since the foundation of the City, permission to ride to the senate-house in a chariot whenever he went to a meeting of the senate." Pliny adds this, but as an instance of misfortune suitable for countering the old tendency to self-glorification and for supporting his own contention, *Nemo mortalium est felix,* " No mortal is happy." " Inasmuch as this Metellus passed an old age of blindness . . . he cannot be called happy."

How far the development of the funeral oration among the Romans proceeded beyond the idealization usual in this *genre* and attained a realistic picture of the life of the individual, we are unable to trace. The patricians' falsification of history in the interest of family prestige was pointed out by critics among the ancients.* And the rules Cicero gives for this type of speech as a literary production [47] offer only generalities : he does not proceed from existing documents of the *genre*, in order to analyse their content and structure, but from the generally recognized system of virtues, into which the biographical material has to be fitted, with an eye to effect, things of outstanding nobility or novelty or strangeness being the first to be selected. It can still be seen, however, that an intimate narrative account of the actual circumstances of the home life, similar to the chronicles of more modern times, including a record of happiness in childhood and especially of material things like property and inheritance, was admissible.[48] Something of the same sort is to be observed in the autobiography of Scaurus, where he tells of the smallness of his inheritance from his father.[49] The estate (*res familiaris*) was part of the Roman conception of the family.

---

* Cicero, in dealing with the origins of oratory, writes of the Roman tradition of funeral speeches as follows : " Of these some are, indeed, extant, preserved by the families of the dead as trophies of honour and for use on the death of other members of the family, whether to recall the memory of past glories of their house or to support their own claim to noble origin. Yet by these laudatory speeches our history has become quite distorted ; for much is set down in them that never occurred—false triumphs, too large a number of consulships, false relationships and transitions of patricians to plebeian status (in order to gain the right to stand for the tribuneship), in that men of humbler birth professed that their blood blended with a noble family of the same name, though in fact quite alien to them ; as if I, for example, should say that I was descended from Manius Tullius the patrician, who was Consul with Servius Sulpicius ten years after the expulsion of the kings." Cicero, *Brutus,* xv, 62. Translated by G. L. Handrickson, in the Loeb Classical Library. Further instances in Vollmar, *Laudationum funeb. Romanorum historia,* p. 467.

But the Roman family was not merely a sacramental, social, and political institution—in brief, a historical one,—but also the natural place for the development and expression of the emotional relationships of men and women. We have a touching testimony to married love and loyalty in the speech of a Roman republican, whose name has not been handed down, on his dead wife, the so-called *laudatio Turiae*. The document is of much later date than the laudatory speech on Metellus ; it takes us into the terrible period, two centuries later, of the civil wars, with proscriptions and assassinations, in which the ancient Roman Republic came to its end : the new regime introduced by Augustus was in reality a monarchy. The speaker was one of the many thousands of citizens whom the triumvirs had proscribed in 43 B.C. as supporters of the Republican party ; he owed his escape to his wife. Women's virtue, which is the theme of the speech, appears here against the background of the general corruption of morals that accompanied the dissolution of the old order. We possess the speech almost in full, in the form elaborated for permanent preservation, in a long inscription that was found on the wife's tomb.[50] This historical testimony is for us of special interest as a human document that gives an intimate and realistic picture of personal relations through life, unrhetorical and full of deep feeling.

The speaker tells the story of his wife, who shared his fate, and he uses the more intimate form of an address to the dead woman ; both alike are nameless for us. He begins with a mainly factual account, only accenting her virtues—the peaceful childhood of the well-behaved little girl with her upright parents in the country, " remote from intercourse with corrupted people " ; the vengeance for the murder of father and mother, which the girl carried through with masculine resolution ; the wife's independent pursuit of the common interests of man and wife in the difficulties over the inheritance, which are retailed at length ; the general womanly virtues which she displayed during forty-one years of marriage, modesty, deference, cheerful and kindly energy, unpretentiousness in clothes and ornaments, piety without superstition, and loyalty in all things.

But then, when the " hardest achievement " was reached, through which she saved the life of her proscribed husband, there begins a description full of passionate emotion of the way the young wife kept him informed, warned him, dissuaded him from indiscretions, gave him all her jewellery, prepared a safe refuge for him, betrayed to no one the secret of his whereabouts, and actively and courageously stood up for him.

How shall I delve now from my memory our secret intimate decisions, one by one ? . . . I must confess that the bitterest news I learned in all my life was of thee. When I had been restored full civil rights in my country through the favourable decision of the absent Cæsar Augustus, and his deputy Lepidus was personally approached by thee for my restitution, thou didst throw thyself on the earth at his feet, and wert not raised up but shamefully dragged away by his minions, thy body a mass of bruises ; and when then, with indomitable courage, thou didst remind him of Cæsar's edict, thou wert dismissed with congratulation on my restitution but amid abuse and with cruel woundings.

Finally, now that peace had returned and nothing was lacking for their happiness but the child expected (but mistakenly), comes mention of her pressure for a divorce : she herself proposed to help him choose a new wife, to whose children she would be second mother : without any change in their community of goods or their personal relationship, she would " show me the dutiful-ness of a sister and a mother-in-law ". The picture of his agita-tion at that moment leads to an outpouring of his grief, with the further personal touch that in his solitude he has no child left to mirror the dead : he can only help to perpetuate her memory through this *laudatio.*

The poetic representation of such emotions is familiar in Roman literature ; Propertius created from them a lyric that has been called " the queen of elegies ". The only autobio-graphical work in similar form to this document of which we know comes from the Renaissance—a Venetian, Nobile Giovanni Bembo,* tells his own story in the course of a biography of his wife ; the biography is put into the form of a letter about her written by him to a friend just after her death. The story is more rhetorical in style than the Latin inscriptions, but is dis-tinguished by the variety of adventures vividly narrated, with descriptions of manners ; the style is rather reminiscent of the realistic type of biographical novel that was developing at that time in Spain.

The laudatory speech at the funeral of a near relative is not the only form in which we find in Roman life something of the roots of Roman autobiography. A still broader basis of the development of autobiography comes to light in the inscriptions

---

* Autobiography of G. Bembo (1536), contributed by Th. Mommsen to the *Sitz-Ber. der Münchener Akad.* (1861), I. See below, vol. III.

that were customary on many occasions, some domestic, some political. The two categories are, indeed, intermingled, since domestic life was not yet distinguished, as a private sphere, from public life.*

Among the domestic inscriptions those on tombs predominate. Here we find a characteristic trait that appears to be peculiarly Roman, if, as is usual, the Roman type is compared with the Greek. Wilamowitz writes with regard to the Greek inscriptions : " The Hellene was infinitely concerned about the perpetuation of his name ; therefore it had to be on the tomb. But there was no description of his life in the epitaph, even when it was a poem." [51] In contrast with this was the Roman custom, as defined by an expert in Latin epigraphy who had specially in view the inscriptions in prose :

It was usual to give the dead his names (with attributes, father's names, etc.) and the offices and priesthoods held by him (in this following the inscriptions below the ancestors' busts kept in the house), in the nominative on the gravestone or monument ; to these there could be added narrative elements, written in the third person, if there seemed to be anything exceptionally noteworthy to say about the dead person . . . There is not an entire lack of epitaphs in which the dead person, like Augustus, enumerates his achievements in prose for the public ; and by no means unusual are epitaphs in which he tells in prose of his private life. [52]

Thus it is easy for us to understand why Cato the Elder, who

---

* The great wealth of material assembled in the *Corpus Inscriptionum Latinarum* published by the Berlin Academy—some 100,000 items—called for special examination. This was carried out by an American classical philologist—H. Armstrong, " Autobiographic Elements in Latin Inscriptions ", *University of Michigan Studies, Humanistic Series*, III, Part IV, pp. 215–84 (New York, 1910). He was able to collect " over 2,200 " inscriptions in which " genuine autobiographical forms ", as he calls them, or, as we might say more cautiously, " personal statements ", were found. They range from about the middle of the second century B.C. to the sixth century A.D., the great bulk being from Italy and most of those from Rome. This astonishing mass of testimonies, with a few exceptions with which we shall deal, is not part of the autobiographical production of the Romans, but belongs to a much more elementary stratum of human relations and self-revelation. It consists of inscriptions with a " personal tinge ", mainly expressions of emotions such as love, appreciation, sympathy, thanks, desires, or hopes, such as we naturally meet with in mutual intercourse in the familiar world around us. This sort of intercourse is extended here to the dead by the inscriptions, the current phrases of everyday life being perpetuated in stone ; there they appear in the formal style familiar to us in our Christian cemeteries. Similar items can be grouped together by the dozen ; there was a sort of table of expressions of feeling which was probably placed before those concerned by the masons or other artisans. The great bulk of the epitaphs of the period that concerns us at present—from the second century B.C. to the second century A.D.—comes entirely from the middle and lower classes of society in Rome and in the wide regions of the Empire, while the autobiographies came from the small upper class. Inscriptions of this latter sort are sometimes referred to or quoted by classical authors. A survey of them is given by Sir J. E. Sandys in his *Latin Epigraphy : an Introduction to the Study of Latin Inscriptions* (Cambridge, 1919).

was considered one of " the most ancient historians " of Rome, liked to " read the epitaphs " ; at least, Cicero says he did, and makes him speak on the subject with reference to his intimate knowledge of the past : " I not only know the living, but I recall their fathers and grandfathers too." [53]

In Cato's time it was customary among the ruling nobility to expand the epitaphs, which originally, even in the case of distinguished persons, had contained only the name and the father's name. Thus came the epitaph, and later the prose *elogium* ; that characteristic term, which for us has the meaning " eulogy ", is probably, in the opinion of experts like Mommsen, derived from the Greek *elegeion*. The first person seems to have made its earliest appearance in the verse form and to have been transferred thence into the prose epitaph. One of the earliest poetic epitaphs in Latin that have come down to us is that composed for himself by the poet Ennius (239–170 B.C.) :

> Aspicite, o cives, senis Enni imaginis formam :
> Hic vestrum panxit maxuma facta patrum.
> Nemo me lacrumis decoret nec funera fletu
> Faxit. Cur ? volito vivus per ora virum.*

Here it is not on the career but on the achievement that the man prides himself. Ennius's greatest work was the creation of the national Roman epic, which bore the title *Annales*. He made the history of Rome from its legendary beginnings to his own day, that is to say, after the Second Punic War or the rise of Rome to world dominion, the theme of his great epic in Latin, and chose for his poem the Homeric hexameter instead of the early Latin Saturnian metre. The creator of the Latin hexameter, Vergil's predecessor, had had a Greek education from the first ; in Calabria, where he was born, Greek was the language in common use among the educated classes. He composed the epitaph for the greatest Roman of his day, Scipio Africanus the Elder (237–183 B.C.), whose friendship he had won ; the first lines are extant [54] and may here be quoted, to give an example of the monumental style :

---

* Behold, my fellow-countrymen, old Ennius' sculptured face !
He told the glorious story of your fathers' mighty race.
Let no one honour me with tears or on my ashes weep.
For why ? from lips to lips of men I pass and living keep.

The verses have come down to us through Cicero, who quotes them as evidence of the desire for posthumous fame with which the men of the greatest genius and the loftiest spirit are filled.—" Tusculan Disputations ", Book I, xv, 34. English translation by J. E. King, in the Loeb Classical Library. In Greek poetry we find epigrams in the first person from the sixth century B.C. onward. *Cf.* Kaibel, *Epigrammata Graeca.*

Hic est ille situs cui nemo civis neque hostis
Quivit pro factis reddere opis pretium.

("Here lies the man to whom nor citizen
Nor foe could give fit praise for his great deeds.")

In the family vault of the Scipios were found the most important epitaphs of the Republican age that we have. In addition to the offices and dignities of the dead person they mention particular titles to fame such as victories and conquests of cities ; but they are in the third person and in prose, with one exception, which concerns a not particularly eminent member of the great family, Gn. Cornelius Scipio Hispanicus (c. 150 B.C.). Several slabs of this man's sarcophagus have been preserved ; on one of them is the *cursus honorum*, the sequence of his public offices, beginning with the highest he attained (not the Consulship but a Prætorship, in 139) ; on others there are two elegiac couplets in which he praises himself as a worthy heir to his ancestors :

Virtutes generis meis moribus accumulavi,
Progeniem genui, facta patris petii.
Maiorum obtenui laudem, ut sibi me esse creatum
Laetentur ; stirpem nobilitàvit honor.*

Here the use of the first person is obviously poetic licence : the subject of the verses certainly did not write them himself. The same form appears about half a century later on the tombstone of a freedwoman ; there it is used in order to let the dead woman herself give expression to the feelings her husband entertains toward her, and to put into her mouth the praise of her womanly virtues, such as chastity, modesty, decorum, and marital loyalty.†
Such use of the first person is frequently found in later epitaphs of the lower classes.[55] Their contents are reminiscent of the

* " I added to the virtues of my house by my way of life, I begat progeny, I emulated the deeds of my father. I gained praise from my ancestors so that they rejoiced in having created me ; public office ennobled my house." Bücheler, *Carmina Epigraphica*, no. 958 ; *cf.* Sandys, p. 61.

† Viva Philematium sum Aurelia nominitata,
Casta, pudens, volgi nescia, fida viro.
Vir conlibertus fuit eidem, quo careo eheu,
Re fuit ei vero plus superaque parens.
Septem me natam annorum gremio ipse recepit ;
Quadraginta annos nata, necis potior.
Ille meo officio assiduo florebat ad omnes.

(" When alive, I was called Aurelia of the Philemates, chaste, modest, knowing nothing of the crowd, faithful to my husband. My husband was set free together with me by the same man of whom, alas ! I am deprived, who indeed was more than a parent to me. He took me to his bosom when I was seven years old ; at forty I died. He flourished in every way owing to my constant service.") Bücheler, *op. cit.*, p. 257. In another example, of A.D. 29, the deceased boasts of his honesty, though poor, in life. Bücheler, no. 996 ; Armstrong, *Autobiog. Elements*, p. 239.

laudatio Turiæ. We may also recall the Roman epitaphs that are familiar in museums, where sometimes the sarcophagus is surmounted, not as usual by the portrait-bust of the deceased, but by reclining figures representing a husband and wife. In the inscriptions we may see how the actual relations between members of the family, especially between man and wife, find expression in the lower classes of society as elsewhere ; and how as a rule the forms of expression and behaviour developed in higher circles are taken over or imitated.

In the prose epitaphs we do not meet with the use of the first person until about the Augustan age,* and then only by chance in one of the numerous records of their military careers left by officers of the Roman army. A *praefectus cohortum* (commander of an infantry unit), who had served under P. Sulpicius Quirinius, the Consul in 12 B.C. and later governor of Asia Minor and Syria, gives one of these records in an inscription intended for his own grave and that of his wife, a freedwoman. Name and rank, as is usual in these *elogia*, are given at the outset, but then follow the predicates in the first person, without the introduction which we found elsewhere, " He says : I . . ." † He mentions certain notable deeds : he had carried out the census in Apamea in Syria, and had stormed one of the fortresses of a robber tribe in Lebanon, both in A.D. 6.‡ This " autobiographical " epitaph was probably written under the influence of the Monumentum Ancyranum.[56] In this type of records the use of the third person was customary. In this form Petronius introduces in his brilliant satire " Trimalchio's Feast " the inscription which the wealthy parvenu wanted to have on his tomb. The whole passage in this famous romance interests us here as a striking presentation of the social manners of the wealthy freedmen and provincials of the time of Nero (about A.D. 60) : in it the " arbiter elegantiæ " satirizes the custom of self-glorification, which had become a

---

* Apart from the salutations purporting to be addressed by the dead to the living, or to the dead by the passer-by. *Cf.* Sandys, *op. cit.,* p. 63. Armstrong, *op. cit.,* pp. 238–9.

† *Cf.,* for instance, Introduction, above, p. 47.

‡ Quintus Aemilius Quinti filius Palatina (tribu) Secundus, in castris divi Augusti sub Publio Sulpicio Quirinio legato Augusti Caesaris Syriae honoribus decoratus, praefectus cohortis secundae classicae ; idem iussu Quirini censum egi Apameae civitatis milium hominum civium CXVII ; idem missu Quirini adversus Ituraeos in Libano Monte castellum eorum cepi et ante militem praefectus fabrum, delatus a duobus consulibus ad aerarium et in colonia quaestor, aedilis iterum, duumvir iterum, pontifex.

Ibi positi sunt Q. Aemilius Q. f. Pal. tribu secundus filius et Aemilia Chia liberta . . . *Cf. Corpus Inscr. Lat.,* III, Supplement 6687 (Berytus). Dessau, *Inscr. selectae,* no. 2683. Armstrong, *op. cit.,* p. 247.

vulgarity. Trimalchio, the giver of the banquet, addresses one of his friends, a monumental mason : [57]

Now tell me, my dear friend : you will erect a monument as I have directed ? I beg you earnestly to put up round the feet of my statue my little dog, and some wreaths, and bottles of perfume, and all the fights of Peraites,* so that your kindness may bring me a life after death ; and I want the monument to have a frontage of one hundred feet and to be two hundred feet in depth. For I should like to have all kinds of fruit growing round my ashes, and plenty of vines. It is quite wrong for a man to decorate his house while he is alive and not to trouble about the house where he must make a longer stay . . . I beg you to put ships in full sail on the monument, and me sitting in official robes on my official seat, wearing five gold rings and distributing gold coins publicly out of a bag . . . I should like a dining-room table put in too, if you can arrange it ; and let me have the whole people there enjoying themselves. On my right hand put a statue of dear Fortunata,† holding a dove, and let her be leading a little dog with a waistband on ; and my dear little boy . . . And a sundial in the middle, so that anyone who looks at the time will read my name whether he likes it or not. And again, please think carefully whether this inscription seems to you quite appropriate :

HERE LIETH CAIUS POMPEIUS TRIMALCHIO, FREEDMAN OF MÆCENAS. THE DEGREE OF PRIEST OF AUGUSTUS WAS CONFERRED UPON HIM IN HIS ABSENCE. HE MIGHT HAVE BEEN ATTENDANT ON ANY MAGISTRATE IN ROME, BUT REFUSED IT. GODFEARING, GALLANT, CONSTANT, HE STARTED WITH VERY LITTLE AND LEFT THIRTY MILLIONS. HE NEVER LISTENED TO
A PHILOSOPHER
FARE THEE WELL, TRIMALCHIO, AND THOU, TOO, PASSER-BY

Of the other groups of inscriptions, we are concerned with those in honour of men of mark, whether placed on publicly erected portrait-statues or on public works. The honorary inscriptions in Latin are scarcely distinguishable from Greek ones. We learn, indeed, expressly from a scholar of the early imperial period,[58] who had before him the statues in the Forum of Augustus, that this custom came from Athens, and spread from there " throughout the world ", a sign, as he says, of the *humanissima ambitio*, the most human of ambitions, since the honours and dignities of memorable men should not be simply recorded in their tombs but " placed on the pedestal of their statues ". Livy tells us of a golden portrait-statue, the first of its sort seen in Rome that represented not a deity but a man ; it represented Manius Acilius Glabrio, the victor over Antiochus,

* A celebrated gladiator of the period.
† His wife, a woman of the humblest origin.

king of Syria (192 B.C.), and was erected by his son in a temple which, in fulfilment of a vow of his father's, he dedicated to Pietas (in 181).[59] The satisfaction of family pride by means of historical monuments of this sort accorded, it is true, with an older Roman tradition. We hear, once more from Pliny, that Appius Claudius (about 300 B.C.), a man of the high nobility, who built the famous road and aqueduct named after him, was the first to place the images of his ancestors in the form of portrait-medallions, with the record of their public offices, in a temple which he had vowed to erect.[60] The temples which generals vowed in time of danger to build, and afterwards built, partly at their own and partly at the public expense, served, as a modern historian puts it, "not a religious purpose but as a standing proof of the victories they declared that they had gained". He sums up : [61]

To see the name of one's family commemorated on public buildings, in streets, aqueducts, halls, basilicas, temples, and theatres, was the great desire of every man who could hope to attain to the high offices of the state. Whoever failed in this object sought at least to erect a statue or a portrait somewhere in honour of an ancestor, if not of himself. The Roman Forum and the places round the temples gradually became crowded with monuments of this sort, so that the censors were repeatedly obliged to interfere and to remove all monuments erected without public authority.

An example of this self-glorification of republican dignitaries is given by a monument which Tiberius Gracchus, the father of the two famous reformers, erected to himself in a temple. He had moved with a strong consular army against a revolt that had broken out in Sardinia in 179, and in two years' warfare he had overcome it. He caused a picture to be painted representing his victories, and placed it in the temple of Mater Matuta, with an inscription under it which Livy has recorded : [62]

Under the command and auspices of Tiberius Sempronius Gracchus the army of the Roman people conquered Sardinia. In this province more than eighty thousand of the enemy were slain or captured. Having administered the State most happily, set free the allies, and restored the revenues, he brought the army home, safe and secure and enriched with booty : for the second time he entered the city of Rome in triumph. In commemoration of this event he set up this tablet (i.e. the picture of Sardinia) to Jupiter.

In this group of inscriptions the use of the third person was traditional. But it happened occasionally that a particularly vainglorious aristocrat chose the first person for the speech when he erected a memorial to himself.   The only example now existing is a milestone of the time of the Gracchi.   It is four feet high and two wide, and was found near a village in Lucania, on the road from Regium to Capua.[63]   The builder of the road, a certain P. Popillius Laenas, who had also laid out the village, set up the stone as a record of these works (probably about 132 B.C.),[64] but the inscription does not give his name, though it is put into the first person, " in an entirely unprecedented way for Rome and Italy ", as one of the best experts remarks.[65]   It begins : " I built the road," and ends :   " I erected the Forum here and the public buildings."   In between are first, taking up half of the inscription, the details for which the milestone was set up, giving the distances of the principal places along the road, and then a bit of reporting of activities :   " During my prætorship in Sicily I caught fugitive slaves from Italy and returned 917 of them.   And I was also the first to ensure that shepherds gave place to farmers on the State lands." *

The first claim to distinction refers to the suppression of unrest that preceded the First Servile War in Sicily (135 B.C.) ; the other probably to the land law enacted by Tiberius Gracchus in 133, which combated the economic crisis by the division of latifundia into peasant farms.   Popillius, who was one of the most bitter opponents of the Gracchi, claims credit, in the same breath in which he represents himself as having suppressed the rising of the slaves, for making a beginning with the land reform that was to make an end of a pernicious servile economic system. Thus we see here how the politician's need for placing on record his attitude in the party conflicts of the time could ultimately break through the limitations set to this sort of inscription by the purpose they were to serve and by the place at which they were set up.   Wretched as is its style, this document is nevertheless on the road from the routine of practical life to autobiography, though it may not itself be properly regarded as an autobiographical production.†

If we pursue this path further we are led out of the realm of

---

* Viam feci ab Regio ad Capuam, et in ea via pontes omnes, miliarios tabeliariosque posui. Hinc sunt Nonceriam milia LI, Capuam XXCIIII . . . summa ab Capua Regium milia CCCXXI.   Et idem praetor in Sicilia fugitivos Italicorum conquaesivi reddidique homines DCCCCXVII. Idemque primus feci ut de agro publico aratoribus cederent pastores.   Forum aedesque publicas hic feci.

† Armstrong, *Autobiog. Elements*, p. 262, declares the milestone of Popillius to be " our earliest prose autobiography ", emphasizing that " here on enduring stone is a true autobiography which antedates by full twenty years any literary autobiography recorded."   On the strength of this he elaborates the theory that " the Romans created autobiography ". *Ibid.*, p. 215.

inscriptions proper and into that of literature. As to this we may say in general that in Roman literature history preceded autobiography. It is true that the history was of the sort that itself proceeded from the traditions of the ruling families, and drew from them not only material but standpoints for the judgment of men and events.

The distinguished families took pride in the achievements of their members ; on the other hand, they felt themselves to be representatives of the Roman State. In the halls of the aristocratic houses, in which the images of the household gods, the hearth with the family fire, and, kept in cupboards, the waxen masks of famous ancestors were preserved, room had from of old been provided for the preservation of family records. These included not only purely private documents like the family tree and the equally important account books, but also public official documents : the documents compiled by members of the family during their official career remained in their possession and were preserved as family property in respectful memory of them.[66] Consequently the normal course of development, which leads first to the compilation of family chronicles and then in it or through it to autobiography, is here modified in a characteristic way.

It is generally considered [67] that chronicles of the great Roman families existed from the early days of the Republic ; this view is defended on the strength of a remark of Livy, who speaks, with reference to the sources for the earliest history of Rome, of *privatis publicisque monumentis*, which were lost in the burning of Rome. But the traditional interpretation of that passage is scarcely defensible.* Livy himself, writing in the Augustan age, assumes a distinction between " public " and " private " (literally " apart ", i.e. from the State) that can scarcely have existed in

---

* The current view is opposed by von Premerstein (article " Commentarii " in Pauly-Wissowa, *Real-Encyclopädie der Classischen Altertumswissenschaft*, vol. 4, col. 756): " The *privata monumenta* (Livy, VI, 1, 2) traditionally regarded as family chronicles, where they are not *laudationes* or late antiquarian compilations, are probably nothing more than the official records of the former magistrates, preserved in the *tablina* of their families in memory of them and as practical lessons for their descendants." A work of this sort was compiled, for instance, by Cicero's friend Atticus, at the suggestion of M. Brutus, in order to prove by means of a very questionable family tree that the Junii, from whom Brutus was descended, were an old patrician family. *Cf.* Nepos, *Atticus*, 18, 3 : " Juniam familiam a stirpe ad hanc aetatem enumeravit, notans quis a quo ortus quos honores quibusque temporibus cepisset . . . Nihil potest esse dulcius iis qui aliquam cupiditatem habent notitiae clarorum virorum " (" He gave a list of the family of the Junii from its origin to the present time, noting who was born of whom and what honours he gained and at what times . . . Nothing can be more delightful to those who have any itch to possess the celebrity of distinguished men ").

the early days. The historical literature of the Romans, though based on the tradition of the patrician families, was concerned not with the history of those families but with that of the Roman State. This is true of the work of the earliest prose writer of Roman history, Q. Fabius Maximus (born 254 B.C.), who belonged to one of the most eminent families. He made use of his record of the national history in order to show the celebrity of his own family ; but this celebrity was based especially on the fact that in one of the critical wars for the dominance of Rome over Italy all the males of the *gens Fabia* died fighting for their country, with the exception of a boy who had been left in Rome.

The type of historiography introduced by Fabius Pictor into Roman literature—or, rather, into Hellenistic-Roman, for Fabius, Roman senator though he was, wrote in Greek, probably because he wrote for the educated world—is thus described in one of the great modern histories of Rome published in the nineteenth century :

> The greatness of the Roman aristocracy, which characterizes the whole internal and foreign policy of the republic, has impressed its peculiar stamp on the national annals. As the history of despotic countries is to a great extent the personal narrative of the doings of the successive despots, so the history of Rome is the sum total and the working up into one connected story of chronicles* which recorded the exploits of the great families.[68]

On the other hand, this historical literature, which is entirely lost to us, seems to have been allied to the class of political memoirs ; for a large part of the works was concerned with contemporary events, of which the writer had knowledge not only as spectator but as participant. This applies to Fabius and to Cato the Elder (born about 234 B.C.), who is usually regarded as the real father of Roman history. Cato carried his work, which he called *Origines*, from the legendary founding of the city to 150 B.C., that is to say the year before his long life ended. Cicero, who made him one of the principal characters in one of his dialogues, makes him speak there of his historical labours ; he tells, as we have already mentioned, of his interest in the epitaphs of men's forefathers, and adds : " I am collecting all the records of our ancient history, and at present am revising all the speeches made by me in all the notable causes which I championed." [69] This has reference to his political orations,

* Instead of " chronicles " we should prefer " traditions ".

which, as we saw,* he inserted into his Annals of Rome ; they formed so important and so large a part of the Annals that they were later brought together in a separate work. Thus official activities, as well as the pride of the aristocratic families in their achievements for the State, contributed to the growth of historical literature.

In the literature of modern times, where we have a wealth of genuine family chronicles, we can pursue the natural course of their growth out of family traditions, to which this or the other head of the family has added the story of his own life for his descendants.   In this process there comes into existence a peculiar sort of autobiography.   It makes its appearance not only in the mediæval cities but also in the English aristocracy, with typical traits, and the Florentines in developing it were fully conscious of a link in it with their Roman forefathers.†   Concrete rules based on experience of life, example and warning, presentation of parents and forefathers and relatives in the form, among others, of character-studies ; a revelling in all the detail of everyday life in a chronicle-like record or with a natural art of story-telling—all these things are characteristic of it.

It is difficult to judge of the style of the older Roman auto-biographies, as not one is extant ; and it must remain uncertain how far their reflection in Cicero and Tacitus does them more than justice.   But one thing is clear, that the region in which they were elaborated, in the shadow of those domestic traditions, was not the " private " family life, in which a man's experiences are told for their own sake, and not a purely Roman practice of public self-portrayal such as may be found in the inscriptions, but the Hellenistic civilized world with its political memoirs and its conception of personality and forms of presentation of it.‡

---

* See above, p. 214.

† See below, vol. III.   A general indication of the analogy between the Florentine chronicles and the Greek tradition of the Roman noble families is given by Abbate Salvini in his edition of Pitti's Chronicle (1720), pref., pp. xii *sqq.* : " Cicero non solo lodò ma dette per precetto il leggere i libri domestici e familiari de' lor vecchi spezialmente " (" Cicero not only praised the domestic and family books of the ancients, but advocated the special reading of them ").

‡ There is a similar development, influenced by Greek literature, by the Greek forms of the *enkomion* or of biography (Leo, *op. cit.*, pp. 225 *sqq.*), in the literary treatment of an individual life in works written in honour of the recently deceased, and in one case (the *Atticus* of Cornelius Nepos) of the still living—in contrast with the national Roman custom of the laudatory speech at a funeral ; though the regular connexion continued between portrayer and portrayed, that of close relationship or of indebtedness, the son writing the life of his father, the friend that of his friend, a follower and comrade that of the party leader, a client that of his benefactor. Examples in C. Wachsmuth, *Einl. in d. alte Geschichte*, p. 207.   Leo, p. 226.   H. Peter, *Die gesch. Literatur der Kaiserzeit* I, pp. 184–5.

III.   ROMAN STATESMEN BEFORE AUGUSTUS

It is usual to dismiss the autobiographies of Roman statesmen of the old aristocratic Republic, together with those of the imperial age, as propaganda literature, and to attribute their origin to political pamphleteering, which had already been introduced into the literature of the Romans.[70] This view is in conflict with the picture of the *ethos* of those first Latin autobiographies which we get from the statements of Cicero and Tacitus concerning them, but it may complement that picture, the background of which we have tried to describe.

The appearance in Rome of what may fairly be called political pamphlets is bound up with a great name. Scipio Africanus the elder (237–183), the conqueror of Hannibal, published a pamphlet about 190 B.C., in which, probably among other things, he dealt with his military operations in Spain against the Carthaginians, by means of which, when he was scarcely twenty-seven years old, he had given the war a fresh turn and had rescued Rome from an apparently desperate situation (210 B.C.). The document was written in Greek, as was the history of Rome compiled at the time by Fabius Pictor, and was in the form of a letter addressed to the king of Macedonia, a ruler whose influential position we noted when we were dealing with the autobiography of Aratus of Sicyon. We know of this missive of Scipio's through Polybius (X, 9, 3), who was familiar with the traditions of Scipio's family. He refers to the document because in it Scipio laid emphasis on the careful planning of the operations which had ended in his victory, a point which Polybius defends against other historians, who, he says, " attribute his success not to the man and his foresight, but to the gods and to chance, or good luck (Tyche) ". The point is of special interest for us in view of Sulla's autobiography, in which we find the very conception of success through good fortune which Polybius rejected. Among Scipio's soldiers the belief was current that he was a special favourite of the gods, and the general opinion is that he shared this belief, or at all events promoted it. In the " letter " in question he seems to be defending himself from the suspicion of doing so. It is also possible, however, that the attacks to which he was subjected in his old age induced him to write a sort of apologia. He had not been able to maintain permanently the dominant, indeed royal, position he had won as leader of the senate, *princeps senatus* ; after he had removed the danger threatening from Hannibal, his political opponents, who stood for the " freedom " of the Republic—that is to say, for equality among all the noble houses—began an attack against the all too powerful family of the Scipiones. A public trial for bribery was started first against his brother and then against Scipio himself. Scipio, embittered, withdrew to his country seat in his native Campania, where he hoped to be buried, far from Rome—as is expressed by the epitaph attributed to him : " *Ingrata patria. Ne ossa quidem habeas* " (" Ungrateful mother-country. May you not have even my bones ").

The literary form of the missive (which is one of the forms developed in Hellenism) was also used at this period for auto-biographical purposes by another member of the family of the Scipiones ; and again the letter was addressed to a foreign ruler. Scipio Nasica, who distinguished himself under Aemilius Paulus in Rome's critical struggle against Macedonia in 168 B.C., wrote on these exploits of his, as we learn from a chance reference in Plutarch,[71] in " a short letter which he wrote to one of the kings " (probably Masinissa of Numidia).

Of more importance is a note that we have of a political pamphlet published in letter form by Gaius Gracchus (153–121 B.C.), the younger of the two famous brothers, themselves aristo-crats and men of birth and culture, who worked for social reform and whose failure resulted in the downfall of the Roman Republic. In this " letter ", which he addressed to one of his Roman friends (M. Pomponius), Gaius spoke of the influences which had led his brother to their bold enterprise, and selected as the decisive influence an experience which Tiberius Gracchus (163–133) had had in his twenty-sixth year, when in his first public office, as quæstor, he marched through upper Italy to Spain in the Numan-tine war (137 B.C.). Plutarch quotes the following passage from the document because it is in opposition to the view he himself advanced, that simple ambition was the motive for Tiberius' " bold political measure " : [72]

> But his brother Gaius, in a certain booklet, has written that Tiberius was passing through Tuscany on his way to Numantia, and observed the dearth of inhabitants in the country ; he observed also that those who tilled its soil or tended its flocks were imported barbarian slaves ; he then first conceived the public policy which was the cause of countless ills to the two brothers.

What Plutarch regarded as the cause of ills to the Gracchi was in their view the recognition of the cause of the sufferings of their country. The " booklet " in which Gaius expressed this view was apparently of biographical character ; in it he also spoke of their father, the famous Consul whose inscription recording his victory we have mentioned, and of their mother Cornelia, daughter of Scipio Africanus.[73]

With this series of political missives may be associated the autobiographies, so far as they, too, directly pursued a practical aim. This they mainly did, in the opinion of the eminent scholar who collected the fragments and dealt with this *genre* as a branch of the historical literature of the Romans. He writes : " The Romans knew nothing of the pleasure of giving an honest and unvarnished account of one's own experiences and so providing enjoyment for the reader ; their autobiographies, so far as can be judged from the scanty vestiges of them, always pursued a political aim : they set out to create opinion in their favour, and in favour of their memory." [74] The question remains, however, how it was that this political aim was pursued not simply by means of pamphlets or historical accounts of contemporary affairs, but by means of autobiographies. This may have been mainly due to a convention of personal self-expression that had struck root in the political life of the Roman Republic. It was a habit connected not only with the official conduct of affairs but with the aristocratic craving for what might be called earthly immortality, that is to say, enshrinement in historical archives. A defensive attitude or, in general, the treatment of autobiography as a task embarked upon not for its own sake but for other purposes, such as the implanting of a definite conception of historic events in the minds of contemporaries or of the next generation, is characteristic of the class of political memoirs in general as they develop in revolutionary times and during civil struggles. Such practical aims, or " political " aims in the widest sense of the word, were certainly present when a Roman senator, in his old age, at the end of his military and political career, took up the pen, no longer as a weapon in the actual party struggle, but in order to write his life. The autobiographers attained their purpose : their account dominated the historical tradition concerning the time of Marius and Sulla, except for the independent historian Sallust.[75]

Nearest to the political brochures seems to come the work of Lutatius Catulus " on his consulate and his deeds ", which preceded the appearance of the full autobiographies. His purpose was to place on record his share in the victory over the

Cimbri at Vercellæ, in opposition to Marius, who was claiming the whole credit for the victory for himself alone. It was a short work, comprising only one " book ", while the autobiography of Scaurus, with which Cicero bracketed it, contained three books and that of Rutilius at least five. In the case of Scaurus, however, the customary official procedure comes also into consideration. It was customary in the Roman Republic, and remained so down to the time of the emperor Augustus, for army commanders and governors to send to the senate a written report of their activities. Such reports could be used by their writers to present their deeds to the general public in case of need. Thus, for instance, Cæsar's reports to the senate were the basis of his " Commentaries " on the Gallic war.

The element of apologia is plain in Scaurus (162–89 B.C.). He is one of the most prominent figures of the time of the restoration of the senate's dominance after the destruction of the Gracchi and before the rise of Sulla. As leader of the reactionary pro-senate party he played an important part, but a part so obscure that diametrically opposite judgments of his character have come down to us. Cicero describes him as a Roman of the old type, a wise and upright man of great dignity and authority, and praises above all his trustworthiness (*fides*), a quality which, as Cicero emphasizes, " holds the secret of success." [76] Sallust, on the other hand, declares that Scaurus was a clever intriguer, the organizer of the corruption that was spreading in the ruling class of the imperial Republic. Scaurus, he says, " craftily concealed his vices "—ambition, acquisitiveness, and lust for power.* These vices, however, were typical, in our view, of the Roman lords of the world. This judgment certainly has reference not only to Scaurus' conduct in political life but also to the autobiography in which he wrote it. Scaurus was, indeed, repeatedly prosecuted by his opponents for corrupt practices in home and foreign policy ; he was suspected of allowing King Jugurtha to bribe him. In his old age he found himself exposed to a still worse charge, when the so-called Social War, that is to say, the rising of the Italian allies, broke out (90 B.C.) ; he was held responsible for the short-sighted policy that had withheld from the allies the often promised right of Roman citizenship. To that extent Scaurus' autobiography may be regarded as a symptom of individualism in the bad sense of the word, the

---

* Sallust, *Bellum Iugurthinum*, xv, 3 : " Homo nobilis, impiger, factiosus, avidus potentiae, honoris, divitiarum, ceterum vitia sua callide occultans."

neglect of the common good for the sake of personal and party interests. On the other hand, Cicero's judgment set the work on a par with Xenophon's *Cyropædia*, and this judgment, however exaggerated it may seem, cannot have been arrived at without some ground. Scaurus had behind him a political career of which he could be proud. Born of an old but impoverished and no longer influential family, he rose through his own merit to the highest office and to supreme prestige ; after his consulate (115 B.C.) he held for twenty-five years the position of *princeps senatus*, leader of the senate. Thus, as one of the first if not actually the first of the Latin autobiographers, he was able to convey an exceptional wealth of political experience.

The motive of self-defence is also clear in Rutilius Rufus (158–77), but no longer in the purely political field. He too, as an old man, ten years after his consulate, was prosecuted—for extortion ; he was alleged to have been guilty of this as adminis-trator of Asia Minor, the wealthiest Roman province ; he was sentenced to exile in addition to a heavy fine (92 B.C.). But this judgment was a public scandal. Rutilius was a victim of the capitalists of the knightly order (*equites*) who since the revolution of the Gracchi had dominated the courts ; they had charged him with extortion because he had tried to make an end of their own system of extortion and usury. There is a rare una-nimity among the ancient historians as to his high moral and intellectual quality. Cicero says that by that trial of an innocent man the State was shaken to its foundations (*convulsam penitus rem publicam*). He says that Rutilius refused the support of the most famous advocates and conducted his own defence ; thus he preserved the self-reliance characteristic of the Stoic school.*
His speech in his defence may have been the point of departure of his autobiography. Roman critics may have compared it with the Apology of Socrates, but we think rather of that of Isocrates, which was a true autobiography, though cast in the form of a speech in court. What among the Greeks had been an artistic form seems here in Rome to have been a bitter reality. As an exile, Rutilius went to Asia Minor, the very province which according to the judgment of the court he was supposed to have exploited, whereas he was received there with every honour. He had still fifteen years to live. He regarded his fate objectively, as a philosopher. This was appreciated by Seneca,

---

* Cicero, *Brutus*, xxx, 114 *sqq.* : " Itaque illa quae propria est huius disciplinae philosophorum de se ipsorum opinio firma in hoc viro et stabilis inventa est."

who in one of his epistles, the subject of which is the contempt of
death, adduced him with other historical personalities, especially
Socrates, as an example of high achievement or high endeavour : [77]
"Sentence of conviction was borne by Rutilius as if the injustice
of the decision were the only thing that annoyed him. Exile he
endured even with gladness ; for he refused to return when Sulla
summoned him—and nobody in those days said 'No' to Sulla."

There is express testimony to the defensive purpose of the autobiography of Sulla (138–78). These *hypomnemata* were a real
autobiography, for Sulla gave in them the history not of his
time but of his own career. Plutarch speaks of their apologetic
tendency in his biography of the dictator, with reference to the
Mithridatic War (87–80 B.C.), in which Sulla fell under suspicion
of playing a double game because, after his overwhelming victory
over the armies of the hereditary enemy, he did not impose
excessively harsh conditions of peace ; he even treated the
negotiators with friendliness. "On this point", remarks Plutarch,
"he defends himself in his Commentaries." [78] He defended himself by abusing with apparently ruthless candour the Cappadocian
general who was the negotiator.* It was a small matter in comparison with the fearful atrocities he had on his conscience and
may have wanted to justify—assuming that we may attribute
to him such a thing as a conscience. He occupied himself with
his autobiography after resigning the dictatorship, which was
in his hands for only three years (82–79), although he had been

---

* This may be seen from Plutarch's account of the negotiations that led up
to the conclusion of peace with Mithridates. After the great victories he had won
at Chæronea (86) and Orchomenus (85), Sulla wanted to bring the war to an end,
in order to have a free hand for the overthrowing of his opponents in Italy, the
revolutionary Marian party, which had declared him to be an enemy of the people.
Mithridates sought to take advantage of this situation. His negotiator was a general
named Archelaus. Sulla invited him to come to see him. Plutarch describes the
interview, obviously following Sulla's account : "They had a meeting on the sea
coast near Delium, where the temple of Apollo is. Archelaus began the conference
by urging Sulla to abandon Asia and Pontus and sail for the war in Rome, on
condition of receiving money, triremes, and as large a force as he wished, from the
king. Sulla rejoined by bidding him take no further thought for Mithridates, but
assume the crown himself in his stead, becoming an ally of the Romans, and sur-
rendering to them his ships. And when Archelaus expressed his abhorrence of
such treason, Sulla said : ' So then, thou, Archelaus, who art a Cappadocian, and
a slave of a barbarian king, or, if thou wilt, his friend, wilt not consent to a disgraceful
deed for such great rewards : but to me, who am a Roman commander and am
Sulla, thou darest to propose treachery ? As if thou wert not that Archelaus who
fled from Chæronea with but a few survivors out of 120,000 men, and who lay
hidden for two days in the marshes of Orchomenus, and who left Bœotia impassable
for the multitude of dead bodies ! ' Upon this, Archelaus changed his tone, and
as a humble subject besought him to desist from the war and be reconciled with
Mithridates. Sulla granted the request." Plutarch, *Sulla*, xxii, 3–5. Translated
by B. Perrin in the Loeb Classical Library.

made dictator for an indefinite period—a voluntary renunciation of power that is as mysterious as the man himself. He was then sixty years of age. On his retirement from official political life he is said to have led a merry existence in his villa in Campania, in anything but distinguished society, but also spending his leisure on so un-Roman a knightly sport as hunting. Among his other occupations was the compilation of his autobiography, in which he was helped by an educated Greek freedman. He was writing this only two days before his death, which came suddenly, probably through hæmorrhage following a fit of rage.

For us Sulla's name is associated with the savage proscription with which he annihilated his political opponents. He certainly made no secret in his autobiography of the terror with which he surrounded himself. How he wished to be remembered may be seen from the epitaph which he is supposed to have written for himself : its substance, according to Plutarch, was that " no friend ever surpassed him in kindness, and no enemy in mischief ".* This is the primitive political standpoint which Plato opposed, when in discussing in the *Republic* the nature of justice he started with the conventional formula that justice consists in " doing good to friends and evil to enemies ".[79]

The purpose of the Roman statesmen in their political autobiographies was to determine the picture of them left in the nation's memory ; but in so far as they were under Hellenistic influence this purpose came into conflict (if the phrase is not too strong) with the Greek sense of propriety which required that a man of eminence should not sing his own praises. A conventional solution of this difficulty was found in the æsthetic point of view, drawn from Greek rhetoric, with regard to political literature. From this point of view the autobiographer was not regarded as the writer of a literary work. This conception found expression, both in the earliest Latin autobiographies, already mentioned, and in the later ones, in the rule that they were presented, like the Hellenistic *hypomnemata*, as non-literary. Sometimes they were " sent " (that is to say, dedicated for the purpose of being put into literary shape) direct, as material, to an epic poet or a historian.† But a general conclusion as to the

* Plutarch, *Sulla*, xxxviii, 4.

† Lutatius Catulus " sent " his book to a poet belonging to his circle, A. Furius, probably for working up in Latin verse. *Cf.* R. Büttner, *Porcius Licinius u. d. lit. Kreis um Q.Lutatius Catulus*, pp. 176 *sqq.* H. Peter, " Der Brief in der röm. Literatur," *Abh. der philo.-hist. Klasse der sächs. Ges. der Wiss.*, XX, 3, p. 243.

Sulla dedicated his Commentaries to his friend Lucullus (114–57 B.C.), a man whose name became world-famous as a symbol of great wealth and its refined

character of the Latin political autobiographies cannot be based
on this ; for the unliterary quality is obviously make-believe in
Cicero, who himself says of the *hypomnema*, written in Greek,
on his consulate that this book " had exhausted the scent-jar of
Isocrates, and all the rouge-pots of his pupils, and some of
Aristotle's colours too ", and this with entire success : " I sent a
memoir to Posidonius too, asking him to write something more
elaborate on the same subject ; but he tells me that, far from
being inspired to write by the perusal of it, he was decidedly
put off.   In fact, I have confounded the whole Greek nation "
(" *Quid quaeris ? conturbavi Graecam nationem* ").[80]

And then, Cæsar's *Commentarii* ! These, too, are offered as
mere materials, or, rather, sources for history, and indeed they
dispense with any claim to literary quality through the deliberate
avoidance of the ornaments of oratory ; yet they were masterpieces of Latin literature, and were generally recognized as such,
by friend and foe alike, immediately on their appearance.   This
we learn from a witness in Cæsar's camp, A. Hirtius, one of his
lieutenants-general and confidants, who after that great man's
assassination took upon himself the heavy task of adding a supplement to the Commentaries on the Gallic War.   He makes this
comment of his own :

> It is universally agreed that there is nothing that was finished by
> others, however elaborately, that is not surpassed by the refinement
> of these Commentaries.   They have been published so that historians
> may not lack knowledge of those great achievements ; and so emphatic
> is the unanimous verdict of approval that it appears that historians
> have been robbed of an opportunity rather than enriched with one.*

Cicero, the most authoritative of judges in matters of Latin
prose style, bears witness to the same effect.   In the history of
Roman eloquence which he published two years before Cæsar's

---

* *De Bello Gallico*, VIII, Praefatio A. Hirtii : " Constat inter omnes nihil tam
operose ab aliis esse perfectum, quod non horum elegantia commentariorum super-
etur : qui sunt editi, ne scientia tantarum rerum scriptoribus deesset, adeoque
probantur omnium iudicio, ut praerepta non praebita facultas scriptoribus videatur."

enjoyment, but who also had other qualities.   He was a politician distinguished
by his uprightness, and a successful general, a member of one of the old noble
families, and a representative of Hellenistic culture ; his house was a meeting-place
of Greek men of letters, and he himself had written in Greek a work on his own
times, a history of the war with Marius.   Plutarch, who in his biography of Sulla
(vi, 6) mentions the dedication of Sulla's *hypomnemata* to Lucullus, writes in his
biography of Lucullus (i, 3) : " He was a fluent speaker in both Latin and Greek,
so that Sulla, in recording his own deeds, addressed the record to him as a man
who would be better able to arrange his narrative and put it in order."
On the spread of this device as fiction, see H. Peter, *Die geschichtl. Lit.*, I, 201-2,

assassination he wrote an estimate of Cæsar—who then was at the peak of power—as speaker and writer, and incidentally he gave this judgment on the *Commentarii* : [81]

Admirable indeed ! They are naked in their simplicity, straight-forward yet charming ; stripped of all rhetorical adornment as of a garment. But while his aim was to furnish others with material for writing history, he haply gratified the inept, who may wish to apply their curling-irons to his narrative ; but men of sound judgment he has deterred from touching the subject, since in history there is nothing more pleasing than brevity, pure and lucid.

The æsthetic point of view in regard to the writing of history, which as a rule belittled autobiographical writing by handing it over to the rhetoricians, had the result in this case of veiling the political character, though it was an essential element, of these war-memoirs of the great statesman's. Cæsar (102–44 B.C.) pub-lished the Commentaries on the Gallic War, which he had dictated in camp during the military operations, at a critical moment (51 B.C.), when the long war of conquest (since 58 B.C.) was over, or nearing its end, and the great struggle in home politics, the struggle with Pompey for dominance in Rome, was impending. His purpose was to influence public opinion in his favour ; he had to defend himself against the suspicion of lust for conquest and greed for power. But once more, although the work belongs to that extent to the literature of political pamphleteering, or, if the term is preferred, offers an example of the conduct of political affairs (in its compilation Cæsar made use of his annual reports to the senate), nevertheless, inde-pendently of the time and place and purpose of its origin, it gives us a vivid impression of the personality of this unique man. The simplicity and directness, clarity and brevity of his diction, which Cicero attributes to the historian's art, seem to us to reflect corresponding qualities in this statesman and army com-mander, with his sureness of aim in all he did.

Cæsar's *Commentarii* are not an autobiography. They deal with only a bare nine years of his life, seven of them being covered by the Gallic War and the remainder by the civil war, or, more precisely, its first period (49–48 B.C.), down to the battle of Pharsalus and the death of Pompey. The gap between the two wars was later filled by Hirtius, who added a " book " to the seven on the Gallic War. He extended the work on the civil war " as far ", as he says, " as the conclusion, not indeed of civil strife, of which we see no end, but of Cæsar's life ".[82] This biographical point of view is an additional element introduced into the work, which is a factual military report, beginning : " Gaul as a whole is divided into three parts." But Cæsar provided more in his Commentaries than an ordinary auto-biographical work. They offer an example of self-revelation of the man of action that could serve as a pattern for the auto-biographies of historians and politicians of later ages, who in their self-portrayal sought to adopt an elevated style in the ancient classical tradition. The characteristic of this attitude is objec-tivity in regarding the self. Cæsar speaks of himself in a detached way in the third person, but using his own name, which he likes to give repeatedly—for instance, " Cæsar, having antici-pated that this would be the natural course of events, halted for two days at . . ." He does not absolutely avoid the use of the first person, but, as a Roman, speaks of his soldiers as " our men ", *nostri*, and as author uses the *pluralis majestatis*, the " royal We ", in subsidiary phrases such as " We have shown that . . ." Thus the person regarded and the person regarding are separated, while for us the identity of the two is the essential mark of auto-biography. But this device as Cæsar uses it is in no way artificial but seems the natural way of expressing himself, for it is based on a sound purpose, applicable alike to the historian and to the statesman--to stick to the facts and to let them speak. It is the facts and not he himself that proclaim his fame. He will have nothing to do with rhetoric, and calls a spade a spade, without frills of any sort ; and similarly he refrains from any expression of feeling. This objectivity includes precision of mili-tary detail, but it also includes human and moral qualities : instead of attributing every success to himself in the style of political memoirs, Cæsar brought into prominence the services rendered by his helpers, and his memoirs are free from the abuse of his enemies which is an outstanding feature of the auto-biography of Sulla, his predecessor in the possession of dictatorial power, and with which we meet also in the autobiography of his successor Augustus Cæsar.

The cold, clear, even artistic atmosphere of understanding that we breathe in Cæsar's work is of a Greek rather than a Roman nature. He adopted [83] the characteristic form of the factual and unrhetorical report of events introduced into Hel-lenistic literature by the practice of the General Staff of Alexander the Great.* But he adapted it to his political purposes, or,

* See above, p. 203.

rather, his own political nature, for to him all that he did and observed had a political meaning. Thus the purposefulness of his narrative did not impair its objectivity. Moreover, this attitude corresponded to the individual trend of his mind ; for he was capable of looking at things with the artist's eye, even if they were the results of his own action. With effortless skill and unfailing sureness of touch he sketched historical events and explained his plans. Hirtius reveals this to us—a fact that only those in close touch with Cæsar could know, and which filled them with astonishment : " The world knows how well, nay, how faultlessly, but we know also how easily and quickly he composed his Commentaries." [84] The unprejudiced reader is carried on by the powerful flow of the narrative ; he does not notice the purpose at the back of it. One single voice from the camp of the opponents of the policy of Julius Cæsar and the emperor Augustus warns us to be on our guard : Asinius Pollio (75 B.C.–A.D. 4) thought, as Suetonius tell us, that Cæsar's *Commentarii* " were put together somewhat carelessly and without strict regard for truth ; since in many cases Cæsar was too ready both to believe the accounts which others gave of their actions and to give a perverted account of his own, either designedly or perhaps from forgetfulness ".* Modern historians, in possession of all the resources of historical criticism, nevertheless place faith in his credibility. He does not falsify the facts, but merely leaves out those that tell against him. And so far as his explanations of his actions are concerned, the fundamental motive which he reveals is consistent with adherence to the facts : he did not want the war, but simply recognized the inevitable and acted accordingly. *Voir pour prévoir.*

But Cæsar's Commentaries have not won their great standing in Latin literature, and, indeed, in world literature, through their literary or historical merits, but as the work of a great man whose every word is of importance. Thus the value set on them in ancient times did not result in any increase in the prestige of autobiography as a *genre* or in the interest in it. Autobiography never secured the full recognition that it has among us. This is partly explained by the customary depreciation of autobiographers in comparison with rhetoricians and historians. Cicero testified to this in the matter of the earliest Roman autobiographies—directly in the cases of those of Scaurus and

---

* Suetonius, *Divus Julius*, lvi : " Pollio Asinius parum diligenter parumque integra veritate compositos putat . . ."

Catulus, of which he complained that nobody read them,[85] and indirectly in the case of Rutilius : he makes no mention at all of the fact that Rutilius wrote a work *de vita sua*, although he writes at length of the man, his character, and his eloquence, in the same connexion in which he speaks of Scaurus and his autobiography in high praise.* Some forty years after their publication these works had disappeared, while amusing court memoirs like those of the Egyptian King Ptolemy Physcon were still widely read in Pliny's time, as we learn from him. This indifference among the public and among authors themselves to the value of a work of pure autobiography shows itself at times in the imperial Republic even in an exaggerated form : Hadrian published his *vita* under the name of one of his freedmen.[86]

But these facts are not enough in themselves to decide the positive significance of these autobiographies. Various possibilities remain, as is shown in modern times by certain political memoirs in which historical facts are deliberately distorted, and which do not set out to be literary works and yet belong to literature, because they give an impression of life in general through the peculiar traits of human beings. In view of the condition of the material, it is only possible to speak in general terms of the Roman autobiographies of the last century of the Republic ; nevertheless, they expand and enrich our conception.

The first thing to point out is the all-important fact that the men associated with the first appearance of autobiography among the Romans were directly connected with the intellectual movement that began in the period of the imperial Republic, in the " Scipionic circle ", that is to say in the intercourse of Scipio the younger (185–129 B.C.) and his friend Lælius, and of the young Romans who collected round these two eminent men, with the representatives of Hellenistic culture, especially with the great historian Polybius and the Stoic philosopher Panætius. This movement, in addition to all the important influences of Greek philosophy on Roman life and the adjustments of that philosophy to the realities of the Roman State, had the further effect that the self-confidence of the aristocrats who were born to rule the world was touched by the awakening hand of the philosophic spirit : the old Roman asset of the nobleman's *virtus* was deepened into a consciousness of the personality of the individual who freely accepted the existing conditions of dominance, as these were philosophically interpreted from the Stoic

* See above, p. 210.

idea of the natural moral order of the universe. The inborn strength and independence of will that were characteristic of the Roman rulers were thus rounded off with humanity and harmonized by combination with the free mobility of the Greek intellect with its enlightened attitude to life.

As regards Rutilius, we know of his relations with the " Scipionic circle " from Cicero's work on the State. In that work, which was in dialogue form, Scipio appeared as one of the chief speakers ; and he mentioned his conversations on philosophy and politics with the young officer Rutilius at the time when Panætius was with him. Cicero himself speaks there of Rutilius as the intermediary through whom he had learned, when he visited him in past years in his exile, of the discussions of those " eminent sages ", represented in his *Republic*.[87] In the selflessness of his proconsular administration Rutilius gave evidence, as Catulus had done, of the practical moral influence of Stoic idealism ; the most outstanding disciple of Panætius, Posidonius, who was the greatest intellectual force of the age, was a friend of Rutilius, who dedicated one of his works to him. Rutilius wrote his autobiography in an exile that only added to the nobility of his personality, an exile occupied with historical works, the outcome of a philosopher's leisure.[88] And Catulus, into whose mouth Cicero puts the saying that without philosophy there is no life,[89] is shown as the direct heir of Scipio, Lælius, and their circle,[90] devoting himself to its continuation. He was justly so regarded because of the straightforwardness and openness of his nature and the candour and grace of his speech, and his active sympathy with and assistance to the literary efforts of his circle of friends, with which Scaurus was also in touch ; and because of his joy in beauty and art, especially the art of Pheidias, and particularly his leaning to scepticism. For the type of scepticism that came from the Platonic school of thought fitted the Roman gentleman, as it supported the independence of the personality of the individual.

Thus the rise of autobiography among these political personages is to be attributed not so much to the particular motives of self-defence we have noticed as to the central intellectual movement into which it fits ; and the judgment of Cicero and Tacitus, who found in the political autobiographies the documents of Roman integrity, may be regarded as evidence that the consciousness of personality had found here an important means of expression. This aspect is confirmed by what we learn from

Cicero about the literary individuality of those early Roman autobiographers. He describes Scaurus as a senator of the old stock and Rutilius as a perfected Stoic, both " rough vigorous characters " (*uterque natura vehemens et acer*), whereas he writes in appreciation of the " gentle Xenophontic style " [91] of the memoirs of Catulus and the elegance and flexibility of his language, which is that of high society and not of the market-place.

We are confronted with another type of the Hellenistic view of life when we approach the self-glorification which Sulla adopted in his autobiography, whose twenty-two books formed apparently the most comprehensive work in the literature of Roman political memoirs. In his biography of Sulla Plutarch made extensive use of this work, quoting at times from it. He liked to use works of this kind not only for the sake of the facts or of points of grammar, as the antiquarians did, but with a sense of the human element. Thanks to the evidence he offers of Sulla's memoirs, at least one fundamental characteristic of the lost original is discernible to us alongside the defensive or at times aggressive tendency already mentioned * and what looks like a cynical pleasure in the disclosure of political machinations. Plutarch himself refers to this fundamental characteristic in discussing the man's character and especially his religious attitude.[92] Sulla, who at the height of his triumph assumed the cognomen " Felix " (" fortunate "), had made his own, says Plutarch, the depreciatory explanation of his successes as due to pure good fortune, and had taken pride in that interpretation. Either in self-glorification or out of piety he had attributed his achievements to the favour of Tyche, and had thus given his deeds the heightened significance involved in such a relation to the gods. We may quote this characteristic passage from Plutarch's biography of Sulla :

He did not feel about this as Timotheus the son of Conon did, who, when his adversaries ascribed his successes to Fortune, and had him represented in a painting as lying asleep while Fortune cast her net about the cities, was rudely angry with those who had done this, because, as he thought, they were robbing him of the glory due to his exploits . . . Sulla not only accepted with pleasure such felicitations and admiration, but actually joined in magnifying the aid of Heaven in what he did, and gave the credit for it to Fortune, either out of boastfulness or because he had such a belief in the divine agency. For in his Memoirs he writes that of the undertakings which men thought well-advised, those upon which he had boldly ventured,

* Plutarch, *Sulla*, 23. See above, p. 236.

not after deliberation but on the spur of the moment, turned out for the better. And, further, from what he says about his being well endowed by nature for Fortune rather than for war, he seems to attribute more to Fortune than to his own excellence, and to make himself entirely the creature of this deity, since he accounts even his concord with Metellus, a man his equal in rank, and a relative by marriage, a piece of divine felicity.[93]

It was a new turn in the typical method of expression of a ruler's sense of his own worth to base his personal supremacy on nearness to the gods, to compare himself or associate himself with them. Tyche, the goddess of fortune, was elevated, in that period in which human destiny had become so insecure, to the company of the comprehensive single deities which were competing for sole dominance in the early struggles of monotheism ; [94] the works of this goddess had been proclaimed by the Hellenistic historians and philosophers, and Posidonius had just given impressive pictures of her : according to the writers' horizon, enlightened or mystical, she was represented as blind and capricious chance or as the representative of the powers of guardianship and beneficence, or as " the human Moira, who in a sudden turn springs up in dénouements ".[95] Sulla's Fortuna was not the Tyche of popular belief, who " before the eyes of the world raised kings up and threw them down ",[96] and who also bore the responsibility for the incomprehensible changes of good and evil fortune in the life of ordinary mortals ; she was a power akin to Aphrodite, the goddess of love and of victory, incorporating the man of action's characteristic belief in his own star. The dictator's character was composed of cunning and courage ; those who knew him depicted him by the famous phrase " half lion, half fox " ; * and he displayed that belief with a sort of brilliant levity. He represented that irrational divine power, against which no calculation of the army commander and statesman could do anything, as smiling upon himself, Sulla,

* The famous phrase, rendered familiar by Macchiavelli's " Prince ", was first coined and applied to Sulla by Papirius Carbo, one of the leaders of the Marian party. Plutarch (*Sulla*, xxviii, 3) mentions the situation in which " Carbo was said to have remarked that in Sulla he had to encounter at the same time a lion and a fox, and that he was more annoyed by the fox." Macchiavelli writes in *Il Principe*, chap. 18 : " There are two kinds of combating or fighting, the one by right of the laws, the other merely by force. That first way is proper to men, the other is also common to beasts ; but because the first many times suffices not, there is a necessity to make recourse to the second . . . A prince, then, being necessitated to know how to make use of that part belonging to a beast, ought to serve himself of the conditions of the Fox and the Lion ; for the lion cannot keep himself from snares, nor the fox defend himself against the wolves. He may need then be a fox, that he may beware of the snares, and a lion that he may scare the wolves." (Translated by E. D., London, 1640.)

the darling of the gods. In this way his deeds and successes, which revolutionized the old Republican Constitution, were given the semblance of a manifestation of his higher mission, so that his personal existence with all its acts of violence became irradiated with the splendour of an effortless achievement, unerringly pursued because directed from above.*

To carry through this view he made use of wonders and signs, oracles and dream visions, traditionally the chief expedient for the suggestion of divine guidance. In the announcement of the divine kingship of Alexander the Great his historiographer Callisthenes, nephew of Aristotle, made use of this expedient, and we shall meet with it again in the autobiographies of the Roman emperors. In Cicero's collection of prodigies of this sort in his work attacking divination, Sulla's autobiography is set alongside the history of the Syracusan autocrat Dionysius I,[97] written by his Minister Philistus, a prominent politician of that time. The effect of this Greek literary tradition was reinforced by the hold of the belief in auspices and omens over Roman life and worship. Its political utilization for self-glorification is the first form in which it makes its appearance in the history of autobiography. It took another form when serving to present the life of the individual as a consistent whole. This use in biography of oracles, dreams, and other signs was supported by the Stoic theology, which since the time of Posidonius had swept through the Greco-Roman world. The Stoics had a rationalized interpretation for this as for other parts of popular belief, an interpretation drawn from their leading scientific idea of the causal interconnexion of all things that happen ; thus the next stage of the technique of foreordainings will be shown to us in an autobiography from the circle of Origenes, the great Christian theologian of the third century, who represented the Hellenic culture of that time.

Sulla was the first to concentrate on his own person attention to the " prodigies " of which it was customary to tell, in the writing of the history of the Republic, so far as concerned the State, to which the gods when officially consulted proclaimed their will through signs and wonders.[98] In taking this line he appears to have been influenced by the consciousness of the great upheavals he had produced. For there was not at work here

---

* Cf., for example, the naïve adoption of this self-portrayal, with duly harsh criticism, in Drumann, Geschichte Roms, ii, p. 495 : " He had made no effort, either now or at any time, but had simply accepted what destiny, his fortune as he called it, brought him."

simply the superstition that led him to maintain, and to represent as a crucial point in the interpretation of his life, that nothing was so inviolable as that which the *daimonion* commanded in a dream.* In a remarkable passage in Plutarch, which almost certainly comes straight from the autobiography,[99] the clear and distinct meaning with which the divine signs appeared in Sulla's day is related to the historical situation of that time of social and political dissolution : according to the ablest soothsayers, a universal change in the world, the rise of a new race of men with other customs and other ways of living, was being announced by those signs. This is strangely reminiscent of oriental conceptions, in which a king's rule might be hailed as the dawn of a new age.[100]

Of the soothsayings which have come down to us from Sulla's book, some had the function of foreshadowing the future greatness of the dictator. A Chaldean in the embassy of the Parthians, who watched him in accordance with the rules of the science of physiognomy, declared : " This man is simply bound to become the greatest of men, and I am only amazed that he can endure not to be even now the foremost among all." Sulla himself undertook the interpretation of a portent that came at the beginning of the Social War : the hero with the uncommonly imposing appearance, to whom the interpreters of signs pointed after the outbreak of a volcanic fire—saying of him that he would attain dominion and would liberate the City from the disturbances —was, said Sulla, he himself, he with his light golden hair and his manly virtue, which after such great and noble deeds he could demonstrate without shame. In the other omens, which referred to a single coming event, such as the success of an impending battle, there appeared, in addition to the other signs, effective pictures. When he faced Marius outside Rome, the goddess of war appeared to him in a dream and gave him the lightning to hurl against his enemies, and he could still see how they fell before it. Or before an engagement, when his deputy commander hesitated to attack, a mild wind brought from a neighbouring meadow blossom that blew up against shields and helmets and stuck to them, and, thus garlanded, the troops marched to victory.[101] That the enemy suffered in the fighting at least a thousand times his own losses [102] is a magnification

---

* Plutarch, *Sulla*, 6 : " In the dedication of his Memoirs to Lucullus, he advised him to deem nothing so secure as what the divine power (*daimonion*) enjoins upon him in his dreams."

proportional to that self-glorification by means of divine signs. Two days before he died, he wrote in his autobiography, in anticipation of death, that the Chaldeans had prophesied to him that it had been ordained that after a glorious life he would die at the height of his good fortune.[103]

A further insight into the character of political autobiography in this period is given by Cicero in the work chiefly devoted to the glorification of his consulate and of his rescuing from destruction in that year (63), as he was convinced, of the Roman State (by his disclosure of the conspiracy of Catiline). In his case we have a whole series of autobiographical works in various literary forms by a single individual and for only one side of his life —which, though it was in his judgment the principal one, did not exclude other sides with corresponding self-portrayals : we are here afforded a glimpse of the various ways of portrayal of a man's own deeds. And while the vanity to which Cicero here allows play does not tempt us to dwell on those works, it is of importance to observe how a more individualized self-importance found free expression in various literary forms chosen for one and the same purpose.

The series begins with a political missive " On his deeds and the highest affairs of state ", straight from the winter of 63–62. Cicero addressed this " voluminous epistle ", which he distributed in Rome, to Pompey, in association with whom, as the other great contemporary statesman, he proposed to rule the Republic under the old Constitution, much as Lælius had done in the past with Scipio ; at the end of his year as Consul he had called Pompey back to Rome from the East, where he had been conducting military operations, in order that he might assume the leading political rôle as was his due. He also had already in view an epic poem as the due form for the celebration of his deeds.[104] He expected a " Ciceronias " from the Greek poet Archias (who wrote epics about Roman family histories) when he undertook Archias' defence (62 B.C.).[105] In face of the triumvirate, which implied the beginning of his fall, he took up again the writing of works in praise of his consulate (60)—three at once : a highly rhetorical work in Greek (though it was issued as a *hypomnema*), a Latin work, also in the form of *Commentarii*, and thirdly—" so that no medium may remain unavailed of for my praise of myself " [106]—a heroic poem : three books of Latin verse, which he completed in the same year. Even that was not enough : in the following year (59), finding himself pushed out of office, he began a work in the style of large-scale history, a contemporary account in the manner of Theopompus, a pupil of Isocrates, and if possible " much more scathing " in its personal criticism. On this he worked for a further fifteen years : in his own words, he found it consoling to have an outlet for the bitter feelings to which he had now to confine his political existence, for his " hatred of evil persons ".

Interest centres mainly in the three works of the year 60, and can in some degree be satisfied.* The first was the rhetorical *hypomnema* written in Greek. Here it is primarily the literary element, the perfect mastery of Isocratean artistic prose, that appears to be his great pride. The work is said to have been circulated in Athens and the other Greek cities as a sensation, and he is able to quote Cæsar's statement that in his opinion he had never read better Greek.[107] Cicero gives delicious evidence that it was customary in a work of self-glorification to undertake only the compilation of the material and to leave its working up in the formal style to someone else : he rejoices that through his own elaboration of this work he has saved himself from the burden of the customary collection of material for decking out.[108] And yet it was from him that the appeal came again and again, *Orna me !* Atticus himself had recorded his friend's deeds in a normal Greek *hypomnema*, written without elaboration.[109] It is characteristic, however, of Cicero's high ambition that it was to no less a person than Posidonius that he transmitted his memoir, inviting him to undertake a " more decorative " exposition of the subject. Posidonius was then foremost in the art of pushing a great personality into the centre of a historical narrative ! We are also afforded an insight into the style of this autobiographical sketch by Plutarch, who used it in his biography of Cicero.[110] We find there that the autobiographer in decrying his opponents made play with charges of immorality—incest, profligacy, piling up of debts, and so on—showing reserve only in regard to Cæsar. In order to increase the importance of his deeds he accumulated the conventional omens, lightnings, earthquakes, ghosts. He gave a full account of his reflections and anxieties at critical moments. He included in the motives of his actions the political ambition of his wife Terentia and instigation from other persons in close touch with him. And he added for effect such things as the description of his procession at the consular election : he

* Only of the *hypomnema* (*Commentarii*) written in Latin are we without any detailed knowledge.

had ripped open his under-garment at the shoulders, to show the cuirass he was wearing, so that the crowd should appreciate the danger by which he knew himself to be threatened. The conclusion [111] was probably formed—as it was later in the famous record by the emperor Augustus of his own deeds—by the conferment on him of the title " Father of his country ". Cicero dwelt on the magnificence of the occasion, and on the illumination, and so on, and especially, as the crowning element of fame, on the judgment of the most eminent men of Rome that the City owed more to Cicero than to any army commander, more than wealth and booty and power—the saving of its very existence. He did not confine his own glorification to virtues in general, but made special mention of the power of his oratory. Plutarch, after the chapters for which he had used the *hypomnema*, could not refrain from giving at once his view of the eternal self-praise and vainglory that were the weakness of the great orator.

It is possible to speak in more detail of the history in verse on which Cicero had worked with such enthusiasm. Owing to the pleasure the author had in making quotations from this poem in his other works, several fragments are extant from which the composition is recognizable as a whole.[112] Amid the inventive incapacity and the mechanical way in which he made use of the resources of Greek epic, the verses show at least his endeavour to work in the grand style that seemed appropriate for this autobiographical undertaking. For in an " epic " the demand in Aristotle's *Rhetoric* that the historian should compete with the poet could properly be complied with, and not left to others to fulfil as in a modest *hypomnema*. Here again we have the conception of the hero's divine mission. There are signs galore from the gods. The chief action takes place on Olympus itself, where Jupiter, Apollo, Minerva, Urania, and Calliope talk to Cicero and about him. But this is pure empty fiction, an abstract form imposed by the literary tradition from Homer, or rather from the Hellenistic epigoni of the great epic art. Tradition says also of Pompey that one of the historians of whom he made use for the publishing of the fame of his deeds chose the form of the great epic with the staging of the Olympian gods. We may see from Cicero's use of it how conventional this form was. The enlightened author himself in his dialogue *On Divination* belittled the signs and wonders he had earlier accumulated for himself.[113]

There exists a lengthy series of verses from the second book, in which the story reached the crucial act, the judgment on the conspirators. The verses show the hero at a council meeting of the gods. Here, in a long-winded address, the muse Urania gives a list of the mass of prodigies that showed the greatness of the danger overcome,* and the situation is used by Cicero to enable the gods to illuminate his life, showing how Minerva herself taught him the arts, and how he, a worthy scholar of the Academy and the Lyceum, held to his philosophic ideals at the height of his fame and amid the cares of his statesmanly activity, and devoted his leisure to studies and to the worship of the gods. These exalted periods, and especially a speech which Jupiter makes to him at the end of the book, seem to have had a basis of truth for Cicero ; for five years later he told his brother that he took to heart all that he had said in those verses, and had written more for himself than for the public.[114] The notorious line that brought him so much mockery, *Cedant arma togae, concedat laurea laudi*, he included later in his work on Duties as an admirable expression of the fact that the achievement of the statesman ranks equally with the deeds of the army commander.[115] Finally, the last book contains an exhortation from the mouth of Calliope, that he should continue to preserve the attitude he had adopted from his earliest youth and now maintained as Consul with such fine integrity, so that his fame and the gratitude of patriots should grow yet further. In a difficult political situation he recalled these lines : they became for him, he confessed, an encouragement to be guided in his attitude not by personal expediency but by his patriotic ideals.[116]

Cicero declares expressly, in consonance with rhetorical theory,[117] that these three eulogistic works were not intended as biographical tributes, were " not encomiastic " but " historical ". This technical definition does not, however, imply any insistence on their entire truthfulness.† Imaginative writing played in historical narrative the part that fell in the *enkomion* to the art of direct exaggeration. It is only in regard to that element, or to what we termed the " inner form " ‡ (as distinguished from the literary form), that a *hypomnema* and a poem could both be characterised as historical in contrast to the *enkomion*.**

* Cicero did not make artistic use of the portent for purposes of prophecy. The miracle at Terentia's sacrifice, which according to the report of Servius foreshadowed the glorious consulate, is erroneously antedated by the grammarian who assigned the verses in question to the first book of Cicero's epic instead of the second. Buresch, *op. cit.*, p. 226.
† See above, pp. 188 *sqq*. ‡ *Cf.* Introduction, p. 11.
** Apart from the limitation—scarcely observed by Cicero—of the biographical material to the period of his consulate.

So far as concerns the truthfulness of a historical work, Cicero sees no difficulty ; " for who does not know ", he declares, " that the first law of history is that one must not dare to tell anything untrue ? And its second that one must dare not to conceal anything true ? That there must be no suggestion of partiality in one's writing ? nor of malice ? These fundamental principles are familiar, of course, to everyone." [118] The problem lay for him in the importance of the particular historical matter and in diction—*in rebus et verbis*. In regard to the latter he distinguishes two levels of historical writing, a lower one, represented by the old Roman historians such as Cato and Fabius Pictor, and the higher level attained by the Greeks. Thus he puts the question : " What kind of orator, and how great a master of language, is qualified to write history ? " and he replies : " If he is to write as the Greeks have written, the highest kind of orator is required ; if he is to write as our own countrymen have done, he need not be an orator at all ; it is enough that the writer should not be a liar." This applies to the primitive annalistic form of history, which he describes as " simple records, without any ornament in their composition, of dates, persons, places, and events ". On this level, on which he looks down, historians regard " brevity, provided that it does not impair understanding, as the only merit of diction ".[119] Was it, we ask, mere flattery when in regard to Cæsar's Commentaries he declared that in history there is nothing more pleasing than brevity, pure and lucid ?

And now a final testimony of Cicero's gives a full explanation of the nature of the historical treatment [120] which seemed to him to be desirable in self-glorification. The passage throws a strong light on the position of autobiography at the time. After his return from exile, and before he himself, in a continuation of his epic " on his times ", pictured his deeds and sufferings and especially the services rendered to him by his friends (54), Cicero wrote to his party comrade Lucceius, who was at work on a history of Rome during the last forty years, to induce him to take out the section about him and to form it into an independent work. In this epistle (Fam., V 12), which he praises as " exceedingly pretty ", *valde bella*, and recommends Atticus (IV, 6, 4) to read, he expounds to the historian the point of view for the desired exposition, and this is now entirely in the style of the type of Hellenistic historiography which was poetic or imaginative, emotional and sensational,

The various events and the changes of fortune in his life—
from the Catilinarian conspiracy to his return from exile—
make it, he emphasizes, highly profitable material ; effectively
presented, it would grip and move the reader as nothing else
could ; the sufferings to be described would arouse the agreeable
feeling of sympathy. Cicero himself, in reading the work, would
have the enjoyment of peaceful recollection of the times that were
so hard to live through.

The fact is that the regular chronological record of events in itself
interests us as if it were a catalogue of historical occurrences ; but
the uncertain and varied fortunes of a statesman who frequently rises
to prominence give scope for surprise, suspense, delight, annoyance,
hope, fear ; should those fortunes, however, end in some striking
consummation, the result is a complete satisfaction of mind which is
the most perfect pleasure a reader can enjoy.[121]

Cicero, on this principle, describes his story actually as
drama, *fabula*. This element is dealt with at length ; the
other elements, pragmatic explanation and political judgment of actions in state affairs, and criticism of other persons
involved, including the charge against them of " perfidy,
persecution, and treachery " to the hero, are touched on only
briefly.

What Cicero here demands for himself existed in Hellenistic
historical compositions as a definite form for the " tragic "
presentation of historical personalities : this was a class of
historical monograph, the typical features of which were described
by rhetorical theory, as is done by Cicero ; it had a technical
name,[122] and the revealing comment has been made [123] that a
strong link may be found in it between the drama and the
" novel ".

For the narrative of his life in this form, Cicero was ready to
supply Lucceius with comprehensive " commentaries ", if the
latter decided to undertake the work. " If I fail", he writes,
" to induce you to grant me this request . . . I may be forced
to do what some have frequently found fault with—to write
about myself; yet I should be following the example of many
distinguished men." [124] Thus, here again autobiography is
regarded as of a secondary order, and the theoretical requirement
that the colours should be more discreetly applied in it further
reduces its value.

This application to autobiography of a method of treatment

which we know as that of the historical novel, is one of the most important things that happened to it in ancient times. The romantic narrative which was to serve for the idealized representation of Cicero's deeds corresponds in its intellectual attitude to the seventeenth-century historical novel on the grand scale which elaborated the picture of the French aristocracy, the Fronde and its supporters, and introduced the *honnêtes gens* with their exalted virtues and lofty ambitions, under a transparent disguise of antiquity, in dignified situations and with sonorous speeches. In the seventeenth-century the so-called Greek novel, of which we have definite knowledge in a later period of the Roman Empire, was consciously adopted as one of the models to be followed ; this is further evidence that the effect of those ancient models was due not to their special literary feature, the love-stories they contained, but to their conveyance of the Hellenistic traditions, their general poetic and rhetorical treatment, the usefulness of which for the idealization of his own political personality was appreciated by Cicero. This is further made plain by the versified " historical " books on his consulate and by the " Isocratean " *hypomnema* with the features referred to by Plutarch. Later on we shall realize more clearly the relation of autobiography to those " romantic " narratives in contrast with its relation to the realistic novel based on the observing and reasoning power of the intellect.

Cicero, who was the first, apparently, to use the " tragic " style for the glorification of his deeds, seems to have been started on this course not only by the literary theory of that class of historical monograph but also by his own art of oratory ; for the very core of this forensic art was the effective representation of the emotions and the moral considerations arising out of the typical situations with which the orator had to deal in the political struggle or in the law courts. As the greatest orator of the Roman Republic, Cicero made the Latin language a perfect organ for such impressive and lively descriptions of those actualities of social and political life.[125]

In its appeal to the emotions the rhetorical art taken over by the Romans from the Greeks was associated with imaginative writing. The distinction we are wont to draw between rhetoric and poetry does not therefore apply here. Thus the first autobiography known to us that really gave poetic form, drawn from genuinely passionate experience, to the record of an individual life, the poem " On his Life " by Gregory of Nazianzus, was written by a great preacher and orator, who had come straight from the oratorical combats of ecclesiastical dignitaries.*

IV. THE ROMAN EMPERORS

In the fundamentally different conditions of State and society in imperial Rome, political autobiography underwent a change. Even in the scanty vestiges still extant, change is evident in important features, though it is difficult to say how far these features determined the physiognomy of the *genre*. The writers of these works were now the emperors. Only Augustus still permitted the writing of reminiscences by his helpers, and, indeed, reminiscences of other than specifically courtly character. Agrippa, the friend of his youth, who had such regard for him that he declined, although he had the Senate's authorization, to celebrate a triumph at a time when Octavian was in difficulties, was able to write, without any fear of the consequences of so doing, of the steps he had taken to rescue Octavian. 'He told how, when Octavian's fleet was destroyed in the war with Sextus Pompeius, he had built a new one, provided harbourage for it by connecting the lakes Lucrinus and Averno with one another and with the sea, and finally fought a successful naval battle for him (36 B.C.). On the other hand, Agrippa is said to have remarked to intimate friends that " most men in positions of power wish no one to be superior to themselves " ; his advice, therefore, was " that the man who expects to come out alive should relieve his masters of undertakings which involve great difficulty, and reserve for them the successes ".[126]   And it was Agrippa who broke with the republican custom that had favoured the writing of memoirs by army commanders and statesmen ; in 14 B.C., when he was fighting in Pontus, he made no report to the Senate on his activities.[127]   It seems that once more in Nero's time a Roman general, Domitius Corbulo, ventured to write in praise of his own famous deeds ; he paid for the indiscretion

---

* The last autobiographical work from the Republican period was the *vita* written by Varro (116–27 B.C.), who is known as Polyhistor (among his many writings is a life of Pompey, under whom he commanded an army). Of this work there exists only a chance mention, giving only its title.   The work may have dealt not only with military and political experiences of this incredibly industrious antiquary, and with his famous exploits, but also with his learned works and other things on which he prided himself.   But even its form is unknown, especially as nothing is known of any Hellenistic model that Varro may have had.   It also remains uncertain how far his humanistic or antiquarian interest in all sorts of curiosities of natural history, geography, or history found mention in the autobiography.   Conjectures as to this are offered in Ritschl, opusc. III, pp. 436–7, and F. Münzer, *Beiträge zur Quellenkritik der Naturgesch. des Plinius* (1897), pp. 275 *sqq.*

by suicide (A.D. 67).* Thus, apart from the emperors, this production of autobiographies came to an end ; it reappeared only with the struggles for power in the Church.

The fact itself, the appearance of several autobiographies of emperors, is not, as is usually supposed, the actual problem, since autobiography had already made its appearance in the Republic, and the concern of a ruler for a permanent record of his personality was a lasting source of autobiography, especially in ancient times. Thus there is little need to assume any special motive such as the anticipation of a court of judgment on the dead, with the function of deciding upon the deification or the anathematization of an emperor after his death—a court which might be influenced by an autobiography.[128] And even tendencious recording, with discreditable facts suppressed or glossed over or twisted, as might, of course, be ordered by an autocrat, is not the characteristic element ; not all these autobiographies are historical works. The strange thing is, indeed, what might almost be called an unkingly spirit in these works : judging, at all events, by the fragments, they all had room for trifles and the commonplace. It must, of course, be remembered that, in that monarchy disguised as a republic, dealings with the personal affairs of the ruler were regarded as acts of state. Thus it is reported of Octavian that " when he shaved off his beard

---

* *Cf.* H. Peter, *Die gesch. Lit.*, I, pp. 202 *sqq.* But his *Commentarii* were probably only edited official documents of the campaign ; in any case the work was based on his official reports to the emperor.

War memoirs may also have been published by L. Antistius Vetus, who was *legatus* (commander) in Germany for three years after his consulate (A.D. 55). He, too, aroused Nero's suspicion, and escaped punishment by killing himself. Suetonius Paulinus, the father of the biographer of the emperors, seems to have been more cautious. He wrote on the campaign in Mauretania with which he had been entrusted, after a rising had broken out in that province, but so much of the work as is extant (thanks to Pliny's Natural History, V, 14 *sqq.*) is confined to geographical and ethnographical features of the country. The same may have been true of the *De Judaeis* of M. Antonius Julianus, who was commander in the Jewish war under Titus.

In the time of the soldier emperors there is mention of two eminent generals who took the side of Vespasian in the civil war (A.D. 69)—M. Vipstanus Messalla and C. Licinius Mucianus. Messalla's work on that war was made use of by Tacitus in his Histories (III, 25 and 28). He says there that Messalla, a man of eminent family and of personal distinction, was " the only one who had brought with him to the war some honourable pursuits ". It is in consonance with this high estimate that Tacitus assigns Messalla a part in his Dialogue on Oratory ; the general appears there as a champion of antiquity, a convinced classicist.

Mucianus was the champion of the Flavian cause ; he was three times Consul and then governor of Syria, and he played the principal part in the elevation of Vespasian to the throne ; he regarded himself, according to Tacitus (*Hist.*, II, 83), as *plus socius imperii quam minister* (" a partner in the imperial power rather than its servant "). But judging by the mention of his memoirs in Pliny, the work was concerned only with *mirabilia*, curiosities. *Cf.* Pauly-Wissowa, *Real-Encyclopädie*, xiii, 437.

for the first time, he not only himself gave a magnificent entertainment but also granted to all the other citizens a festival at the public expense ".[129]

The ancient self-portrayal in the Greek style, aiming at idealization, attained that end by excluding the merely personal and particular and confining itself to a general statement of virtues, and by exaggerating these into a general norm. Since there was a tradition of autobiography among the Roman emperors, it might have been expected that a grandiose form would develop here, in which the ruler's ideal, determining his interpretation of his own life, could be put forward with the assurance of a man who, relying on his might, exerted it in framing his history as in all his utterances and actions. Instead of this, the extant fragments reveal nothing in the grand style and no trace of the weighty manner of a writer with a sense of his own pre-eminence, but an approach to moralizing in the spirit that reigned in the society of that time. Here and there the record is very close to the average commonplace existence. One is reminded of forensic eloquence and of the treatment customary in the Forum of intimate human relations, but one is also reminded of courtiers' diaries, and we may assume some influence from the type of memoirs that flourished in Hellenistic courts. The common human elements that produce a pleasant fellowship between ruler and people make their appearance in the self-portrayals of these world rulers alongside political acts and the conduct of wars, and here more than anywhere in earlier times one detects something of the peculiar character of memoirs—in the narrower sense of the word, implying products of court life —which usually is found in the works not of the ruling personages themselves but of their entourage. The material does not exist for a general assessment that could decide whether the broad outline conveyed was nevertheless that of a proud and dignified personality, as in some autobiographies of Spaniards, of whom in their great period many remind the reader of the Romans of the imperial age.

These six or seven emperors' autobiographies [130] are not, of course, to be regarded as a body, like the records of the deeds of the early Assyrian and the Babylonian rulers with their characteristic " court style ",* although the model provided by Augustus certainly had a considerable influence. Even the scanty information we have as to their size and their literary quality indicates variety.

* See above, Introduction, p. 35.

The autobiography of Augustus, whose exclusive concern " with his own deeds and not those of other persons " is expressly stated (fr. 14), consisted of thirteen books, though it dealt only with the first half of his life.   Beginning with his birth and descent, it was continued as far as his thirty-eighth year, that is to say, some two years after the definite establishment of the monarchical State, which was indicated by the conferment on him in 27 B.C. of the name Augustus.*   Probably he wrote this substantial work at some time between 27 and 22 B.C., after a long and tedious illness [131] in Spain during his war against the barbarians, which he had determined to conduct himself.   From Spain he had corresponded with Virgil, who was already working on the Aeneid, the epic poem which was to provide a grandiose poetic exaltation of his historic achievement.   He himself, however, was also claiming literary laurels with his autobiography.   We are told [132] that the characteristic quality of his manner of speaking and writing was clearness of expression, without adornment and with more attention paid to intelligibility than to smoothness and neatness of style.   But the emperor did not despise the ordinary devices of the historian ; this is shown by the fictitious speeches, cleverly arranged, by means of which he described the motives of the Perusine civil war when telling of his acceptance, as victor, of the submission with honour of L. Antonius, brother of the triumvir Mark Antony. [133]   Thus his autobiography is mentioned by Suetonius as one of the literary productions of which Augustus read several to his intimates " as in a lecture hall " [134]—an indication of rhetorical treatment that once more suggests a slight variation in the sense of the word *hypomnema*, applied to all these works *de vita sua* in the Greek quotations.

Of Tiberius, on the other hand, it is stated by Suetonius that he wrote his life " summarily and briefly " ; this autobiography is said to have been Domitian's favourite book.   In the case of the eight books of Claudius on his own life the style is praised in contrast with the ineptness of the contents ; in the case of Hadrian (about A.D. 135) the publication under the name of a freedman gives some indication of the literary standard, and in that of Septimius Severus (after 197), where the fuller title " on his private and public life " is given, there is a direct reference

---

* The work ended with the Cantabrian war, which broke out in 26 B.C., and perhaps, as is conjectured by a modern historian, with the second closing of the temple of Janus in token of peace in the Roman world empire (25 B.C.).

in Suetonius to the " elaboration " of the narrative, and to its trustworthy character. Agrippina, who wrote her memoirs when she was only forty-four years old, adds a new element, her family history ; Tacitus mentions that she had " described her life and the fate of her family for posterity ".

But these differences, as gleaned from the tradition concerning these autobiographical works, are not tangible enough to permit of the individual treatment of each work. Only in the cases of Augustus, Hadrian, and Septimius Severus have we any considerable number of definitely attested quotations, or, indeed, more than just one or two ; the similarities in these quotations may be largely attributed to the narrow range of interest of the writers making them, though it must have been to some extent connected with the character of the autobiographies of emperors. Thus it is possible to try to indicate the common traits in the extant passages, which may, however one-sidedly, throw light on this type of political memoirs.

Of the autobiography of Augustus, which heads the list, it may probably be said with assurance that it did not belong to the type of Cæsar's Commentaries, as may be maintained of his later, monumental record of his deeds. We may more appropriately apply to it Humboldt's dictum concerning the usual quality of political memoirs, that they " degrade the tragedy of world history to a drama of everyday life ". The effort has been made to reconstruct the course of the comprehensive narrative in order of time from birth onwards, by collecting from the ancient historical and biographical works on Augustus, in which use is made of his autobiography, the sections drawn from that source, and by comparing this " official " picture of the emperor with the picture drawn from another tradition less favourable to him.[135] This investigation confirms the impression gained from an unprejudiced reading of the fragments.

We may take as an instance the description, based on the autobiography, of the way he came to power. It was the typical course of violence and double-dealing—typical in the sense in which Macchiavelli paints the prince who desires, at a time of dissolution of morals, to establish order and peace in his realm.* Needless to say, Augustus did not openly admit pursuing this course, just as he did not admit that his position was that of a monarch ; he disguised it by the grandiose fiction of the restoration of the old Republican Constitution, under which he

* See above, p. 245.

himself was simply the *princeps senatus*, the leader of the senate. But he seems also to have denied the strength of will, the purposefulness, and the equally pronounced versatility of the calculating intelligence that was able to suit action to the circumstances ; in the true style of a writer of memoirs, wherever there was a question of illegality and violence he made a point of appearing not as the driving force but as the instrument used by others, friends or foes, for a step for which he could not himself answer. For instance, he started his political career with violence when, as a young man barely nineteen years old, he took over Cæsar's heritage after the assassination of the dictator.   He had collected an army without any authority, like an insurgent—unless Cæsar's heir had not only the duty of avenging his murder, but, as in a monarchy, a right to the position attained by the murdered man. His bold challenge of political forces opposed not only to him but to one another brought success.   The senate thought it could make use of " the young man " in order to break the power of Mark Antony, the other leader of Cæsar's party ; but Octavian cut across that policy, the purpose of which had been betrayed by Cicero through the pun he made in the senate, pointing to Octavian as *laudandum adulescentem, ornandum, tollendum,* " the young man who deserved to be praised, decorated, and "—either elevated or got rid of, according to the interpretation put on the word *tollere* with its double meaning, " to raise " and " to put out of the way ".

In 43 B.C., after Antony had been defeated at Mutina by Decimus Brutus, Octavian contented himself with that humbling of his rival and sought to come to terms with him as his collaborator in the avenging of Cæsar.   He broke with D. Brutus, who was the legitimate commander-in-chief but had been one of the Republican conspirators at whose hands Cæsar had fallen. Instead of transferring the legions he had recruited to Brutus as ordered by the senate, he marched on Rome at their head, seized the treasury, and forced the senate to elect him as Consul in spite of his youth, which legally and traditionally should have stood in the way of his election.   As Consul he secured the formal confirmation of his succession to Cæsar ; after this he was able to face Mark Antony on an equal footing.

In the autobiography he gave expression, it is true, to the pride he had always felt at attaining the highest office in the State so early in life, but he not only glossed over the hard political facts but transferred them to another plane, that of civic morality or even sentiment. Instead of pretender to the throne, he represented himself as an innocent man suffering from persecution. He declared that he had been persecuted by his uncle Mark Antony, a man twenty years his senior, who in the year of Cæsar's assassination (44 B.C.) was in possession of power as Consul ; Mark Antony, as friend and comrade of Cæsar, had himself hoped to succeed him, and immediately after the assassination he had secured all Cæsar's papers and funds. According to the official tradition, probably derived from Augustus' autobiography, Antony despised and hated, and slandered, the modest young Octavian, who had come to Rome as Cæsar's legitimate heir, and when Octavian put forward his legal claims in the Forum Antony so threatened him that he felt in peril of his life and preferred to withdraw entirely from public affairs. But his very modesty and perplexity touched people and brought him not only popular sympathy but the adhesion of Cæsar's veterans, who compelled Antony to negotiate with Octavian. When the powerful Antony continued to revile his nephew, the veterans went over to Octavian in a body.

Apart from this touching version of the incidents, Augustus defended his acquisition of the army on the ground that his purpose had been to secure protection not only for his person but for the threatened Republic. In explanation of his collaboration with D. Brutus for a time in the struggle against his rivals, he stated that Brutus had declared to him his genuine regret at his participation in the conspiracy and, indeed, had asked his forgiveness. Then came his change of attitude after the engagement at Mutina. He stated that he did not transfer his troops to D. Brutus, as he should have done under the Constitution, because they refused to serve under an army commander who had been one of Cæsar's assassins ; he further stated, in defiance of the facts, that in view of the loyalty of his legions to him the senate had not dared to order their transfer, but had tried to incite them against him—and had completely failed. Instead the veterans sent a deputation to Rome to demand the payment promised them for their victory and to demand the Consulate for Octavian. The senate rejected both demands. At this the leader of the deputation pointed to his sword and shouted : " *Hic faciet si vos non feceritis* " (" This will do it if you do not "). After this his victorious legions demanded of Octavian that he should lead them to the capital, and he had to comply—thus happened his march on Rome in 43 B.C.

He offered a similar explanation of his approach to Antony after Antony's defeat : his legions declared of their own accord, and, indeed, swore, that they would not allow themselves to be used against an army which, like that of Mark Antony, had fought under Cæsar ; they also compelled him to give his assent when the senate, also of its own accord, resolved to end the outlawry of Antony, who had been declared an enemy of the State. In order to palliate his change of allegiance, he stated, once more in defiance of the facts, that the senate had withheld from him the honours due to him. This ingratitude drove him —such was the official tradition—into the path that led to the triumvirate.

The distribution of power and of regional authority between Antony, Lepidus, and Octavian that was effected in 43 B.C. under the title of the " Triumvirate for the restoration of order in the State " began with terrible proscriptions in the style of the dictator Sulla. Cæsar had exercised leniency toward his enemies when the safety of the State allowed it. Augustus, who held up Cæsar to approbation, tried in his autobiography to shift the responsibility for these atrocities from his shoulders on to those of the two other autocrats, contending that they had compelled him to take part in them against his will. The moral character which he intended to impress on his own picture may be inferred from the inscription on the golden shield of honour which the senate dedicated to the restorer of the Republic in 27 B.C.—*virtutis, clementiae, justitiae, pietatis causa* ("for virtue, clemency, justice, devotion "). We do not know whether he mentioned, and if so in what terms, that after the victory over Cæsar's assassins won by Antony at Philippi (42 B.C.), he had the head of M. Brutus cut off his corpse and sent to Rome to be cast at the feet of Cæsar's statue.[136] Nor do we know whether he mentioned the vengeance he took after the capture of Perusia in 40 B.C. in the Perusine war : three hundred senators and knights were selected, we are told,[137] from the prisoners of war and killed on the Ides of March, the day of Julius Cæsar's assassination, like so many victims sacrificed to the god Julius. Atrocity of this sort was characteristic of the young Octavian in his capacity of Cæsar's avenger. In his great epic, Virgil did not suppress this trait when he created the idealized picture of Augustus in the form of *pius Æneas*. But he gave this human weakness an element of greatness by writing of it in heroic terms. Æneas has the virtues of Augustus, the ruler who had brought peace to the world—justice, clemency, and above all *pietas*, that is to say devotion to the gods and the country, or, in general, goodness ; but there are times when this wise leader, though he has learnt to rule himself, gives free play to his anger, and in wrath he is as terrible as Achilles.

There may have been a certain effort to represent great matters in the grand style in the treatment of this world-historic subject not only in the epic but in the autobiography. In any case, Augustus made use of traditional means of serving that purpose—wonders and dreams. These were used to accentuate the importance of such events as his arrival in Rome after Cæsar's assassination, or the destruction of the assassins, Brutus and Cassius, at Philippi. We saw in the case of Sulla how this expedient, used both in the Greek literary form of the *enkomion* and in Roman religious observances and national historiography, was employed by an autobiographer for the exaltation of his personal reputation.* Augustus went further in this direction ; he told of signs and wonders that accompanied his birth— although he was neither of eminent origin nor a man of genius.

But what was it that he picked out from his childhood as so remarkable that it might make him seem a born ruler ? One of the stories he told of himself was that at the customary funeral solemnities in honour of his maternal grandmother Julia, the mother of Julius Cæsar, he delivered the funeral oration, although he was only twelve years old. Another story had reference to his first public office. At Cæsar's wish he was elected when barely fifteen years old to the college of priests, and he goes on to say that he visited the temple only at night, in order to escape from the gaze of aristocratic ladies who were running after him —so handsome was he. According to the classical scholar to whom we owe a clearer impression of Augustus' autobiography, he made special reference to this " in order to combat the rumours, spread not only in his youth, of his unchaste way of living ".[138]

These and other anecdotes of the sort, however, did not merely serve a defensive purpose, but had also a positive political aim. The emperor seems to have wanted to provide in his autobiography a model for the education of a young Roman *more maiorum*, in the ancestral style. To this picture belonged the beneficent moral influence of his parents on the growing child, corresponding to the *ethos* of the aristocratic families, from which we proceeded in the exposition of the political autobiographies

* *Cf.* above, pp. 163, 246.

of the Romans. In ancient biographical and historical works on Augustus, wherever they follow the official tradition, we find a picture of his childhood according to which he grew up in the care of his mother Atia (his father had died early) in purity of morals, protected from all corrupting influences, from ugly things and words, and in a prim seclusion, in an atmosphere of *sanctitas et verecundia*, as Tacitus expresses it—" purity and modesty ".[139] It is probable that he himself offered this picture, the spread and the permanence of which he desired, in his autobiography, so that his youth was interpreted from the efforts of the mature man, who sought to carry out a moral reform in the depraved Roman society. This characteristic was probably peculiar to the autobiography of Augustus and not typical of the emperors' autobiographies.

The same is probably true of the way he brought out in his story of his youth the emotional relationships associated with the life of his family. He seems even to have described in this spirit his relationship to Cæsar, to which he naturally gave prominence. The dictator appeared as the supremely honoured uncle, who for his part showed a tender affection for the delicate and ailing boy, caring for him like a mother, giving him an entirely unearned share in the honours when he celebrated his triumph, but not only spoiling him but educating him ; he adopted him only in his testament, and had said nothing about this intention beforehand. Why ? In order—so Octavian explained—to prevent Cæsar's strange procedure from destroying his nephew's youthful modesty. Octavian also depicted as in a certain sense a family matter the important and difficult decision which he had to make when, as a student at Apollonia, he learned of Cæsar's death, and then, when already on his way to Rome, of the testament. He related that his mother was opposed to his acceptance of the great but perilous inheritance, and that his stepfather, in whose home he had grown up, was also opposed to it ; his stepfather held to his view, but his mother began to waver when she saw that Octavian was determined on acceptance. As regarded himself, he pointed out that he gained strength to make that resolve from the consideration that if Cæsar had regarded him as worthy to bear his name he must probably be so. In that family scene he seems, however, to have adopted a heroic tone. For he tells us that he replied to the warnings from his parents with a verse from the Iliad, where Achilles, resolved to avenge Patroclus, is warned by his mother Thetis, " Doomed, then, to a speedy death, my child, shalt thou be," and answers : "Straightway may I die, seeing that I was not to bear aid to my comrade at his slaying ! " [140]

The old Roman identity between the life of the noble families and that of the State, mentioned at the outset of this section, no longer existed in the time of Augustus. The change must have found expression in his autobiography, although he dealt with both his public activities and his private affairs from moral points of view. The autobiography was the product of the political life which it described. Long before it was written, after the victory over Sextus Pompeius (36 B.C.), at the beginning of his second Consulate (33 B.C.), and in other critical situations, he had taken the opportunity of his speeches to the citizens or in the senate to explain the course of affairs, to defend his own attitude, and to denounce his opponents.[141] The tone of these speeches was obviously continued in the autobiography. This is especially true of his relations with Mark Antony. The two engaged in mutual abuse. According to the official tradition, Antony began it. "He taunted him, for instance," writes Suetonius, "with his great-grandfather, saying that he was a freedman and a rope-maker, while his grandfather was a money-changer." [142] The blow struck home. In the autobiography the emperor said nothing about his father's ancestors and wrote of his father, as Suetonius tells us, only " that he came of an old and wealthy equestrian family ", while he dealt at length with the ancestry of his mother because of her relationship with Julius Cæsar. To other charges made by Antony he replied in his autobiography with similar charges of personal ambition, cowardice, quarrelsomeness, irresponsible courting of popular favour, and so on. In these polemical passages he seems to have followed the old and tried method in political propaganda of attributing to his opponent disreputable activities of which he was well aware that he himself had been guilty.* Thus, for instance, he contended that in the period before the triumvirate Antony had protected Cæsar's assassins, while at that time he had himself joined with Decimus Brutus in fighting Antony.

Of another character, though at an equally low level of political history, is the part attributed to women in the political game, a part that is again characteristic of memoirs in the

---

* Cf. Isocrates, *Antidosis*, 14 : " I consider that in all the world there are none so depraved and so deserving of the severest punishment as those who have the audacity to charge others with the offences of which they themselves are guilty."

narrower sense of the word—of court memoirs. In the case of Cleopatra, it is true, the relations between Augustus and that dæmonic personage are not clear. All that is clear is that he represented Antony's passion for her as a simple mania, which made Antony morally irresponsible, and that he held her responsible for his rival's policy, which he branded as a disgrace to the Roman people. The official version, that he fought not against Antony but against the queen of Egypt, may have been simply a political subterfuge : some years before the break with Antony, after the destruction of Sextus Pompeius, he had announced that the terrible time of the civil wars was over. But the personal rancour so closely associated with memoirs is clearly visible in the reports drawn from the autobiography concerning another woman, who played a political part at the time of the triumvirate —Fulvia, Mark Antony's first wife (he was her third husband), who has been called " Rome's first princess". It was said of her that she dominated not only her own husband—until he fell under the influence of Cleopatra—but also his younger brother Lucius, who at that time, at the outbreak of the civil war in Perusia, was Consul (41 B.C.) ; indeed, it was said that the whole senate followed her blindly. Augustus held her responsible for the war that broke out when he had carried out the most appalling of the mass proscriptions, which the two other triumvirs had left to him—the expulsion of the population of eighteen prosperous cities of Italy, in order to divide their possessions among the veterans, who had been promised this land in reward for the victory over Cæsar's assassins. Fulvia's husband was at war in the East, and she was watching his interests in Rome ; in her hatred of Octavian, who had deprived her husband of Cæsar's heritage, she took the part of the expelled population and incited them to resistance, so that he was compelled to suppress the revolt by harsh measures. It has been said [143] that " Fulvia was the first ruler's wife who felt and behaved as such ; since the Romans of her time had never heard of such a thing, they were utterly shocked, and on this point the moderns have not corrected the judgment of the ancients but have been even more severe "—with the exception of Shakespeare, who makes Antony exclaim at the news of her death (40 B.C.) : " There's a great spirit gone." [144]

We are inclined to think that the harsh judgment is to be traced to the emperor's memoirs. There is an extant epigram on Fulvia, attributed to Octavian, which runs as follows :

> Quod futuit Glaphyran * Antonius, hanc mihi poenam
> Fulvia constituit, se quoque uti futuam.
> Fulviam ego futuam ? quod si me Manius oret
> Pedicem, faciam ? Non puto, si sapiam.
> " Aut futue, aut pugnemus," ait. Quid si mihi vita
> Carior est ipsa mentula ? Signa canant ! †

Martial, that master of the art of the epigram, notorious for his indecency, says that he " had these six wanton verses from Cæsar Augustus ". He framed them in verses of his own, in which he addresses Augustus :

> Absolvis lepidos nimirum, Auguste, libellos,
> Qui scis Romana simplicitate loqui. ‡

Martial said of himself, " *Lasciva est nobis pagina, vita proba* " (" Lewd is my page, but virtuous my life ").[145] From his friend Pliny the younger we learn that at that time, in Nero's day, it was fashionable for *summi et gravissimi viri*, " eminent and highly responsible men ", to write licentious verses.[146] There is no accounting for tastes. One of Mark Antony's insults to Octavian, quoted by Suetonius,[147] was to taunt him with having " earned adoption by his uncle Julius Cæsar through unnatural relations ". We need not enter into these things. Octavian's epigram concerns us only in so far as it shows that he did not shrink from putting forward that explanation of a war, even as a joke, as a point in the play of a tainted fancy. The verse is usually taken seriously.[148] Montaigne, the great French thinker of the Renaissance, quotes it in a chapter of his essays in which he sets forth philosophical considerations on war.[149] He proceeds to show by the example of Augustus, *le plus grand, le plus victorieux empereur, et le plus puissant qui fut onques*, " the vanity of the occasions by which war is produced . . . which is the greatest and the most stately of human actions ". But Augustus' example does not show, as Montaigne supposed, the small causes for which a great emperor will go to war, but that the view that wars can have such origins was common at that time—the time when Cleopatra was pursuing her dæmonic course. Augustus must

---

* A courtesan, mistress of Antony. He made her son by an earlier lover king of Cappadocia.

† Martial, Epigrams, XI, xx. " Because Antony handles Glaphyra, Fulvia has appointed this penalty for me, that I should handle her. I to handle Fulvia ? What if Manius were to implore me to treat him as a Ganymede ? I trow not, if I be wise. ' Either handle me or let us fight,' she says. And what that my person is dearer to me than my very life ? Let the trumpets sound ! " Translated by Walter C. A. Ker in the Loeb Classical Library.

‡ " There's no doubt about it, Augustus : with your gift of Roman forth-rightness you exonerate my bright booklets."

have shared the view if he seriously attributed to Fulvia the responsibility for the Perusine war.

In any case, this imperial autobiographer imposed no reserve on himself in his statements about women associated with him. When the triumvirate was set up he had betrothed himself— though already betrothed to another—to Clodia, the adolescent stepdaughter of Antony, in order to set the seal on his reconciliation with that powerful man. When the conflict between the two broke out two years later, he sent her back to her mother Fulvia with the remark that she was still a virgin—a statement which he confirmed on oath. This was probably to be found in the memoirs. Then, at twenty-three years of age, he married Scribonia ; he was her third husband. From this marriage, declared Virgil in 40 B.C. in his fourth Eclogue, a boy would come who would give the world the eternal peace for which men long, introducing a golden age. Scribonia gave birth to a daughter, and shortly afterwards Octavian divorced her, because he had conceived a passion for Livia, who was to be his life's companion. Livia was with child, but he took her from her husband—peacefully and with honour. In his autobiography was to be found the statement that he divorced Scribonia because he was " disgusted with her behaviour ", *pertaesus morum perversitatem eius.*[150]

This remarkable style of exhibitionism is not unique, and there was method in it—Augustus' political method of bringing scandalous happenings in the imperial house to the official notice of the senate, as formally, under the Republican Constitution, both the joint ruling body and the centre for public information.[151] Thus he had a report read to the senate on his daughter's dissolute conduct, and he depicted one of his grandsons, whose banishment was under consideration, as a dreadful example of profligacy.* We feel in this unkingly procedure a mixture of court atmosphere and the old republican publicity of family life, which may have served to enliven the political autobiography in imperial Rome. The only extant fragment of Agrippina (in Tacitus) takes us into intimate family history. It is a scene made by her mother, the widow of Germanicus, in front of the emperor Tiberius. Ill and weeping bitterly, she implored him to grant

---

* Suetonius tells us (64) what amounts to another aspect of the same attitude : Augustus " organized the education of his daughters in this way : he accustomed them even to woolwork, and forbade them to say or do anything that could not be permitted to become public and to be reported in the court journal "—the equivalent of the Official Gazette. (*Cf.* Wilcken, *op. cit.*, p. 116.)

to her unconsumed youth a second husband.   Tiberius gave her no answer.

One may quote further examples of this style.   In his *vita* [152] Hadrian denied his Spanish origin, bowing to the current prejudice.[153]   He dealt with his earlier drunkenness, again with an explanation characteristic of his self-consciousness : he had indulged in wine-bibbing only out of regard for Trajan, who in turn had richly rewarded him.   Of Septimius Severus it is said that in his otherwise credible autobiography he " made excuses for his vice of cruelty ".   It is possible that the eight books of the autobiography of the emperor Claudius, with what Suetonius calls their rubbishy contents, followed the example of Ptolemy Euergetes II in digressing into stories of court dwarfs, precious tables of citrus wood, marvellous Arabian trees, and a newborn Centaur.[154]   The strangest thing of this sort is found in fragment 19 of Augustus' autobiography—a detailed, precise recipe for a household remedy for failing eyesight : " This composition has been copied from the Commentaries of the emperor Augustus, who regularly used it himself and recommended it to other people."   It might be supposed that that was simply a " puff " for an " Every Man's own Doctor ".   But an analogy is offered by the biography of a Spanish grandee, which concerns itself mainly in the style of ancient histories with political and court affairs : among its miscellaneous recommendations for the good of the soul, for distinction, and for well-being is a remedy for toothache.[155]

This pettiness extends to the treatment of other persons. There does not seem, as a rule, to have been in these autobiographies of emperors any twisting or lofty evasion of facts, any strong denial of atrocities, or simple branding of rivals as rebels ; instead there is a complicated process of self-justification and backbiting, and here and there one can still see the insults heaped on political opponents, such as " push, mendacity, abusiveness ", or " infamous, vicious, nefarious, dishonourable, lascivious, debauched ".[156]

The plainest evidence, however, of the rather low level of these imperial writings is the treatment of signs from Heaven. These have come down to us in considerable number from the *vita* of Augustus.[157]   In them the autobiographer had a means both of elevating his own person and his position as ruler by virtue of the religious tradition or imagination, and of exhibiting the sense, appropriate to a royal will, of the inevitability or the fated nature of events, including his own deeds. Augustus had this belief. He spoke, like the dictator Sulla, of his Tyche. There has come down to us among his dicta an expression of good wishes [158] for a grandson of his who was going on active service —that " the popularity of Pompey, the daring of Alexander, and my own good luck " might attend the young man. In his autobiography he dwelt in this sense on his narrow escapes from grave illness and other mortal dangers, lightning and so on. But, so far as we can see, he used the omens to make plausible the divine care, the predestination and sanction of his rule, in the manner of a rationalized superstition, keeping to that orthodoxy which he had himself established when restoring the old national religion as a means of maintaining the Roman State. A feature of this use of omens is the lack of poetical imagination in the pictures, which only approach greatness where old traditional or literary assets of reported miraculous signs were available, or tremendous natural phenomena, such as the comet of 44 B.C., which is mentioned in Augustus' autobiography as a sign of Julius Cæsar's entry into the world of the gods. We may judge of this pedestrian sort of invention from a dream vision that was one of the many omens of his future greatness, clearly an invention of Augustus' : a youth was let down from the sky into the Capitol by a golden chain, and there he was handed reins sent by Jupiter ; Cicero is said to have had that dream and at the first sight of Octavian to have recognized the youth in him. Or a premonitory sign of victory in a naval war : Augustus was wandering along the shore when a fish jumped out of the water and lay at his feet. In Severus' autobiography, which related all the dreams, oracles, and prophecies indicating his rise, the principal premonitory sign mentioned, again a dream vision, has a military tinge : a huge thoroughbred horse, with royal trappings, bore the emperor Pertinax through the Via Sacra, and just in front of the market-place it threw him, and allowed itself to be mounted instead by Severus, who had been standing apart, so that Severus towered, proudly and firmly seated, above the crowd in the Forum.

Especially characteristic, however, is the way the mention of heavy strokes of fate is robbed of its effect by the introduction of everyday trifles into the omens. Augustus considered it worth mention in his *vita* that on a critical day he had put on his left shoe first—a warning of a military mutiny that became a mortal peril to him. Agrippina, writing of the birth of her son Nero, mentioned the ill-omened detail that he came into the world feet first. Hadrian adduced as an omen of his ascent of the throne that once, when he was tribune of the people, he had lost the cloak which those officers wore in the rain : emperors never wore such a cloak.

The dream that brought the signs could also give them a picturesque character, though this resulted not from an elevated state of mind but from frights and shocks. Nero, after the murder of his mother, saw the earth rock and open, and the souls of all those whom he had murdered climbed out and crowded round him.

v. Augustus' Monumental Record of Deeds

" The principal element of heroic actions is the happy instinct that inspires a man with the desire to enjoy a good reputation." So said Frederick II of Prussia. The king had hard things to say of the loss of dignity involved in the arguing of political issues in public : " Let it suffice for rulers to settle their disputes by armed force, without prostituting themselves before the world by writings, which are suitable for the markets and not for the throne."

The self-portrayal, however, of rulers and men of action, which seems to be justified entirely by the gravity of the subject-matter, stands in greater need than other sorts of autobiography, if it is to have greatness, of a concentrated state of mind, in which the man of action, lifted out of the practical relationships of ordinary life, is alone with his strong will, so that he may form his picture from within. There are many ways of doing this, and often a work planned on a big scale fails of achievement owing to defective organization of the royal literary labour. Prince Bismarck gave us in his *Gedanken und Erinnerungen* an autobiography covering the whole of his long life, in which the great statesman, founder of the new German Reich which for two decades he ruled as a faithful servant of his king, stands before us at full length after his loss of power, still exercising the power of his personality and the authority of his political vision in free, natural, passionate speech with a religious sense of responsibility. Lord Clarendon, the leading statesman of the Restoration period, maintained a dignified philosophical attitude of the classic ancient type when after his fall, in exile, he set out to write his autobiography as a pendant and complement of his great *History of the Rebellion.* Based on firm ethical convictions, this apologia, although treated as a private undertaking, a testament for his children, aimed at objectivity in its judgments and in the characterization of his own person and of friends and enemies alike, the portraiture of whom is the most brilliant feature of the famous book.

Other examples of literary excellence are offered by Cardinal Retz, whose brilliant autobiography drew its artistic quality from Corneille's tragedies, or Maximilian I, who emulated the forms of the poetry of chivalry. Frederick II himself, in his Memoirs, aimed at high historical art and at philosophical interpretation of the causes of historic evolution. In Richelieu's Memoirs, and especially in his political testament, a powerful and assured political intelligence was directed to the perpetuation of his life's work by means of general principles and maxims drawn from it ; their inculcation was to assure the continued dominance of his will in the future conduct of the State. His shadow, he said, must show itself and remain active ; the words of his testament, spoken with the candour of the dying, should be timeless, endowed with ever vigorous force as coming from the Beyond.

Self-portraits of kings, in which the rulers present themselves as ordinary human beings of flesh and blood, portraits striking in their freshness of colouring, confront us from times and places where we might least expect them. In mediæval Spain there is the Book of Deeds, *Commentari del Feyts*, of King James I of Aragon and Catalonia (1214-1276), who was called the Conqueror ; and in central Asia there is, early in the sixteenth century, the autobiography of the Turkish conqueror Babur (" Tiger ")—a successor of Timur—who founded in India the so-called Mogul dynasty. Conventional elements of elaboration were to be found from of old in the self-glorification of the rulers of the Near East—a stock of imposing formulæ, or the erection of vast buildings, or association with the monumental art in the simple style adopted by the inscription of Darius, or the splendour of resounding phrases as in that of Antiochus of Commagene. Among the Roman statesmen of the pre-Augustan period autobiography appeared in various forms, achieving greatness, or at least striving after it, in the conscious presentation of the moral personality, or the relating of the will-to-power to divine favour and destiny, or through literary style. And although the actual emperors' autobiographies—scraps which,

however carefully approached, can at any time be so easily distorted
—are incoherent and unimpressive, we have the one surpassing
monument, standing in quiet majesty, the Roman greatness
of an emperor who lived in supreme fullness of power, described
in his own words by the ruler himself—the *res gestæ* of
Augustus.

In consecrated ground on a quiet spot not far from the
centre of the City, on the edge of the Campus Martis, which
Augustus and Agrippa had made the most magnificent quarter
of Rome, this record of the emperor's deeds was erected. Here
Augustus, soon after his return from the East and forty years
before his death, had built a monumental tomb for himself and
his house. A high wall of marble blocks surrounded the burial
chambers : Goethe estimated that the enclosed space could have
held four to five thousand people. Above this wall sloped the
tumulus, planted with cypresses to the top and crowned with a
colossal bronze statue of the ruler ; in front of the memorial
stood two granite obelisks, which the conqueror had brought
home from Egypt.[159] Here Augustus, who was always ailing
and always contemplating death and who yet lived to so advanced
an age, had buried his sons and heirs, Marcellus, Agrippa,
Drusus, Caius, and Lucius Cæsar. He had composed the inscriptions for their funeral urns, or had placed a fuller obituary record
of one or another on the outer wall.[160] Now, in accordance
with the directions in his will, there was inscribed on the inner
surface of the two tall doors of his mausoleum, which opened
toward the city, his own record of his deeds, in three columns
of about fifty lines each on the broad bronze covering of each
door. The document, prepared long before but drawn up at
a sitting,[161] included the statement that it had been written in
his seventy-sixth year—the year of his death. He had deposited
it in the temple of the Vestals in Rome, together with other
holograph documents containing his directions for the eventuality
of his death. These documents, with the *res gestæ*, were opened
and read in the senate after his death. They consisted of full
instructions in regard to his solemn burial ; his personal will, a
business report on the financial resources and the military per-
sonnel of the State, and perhaps in addition a separate document,
a sort of political testament, indicating to the regent acting for
his successor the general principles of his rule.

The appearance of the *res gestæ* among these documents shows
clearly that it was one of the ruler's last acts to give posterity a

definite picture of himself as he wished to be remembered. The method of publication he chose—not book form or any independent presentation, but association with the mausoleum—gave the written words a firm background that drew not only upon the solemnity of the monumental edifice but upon the religious conceptions that surrounded the name Augustus and the idea of his imperishable existence.

The provision of massive architecture to throne their words was habitual among oriental rulers. Mommsen pointed out that the royal inscriptions of the Middle East, and especially that of Darius, offer the only analogy to the memorial to Augustus—corresponding to the effect of the oriental regime, tempered by Hellenic influence, on the transformation of the Roman State system into the Augustan Constitution, the personal rule of the first citizen in the State.[162] Moreover, the environment of this memorial recalled the old Roman religious ideas that gave expression in the interment ceremony itself to the overcoming of death through perpetuation in history. Near the mausoleum, and connected with it by a park, was to be seen the cremation station Augustus had laid out ; thither, in accordance with his will, the funeral procession had gone from the Forum, headed by the cavalcade of the forefathers in an unending line, all the historic figures from the Forum of Augustus, represented as living persons, Romulus among them ; Cæsar, his father, had to appear as a god among the pictures of the gods. Then the pyre flamed up, and the eagle captive in it was released and flew toward Heaven. The funeral was followed by the apotheosis, by resolution of the senate declaring Augustus to be a national god. Thus his record of his deeds in front of the mausoleum, and later in the already existing temples of Augustus and temples of Rome in the Italian provinces and in the cities of Asia Minor, bore the superscription drawn up by Tiberius : " The deeds of the god Augustus, through which he subjected the world to the sovereignty (imperium) of the Roman people, and his expenditure for the State and people of the Romans."

Whatever may have been Augustus' own attitude to the idea of his deification, he must have known that it was intended. There was nothing so monstrous about it as there might seem to be to us, with our conceptions of religious faith and of monotheism ; it was an expression, intelligible in view of the interconnexion between politics and religion, of the actual historical function the ruler and organizer of the empire had exercised and was still to exercise. He had enjoyed divine honours in his life-time, acknowledged and, indeed, promoted not only by subject peoples but by Roman citizens, who had to swear by the god Augustus ; only in Rome had he permitted during his lifetime no temple but only the honours of a hero.[163] In the words of the *res gestæ*, which were intended for Rome, there is not the language of a god and nothing of divine grace or reference to a world above human activities ; there is a unique combination of self-confidence and restraint in the monarch's matter-of-fact way of presenting the historical facts ; the picture he deliberately paints of his personality reveals a self-reliance and a strength of will that need no boosting. The higher, super-personal order from which the ruler's power receives authority for its legitimate exercise is not a divine right of his own, but the enduring Con-stitution of the Roman State, and the standard by which he measures his own achievement is determined by the national traditions, the customs and character of the forefathers.

But that strange religious belief, which after all was widely and genuinely held, raising a man, because of superhuman deeds, to a hero and to a god, must be taken into account in order not to judge by ordinary standards the close association with death in which the monument was intended to produce its effect. To interpret the memorial as nothing more than an epitaph accessory to the monument is to belittle it.[164] So would be its attribution to an apologetic motive as in the ordinary type of political memoirs. In following the native development of autobiography in the political life of the Roman Republic,* we came across inscriptions more or less comparable with the monument of the emperor Augustus, but the comparison should not mislead us into classing it with other inscriptions ;[165] it should serve to measure its distance from all that preceded it. It will not be possible to find a superior category for the individual elaboration that found here a permanently effective method of self-portrayal for a great ruler ;[166] autobiography is not a *genre* determined merely by its form, and just where it comes into existence of necessity and with greatness it produces a form of its own. The form chosen by the emperor corresponds to the importance of the place, which was naturally and tradition-ally devoted to remembrance, and which provided for the inde-pendent memorial a fixed and deliberately chosen frame. Out of the deep silence that surrounds death and transfiguration

* See above, pp. 222 *sqq.*

proceed the words of the immortal man, starting without preface as if spoken by one present, words whose truthfulness is assured by the fact that they were spoken in the face of death :

" At nineteen years of age, on my own initiative and with my own means, I recruited an army and gave back to the State, which had been oppressed by the dominance of a party, its freedom."

What a grandiose beginning ! And how different a level from that of political memoirs ! All that is petty has fallen away. The historic achievement alone finds expression. It has retrospective effect. There remains the pride that he was so young when he assumed the great responsibility. But the deed with which the nineteen-year-old youth started gains its importance, and indeed its purpose, from the achievement of the mature man, or what he regards as the essence of his achievement, or, in still more political terms, wants to be regarded as its essence —the " liberation " of the State. Who will quarrel with the man who made history, and, indeed, in stern self-discipline made himself what he was, if he also placed his own interpretation on the historic facts ?

That is the character of the narrative. Augustus presents his account not, as is so often said,[167] to the *plebs Romana*, to the broad mass of the city population, but in sight of eternity. This sublime standpoint did not induce him to disclose the state of mind of the man who realized his proximity to the divine. But this reticence was due not to any tendencious inclination to give the public what it wants, but to the positive attitude we have described : it was for the historic facts to speak ; the human, personal element, the man's hidden energy, remained undisclosed as concerning only the solitary ego. The consciousness of achievement, in the ordering of the State which he had effected in his long rule, to the salvation of Romanism and the lasting good of the world, provides the basis on which his deeds, which, regarded morally, seem so discrepant, form a consistent whole. In this lies the truth of the account ; it is not historical in the sense of reproducing the events as they happened—autobiographical documents scarcely ever have the value of truthful records—but in a practical sense. The state of things achieved in the development of his person and of the State, which was to determine the future of Rome, leaves everything of the nature of egoistic courses, usurpations, atrocities and bloodshed, far behind itself as impotent shadows. The record is concerned with lasting realities that will make history, and from this higher standpoint the past is not reproduced but lived through again and re-formed.

Here there was no room for subjective considerations, whether of surface biographical details or of the ruler's Stoic duty-ridden life or of his personal sense of power. Augustus does not mention his name, or his father's or mother's ; he does not begin with birth or adoption but with his first political successes, and he makes no mention of the supreme authority in virtue of which he ruled. He has no desire to place on record the way successes were achieved, but only the achievements. Similarly the independent efforts of other persons gain no mention ; as Cato did before him, he leaves out their names, and speaks of them only in general, though definite, terms, which make of the political situations from time to time only so much visible as is of importance to the final development, so that the cause of the Fatherland is always in view. Where there is no escape from mentioning his enemies and rivals in the civil war, he indicates them impersonally as the leaders of opposition moves—for instance, " the man with whom I went to war "—or a deed that aroused human or national feeling is mentioned without calling up the picture of the doer by giving his name : " those who assassinated my father ", " those who had suppressed the constitutional order through party rule ", " he who had pillaged the temple and placed its treasures in private hands " ; or, still more briefly, a subordinate interpolation : " when the kings " (Cleopatra and her sons) " held the greater part of our eastern provinces ", or, in a direct reference to the hard war against Sextus Pompeius, " I cleansed the sea from the pirates ".

The general custom was to brand rivals and rebels as enemies of the realm, but Augustus, in dealing with the critical battle at Actium, confined himself to stating that " all Italy " chose him as leader and flocked to his standard. There is not the slightest trace of rancour left from his hard and violent struggle to secure sole power. Similarly he makes no mention of the persons who collaborated in his rule, as did Darius, who gave at the end of his inscription the names of his helpers. As if unconcerned with the moral relation between man and man, Augustus concentrates on the political actualities, showing the functioning of the State-maintaining organs, *Senatus populusque Romanus*. The senate, always referred to with respect, is mentioned only as a body ; not a single member is named. Senate and people appear even in those violent times before the founding of the constitutional monarchy as determining factors who sanctioned his power—not that he has any feeling of a need to defend himself against charges of usurpation, or any desire simply to spin phrases ; the Constitution as he had restored it, with its lasting efficacy in view, could give back content and force to what had become a mere conventional form. The new, monarchical Roman State which he had founded, and which he represented in his own person, was in a genuine Roman sense intended to maintain continuity as far as possible with the institutions of the ancient Republic which had slowly developed in the course of history. The Roman *virtus*, fostered by these institutions, was once more to be made fruitful by them as the germ of the State, destined to live on while the Republic changed into a universal State, and even to dominate that inevitable evolution.[168]   In this sense the *res gestæ* stood for the eternal city, and Augustus spoke as the *princeps* of the Republic and not the *imperator* who carried on the imperial regime. He confined the enumeration of the benefits for which the world was indebted to him to what he had given the Romans, and based his proudest phrases on the inherited *ethos*, the example of his forefathers, which he was restoring and elevating, and on the weight of personality on which alone his worth as ruler was founded.

Here is style without fantasy or passion. That which seems possible only through direct intervention and construction, the penetration of the past with the consistent conception that has its essential truth in the current life of the author, is here attained, to all appearance without any auxiliaries, by simple, bare factuality, by *imperatoria brevitas*, an emperor's brevity. The subjects are so massive that they demand clear and precise expression. But it is just this that produces strength. Concise, calculating, characteristic, hard at times, without superlatives, he is sparing of words lest any excess or looseness should interfere with objectivity. All is nerve, assured and deliberate will, clear robust intelligence. When the record has to go into details, as in dealing with grants of money, he gives the figures to the *denarius*, so that the dimensions of his deeds are sharply defined. Since the body of his work rests on the national traditions, he can measure his achievement throughout in its relation to the historic past, as something in no way qualitatively different, by emphasizing what he did first, or alone, among the Romans. This emphasis is very reminiscent of the laudatory speech delivered at the funeral of an ancient Roman republican of the third century B.C., whose success was described as " unique in the whole history of Rome ".*

The masses of facts which the first Roman emperor has to record are held together in a simple, characteristic way. The scaffolding is not chronological order, and no direct means of connexion, transition, and the like are used, rarely a " thereafter " or " therefore ". Yet it is not a mere register with separate headings, such as honours, expenditure, or victories, under which the facts are classified.† It is like a structure in which the stones balance owing to their differing but well-proportioned weights and so form a whole. Facts which through their content have greater weight and more general significance serve as massive beams, as foundation stones and crown stones, and also as pillars within the more uniform individual masses.

The record opens with three crucial statements which, packed together in lengthy main sentences, and given a more general character through leaving out the date, provide at the very outset of his political career the measure for the whole (c. 1–3). " At nineteen years of age I . . . gave back to the State its freedom." The offices in which the growth of his power is registered, up to the triumvirate, follow logically on this as the sanction accorded to him by the pillars of the old Constitution, senate and people. Then come the twin events, concisely reported as his personal affair, of the outlawing of Cæsar's, his father's assassins as his just vengeance and the victory over them as the deed of himself alone. Finally " I undertook wars on sea and land, civil wars and foreign wars the world over "—thus are the struggles for power embraced in a general statement of his wartime eminence ; there follows the complementary fact of his mildness as victor everywhere, and at the end he calculates scope and measure, giving the number of soldiers—500,000—who served under him, and of ships he captured.

After this beginning comes the development of details under three heads, arranged in groups. First the offices and honours in which his position found expression. They appear to be thrown in indiscriminately, and yet they are systematically arranged,[169] so that a certain order is made visible in the position he attained as sovereign ruler. The account starts (c. 4) with

---

* The pontiff Metellus. See above, pp. 217–8.

† Unaware of this composition, some historians have wondered that the most characteristic distinctions—Augustus, *pater patriae*, etc.—come at the end. These scholars tried to improve the text handed down to us by placing those distinctions in the *cursus honorum*, which makes the first section !

the highest regular dignities of the Roman commander and states-man,* at one point it goes beyond them.† It then rises (c. 5 and 6) at once to the prerogatives offered to him, which were equivalent to those of absolute monarchy. At this critical point he sets forth the decision by which without any such encroach-ment he carried out the required services within the limits of the republican magistrature. He then (c. 7 and 8) proceeds from the triumvirate period by way of contrast to the forty years of his status of *princeps*. Here come his permanent civil and priestly offices and his statesmanlike measures aimed at the regeneration of the Roman people and at estimating, through the censuses, its existing and increasing vitality. The section ends with the honours that culminated in the recognition that the realm of Augustus was peace.

Where he is concerned with traditional things, he contents himself with the simple mention of the office or distinction, and often there are no actual sentences but simply figures—how often, when, and for how long ; the imposing list is also directly given by means of summary enumeration, for instance seven priestly offices : " Pontifex, Augur . . . Fetial have I been." Thus a predicate that has full content suffices for pregnant emphasis ; compact sentences defining a service, such as the feeding of the city at times of dangerous inflation, have weight and gravity ; and running through the list at short intervals, like a strong embankment holding back the surging floods, are such phrases as " I refused ", " I did not accept ", " I rejected ", indicating his self-command in declining excessive triumphs or unusually extended official prerogatives. In the last main passage, dealing with his position as virtually a monarch— the lifelong supervision accorded to him over laws and customs, with unrestricted plenary power—he expressly sums up the sense of these negative sentences (c. 6) : " I refused to accept any office that was against the custom of our forefathers."

Similarly he sums up his intention as to the measures of reorganization that follow as a special group (c. 8) : " By means of new laws I reintroduced many standards of our forefathers that had fallen out of use in our practice, and I even supplied for many things a standard for emulation by posterity." This refers to the increase in the patrician families, the framing of a Con-stitution for the senate, and the triple census showing the in-

---

* The triumphs, the title of *imperator*, the festivals of thanksgiving, the consulates.
† The 37 years' office as tribune.

creasing total number of Roman citizens. In the honours that
come now (c. 9–14) there is no longer an accumulation, but the
few distinctions he mentions give at once through their characteristic names a picture of the achievement acknowledged. Of
the honouring as a hero implied when his name was given in
the hymn of the Salii next to those of the gods, there is the simple
statement that " By resolution of the senate my name was entered
in the Saliar hymn." Then comes the grant by the senate of
an altar to " returning Fortuna", and the naming of her festival,
falling on the day of the ruler's return, as " Augustalia " ; and
then the dedication of an " Altar of Augustan Peace ". Of the
public demonstrations he makes only summary mention, without
dwelling on pictures of his enjoyment of fame—how, under a
resolution of the senate, on his return from the East the foremost
men in the State, some of the prætors and the tribunes with
one of the consuls and a deputation of senators, went as far as
Campania to receive him, " an honour accorded to none but
me, down to this day " ; how at his acceptance of election to the
office of *pontifex maximus* " a crowd assembled from all over Italy,
vaster than is believed ever to have been seen in Rome ". Here,
too, is a concentrated final sentence :

The gates of war (of the temple of Janus), which in accordance
with the will of our forefathers are to be closed when in the whole of
the Roman empire peace has been won by wars on sea and land,
were closed in the time before my birth only twice in all since the
foundation of the City, and during my period of office as *princeps* were
three times closed by resolution of the senate.

The next group (c. 15–24) is formed by the striking evidences
of the ruler's munificence, economic achievements which under
the peculiar system of State finance had to be covered from private
resources, and which as a rule represented the emperor's presents
to the people in compensation for its loss of its freedom—the
personal expenditure of the " first citizen " for the material welfare of the Roman plebs and the soldiers, for finances and buildings, religious worship, and the public amusement so important
to the southern lands. Here everything is set out quantitatively.
At the outset come the immense sums—in all 600 million denarii,
but he does not himself give a total—which he disbursed among
the populace of the capital (every item per head with the number
of recipients—usually a quarter of a million), in land or money
to the veterans, and also for the chronic deficit in the treasury,
for the starting of the new military fund, and for the relief of

the taxpayers. At the end come new sums and presents in gold which he granted to the Italian towns or the great temples out of war booty or out of the proceeds of sales in Rome of the eighty silver statues of him on foot, on horseback, and in war chariots. There stands out among the figures the " I first and alone among all " with which he ends the record of the compensation of the former owners in connexion with the land grants. Like the eastern despots, he gives a list of the public works and temples erected or restored by him, by means of which he had made Rome an imperial city, the enormous aqueducts, the Via Flaminia with its many bridges—but here again without predicates of vastness or sunning himself in magnificence, but with the names soberly stated and, for instance, with some fifteen different buildings as objects of one *feci*. Then come the titles of the festivals and spectacles he had given the people, with details of scale and frequency ; in the gladiatorial combats there were " some 10,000 men " whom he had sent to fight, and in the animal-baiting " some 3,500 African beasts " that were killed. A magnificent naval spectacle, which Ovid had described, is recorded simply in figures : the lake excavated for it was " 1,800 feet long and 1,200 feet broad " ; there were 30 big warships and still more smaller ones ; the crews totalled 3,000 combatants. Alongside the mere popular amusements come the secular plays, in the celebration of which the religion of the State reached its climax, and for the Martialia, recalling the subjection of the arch-enemies, the Parthians, there comes once more the proud *primus feci*, " I was the first to do it."

There follow in the next section (c. 25–33) the wars in which he destroyed his opponents in home politics and set up the Roman Empire, or, as he terms it, brought peace to the world (*pacificavit*). In this section there is a massive progression from group to group of sentences, corresponding to the historic process in which he established his power and expanded the power of the State ; but he does not present the wars in this way, he has no desire to be accounted simply the conqueror that he was : the *leitmotiv* is Peace.

First comes the victory over Sextus Pompeius, who had dominated the Mediterranean with his fleet, cutting off Rome from her grain imports. His phrase, as already mentioned, is : " *Mare pacavi praedonibus* " (" I gave the sea peace from the pirates "). But the precariousness of that time sticks in his memory, as in that of the people. He had granted an amnesty to Sextus' army, which had surrendered after the decisive naval battle

(36 B.C.), but he gave no pardon to the slaves who had taken service with Pompeius in thousands, fleeing to Sicily and thus injuring the capitalist economy in Italy. In view of this he added the following sentence : " In that war I captured slaves, to the number of some 30,000, who had fled from their masters and taken up arms against the State ; and I handed them over to their masters for punishment." This sentence is reminiscent in content and tone of the inscription on the milestone of Popillius Lænas *—but it is only a single sentence, like an old stone on a new wall. Octavian had had 6,000 runaway slaves, whose masters could not be ascertained, crucified in the places they had come from. This he does not mention. Instead he jumps from the war with Pompeius, officially the last civil war, to the critical struggle with Antony ; and here, where the existence of the Roman State was at stake, he shows the victory as the outcome of the general political situation, in which he himself was borne on a popular movement. He makes no mention of the danger of a Greco-Oriental empire, or of the names of Antony and Cleopatra ; only the name of the great decisive battle is given, and even that only in a subsidiary sentence : the main point is the great demonstration of confidence, the *coniuratio*, by which his mission as saviour of Rome was virtually confirmed by the people. " All Italy voluntarily swore allegiance to me and demanded that I should be the commander in the war I won at Actium. The same oath was taken by the provinces of Gaul, Spain, Africa, Sicily, and Sardinia." He adds that at that time there were 700 senators fighting under him, and that of this great number of dignitaries 83 had been or later became consuls, and 170 held priestly office.

The zenith in this rise is formed by the sovereign position he assumed after the conquest of Egypt ; he describes it thus : " When I had extinguished the civil wars, I was in possession by general consent of universal power." But this significant sentence comes later ; first he continues his survey of the wars, proceeding from the civil wars to the wars abroad ; this again is done without any noise of arms, not in the tone of a conqueror, but with the express declaration that he had " waged war with no people without just cause ".† He records in detail, but with the utmost

* See above, p. 227.
† This is in harmony with the wise moderation he imposed on himself in the conquest of Germania after the defeat of Varus, and in general with the maxims of rule which he particularly recommended to his successor in one of the testamentary documents—to confine the empire to the status quo and to undertake no policy of conquest. Dio Cassius, 56, 33. *Cf.* Tacitus, *Ann.*, I, 11.

brevity, the safeguarding ("*pacificatio*") of the frontiers on west and north, the expansion of the empire in the east and south —" Egypt I added to the Roman Empire "—and the places or the number of the military colonies, for the prosperity of which he then does allow himself one superlative. Roman legions pushing on in Pannonia and Arabia, Roman fleets east of the Rhine estuary and on the Danube, kings of the Parthians and Medes and Germani as petitioners in Rome, Augustus as the man who gives the Parthians and Medes their kings, remote peoples, even India, represented with him by many royal embassies, in order to assure the friendship of the Romans—four times he is able to introduce the " never before attained " into this outline of the nation's sphere of power and fame.

And now comes the conclusion of the whole : Augustus sums up his life's work in facts of the most general order. First he refers to the crucial act of the year 27 when he laid down the extraordinary prerogatives of the triumvirate, to make an end of the period of emergency and bring back into force as far as possible the old constitutional system. Of this particular event he places on record its general and lasting meaning as an expression of the consciousness he has of his self-ordained position in the Roman State and of his supreme fame. In the years 28 and 27, " after making an end of the civil war, when with general consent I had power over all, I transferred the State from my dominance to the free rule of senate and people.* . . . Since then the element that has given me the supreme position has been the dignity of my person. But I had not one prerogative of office of greater scope than my colleagues in the magistracy." Inserted between these two sentences and supported by these statements of his own, and giving them support in turn, are placed the public pronouncements presenting the same substance in the verdict of senate and people—the honours conferred on him in lasting evidence of his triumph over enemies and rescue of the State, the great virtues he was acknowledged to have, and the eminence of his person in general ;

---

* This sentence of the *res gestæ* is the main point of attack for the judgment of the record as deception, hypocrisy, phrase-making. If one single proof of the error of such a conception of the monument is wanted, it might be remarked that Augustus, in spite of his notorious caution and deliberation in writing as in other things, would here have unnecessarily taken upon himself the responsibility for a lying statement. The fact that " rem publicam populo Romano restituit "—that he had " restored the State to the people "—had been testified to him by the senate at the conferment on him of the golden wreath of oak leaves.—*Corp. Inscr. Lat.* (2nd ed.), p. 231. *Cf.* Gardthausen, *Augustus*, I, p. 1337.—Thus, in this connexion Augustus would have been able to refer to this distinction in " oratio obliqua ".

the decoration of the entrance to his house with laurel, the fastening of a citizen's crown over the door, the consecration of a golden shield of honour, which, " as the inscription itself shows, was given to me by senate and people for my *virtus* and gentleness, justice and piety ", and the conferment of the name Augustus, meaning " venerable " or " majestic ".

This document was not a mere last move in a subtle policy : Augustus needed a monument of this sort in order to publish, unhampered by circumstances which might be stronger than he, the ideal aim he cherished, without which his work would be an enigma.* In this self-portrayal, in which, as was customary, there was no place for the dishonourable, there were plenty of inaccuracies.[170] On the main point, concerning the situation in foreign affairs, the apparent inconsistency disappears on closer examination.[171] Other objections have reference to the picture he gives of his internal policy. He represents its course as a consistent whole, regardless of the cruel and despotic methods of his youth, which he outgrew, overcoming his passions by means of Stoic self-discipline. This aspect involved misrepresentations of some facts, but such distortions are far fewer than is usual in autobiographies. If Augustus' record of his deeds is measured by the untruthfulnesses, the deliberate and the inadvertent deceptions, which, when one inquires into details, make autobiography generally the least reliable of historical sources, this document excels in honesty most of those of its type, whether the work of literary or of political personages.

Starting from these inconsistencies, some historians have imputed to Augustus an ingenious tactic which would reveal the record as essentially a " tendencious partisan document ".[172] This view corresponds to a rather mean picture of the emperor, in which the achievements of one of the world's historic personages are assumed to have been attained by petty means of misrepresentation and intrigue, and the preservation of the republican institutions, through which the emperor intended to give his Constitution the strength that comes from continuity, is regarded as an empty form. To defend him from that imputation, and to show the truthfulness of the great historic document, it is not

---

* On an imitation of this monument by Hadrian, *cf.* von Wilamowitz in *Hermes*, 23. Hadrian had an inscription set up in the Pantheon which he had erected in Athens, and sought to outbid Augustus' *res gestæ* by dispensing with warlike fame —he declared that he had not voluntarily begun any war—and by giving a list of benefactions covering the whole world, temples built, restored, and beautified, and presents given to Greek and barbarian communities.

enough to establish the absence in it of any direct lying and the general accuracy of the laconic phrases, the manufacture of lies being carried out only through the way the reader absorbs the cleverly presented facts. The thing that matters is that a self-portrayal that possesses this completeness, this solidity, this form, could not have been produced if the point of view represented had not lived in the consciousness of the author as utter reality. Man would have had to be made differently to be able to do that.

CHAPTER II

WRITERS' AUTOBIOGRAPHIES AND CHARACTER
ANALYSIS

In the literature of the Augustan age we meet, for the first time in our story, with poets. From Ovid we have a lengthy autobiographical poem ; he placed it at the end of his *Tristia*, the books of elegiacs which he sent to Rome from the exile imposed on him in A.D. 10 by the pitiless wrath or moral indignation of the emperor. We have shorter poems from other Augustan poets, including Propertius and Horace, telling of their lives. We have also an autobiographical sketch from the eminent historian Sallust (86–34 B.C.). A resolute partisan of Cæsar, he had withdrawn from political life after Cæsar's assassination, to devote his " precious leisure " to the study of recent Roman history, instead, he writes, of such " slavish occupations " as farming or hunting. In the introduction to his first historical monograph, on the conspiracy of Catiline, he sketched his own path from politics to political history in a manner reminiscent of the moral point of view from which Plato's path from politics to philosophy is sketched in his famous so-called Seventh Epistle. Aiming at the revival of the old Roman *virtus*, and at the same time filled with the sense of the dignity of the intellectual life. Sallust claimed for the true, the impartial historian no less fame than is enjoyed by the doer of great deeds. Before this, Cicero, whose vain effort to glorify his deeds as statesman we followed, had written a record of the truly great position he held as orator and writer. In connexion with his history of Roman eloquence, in his *Brutus* (46 B.C.), written in dialogue form in imitation of Aristotle, at a time when civil strife had put an end, in his judgment, to a free and unconstrained eloquence, he gave a profound analysis of the development of his own oratory.

In the Greek-speaking world, autobiography was represented at that time by a politician and man of letters from the Middle East, Nicolaus Damascenus, who lived from about 64 B.C. until after A.D. 14. As a confidential adviser of Herod the Great he had played a part in the diplomacy of the Roman Empire, but he enjoyed special celebrity as a court historiographer.

Among his many works there stand out two—a Universal History which he wrote at the suggestion of Herod, its 144 books reaching from the time of the Assyrian world empire to his own day, when Rome had entered Syrian and Palestinian territory ; and a biography of Augustus, which was probably commissioned by that emperor, and in any case made use of his autobiography. In consonance with his philosophical training, his own autobiography, of which several excerpts have been preserved, was constructed according to the rules of the biographical art ; it also bore the formal title " Of his own *bios* and his own education ".*

The next autobiographical work that calls for mention here, also by an author writing in Greek who had turned from political life to history-writing, and who made a lasting name by his historical works, is the Memoirs of Flavius Josephus (A.D. 37–100?), as the Jewish notable Joseph the son of Matthias called himself after entering the service of the emperor Vespasian, the Flavian, at the time of the downfall of his people : Vespasian rewarded him with Roman citizenship. We may complete this varied list with the autobiographical writings of Galen (A.D. *c.* 130–*c.* 200), the famous physician and physiologist, born at Pergamum in Asia Minor. In these writings " on his own books " Galen devoted special attention to an account of his course of studies.†

These autobiographical works differ among themselves and made their appearance individually, scattered through two centuries ; they may, however, be regarded as parts of a whole, and then, each in its own place, they fill a certain definite category of self-portrayals of personality in the Hellenistic epoch, which we may call that of the autobiographies of writers. All of them have a Hellenistic character, and though one or another of them has originality they are more or less directly the outcome of Hellenistic literature. That these autobiographies of writers are not chance products but have representative significance is confirmed by the fact that successors to them appear in similar form, changed and deepened, in more modern times, especially among the humanists.

But the distinctive element that associates them together is that they depend on methods of biographical treatment developed earlier, and point back to the philosophic conception of man

---

* Περὶ τοῦ ἰδίου βίου καὶ τῆς ἑαυτοῦ ἀγωγῆς (Suidas). On the title *cf.* Leo, *Die griech.-röm. Biographie*, pp. 190, 253.

† Lucian's autobiographical works, which in some respects are akin to this group, belong to another literary class. See the next chapter, Vol. II.

underlying those methods. The forms of biographical literature which had been elaborated at the outset of the Hellenistic period are rooted in a conception of man that belongs to the great historical types of psychological vision. That conception provided the basis for a systematic analysis of human character. Just as the development of such a psychological analysis was of general importance to the growth of human studies in European culture, so also there proceed from it in the history of autobiography far-reaching influences of lasting importance. Autobiography as a literary *genre* received here more than the individual self-portrayals that came into existence in this connexion, which represent for us the multifarious class we termed the autobiographies of writers : these are mere fruits and in some cases mere small shoots of a many-branched tree, whose roots extended also into the other fields of the *genre* of autobiography. Generally speaking, the various types of biography evolved in the Hellenistic epoch maintained their position with the firmness of Greek art forms down to modern times, when they were superseded by a truly historical conception of man. They were also used again and again by autobiographers. In ancient times it is only the few extant examples enumerated above of the autobiographies of writers that give us news of these relations : even these works can only be comprehended from the connexion we have indicated between biography and the philosophic conception of man.

1. ARISTOTLE AND THE SHAPING OF BIOGRAPHY

The point of departure lies here in the analysis of human character by Aristotle. In his thoroughly clear mind the way of seeing things plastically that characterized the classical Greeks (who, as we have pointed out,* grasped amid the vicissitudes of life the typical outlines of individual existence) became a method of comprehending the individual philosophically. This method assumes that at the back of a man's actions a consistent self-determined character is to be sought ; his various states of mind and activities, which often appear to us to be at variance with each other, are all referred to some few characteristics, considered represent his nature. Static though it was, this vision of human nature was the first methodical philosophical approach to the problem of the unity of life in the individual person.

* See above, pp. 61–2.

Eventually, it is true, it was replaced by the historic method of analysis, which allows us to penetrate more deeply into that unity and to grasp its dynamic character. But there remains from that classical vision of the permanent *ethos* * of the individual the idea of a law of its own creating the separate individuality of the human person and determining its development, an idea that prevents Western thought from denying the reality of the apparently separate existence of the individual, as do so introspective a people as the Hindus [1] in their metaphysical conception of reality.

We can still trace the inner links in the process that leads from Aristotelian psychology to the shaping of biography.[2] The influences at work have their basis in the metaphysic of the *maestro di color che sanno*,† which Aristotle himself called πρώτη φιλοσοφία (" fundamental science "). It has often been described, and must be mentioned here, how his pioneering effort to assess empirical reality with its particular observable data as full reality, instead of attributing to it, as did Plato, only apparent as opposed to real existence, and nevertheless to subject it entirely to scientific thought, led Aristotle from Plato to the conception that the so-called Ideas, underlying everything that is, subsist in the things themselves as their " forms ", either actual or potential. Conceived in terms of genus and species, the immanent " form " of anything accounts for its existence and true function. Though the individuals are the primary and only *substances*, they do not exist independently of their " form ", that is, of the universal within them. It was owing to this conception of the " *substantial* forms " of things that Aristotle succeeded in rationalizing the material of the individual life-story, which might seem to withstand rationalization. He did so by means of his characteristic concept of evolution or development (*genesis*). He conceived development as a process through which the individual attains to his own essence or true " nature " in the course of his life— in fact, as an eternal " pattern imprinted in the individual and growing in the vital process," ‡ as the biologist sees it, instead of the outgrowth, as we conceive it historically, of the characteristics and the many possibilities of human nature, which in the relations of its existence to the world create the form of an individual personality. In this sense he defined the " nature "

* See above, p. 62.
† " The master of those who know ", as Dante called Aristotle.
‡ " Geprägte Form, die lebend sich entwickelt " (Goethe).

of things as " that which each thing is when fully developed ", and evolution as a movement in the individual both determined by the immanent form of the individual and directed toward this form, which is the " end and aim " of all growth.

Through this Aristotelian conception of development was revealed the structure, as it were, of biographical vision, which was to be observed from the first in classical antiquity and long maintained itself as if obvious : it directs the first glance to the individual actually in maturity so as to apprehend his essence and function from an idea of completion ; all that lay before this, the whole youthful career, is then an irrelevance, or at most to be stated in advance as a forecast of the traits of character of the grown man. Thus the real task of a description of development—the demonstration of the way the unity of the personality is formed in the course of life, in the individual's dealings with his environment—remained essentially beyond the horizon of this ancient type of biography. Indeed, even St. Augustine's " Confessions ", that most intimate narrative of an individual life, which at the same time comes closer to our modern idea of true history than any other autobiography written in antiquity, was still, in its general composition, strongly influenced by the Aristotelian conception of development.

But the way Aristotle analysed the actual formation of the moral character influenced the psychological deepening of auto-biography in other directions. For these analyses [3] kept close to empirical reality ; in them he emphasized the importance of the natural endowments in the varying relative strength of inclinations and moods, and so prepared the more individual idea of the moral personality, as reached later by the Stoic philosopher Panætius. [4] Aristotle pointed out that not only reasoned decision but gradual accustoming and practice of the way of acting characteristic of a particular virtue are needed for the virtue really to become also ἕξις, a possession and attitude of the whole human creature as it potentially is. Outlines of a technique of moral self-education thus became visible : they entered into the Stoic method of education and conduct of the soul, where self-contemplation then became such a " practice ", *exercitatio*, for the development of our natural gifts in the pursuit of excellence and for the strengthening of character. Finally, with the recognition of an influence of the social environment on the formation of character the direction was set in which it was also possible for a pragmatic explanation of the story of the writer's own development, as we meet with it later, to come into existence.

The forms of presentation corresponding to this conception of man have had fundamental importance for autobiography. They may be enumerated here at their start, although in auto-biographical literature they make their appearance, elaborated or recast, only later, to some extent only in modern times. From Aristotle's time there first developed biography : it was produced in part through the investigations of his pupils, the so-called Peripatetics, into the history of civilization,[5] and from the third century B.C. onward it was established as a literary *genre*. Its design of giving the record of a man's life with his permanent *ethos* in view could be tackled in various ways, and we know two ancient basic forms [6] of biographical treatment, while the introductory story of forebears and of youth was kept to a single form.

On one side the form of biography was determined by what Aristotle had laid down with his conception of " energy ", that is, action as opposed to mere potentiality—that the essence of anything that exists attains its perfect form only in operation, as the means of fulfilling its true function. Even the essence of God is energy in this sense of *actus purus*. Accordingly a man's character is to be seen developing in his *bios*, his way of living, in action ; for his activities were considered not as mere signs of his character, which without them would be beyond the reach of an observer, and still less as external facts, but as holding the man himself within themselves, because there did not yet exist the conception of the reality of the inner life in inde-pendence of its manifestations. Thus was individual life to be portrayed : " not by an enumeration of characteristics, but the man's acts were to be placed on record so that his character and nature were revealed by them ".[7] By means of this mode of seeing life in action, the abstract element associated with every description of a human being that approaches the individual from without, in the belief in characteristics fixed once for all, could be brought into as close proximity to living reality as possible within the limits of that method of approach. Witness is borne to this by the great effect which the " Characters " of Theophrastus, written in accordance with the master's model, had on dramatic art, down to Molière. And although the more differentiated psychological interest of Plutarch's biographies, works unrivalled in ethical and artistically stimulating influence, belongs to a later age, their technique belongs to this sphere. Such an art of bringing to life the individual human qualities remains, however, always a personal gift, and even the occasional Renaissance autobiographies modelled on Plutarch did not attain their highest level in this form of ancient biography.

The other and naturally the predominant form of biography was based directly on the characteristics and types that offered a theoretical handle for capturing the individual traits, whether a famous man was to be considered with regard to his conduct of life or a particular way of living was to be presented through an individual.[8] How convenient a method of idealization became possible in this sphere is strikingly shown in the autobiography of the Peripatetic court historiographer Nicolaus Damascenus. On the other hand, as philologists and critics became the chief representatives of this literature, amid all the anecdotes and gossip the habit of investigating and analysing a man's character could spread, and with it the intellectual attitude of the investigator of human nature, standing above the investigated subject. In Cicero this tendency, probably developed from pragmatic history-writing, bore fruit for autobiography. But it was also operative in the realistic novel with its first-personal narrative. Moreover, we may place here the well-known method of describing a man's character by enumerating his marked propensities. This method corresponds to the aloof scientific approach to human nature, as it does not require an intimate relationship between observer and observed as does the true historian's method of interpreting an individual life. Since the Greek artistic interest no longer prevailed, this analytical tendency turned into a dissection of individuality. The various aspects of a man's attitude to life and the world were dealt with by treating each separately and giving with it several traits, making clear his usual behaviour from one aspect or another. With this cumulative sort of analysis the task of representing individuality was regarded as fulfilled. It might almost be summed up in Taine's words : * " Every person is reduced in the eyes of the man who has a knowledge of men to three or four principal traits, which find full expression in five or six activities." A definite scheme was elaborated giving the aspects from which a man was to be regarded, in the form of optional heads for the arrangement of the material—such headings as public and private existence, conduct in official business, in war, in the family,

* Retranslated from the German.

toward friends, toward society, toward women ; method of work, studies, writings, memorable sayings ; moral qualities or defects, specified under the various conceptions of virtue ; outward appearance, physical and mental constitution, behaviour in daily life, and so on. This type of characterization is presented to us in Suetonius' biographies, where it is applied, in accordance with the abstract method of analysis, to Roman rulers as well as to literary men, with differences only in the headings. In the auto-biographical *genre* this Suetonian form is not exemplified in antiquity ; it is to be found here, in addition to the *enkomion*,* only from the Middle Ages onward. The strength of the analytical tendency from which it was drawn was yet so great that even Cardano drew benefit from this form, giving it marrow and internal structure in his own *Vita*.

Finally, the starting point is to be sought in this historical context for the type of description of people to be defined as a literary portrait.[9] When literary self-portraiture came to be the fashion of the day in the salons of the French aristocracy of the seventeenth century, its representatives were aware of their debt to ancient models.[10] This method of treatment differs from the integrating characterization with which we are familiar as a part of the *enkomion* : it differs in this way, that the external or internal traits, which do not at all need to be always fixed by means of descriptive terms, are displayed as close together as possible, and thus often asyndetically in order to convey the impression of a complex whole, observed trait by trait instead of being cut up into its various parts. As the descriptions of types in Aristotle—the picture, for instance, of the magnanimous man in the Nicomachean Ethics (II, 8)—and in Theophrastus reveal a particular quality in the more or less many-sided form of observable traits, so here the entire *habitus* of a man, his whole disposition, is intended to be shown. As a rule this complex of traits has no structure, but in this form there is room not only for a random accumulation but for any sort of internal association. And equally variable is the method of presentation : it extends from the routine list of attributes, reminiscent of a warrant for arrest, to the depicting of a man at a climax in his life. As an attempt to do with words what the painter can do visually in a portrait, this sort of personal description was no mere literary curiosity, but was bound up with practical life, as its use in the courts of justice or in astrological horoscopes

* See above, p. 161.

shows.* Thus it was possible for it to be introduced into autobiography from various sources, from literature as well as from the
customs of ordinary life. This influence, however, is observable
only in a late period. The first self-portrayal we have in the
manner of the literary portrait is a work by Bishop Rather of
Verona, of the tenth century, a "Description of Somebody's
Character",† and not until Cardano are there signs of any
influence of the astrological literature of late antiquity, with the
characterizations of this sort which were customary in it.

II. SELF-REVELATION AMONG THE POETS

How, then, in the Hellenistic age, in which such methods and
forms of presentation of personality developed in an international
literature that embraced the various peoples of the Mediterranean,
did the type belonging to this literary world form itself, the type
we call that of writers' autobiographies? We have no documents that might reveal the process directly. The few extant
writings of this widely ramified type, which we enumerated at
the outset of this chapter, date from the middle of the first century
B.C., and two out of the three earliest belong to Latin literature,
which was forming itself in the comprehensive historic process
of the Romans' assimilation of Greek culture. Thus we are faced
here, as in the autobiographical works that came from political
life, with the question of the Roman element in this production.
This question, however, is not so crucial here, because the autobiographies of writers were not built up on native forms of
life, but on stereotyped ways of thought and conventions. This
applies especially to the relation between this production and
imaginative writing.

One of these two Latin works is a poem by Ovid—the first
poet's autobiography known to us in ancient literature. It might
seem unjustifiable to take cognisance of this document in the
present connexion instead of examining the poetic product in

---

* Characteristic of the popularity of this practice is a passage in Apuleius'
Metamorphoses (about A.D. 160), in the famous story of Cupid and Psyche. Venus,
who was pursuing the wandering Psyche in order to punish her, but was unable
to find her, called in the crier-god Mercury. "Nothing remains to be done," she
said, " but for you to proclaim her in public and announce a reward to him who
shall find her. Take care, therefore, that my commands are speedily executed,
and clearly describe the marks by which she may be recognized ; that no one may
excuse himself on the plea of ignorance, if he incurs the crime of unlawfully con-
cealing her." So saying (the story proceeds), she gave him a little book in which
were written Psyche's name and sundry particulars.
† Qualitatis coniectura cuiusdam.

its own field of poetry. But in this autobiography of a poet the question is precisely whether the incentives to its production were specifically poetic. As already remarked, Ovid placed this poem at the end of one of his books of elegiacs. In doing so he followed an Alexandrine convention.[11]   In the court poetry which had flourished in Alexandria since the third century B.C., in a literary and, indeed, a learned atmosphere, the custom had grown up of permitting a poet to accompany the publication of his work with verses of an autobiographical nature, in order to make himself known to the public. We thus see in these poems a variety of writers' autobiography, in contrast to the poetic treatment of the poet's experiences not in a separate poem concerning the author in person but in his work as a whole in what may be termed personal poetry. We find both sorts of poetic self-portrayal in the Latin poetry of the Augustan age, taking the Alexandrine poetry as their model but transforming it in a characteristically Roman fashion. How deep the transformation went depended naturally on the individuality of the poet. In Horace we may see how personal poetry flourished under the liberating breath of the Greek spirit. To this we shall return later. In those particular autobiographical poems, however, one of which is to be found in Horace's works, the transformation of the Hellenistic type seems less thoroughgoing. There remains the general question how the biographical type of work which is alien to lyricism, entered the field of poetry.

If we look for the point from which this association proceeded, we are led back to the sense of their poetic individuality characteristic of the Alexandrine poets. They were originally concerned, so far as we can see, with the interpretation of their art rather than their lives ; but their æsthetic attitude to art involved the recognition of the value of originality as the mark of true poetry, and this appreciation resulted in attention being extended beyond a work to its author's creative personality, and so to his life-history. This innovation can be shown clearly, thanks to a precious discovery which we owe to papyrus-research.

It is a self-revelation of Callimachus, the representative of the new æsthetic tendency that corresponded to the changed position of poetry in the post-classic period. Poetry, which with the dissolution of the political and religious communal life had lost its original function, freed itself in this period, when it was in danger of acquiring an epigonal character, from all associations outside art, and secured a place apart in culture. This decisive change, which we may define by the modern phrase " art for art's sake ", is reflected in the poet's consciousness of the importance of his work, as Callimachus expressed it. He had issued a new edition of one of his books of poems, in his old age, about 250 B.C., when he was a famous but a much-discussed author ; and he provided this issue with a programme-introduction in which he established, with his characteristic grace, the poetic worth of the direction he had taken, that of refined and elaborate art.[12]

The poem is written in a polemical tone, and to that extent is reminiscent of the literary controversies that played so great a part among the Greeks that even in the great tragedies there was room for it in the chorus. Callimachus turns upon his critics, who interpreted as a sign of impotence his abandonment of the petrified tradition of the epic, which was considered to be the grandest and noblest form of poetry. They contended, he says, that he had not at any time produced " a continuous poem, singing of kings or heroes in thousands of verses ". Mockingly he points out the requirements of the large canvas and of heroic material, exposing the æsthetic incomprehension of the " enviers ", as he calls them. The characteristic purpose of his own work demanded another measure—the true measure of all criticism :

> Measure the poet's gift by art, and not by cubic contents.
> Ask not of me a monstrous song of roars and bangs and rumbles :
> Thunder is no prerogative of mine—'tis Zeus that sends it.

He then proceeds :

> For when I first set a tablet on my knees, Apollo . . . said to me, " Good bard, offer to me the fattest possible sacrifice, but only a slender poem. Moreover, I lay this behest on you : take the path that wagoners do not use, and drive not your chariot along the common tracks of others, nor up the broad road ; but you shall drive on a newer, though narrower, way." I obeyed. For I sing among those who seek the grasshopper's sweet sound, and love not the noise of asses.[13]

So he expresses, in the form of autobiographical reminiscence, his consciousness of the originality of his poetry. The typical motif of the poet's inspiration by the Muses, which we found in the early period in Hesiod, is thus given a new meaning. He attributes the path he followed in his poetry to divine guidance, and so represents it as taken designedly. By unhesitatingly attaching this intention, indeed the principle that in art it is individuality that counts, to his first beginnings, he gathers start and completion,

youth and age, and so the whole course of his life, into a
rounded unity with its centre in the poet's vocation, in the
service of the Muses.   To this self-characterization he adds his
ideal of living—a dream of purely poetic, ethereal existence.   He
does not speak of living on in immortal fame, but of unceasing
production.   He draws the colours for his picture from poems and
stories that told of the cicada, the darling of the Muses.   The
verses continue :   " Let others bray like the long-eared beast,
but let me be the dainty winged creature.   Ah, if only I could
live on nothing but the dew from the divine air and sing on
ever, shaking off the burden of old age that now weighs on me
as heavily as the three-cornered isle (Sicily) on Encelados."

Playfully he exaggerates the burden of his sixty years in this
mythological simile.   He does not sing an elegy on old age,
like the poets of earlier times, who praised youth as the fullness
of life in physical strength, combatant courage, and amorous
passion ;   he is inspired instead by the thought of the self-fulfilment of the creative man who preserves in ripe old age the
enthusiasm of his youth.   He illustrates this idea, in the same
way as he illustrates the ideal of an unencumbered, Zephyr-like
life, not from the gods in Olympus but from the winged creature
that is a symbol of sweet song.   There is, he declares, " nothing
unbecoming " in this poet's aspiration, " for the Muses do not
reject as grey-beards the friends on whose childhood years they
smiled ".   So ends the rediscovered fragment of the poem.

The course of subsequent development may be seen from the
later testimony of poetic self-portrayals.   In giving his book of
verses an autobiographical introduction or conclusion, a Hellenistic poet was influenced not so much by the reflected subjectivity of Hellenistic poetry as by the need to meet the personal
interest of the court society in which he moved by giving information about himself, such as the philologists gave of the classic
writers.   In the French salons of the seventeenth century self-
portrayal was similarly practised by authors.   And from the
Roman literature in which such verses are extant we know also of
editions with the portrait of the author facing the title : [14]
" Here is he whom you read, he whom you ask for, Martial,
known throughout the whole world for his witty little books of
Epigrams.   To him, while he lives and feels, you, studious
reader, have given the glory that poets win but rarely when they
are dust."   Thus does an epigram of Martial's at the outset of
the collection illustrate such a title-portrait.[15]

The motives here visible, contained in the relation between the author's life and his work and in the curiosity of the public, are typical of the whole class of writers' autobiographies. The desire for a direct explanation of their own literary achievement is a motive both of Cicero's and of Galen's. And the formal autobiography that we have of Nicolaus Damascenus seems to have been placed at the beginning of his chief work, a world history. Similarly the autobiography of Josephus was appended to his *Jewish Antiquities*.[16]

In this context we might expect to see the rise of literary memoirs, but among third-century works we know only of the book of Antigonus of Carystus on the philosophers of Athens.[17] The treatment of contemporary celebrities, instead of the already historical great who were almost the exclusive subject of the Hellenistic biographers known to us, and the accumulation of material from personal observation and recollection, give this book something of the character of memoirs, and the intimate touch with the human element that is the virtue of memoirs; but in its construction, as the limitation of its subject to philosophers shows, it is not so near to that type as the earlier travel pictures of Ion of Chios. Of similar nature is a work by Seneca the Elder, which has been described as " memoirs of the rhetorical school ". In this work there are excellent literary portraits of friends of the author, but as a whole the book reveals the type of rhetorical declamations that served for practice in style in the school, with the more or less fanciful delineation of the moods and feelings that influenced men in a particular situation.[18] Occasionally we see also how the reciprocal invectives of neighbouring schools of literary men and philosophers, the evil calumnies familiar from the biographical reports of the time, gave an impulse to autobiography. Thus in the first half of the third century there is an autobiographical fragment by the popular philosopher Bion of Borysthenes, of the school of the Cynics, who was famous for his diatribes. The fragment comes at the beginning of the extant biography,[19] as an account of his origin and youth, and is followed by a characterization drawn from a hostile source; it is an extract from a missive from Bion to the Macedonian king Antigonus Gonatas, and in it Bion replies to the evil things said of him by the Stoic court philosopher : " Let Persaeus and Philonides desist from their fabrications : observe me in my own story ! " The use of epistles for autobiographical purposes, seen here in sporadic examples, was certainly nothing

unusual at that time, as Plato's self-justification of a century
earlier in the so-called Seventh Epistle shows ; it has also an
analogy among the humanists, with whom the letter became a
favourite form for autobiography.

And now the literary forms. It is in consonance with the
standing, already described, of autobiographies that in them
the treatment of the ego does not differ substantially from
portrayal by another person. In his book on oratory Aristotle
laid down the rule that " in speaking of ourselves . . . we
must make another person speak in our place "—in order to
avoid bombast and gross vilification of others (" Rhetoric ",
p. 1418 *b*). In saying this he pointed to the autobiographical
essay of Isocrates as one of the best examples of the indirect
method of self-praise. The principle underlying this " ethical "
requirement of good form remained generally accepted, while
the rule itself lost its generally binding character. Undisguised
self-portrayal, and the reliance on the autobiographical intention manifest in the use for it of expressly biographical forms,
is the common advance in contrast with the fictitious defence
pleading of Isocrates, although the narrative in the third person
appears alongside the first-personal method. With this came
at the same time the natural commencement with origin and
youth. And since the ancient autobiographer did not proceed
from his own experience, but from existing literary forms which
he had in front of him in a model work or in the rules of
rhetorical theory, the few extant works now to be mentioned
reveal a formal variety, but this does not go hand in hand with
an individualization.

The thing that is plainest in the autobiographical poems is
the association with the developed biographical form. Here a
poet's purpose—though he had not yet become a classic—was
to provide an imitation of the sketches of the authors' lives
with which the Alexandrine philologists prefaced their editions
of the classics.[20] The " I " form is here naturally dominant,
and it seems that there was a special opportunity for this when
the poet came before the public with his first book or when he
proposed to give up writing or a particular style of work. Virgil,
Horace, and Ovid give us an idea of this custom, and also of the
elaboration the autobiography acquired from it in the Roman
poetry of the " golden " Augustan age.[21]

Virgil gives his name and home at the end of his first large
work, the *Georgica*, a didactic poem on rural life that preceded

his greatest and most famous work, the Aeneid. He was probably occupied already in planning that national epic of Rome ; but as he speaks of himself here, and describes his poetical work (the Georgics and the Eclogues that had preceded them), he brings out the contrast between its subject and the ruler's deeds that were to be celebrated in the Aeneid :

> This, the care of the herds and the work in the fields and the vineyard,
> This did I sing the while great Cæsar fought by Euphrates,
> Setting as victor his mild just sway over reconciled peoples.
> Thus he makes for Olympus. And I in those years, I, Virgil,
> Rested in Parthenope, sweet village, and there, unheroic,
> Laboured at ease on my pastoral pastime—with youthful presumption,
> Tityrus, singing to thee 'neath the boughs of the sheltering beeches.

Horace, Virgil's friend, a little younger than he, made a different use of the traditional form of author's self-portrayal. Horace took over the Scholastic style of those Alexandrine biographies of the classics in delicate miniature, in order to spice the expression of his sense of his poetic individuality. The well-known short poem at the end of his first book of Epistles (20 B.C.), cast in the form of a covering letter for the book, and in a bitter-sweet mood prophesying the destiny of Horace's poetic work, gives in its last eight verses this biographical information according to that Scholastic scheme : descent, career and achievement, appearance, character, age. The delineation of character is served by the mention of an ingrained quality also noted elsewhere for characterization [22]—quick to anger but easily mollified—as writers sometimes characterized themselves in more modern times by adducing one of the four temperaments. Horace tells elsewhere of his career at greater length, in the *Sermones* ; this belongs to his " personal poetry ", to be distinguished, as we have indicated, from those introductory and concluding poems. In those an author could also deal with his person several times, at first briefly and then, as his production grew, at greater length. We see this in Propertius and in Ovid. Ovid, in a short poem (*Amores*, III, 15), made use of the traditional details of origin and home to sun himself in his fame :

> Mantua Vergilio, gaudet Verona Catullo ;
> Palignae dicar gloria gentis ego.

(" Mantua rejoices in Virgil, Verona in Catullus : may I be called the glory of the people of Palignum.") Of his mother-city, he sings, it will be said : " Oh thou who couldst give birth to so great a poet, however small thou art, I call thee great." A later poem is a fully developed autobiography ; we shall come to it shortly. Of the two poems of Propertius, the first (I, 22) is obviously planned as a biography. In it he proposes to give a reply to the question constantly put to him by friends, " What is my rank, whence my descent, and where my home ? " Only the beginning, dealing with his home, is extant, but the few lines show the hand of the poet. In the picture he sketches of his home—he came from Assisi—he contrasts the fruitful Umbrian landscape with the graves from the Perusine war (40 B.C.), through which he lived as a boy, and he mingles the lament for a friend who was among the fallen with his memory of those " dark hours of Italy ". The later poem, of 75 distichs (IV, 1 ; about 16 B.C.), contains the same mixture of country scene and political history, together with the poet's self-portrayal ; its form is, however, peculiar.[23]

Propertius, who called himself " the Roman Callimachus ", writes here, on the model of the Hellenistic master, of his poetic endeavour and the paths by which he came to his goal. He had abandoned love lyrics to undertake more important tasks in patriotic elegy, and had had to realize that that was not the true direction of his talent, so that this last book of his, to which the poem is prefaced as a sort of programme, is only partly devoted to patriotic Roman songs and contains further erotic elegiacs. He now summarizes the story of his life in a situation that enables him to give a dramatic description of the expansion of his high national effort and the final renunciation and acceptance of his own limitations. At the same time, by means of comic exaggeration of that contrast of heroic and erotic poetry, he brings out the resigned and yet proud consciousness of his own ability, so that room is found for biographical details concerning himself. The plan of the form is this : he shows himself, like a cicerone, ascending the Palatine and speaking to a foreigner, to whom he expounds the historic past that is revealed by the scene around them : thus he is able to show from the observation of the thing itself the emergence of his plan of Roman versification, which he now rhetorically announces—and then abruptly, in the same declamatory style, introduces with a shrill change of tone the pronouncement of an astrologer, who deduces from the stars a prophecy of the vanity of his effort. In the verbose speech of this soothsayer are interwoven, as prophecy after the event, the details of the poet's origin and career, half in earnest and half in jest. The astrologer is a

prophet of evil ; what he now has to announce to the poet is
" a new tale of woe "—a counterpart of the legendary history
of Rome, beginning with the fall of Troy, in order to tell how
the Trojan ruler Æneas left the country and after long wanderings
was brought to the banks of the Tiber. " Troy, thou shalt
fall, and thou, Trojan Rome, shalt arise anew ! " Into this
patriotic context Propertius brings the story of his youth.

He begins with the picture of Assisi, the famous beauty of
the city's situation, on a height that climbs steeply like a wall
out of the Umbrian plain. The poet's fame, the astrologer tells
him, will still further increase the fame of his mother-city—a
return of the motif we found in Ovid. Then come the sad
events of Propertius's childhood, his father's premature death,
the impoverishment of the distingished family in the course of
the war, the confiscation of its great estates for distribution
among the veterans, and finally the last great misfortune : the
youth who had been destined by his family to a forensic career,
withdrew from that highly esteemed and remunerative profession and gave himself up to poetry. But amid the jesting he
insists on the dignity of his art. When he called himself " the
Roman Callimachus ", he brought out what that implied by
introducing into the autobiographical account the motif of a
divine calling which he found in his model. He makes the
prophet of woe proceed :

Thereafter when the ball of gold was cast from thy young neck,
And the robe of the free man was donned before thy mother's gods,
Then did Apollo teach thee some little of his song
And forbid thee to thunder forth thy speech in the mad tumult of the Forum.
Nay, then, be elegy thy task, a work full of guile—here lies thy warfare—
That other poets may take thee as their model.

As we know the verses of Callimachus which Propertius is
imitating we are able to observe here in detail how an Augustan
poet adapted the Hellenistic model.[24] Callimachus proceeded
from the contrast between the styles of art ; Propertius sub-
ordinates the æsthetic to the biographical point of view. Thus
the divine summons to the poet appears as a sort of choice of
profession, associated with a particular moment in the life of the
Roman citizen, the moment of attaining adult age, which was
denoted by the assumption of the *toga virilis*. When Propertius
describes this aristocratic custom " in solemn and ceremonious
terms ", the characteristic Roman sense of historic facts may
be observed. The youth's rejection of tradition has reference

to the citizen's career and not to the poet's literary choice ; the witticism with which Callimachus writes of the " thunder " of portentous verbiage in his mockery of the epigonoid epic poetry is now applied in full earnest to practical life with the strife of parties and the corresponding " noisy style " of the Forum, as Cicero called it.[25] Apollo himself appears in the guise of a schoolmaster " dictating a little of his song " to his pupil. But this recasting, which, we feel, offers a contrast with the Greek original, only introduces another nuance into the tone of the self-portrayal without changing the poet's Hellenistic attitude to life. The civic solemnity disappears in face of the devotion to the lighter Muse to whom Propertius gives allegiance. Destined by Apollo to be a poet of amorous elegiacs, he describes his life as a ceaseless vain struggle with the moods of the loved one. The " tale of woe " pronounced by the astrologer continues :

Thou shalt endure the alluring strife of Venus' wars
   and shalt be a foeman meet for the shafts of Venus' boys.
For whatever victories thy toil may win thee,
   there is one girl shall baffle thee ever ;
And though thou shake from thy mouth the hook that is fast therein,
   it will avail thee naught ; the rod shall keep thee captive with its barb.
Her whim shall order thy waking and thy sleeping . . .

So the poem runs in a humorous description of a poet's nature ; the outcome is that his horoscope shackles him in bondage to Venus.

Ovid addressed to posterity the long autobiographical poem— 66 distichs—which we have from him. With this proud gesture he gave expression to his awareness of his immortal fame, as Petrarch did in the Italian Renaissance. But Ovid was moved also by another significant motive. He wrote the autobiography during the exile to which the emperor Augustus had condemned the all too successful poet of the Art of Love, when Ovid was at the zenith of his career (A.D. 8). The poem formed the conclusion of one of the books of his *Tristia*,[26] which he sent to Rome from Tomi, the Black Sea village to which he had been exiled, far from the civilized world, to languish in longing for the great metropolis whose stimulating intellectual atmosphere was to him the very breath of life. With its appeal to posterity the elegy rises like an epitaph [27]—the exile speaks like the ghost of a dead man to those still living beneath the sun : " You may know who I was, I the playful poet of tender love, whom you read." In what follows this poet's autobiography is deliberately kept in simple terms, and, indeed, kept in tune with ordinary civil life. Ovid tells first of his home, his descent, and his education ; he gives the year and day of his birth, mentions the knightly rank of his family, and depicts himself in his early years together with his brother, his senior by just a year. He laments his brother's early death : " I was bereft of half myself " ; he contrasts the careers before the two :

> My brother's bent even in the green of years was oratory ;
> he was born for the stout weapons of the wordy forum.
> But to me even as a boy service of the divine gave delight,
> and stealthily the Muse was ever drawing me aside to do her work.

Thus does he depict himself as a born poet. He relates that he was at pains " to write words freed from rhythm ", conforming to his father's practical advice not to try " a profitless pursuit ". In vain ! " All unbidden, song would come upon befitting numbers, and whatever I tried to write became verse."

There follow details of the official career he entered after he had been trained for it in Rome, and his quick resignation, glad to remain a simple knight without any pursuit of offices :

> I had neither a body to endure the toil nor a mind suited to it ;
> by nature I shunned the worries of an ambitious life.

In the service of the Muses and in the game of love he found " the security of a life free from business " to which he aspired. Looking back on that happy time, he speaks of contemporary poetry with the air of one who belongs to it. He gives a picture of the Roman poets' group, into which he entered as into the company of " gods ". He indicates his own position as successor to Tibullus and Propertius, the representatives of the erotic elegy. His star rose early :

> When first I read my youthful songs in public,
> my beard had been cut but once or twice.

He speaks of the criticism to which, as the artist that he was, he subjected his own works :

> Much did I write, but what I thought defective
> I gave in person to the flames for their revision.

Sure of himself, thoroughly confident of his poetic genius, he would have been glad to live for the day that was so beautiful. As he had written earlier, when composing the " Art of Love " : *

> Prisca iuvent alios ; ego me nunc denique natum
> gratulor ; haec aetas moribus apta meis.

---

* *Ars amandi*, III, 121-2 : " Let ancient times delight other folk : I congratulate myself that I was not born till now ; this age fits my nature well." Translated by J. H. Mozley, in the Loeb Classical Library.

The fate that overtook him in the shape of the prudish emperor willed it otherwise.   Thus, while Ovid feels himself to be a poet of love, and so describes himself, he is concerned at the same time to display the honourable course of his own life :

My heart was ever soft, no stronghold against Cupid's darts
    —a heart moved by the slightest impulse.
And yet, though such my nature, though I was set aflame by the smallest
        spark,
    no scandal became affixed to my name.

In this connexion he writes that he was married early, when " scarcely more than a boy ", that he married three times, had a daughter, became a grandfather, and buried his ninety-year-old father and soon after his mother.   He continues :

Happy both ! and laid to rest in good season !
    since they passed away before the day of my punishment.

So he sets in contrast to the picture of his family life the blow of fate that struck him.   He gives expression to the access of emotion with which he recalls his parents, and follows it with a solemn assurance of the innocence of his life :

If, O spirits of my parents, report of me has reached you,
    and the charges against me live in the courts of the lower world,
Know, I beg you—and you 'twere impious for me to deceive—
    that the cause of the exile decreed me was an error, and no crime.

A short account follows of the unhappy turn in his life owing to " the wrath of the injured prince ".   He does not enter into the cause of his ruin ; it is " too well known to all ".   He concentrates on the description of his feelings.   In face of the dull pain of solitude, under which poetic labours are but a means of filling and passing the empty day, he summons up his pride :

My soul, disdaining to give way to misfortune, proved itself
    unconquerable, relying on its own powers.

After a life " passed in ease " he had borne up against the fearful hardships of exile in a barbarian country on the edge of the world :

Here, though close around me I hear the din of arms,
    I lighten my sad fate with what song I may . . .

He has still the will and the strength to live : this, he says,

I owe, my Muse, to thee ! for thou dost lend me comfort,
    thou dost come as rest, as balsam, to my sorrow.
Thou art both guide and comrade : thou leadest me far from the Euxine sea
    and grantest me a place in Helicon's midst ;
Thou hast given me while yet alive (how rare the boon !) a lofty
    name—the name which renown is wont to give only after death.

So he completes the picture of his personality, bringing the end of the poem back to its beginning :

Although this age of ours has brought forth mighty poets,
    fame has not been grudging to my genius,
And though I place many before myself, report calls me not their inferior,
    and throughout the world I am read most of all.
If then there be truth in poets' prophecies,
    even though I die forthwith, I shall not, O earth, be thine.

This, apart from Cicero's epic on his consulate, is the first and, until the fourth century, the only ancient autobiography in verse of which we have knowledge. The literary custom that had dictated it was continued until the end of the ancient literature, in which biographical initial poems served virtually as prefaces.*

III. AUTOBIOGRAPHIES OF HELLENISTIC WRITERS

The prose works in which famous or successful authors told the public about their character and career are on a larger scale. Not until the Renaissance did brief sketches of careers with self-characterization make their appearance, emulating the ancient attitude in their concise prose. An autobiography in the strictest sense is that of Nicolaus Damascenus.[28] It shows such inability of the autobiographer to comprehend his own individuality, or, rather, such lack of interest in it, as can scarcely be imagined to have been possible in that age of the growing emancipation of individuality ; but it is the only work of its sort of which substantial remains exist ; † and from it an idea may be gained of the literary form that was probably the principal one in that environment.

Nicolaus, the son of an influential notable of the Hellenized capital of Syria, was in his time one of the most distinguished representatives of the general Hellenistic type, more rhetorical than philosophical, in the Middle East. He had found the position in the highest society, to which that culture helped him, under Herod the Great ; before that he had been in the service of Cleopatra. The queen of Egypt had chosen him to be tutor to her children by Mark Antony. After her fall the " philosopher " went over to her enemy Herod, whom Antony had made king

---

* In Ausonius and Prudentius—see below, Part III, Chapter IV.

† These have been preserved not through chance quotations but through inclusion in the encyclopædic work of excerpts from all available historians, compiled by command of the Eastern Roman emperor Constantine VII (about A.D. 950).

of Judæa. Herod had also succeeded, however, in winning the favour of the victorious Octavian, so that he was able to maintain his power in Palestine as a client-prince of the Roman empire.

Nicolaus had spent most of his life in Herod's service in various capacities, as adviser to the king and as his spokesman ; the king entrusted him with diplomatic missions which took him several times to Rome, the centre of world politics. Nicolaus was also a *bel esprit*—a figure frequently found in that period— serving the king as adviser in intellectual matters ; Herod accepted his guidance in the cultural affairs that played a part in the political prestige of a Hellenistic-Roman kingdom of Jerusalem. Finally, Nicolaus served as historiographer at this oriental court, though in reality it furnished more material for tragedies than for memoirs. In his autobiography he represents himself as the mentor who " joined the ruler in the pursuit of wisdom " ; and he mentions that Herod was difficult to hold to philosophy, preferring rhetoric. On the other hand, the two helped each other in historical work ; Herod inspired Nicolaus to undertake his vast " Universal History ", while Nicolaus induced the king to write his memoirs—which he did in Greek, and probably in the form of material, as one of the *hypomnemata* that were left to a trained rhetorician-historian (in this case, Nicolaus himself) to put into shape.[29]

He certainly set no small value on his political successes, which he owed to his gift of oratory—that is, of persuasiveness. But if we follow the ancient distinction, laid down by Aristotle, between the life of political action and the life of contemplation, Nicolaus belongs to the latter. This is testified to by Julian the Apostate, who pointed to him as an example of the superiority of the " practical philosopher " over the politician, and said (about A.D. 350) : " Nicolaus did not personally do any great deeds ; he is known rather by his writings about such deeds." [30] Accordingly in his autobiography the character of political memoirs is less marked than the effort to present his philosophical *bios* or the *ethos* incorporated in his life. He wrote this work at some time after the death of Herod (4 B.C.), in retirement from court and politics, in his sixties or later, probably during a long stay in Rome, where he also wrote the biography of Augustus. For this latter he was able to make use of the emperor's memoirs ; these he put into the literary form elaborated by the Aristotelian school.[31]

The extant fragments of his autobiography enable us to determine how he proceeded in presenting his own personality. The dominant tone is the usual self-glorification ; this is made indirect by the use of the third person, and in that guise it is so strong, and the method of treatment that effaces the difference between a self-estimation and the estimate formed by another person is so deceptive, that there have been attempts to deny the autobiographical character of the work.[32]   In reality we have here the most telling evidence of the fact that in ancient times autobiography and self-knowledge or individualization did not have the same roots. Nicolaus, as a Peripatetic of a good tradition, required for his self-portrayal a definite literary form ; as historian and biographical writer he had at hand the means of forming a picture of his personality, and he also made use of the ethic of his Aristotle, but in such a way that he took over from without, as predicates of his *bios*, the virtues analysed in Aristotle's " Nicomachean Ethics ".   The ideal of culture that had to be presented in accordance with the philosophic tendency of biography is here simply left in the general form in which it was laid down in the philosopher's teaching, and declared to have been realized in the author's own person.   In so presenting it, Nicolaus added his moral ideal to the historical material illustrative of his career, so that his autobiography partly dissolved into political memoirs ; but on the whole he carried out the self-idealization which was the traditional concern of the auto-biographer in ancient times in an even more mechanical way than Isocrates had done.

For such a work the *enkomion* was the natural form : the story of origin and education ; then the main narrative, which, as the first fragments show, was carried through with direct introductory or concluding indications of the virtues revealed in the hero's behaviour, until the narrative simply became a kind of memoirs ; and at the end the summing up of characteristics, which remained once more an accumulation of virtues.

The autobiography begins with the praising of the virtues of the father and mother.*   The narrative part, to judge by the fragments, was mainly concerned with complications of diplomacy or of court policy ; here the author made much of the part he played on that rather petty stage of political life, pluming himself

* In Augustus' story of his youth his mother played an important part, unlike earlier autobiographies, where we find no mention of the mother. Propertius, in his autobiographical poem, spoke of his ancestors as " his mother's gods ", because his father had died (IV, 1, 128, 132).

on his moral qualities ; but he also referred to his literary or
" philosophical " relations with Herod, already mentioned, and
to the undertaking of his " World History "—an " incomparably
huge work ", under which " Hercules would have broken down
if Eurystheus had imposed it on him ".   The closing section is
the actual place for the self-characterization.   It is significantly
prefaced with the sentence :   " All that he was accustomed to
teach was continually observed in his own conduct "—and here
follow as predicates of his conduct the various virtues arranged,
with only slight deviations, in the Aristotelian order of gradation,[33]
and described, with few exceptions, in the terms fixed in
Aristotle's book.   Even in the mannerism of repeatedly introducing his statements with " with reference to ", he imitates
Aristotle's method, which identified the individual virtues through
the subjects to which the right behaviour refers—except that
everything is transformed into expressions of admiration of the
writer's perfection in this right behaviour.

In accordance with this arrangement the autobiographer
deals first with the inferior levels of moral life, the upright
attitude " in regard to money " and " pleasures " with the
attendant virtues of " magnificence " and " liberality " ; " self-
sufficiency " is here added at once, and then " simplicity ",
and, from a later arrangement[34] of the Ethics, the antithesis
of unrestraint, and in particular of softness, " endurance " of
labour and fatigue ; " temperance " and " respectability " soon
follow.   Then come " bravery " and, in transition to the social
field, the cardinal virtue, " justice ", together with " fairness " ;
in its honour the author introduces a few individual traits—that,
in order not to deviate from the right, he even put up with threats
from higher officials ; that in consequence of his honourable
reputation he was much sought after as judge and arbiter ; that
in business transactions his word could be relied on, without
witnesses or written agreements.   After a lengthy gap in the
text, in which Nicolaus probably ended with praise of his
magnanimity, come references to honour and distinction, but
this is in court language ; he dwells on his well-earned enjoyment
of princely favour and exhibitions thereof, becoming, as he points
out, to a philosopher if in their use the right, " moderate "
behaviour and the " philanthropic " frame of mind are brought
into play.   The virtue of patriotism is also given a practical
illustration, which in addition is a thrust against a characteristic
vice of the time :   Nicolaus had never denied his mother-city of

Damascus and had not chosen to be called, like " the Sophists ", an Athenian, or a Rhodian, with a bought title to citizenship, still less in general a Hellene.

Finally came praise of his philosophical way of life, the life of contemplation, which according to Aristotle is the supreme, divine fulfilment of human nature. Nicolaus brings this out neatly, in indirect form, on the model of Isocrates, by making another person criticize his way of life because in Rome he " avoided contact with the great and the wealthy and went nowhere, in spite of pressure from many highly distinguished gentlemen, but lived throughout the day in philosophic meditation ". But his loquacity robs him of this conclusion ; he cannot refrain from dwelling on his virtuous behaviour " in regard to giving and getting money " * and in regard to his intercourse with friends in inferior positions who shared his views : a thing that was probably nearer to his real *bios* than was the blessedness of pure contemplation.

Humanly speaking, we should not regard this ending as mere inadequacy—the merits of the man who pretended to be a thinker lay elsewhere. Characteristic of this is, for instance, a fragment in which he tells how he trained, and, indeed, educated his slaves, and so treated them that they became his friends.†
He might, we think, if he needed a type by which to define himself, have represented himself, for instance, as a teacher, " with reference to " his conduct toward the children of Antony

* *Cf. Nic. Eth.*, II, 7, 4.
† The fragment (139, Jacoby) is of some general interest because of the ethical attitude to slavery. Nicolaus appears here as a forerunner of Seneca, of whom it has been said that " He has never risen higher or swept further into the future than in his treatment of slavery . . . No modern has more clearly discerned the far-reaching curse of slavery " (S. Dill, *Roman Society*, pp. 12, 328). A passage from Seneca's " Moral Epistles " offers a direct comparison. In the " book " " On Benefits " he speaks of the cases in which what the slave supplies ceases to be a " service " and becomes a " benefit ", as it passes over into the domain of friendly affection. " There are certain things, as for instance food and clothing, which the master must supply to the slave ; no one calls these benefits. But suppose the master is indulgent, gives his slave the education of a free man, has him taught the branches in which the freeborn are schooled—all this will be a benefit. Conversely, the same is true in the case of the slave." This passage is compared with the fragment from Nicolaus' autobiography in a study by M. Braun, " Griechischer Roman und hellenist. Geschichtsschreibung ", quoted in R. Laquer's article on Nicolaus in Pauly-Wissowa's *Real-Encyclopädie*, XXXIII, 373.
The changed attitude to slavery that was given effect in Roman law in Hadrian's time (early second century) is usually ascribed to the influence of the Stoic philosophy, to its cosmopolitanism and its teaching of the equality of all men in " the city of God ". In the case of Nicolaus this humane attitude is at variance with the teaching of his master Aristotle, and it may be attributed to Jewish influence, the duty of kindness to the slave being inculcated by the Mosaic legislation. This would be in agreement with the often mentioned influence of the Semitic spirit on the development of Stoic philosophy.

and Cleopatra, toward Herod the Great, and also, as we may emphasize, toward his own slaves.

What prevented him from generalizing with regard to his own individuality was not the interest of the Greek mind in the typical but the fact that he proceeded from an existing and authoritatively established form of ethical doctrine, instead of interpreting his own experience.

Details throw the strongest light on this type of self-description, this strange possibility of an autobiography, long before the Middle Ages, being guided by an authoritative book of morals, and not merely by the moral ideals that had been accepted in daily life. The Nicomachean Ethics declare that the " life of indulgence " is a thing for the crowd, to be " regarded as slavish " on account of the choice of the animal *bios*, and that " such lusts " as are common to man and the other living beings have to be set down as slavish and animal ; Nicolaus says of himself under the heading " lust " : " he regarded as slavish those who indulged in such pleasures ".* Aristotle, in defining bravery, mentions the situations in which the brave man is without fear, and alongside the noble dangers of war he mentions those " on the sea and in sicknesses " ; in his autobiography Nicolaus writes : " Whenever he was faced with danger, from enemies in war or from robbers or in consequence of illness or storm at sea or anything else, he was so stout-hearted " that he put courage into his companions in danger.† The extent to which this method was followed ‡ can no longer be ascertained owing to the gaps in the text ; but in the indications of virtues in the

---

* *Nic. Eth.*, I, v, 1 ; 1095b, 17–18 : οἱ μὲν πολλοὶ ... τὸν βίον ἀγαπῶσι τὸν ἀπολαυστικόν ... ἀνδραποδώδεις φαίνονται βοσκημάτων βίον προαιρούμενοι (" The generality of men ... look no higher than the Life of Enjoyment ... showing themselves to be utterly slavish, by preferring what is only a life for cattle "). 1118a, 23–24 : περὶ τὰς τοιαύτας δὴ ἡδονὰς ... ὅθεν ἀνδραποδώδεις καὶ θηριώδεις φαίνονται (" Temperance and Profligacy are concerned with those pleasures which man shares with the lower animals, and which consequently appear slavish and bestial "). (In this and the next note, the translations are by H. Rackham, in the Loeb Classical Library.) Nicolaus : Ἡδονῆς δὲ ... καὶ ἀνδραποδώδεις νομίζων τοὺς τῶν ἀπολαυσέων τῶν τοιούτων ἥττους.

† *Nic. Eth.*, III, vi, 9 ; 1115a, 30–31 : τοιοῦτοι δὲ οἱ ἐν πολέμῳ ἐν μεγίστῳ γὰρ καὶ καλλίστῳ κινδύνῳ ... οὐ μὴν ἀλλὰ καὶ ἐν θαλάττῃ καὶ ἐν νόσοις ἀδεὴς ὁ ἀνδρεῖος ... ([" What form of death is a test of courage ? Presumably that which is the noblest. Now] the noblest form of death is death in battle, for it is encountered in the midst of the greatest and most noble of dangers ... Not that the courageous man is not also fearless in a storm at sea, as also in illness "). Nicolaus : ὅπῃ κίνδυνος καταλάβοι ἐκ πολεμίων ἢ ληστῶν ἢ διὰ νόσον ἢ χειμῶνα κατὰ θάλατταν ἢ ἄλλως πως, οὕτω δὴ σφόδρα εὔψυχος ἦν, ὥστε. . .

‡ Cf. also *Nic. Eth.*, IV, i and ii (ἐλευθεριότης, Liberality), with the repetition at greater length, at the end of the autobiography, of the passage on the use of money : εἰ μέν τις εἰς ἄσωτον ἢ ἀμετάδοτον ἢ ὅλως ἄι΄ρονα κτλ. δεχόμενος καὶ ὅτε δεῖ ταῦτα καὶ παρ' ὧν δεῖ κτλ.

narrative section * and in the glorification of his father † one may also see Aristotle in the background.

In this autobiography one senses several times the author's effort to create the impression of his well-balanced and finished character, especially in the way a particular course is attributed to guidance by principle : " he used, for instance, to say . . ." We meet frequently with this device in the Renaissance with the same end in view. It is used in the classic style in Lord Clarendon's autobiography. And the plan visible here to us for the first time, and the only time in ancient autobiography, the narrative of career with direct self-characterization at the end, was a favourite one with the humanists. They filled this form with adequate content, thanks to their vision of individuality.

The record of the author's education placed at the beginning of this work is also of importance because of its contents rather than as regards the man himself. In so far as Nicolaus deals in this short chapter with the development of his mind, he seems to make use of a typical method of representing it. He speaks of the " unspeakable love " drawing him to the general education that was the result of his bringing up, a love inspired by the example of his father and intensified by superior talent ($\phi\acute{v}\sigma\iota\varsigma$) ; he tells us that he excelled those of his age and was famous at home before his beard began to grow, an indication of time similar to that used by Ovid for his precocious fame ; and that with increasing years went the growth of capacity ($\delta\acute{v}\nu\alpha\mu\iota\varsigma$) which now attained its goal.

This section is of special interest because it offers an example of the system of education, known to us from pedagogical discussion and precept,[35] which was usual at that time. First came grammar : Nicolaus relates that it made possible for him the study of " the whole art of poetry " and also the composition of tragedies and comedies that were received with applause ; of the further progress of his studies in later years he reports without details : " rhetoric, music, mathematics, and the whole of philosophy ". His philosophical attitude compels him to give a general assessment of that education. Here we may observe a utilitarian tendency typical of the average education of the time. The studies, including philosophy, here the Peripatetic

---

* οἷα δὴ φιλόσοφον καὶ ἀμνησίκακον. Φιλανθρωπία. Cf. Nic. Eth., IV, iii ; 1125 (end of the chapter on Magnanimity).

† σωφροσύνη καὶ ἄλλη λαμπρότης. No boasting of wealth and distinction. Justice (in the same way as in the self-characterization but at greater length). In addition an instance of his piety.

philosophy, are considered to be valuable and, in contrast with manual labour, indispensable for a life kept within due measure, because they befit a free man and in their variety are serviceable in every way for life, " but especially bring pleasantness into life alike in youth and age ". A doctrine of moderation based on egoism that strikes us as Epicurean rather than Aristotelian—so much do the distinctions of the schools of thought overlap in ordinary practical life. As Nicolaus' *bios* claims to be philosophical, he feels himself with that standpoint to be above the common literary level : far from him be the Sophists' trading in education ; that would be undignified.

To show his own dignity he uses the form of the *enkomion*, ending with the summing-up of the character. In this he has a concluding word to say on his education, and adopts the device customary in biographies of philosophers : he quotes a saying of his own that makes plain through a comparison the significance of this course of education. It is the picture frequently met with [36] at this time, of a journey, a picture which in its use for religious experience usually describes an upward progress, but which is here used in a more literal sense with reference to the variety of mental impressions gained by a traveller. As on a long journey one stays for a longer or shorter time at various stopping-places, until at last one settles down once more at one's own hearth, so in traversing the whole course of education one must dwell more or less at length on the various disciplines and then, in possession of the values to be drawn from them, find one's home again by the " truly ancestral hearth " of philosophy.

The presence of such an autobiography, not introduced by the author himself with the usual claim of offering something original, justifies the conclusion that the condition for it existed in a broader and probably also more personal practice of selfportrayals in this form among the Hellenistic writers. Julian the Apostate, who, as already mentioned, points to Nicolaus as a politician who made a name more by his writings than by his deeds, and so was an example of the superior merit of the " life of contemplation " in comparison with the " life of action ", mentions with him from this point of view another court philosopher of the early imperial age, who had also written an autobiography—Thrasyllus, once a follower of the Platonic school, known as astrologer to Tiberius. " Thrasyllus," he says, " by becoming intimate with the harsh and naturally cruel tyrant, would have incurred disgrace for all time, had he not cleared himself in the writings that he left behind him and so shown his true character ; so little did his public career benefit him." [37] Of this apologia no further trace remains.

The only work comparable with that of Nicolaus Damascenus is the autobiography, written about a century later, of Flavius Josephus, an author standing even more than Nicolaus on the periphery of Hellenistic culture. After the disaster suffered by his people, Josephus, as already remarked, had become a writer attached to the court in Rome. His formless work, written in the first person, does not deserve the title it bears—*Bios*—if we understand that word in its philosophical sense, referring to the characteristic way of living and not merely as the common expression for the author's career. It is a strange mixture of the historian's military and political memoirs, moral or religious apologia, and self-commendation. But second-rate as this work is both humanly and as literature, it is of special interest to us in one respect. It is the first known autobiographical work of an author of Jewish origin, faith, and training writing for the Greco-Roman civilized world. And in Rome, where after the fall of Jerusalem he lived under the patronage of the Flavian emperors, Josephus held fast to the national Jewish tradition. He brought to notice the dignity and the age of that tradition in a special work, intended to serve for warding off anti-Semitism ; and in it he emphasized that one of the peculiar merits of Jewish civilization in comparison with Greek was its great national historical records, contained in the Old Testament.[38] The general interest of the learned world in Josephus' writings is due to the Jewish origin of Christianity. For us, with our interest in the influence of Christianity on the development of autobiography,[39] it is of special importance to have an autobiographical work by this man, who was born in Jerusalem of a distinguished priestly family in A.D. 37, a few years after the crucifixion of Christ.

In his long work Josephus deals at length only with one short period, but a period that decided the course of his life—that of the beginning of the great rebellion of the Jewish people in A.D. 66, which was ended by the conquest of Jerusalem in 70 by Titus. Of the 430 paragraphs of the " Life ", over 380 (28–413) are devoted entirely to his work as a sort of Governor (so he represents it) of Galilee during the six months of preparation for war and until the entry of the Roman legions into Palestine under Vespasian. For the subsequent events, his withdrawal into the fortress of Jotapata, the siege and reduction of the fortress by Vespasian, his capture, imprisonment, and eventual liberation, and his conduct throughout the campaign and at the siege of Jerusalem, he refers to " the detailed description given in his books on the Jewish War " (412). In addition to this relation of his autobiography to his first historical work, affecting its political content, there is the literary relation to his other main work, a history of the Jewish people ("Jewish Antiquities"), published A.D. 93–4, when he was nearly sixty years old. The autobiography appeared as a supplement to that comprehensive work, probably in imitation of Nicolaus Damascenus, whose " Universal History " was, after the Old Testament, one of the main sources for the " Antiquities ". But even the normal literary motive for the autobiography, determined by the author's relation to his work and to the public, was mingled in his case with the apologetic tendency. He had to defend himself against the charge of lack of integrity in regard both to his account of the Jewish rebellion and to his attitude in the war, and in the latter case in two respects. His compatriots, or, rather, co-religionists, hated him as a traitor to the national cause, and on the other hand it was alleged, and certainly not without justice, that when the Sanhedrin of Jerusalem sent him to Galilee to suppress the rebellion he made common cause instead with the rebels.* On this last point he contended that both he and the Sanhedrin, and with them the whole of the ruling class of the Jewish theocracy, had been in favour of peace with Rome, and that they were only dragged into the rebellion by an extremist minority. He maintained this both in his autobiography and in his work on the Jewish War. In that historical work, which was published a few years after the fall of Jerusalem, he described the fall of his nation from the point of view of the Roman conquerors ; his intention, as he himself expressed it, was " to console those whom they have vanquished and to deter others who might be tempted to revolt ",[40] that is to say especially the Parthians and the Jews of Babylon. In his autobiographical

---

* The charge of responsibility for the insurrection against the Romans was expressly made against him in a work on the war published much later, about A.D. 100, by a rival of his, Justus of Tiberias. Josephus replied to this in a new edition of his autobiographical work with a polemic against his accuser, which he inserted in his narrative as a " digression " (336–367). The distinguishing of the two editions, necessary for the dating of the work, was first made by G. Hölscher, in his article on Josephus in Pauly-Wissowa, IX (1916). Cf. on this the remarks of H. St. J. Thackeray in his introduction to his translation of the Jewish War in the Loeb Classical Library.

work he tried to make that contention more plausible by prefacing his account of his political activity with that of a journey (13–16) that took him to Rome at the time of the political unrest (*c.* A.D. 64). In Rome, he states, he convinced himself of the might of the Imperium, and accordingly he endeavoured on his return to repress the promoters of sedition in Jerusalem.

> I urged them to picture to themselves the nation on which they were about to make war, and to remember that they were inferior to the Romans, not only in military skill, but in good fortune (*eutychia*) ; and I warned them not to expose their country, their families, and themselves recklessly and with such utter madness to the direst perils . . . But my efforts were unavailing ; the madness of these desperate men was far too strong for me.[41]

The extremely ambiguous part he had played, as a young man of barely thirty years of age, in that critical time in which his people's fate was at stake, results in his account revealing a mass of inconsistencies as soon as it is studied in detail. These are particularly striking where he has treated of the same things twice over, in his book on the war and in his personal record. Even a benevolent modern judge of Josephus, who recognizes that in his historical works " the author faithfully follows his written authorities ", states of his autobiographical notes that they " must be pronounced the least trustworthy portion of his writings. The numerous inconsistencies, of a minor or of a major character, between the two accounts of his command in Galilee betray either gross carelessness or actual fraud." [42] For us, with our general assumption of the unreliability of political memoirs, it is of more importance to note that between the historical and the autobiographical work there is a discrepancy also in the method of presentation. Not only is the former written in the third person and the latter in the first, but the style is different.

In the autobiographical sections of the work on the Jewish War, which take up in all just as much space as the whole so-called autobiography, the rhetorical and dramatic manner of Hellenistic history-writing predominates.* This applies especially to the narrative of the defence of Jotapata (whither he had withdrawn in face of the superior strength of the Roman army), and of his capture after the fall of that fortress. This long section (III, 129–288) has the atmosphere of a historical romance

---

* Josephus had published the work first in Aramaic, and had produced the Greek version with the aid of Greek scholars.

written round a hero. The second-rate quality and the intrinsic untruthfulness of this elaboration make the work appear to us all the more suited to illustrate the type of this artificial sort of self-portrayal, of which original examples, if there were any, have in any case disappeared.

In the panic that seized the insurgents when the legions appeared in Galilee under Vespasian and Titus, he appears as a hero who remains undismayed, although he recognizes the desperate situation :

The troops under the command of Josephus . . . dispersed and fled, not only before any engagement, but before they had even seen their foes. Josephus was left with a few companions. He foresaw the final catastrophe for which the fortunes of the Jews were heading, and recognized that their only hope of salvation lay in submission. As for himself, although he might look for pardon from the Romans, he would have preferred to suffer a thousand deaths rather than betray his country and disgracefully abandon the command which had been entrusted to him, in order to seek his fortune among those whom he had been commissioned to fight (III, 129, 136-7).

The enemy knew that everything depended on him, the great general. When his withdrawal to Jotapata was betrayed to Vespasian, the Roman commander went at once to lay siege to the hill-fortress, " because its fall, could he but secure Josephus, would amount to the capture of all Judæa. Vespasian caught at that information as a godsend, regarding it as by God's providential ordering that the man who was reputed the most sagacious of his enemies had thus deliberately entered a prison " (143-4).

There follows at epic length the description of the investment (145-288). The small fortress held out for forty-seven days. Josephus describes the manœuvring and counter-manœuvring by means of which he managed this, and the ruses through which he kept the enemy deceived as to the true hopelessness of the position of the town ; he also relates some heroic deeds of his men. Only here and there does he exaggerate so much that one shakes one's head ; when, for instance, he depicts the power of the Roman engines to which he mainly attributes the fall of the fortress :

One of the men standing on the wall beside Josephus had his head carried away by a stone, and his skull was shot, as from a sling, to a distance of three furlongs ; a woman with child was struck on the belly just as she was leaving her house at daybreak, and the babe in her womb was flung half a furlong away. More alarming even than the engines was their whirring drone, more frightful than the missiles the crash. Then there was the thud of the dead falling one after another from the wall (245-6).

Amid the changing battle pictures he places a pathetic scene between the general and the population of the beleaguered town :

Josephus, recognizing that the city could not long hold out and that his own life would be endangered if he remained there, took counsel with the principal citizens about the means of flight. The people discovered his intention, and crowded round him, imploring him not to abandon them, as they depended on him alone . . . Josephus, suppressing any allusion to his own safety, assured them that it was in their own interest that he had contemplated departure . . . Unmoved, however, by his words, the multitude only clung to him more ardently : children, old men, women with infants in their arms, all threw themselves weeping before him ; they embraced and held him by his feet, they implored him with sobs to stay and share their fortune. All this they did, I cannot but think, not because they grudged him his chance of safety, but because they thought of their own ; for, with Josephus on the spot, they were convinced that no disaster could befall them (193–202).

Shaken by his compassion for their distress, he gives way, and now calls for a desperate struggle, in heroic tones which he borrows from Greek tragedy :

" Making the universal despair of the city into a weapon for himself,* ' Now is the time', he exclaimed, ' to begin the combat, when all hope of deliverance is passed. Fine is it to sacrifice life for renown, and by some glorious exploit to ensure in falling the memory of posterity ! ' " (204).

After the fall of the fortress the interest is concentrated once more on the person of Josephus. The Romans pursued him, thirsting for revenge, but also because Vespasian " considered that the issue of the war depended largely on his capture ". In the story of his capture (340–408) the theatricality is yet further increased, and at the same time he strikes a religious note with a specifically Jewish tone. In picturing the massacre carried out in the town by the Romans he relates that many of his picked men committed suicide in order to forestall death at Roman hands (331). He then relates of himself that he, " with divine aid, succeeded in stealing away from the midst of the enemy when the city was on the point of being taken ". He took refuge in a cave in which forty other " persons of distinction " were already hiding. They, too, sought and found death, as he goes on to tell. He needs to explain how he himself remained alive. The hiding-place was betrayed to the Romans.

* *Cf.* Sophocles, *Electra*, 995–6.

Vespasian called on him to surrender. He could not bring himself to do so, as he feared that he was being summoned to punishment ; finally Vespasian sent an envoy to him whom he trusted, the tribune Nicanor, " an old friend " of his.

While Josephus was still hesitating, even after Nicanor's assurances, the soldiers in their rage attempted to set fire to the cave, but were restrained by their commander, who was anxious to take the Jewish general alive.   But as Nicanor was urgently pressing his proposals and Josephus overheard the threats of the hostile crowd, suddenly there came back into his mind those nightly dreams in which God had foretold to him the impending fate of the Jews and the destinies of the Roman sovereigns.   He was an interpreter of dreams and skilled in divining the meaning of ambiguous utterances of the Deity ; a priest himself and of priestly descent, he was not ignorant of the prophecies in the sacred books.   At that hour he was inspired to read their meaning, and, recalling the dreadful images of his recent dreams, he offered up a silent prayer to God.   " Since it pleases Thee," so it ran, " who didst create the Jewish nation, to break Thy work, since fortune (*tyche*) has wholly passed to the Romans, and Thou hast made choice of my spirit to announce the things that are to come, I willingly surrender to the Romans and consent to live ; but I take Thee to witness that I go, not as a traitor, but as Thy minister."   With these words he was about to surrender to Nicanor.

But when he had come to this decision and justified it, a further conflict broke out.   The other fugitives who shared his retreat forcibly held him back.   In a speech which he places in their mouths, he makes them representatives of the warrior's honour which he was on the point of betraying, and the demands of which had also a religious content for the pious Jew : according to Deuteronomy, they declared, it is a falling away from God if a Jew gives himself up to the enemy and thereby voluntarily accepts slavery.

They came round him in a body, crying out, " Ah ! well might the laws of our fathers groan aloud and God Himself hide His face for grief—God implanted in Jewish breasts souls that scorn death ! Is life so dear to you, Josephus, that you can endure to see the light in slavery ?   How soon have you forgotten yourself !   How many have you persuaded to die for liberty !   False, then, was that reputation for bravery, false that fame for sagacity " .(355-6).

They threaten to kill him if he does not kill himself :   " If you meet death willingly, you will have died as general of the Jews ; if unwillingly, as a traitor."

It is difficult to say whether Josephus did not really pass, within himself, through the conflict he describes by that alternative. He declares that he could not resolve on suicide because " he held that it would be a betrayal of God's commands, should he die before delivering his message ". But while he thus plays the part of the prophet in public—a prophet of weal for the Roman conquerors—he describes his behaviour in the situation in which his companions threatened him with death as the behaviour of a " philosopher ". He " proceeded in this emergency ", he writes, "to reason philosophically with them ". He then constructs according to the rules of the art a long harangue (362–82) which he is supposed to have delivered to them on the theme that " suicide is repugnant to the common nature of all living beings and an act of impiety toward God our Creator ".

He preached to deaf ears. The forty were resolved on death. They were ready to lay hands on him. This yields a highly dramatic scene to the taste of the rhetorician :

They ran at him from this side and that, sword in hand, upbraiding him as a coward, each one seeming on the point of striking him. But he, addressing one by name, fixing his general's eye of command on another, clasping the hand of a third, shaming a fourth by entreaty, and torn by all manner of emotions at this critical moment, succeeded in warding off from his throat the blades of all, turning like a wild beast surrounded by the hunters to face his successive assailants. Even in his extremity, they held their general in reverence ; their hands were powerless, their swords glanced aside, and many, in the act of thrusting at him, spontaneously dropped their weapons (385–6).

The passage that follows throws an unexpected light on his character. He states that in his straits a way of escape occurred to him. He declared himself ready to go to his death with the rest, but suggested a different procedure : instead of killing themselves, let each one kill his neighbour, deciding the order by lots.

This proposal inspired confidence ; his advice was taken, and he drew lots with the rest. Each man thus selected presented his throat to his neighbour, in the assurance that his general was forthwith to share his fate ; for sweeter to them than life was the thought of death with Josephus. He, however (should one say by fortune or by the providence of God ?), was left alone with one other ; and, anxious neither to be condemned by the lot nor, should he be left to the last, to stain his hand with the blood of a fellow-countryman, persuaded this man also, under a pledge, to remain alive (389–391).

This passage is introduced by the religious sentence : " Trusting to God's protection, he put his salvation to the hazard."

The conclusion of the passage is formed by the scene in which, as a prisoner in chains, he stands before the Roman commander and his son Titus and conveys to them the message his God has given him : " You will be Cæsar, Vespasian, you will be emperor, you and your son here."

In contrast with this dramatic composition, which stands out from the historical work as a self-contained section of a personal character, the autobiographical work is made up of disparate parts. The main part, dealing with the military operations and administrative measures in Galilee in the short time between the outbreak of the insurrection and the entry on the scene of the Roman legions, fails, in spite of the length to which it runs, to give any clear picture of the situation, still less of the " general ", as Josephus calls himself here too. The picture falls to pieces because the population of Galilee, which was ruled at the time by Agrippa II, the king of Judæa installed by Rome, had split up into parties which Josephus had been unable to unite. But it falls to pieces not only for that reason but because, in the style of political memoirs, he regards political happenings from the standpoint of personal enmities. He writes mainly of intrigues and plots with which his fanatical enemies pursued him, so that his life was continually in danger, though, thanks to God's help, continually saved from it. His adversaries succeeded in inducing the Sanhedrin to recall him. But he did not leave his post. In writing of this he brings into play the same rhetorical devices as in the part of his historical work that we analysed. He tells of a dream in which the future is foretold to him, but this time it is the future he himself expects :

" There stood by me one who said : ' Cease, man, from thy sorrow of heart, let go all fear. That which grieves thee now will promote thee to greatness and felicity in all things. Not in these present trials only, but in many besides, will fortune attend thee. Fret not thyself then. Remember that thou must battle even with the Romans ' " (209).

There follows a scene of popular commotion. Men, women, and children crowd round him and beg him not to leave them. The colours are less vivid than in the corresponding scene which we quoted from the historical work. On the other hand, later on in this account of his enmities he states that he was actually hailed by the Galileans as " benefactor and saviour " (259). In the same passage he records the testimony of the assembled populace, on the same occasion, to the uprightness of his administration, in reply to calumnies. This is a point that particularly excites him. Elsewhere he gives a formal, almost religious, assurance of his integrity :

I preserved every woman's honour ; I scorned all presents offered to me as having no use for them ; I even declined to accept from those who brought them the tithes which were due to me as a priest . . . And though I took Sepphoris twice by storm, Tiberias four times, and Gabara once ; and though I had John * many times at my mercy when he plotted against me, I punished neither him nor any of the communities I have named . . . To this cause I attribute my deliverance out of their hands by God—for His eye is upon those who do their duty—and my subsequent preservation amid the numerous perils which I encountered (80–83).

With the moral self-justification the literary is bound up in a thoroughly superficial way. When he has told of the capture of Tiberias he interrupts the historical record and interpolates a polemic against malignant critics of his book on the Jewish war, especially against Justus of Tiberias, an old enemy of his, who had come forward, thirty years after the fall of Jerusalem, with an account of the rebellion that contradicted Josephus as a historian and compromised him as a politician. In accordance with the rule that attack is the best defence, he challenges his rival's qualification as historian. This qualification is possessed only by those who have been actors or witnesses in the events described, or who have obtained an exact knowledge of the facts by inquiry from those who knew them—advantages which Josephus claims for himself.[43] In this connexion we learn that in his book he had made use of the Commentaries (*hypomnemata*) of Vespasian and Titus, so that we have here an example of the general relation, mentioned in the preceding chapter, between such memoir-like or documentary works and the writing of history.† As further evidence of the truth, indeed the exactitude, of his historical account he mentions that Vespasian and Titus, who had conducted the campaigns in Palestine, and King Agrippa of Judæa, client-prince of the Roman Empire, had expressed themselves in most favourable terms concerning his work. He declares that he could produce sixty-two letters from the last-named which prove his statement. Above all, he declares, the emperor Titus, conqueror of Jerusalem, was " so anxious that my volumes should be the sole authority from which

* John of Giscala, a rich merchant who dominated that city and who was a passionate opponent of Josephus.
† See above, p. 237.

the world should learn the facts, that he affixed his own signature to them and gave orders for their publication ".

The insertion of approving utterances concerning an auto-biographer's works is not a merely vain custom of writers, as we shall see in the case of the humanists.   And it may be that Josephus is not so much to be blamed for identifying the official record of events, with the production of which he had been entrusted, with historical truth.   For he actually believed that the general recognition of a certain view of history was a guarantee of its truth, and saw the superiority of the Israelite historical works over the Greek not least in the fact that, so far as the historical books of the Old Testament were concerned, " there is no discrepancy in what is written ", while the Greeks " possess myriads of inconsistent books, conflicting with each other ".[44] So little had he of the critical sense which we owe to Greek philosophy.

The formless body of the work, embracing such heterogeneous parts, is provided with initial and final sections that give the whole product the appearance of an autobiography.   The open-ing section gives his origin and education (1–12).   " My family is no ignoble one ", he begins.   He boasts of his descent from the priestly nobility, and, indeed, from the first of the twenty-four classes of priests, and in proof of this he gives a family tree more complete than any other of which we have knowledge in ancient autobiography, going back five generations on the father's side, and carried on to his three sons, all with exact or at least apparently exact dates, such as he also gives in the course of his narrative.   He also mentions his mother : through her he was " of royal blood ", for she was descended from the Hasmonæans or Maccabees, who were kings and at the same time high priests. For his pagan public he brings out the special nature of the Jewish theocracy :   " Different races base their claim to nobility on different grounds ; with us the connexion with the priesthood is the hall-mark of an illustrious line."   He claims to have taken the family tree from the public registers in the Temple archives in Jerusalem ; elsewhere he explains that the registers of marriages served " to ensure that the priests' lineage should be kept unadulterated and pure ".[45]

His education, too, was peculiarly Jewish.   He speaks of the Pharisees, Sadducees, and Essenes, whose schools he attended. But he places the nationally conditioned course of education in a Greek light, probably under the influence of the popular philosophical literature : " At about the age of sixteen I determined to gain personal experience of the several sects * into which our nation is divided . . . I thought that, after a thorough investigation, I should be in a position to select the best. So I submitted myself to hard training and laborious exercises and passed through the three courses." We shall scarcely credit him with this tour of investigation through the various schools of thought or even ways of life. This was a Hellenistic rather than a Jewish aspect of education ; we shall presently find it again in some specimens of the autobiographies of writers.

Josephus was precocious ; this he himself emphasizes, as we have found other autobiographers do, for instance Augustus and also Ovid ; the only peculiar feature is that in this self-praise he places the emphasis on intellectual gifts, memory and quick comprehension. He boasts of his scholarly aptitude :

" While still a mere boy, about fourteen years old, I won universal applause for my love of letters : insomuch that the chief priests and the leading men of the city used constantly to come to me for precise information on some particular in our ordinances " (9).

We are reminded of the finding of Christ in the Temple among the doctors (Luke ii. 46–7). All the more do we wonder why Josephus represents himself as an inquiring youth. He had no time for that. This is clear from his own data.[46] His progress through the three sects was followed, he states, by three years' stay in the wilderness with a Baptist ascetic, whose devoted disciple he had become (11). But at nineteen years of age he was already active in political life in Jerusalem, as a follower of the Pharisaic " school ", which, he considers, was something like the Stoic school among the Greeks. With this the section on his education ends. There follows the journey to Rome, which he made in his twenty-sixth year.

In the equally short concluding section (414–30) he writes of his conditions of existence after his liberation, which followed the fulfilment of his prophecy of the rise of the Flavians to the imperial throne. He tells especially of the proofs of imperial favour that enabled him to live in prosperity in Rome, enjoying his pension and protected from his " Jewish accusers ", who had not forgotten his betrayal or, as he puts it, who " envied him his good fortune ". He also enters into his family affairs. He married three times. Of his second wife he says : " I divorced my wife, being displeased

* Or, schools of thought (*hairesis*).

with her behaviour " (426). It is certainly no mere chance that he uses here the same phrase that struck us in the emperor Augustus when he sought to justify his sudden divorce of Scribonia.

In this work Josephus made a literary claim that is significant of the position of autobiography at that time. He closes with a great gesture by making his own the Greek philosophical relation between *bios* and *ethos* : " Such are the events of my whole life ; from them let others judge as they will of my character." *

iv. Authors on their Works and Studies

Among the elements of an author's career with which his biographer would deal were his works, their scope and their success. This subject might be dealt with independently, and then might itself serve as a framework for biographical data. Such was the case in a number of autobiographical books with which we meet in ancient times and also in the Middle Ages, entitled " On my own works " or, in the fuller form customary among the humanists, " On my books and the course of my studies ", *de libris ac ratione studiorum*. Seen in its historical relationship, this variety of writers' autobiographies is of general importance : it provided in more modern times one of the first starting-points from which the developmental treatment of a man's own life proceeded. For in the succession of his writings the author is confronted with the progress of his thought, which, as soon as the conditions for this method of approach existed, required to be interpreted as a consistent whole.

This variety of writers' autobiographies also made its appearance in the Hellenistic epoch, but once more we have only a few relatively late examples of it. There is a short (barely four pages) but systematic and descriptive list of his books drawn up by Cicero, who so often provides us with examples of Hellenistic conventions. It forms a sort of introduction to his work " On Divination ",[47] one of the many comprehensive philosophical works which he wrote with incredible speed—he was a most prolific writer—in the period of his involuntary idleness during Cæsar's dictatorship. It was a continuation of his *De natura deorum* ; he continued to work on it after Cæsar's assassination, when, with his incurable optimism, he saw before him a new

---

* Ταῦτα μὲν τὰ πεπραγμένα μοι διὰ παντὸς τοῦ βίου ἐστίν· κρινέτωσαν δ' ἐξ αὐτῶν τὸ ἦθος ὅπως ἂν ἐθέλωσιν ἕτεροι.

period of distinguished political service as leader of the republican party. In that situation he inserted in his work a survey of his literary activity ; this personal digression has no further connexion with the work. He entered here—a year before his assassination —all his philosophical works, including those only projected, with title and in many cases with contents, grouped in categories and placed in each category in chronological order. For the principal group, the works on general philosophy, he indicates the order according to subject, showing how, opening with an exhortatory work (*Hortensius*), he dealt first with the fundamentals and then with the chief branches of philosophy. This survey begins with a personal statement on his philosophic writings in general : " After serious and long-continued reflection as to how I might do good to as many people as possible, and thereby prevent any interruption of my service to the State, no better plan occurred to me than to conduct my fellow-citizens along the paths of the noblest learning—and this, I believe, I have already accomplished through my numerous books." [48] Cicero also gives this pregnant expression of his intention : *in libris sententiam dicebamus, contionabamur, philosophiam nobis pro reipublicae procuratione substitutam putabamus.** He gave his whole reason for turning from politics to philosophy, or, rather, excused himself for it to his Roman fellow-citizens :

" The cause of my becoming an expounder of philosophy sprang from the grave condition of the State during the period of the Civil War, when, being unable to protect the Republic, as had been my custom, and feeling it impossible to remain inactive, I could find nothing else that I preferred to do that was worthy of me." [49]

We may compare with this what Sallust said in similar circumstances. Sallust had turned at about the same time from politics to history, though only after the assassination of Cæsar, of whom he had been a supporter : [50]

When I was young, my inclinations at first led me, like many others, into public life. There I encountered many obstacles ; for instead of modesty, temperance, and honesty, hardihood, bribery, and avarice held sway. And although my mind, a stranger to evil ways, recoiled from such faults, yet amid so many vices my youthful weakness was led astray and held captive by ambition . . . After many troubles and perils my mind found peace, and I determined to pass what was left of my life at a distance from public affairs. It was not,

* " It was in my books that I made my senatorial speeches and my forensic harangues ; for I thought I had permanently exchanged politics for philosophy."

however, my intention to waste my precious leisure in idleness and
sloth, nor yet, by turning to farming or the chase, to lead a life devoted
to slavish employments. I resolved to return to the studies from
which ill-starred ambition had diverted me, and to write a history of
the Roman people, selecting such portions as seemed to me worthy
of record ; I was the more determined to do this because my mind
was free from hope, and fear, and partisanship.

We have already remarked that the beginning of this autobiographical sketch seems to be imitated from Plato's Seventh
Epistle. Cicero also refers to Plato in connexion with his
retirement from political affairs, but in another way : in the
passage mentioned he writes :

One thing in particular I had learnt from Plato and from philosophy, that certain revolutions in government are to be expected ; so
that States are now under a monarchy, now under a democracy, and
now under a tyranny. When the last-named fate had befallen my
country, and I had been debarred from my former activities, I began
to cultivate anew these present studies, that by their means, rather
than by any other, I might relieve my mind of its worries and at the
same time serve my fellow-countrymen as best I could under the
circumstances.[51]

As to this patriotic purpose, he declares in this survey of his
writings (mentioning also their success in finding many readers) :
" It would redound to the fame and glory of the Roman people to
be made independent of Greek writers in the study of philosophy,
and this result I shall certainly bring about if my present plans
are accomplished." [52]

We come next, at the end of the second century, to the
independent appearance of this autobiographical variety in some
of the writings of Galen of Pergamum, the famous physician, who
was also a philosophical writer ; these are entitled " On the
series of my books " and " On my books ", and were written,
together with three lists of his works, toward the end of his life
(c. 190).[53] These are among the few ancient works with which
humanist autobiography expressly associated itself. They are
not full biographies, but show already the essential components
of the type of work that later developed into autobiography.
The outward form is the epistle, addressed to a friend described
as having suggested them, and thus addressed not only by way
of dedication, but in the course of the works ; this remained here
the usual convention.

In order to explain how he came to write these autobiographical essays, Galen refers to the situation that existed in

regard to scientific instruction and the sale of books : in consequence of his indifference to formal publication his writings and lectures were circulating on a considerable scale under other people's names, or with alterations and mutilations, so that it was desirable to give information concerning his works. Titles, contents, and scale of all the books, lectures, and published college documents of this incredibly prolific writer are enumerated with a care that makes the product of his personal vanity look almost like that of the meticulousness of a philologist. And at the same time, in spite of the practical consideration advanced, there is a strong tendency to develop the story of the works into that of their author.

In the earlier and shorter of the two essays his main purpose is educational. He intends, on the lines of our academic bibliographies, to advise his readers how to proceed in studying his works, especially the medical ones, which treat of everything from the first elements. In the second work he begins with his first journey to Rome, in his thirties ; he himself defines his subject : " Readers should have knowledge of the age at which I wrote the various books, and of the occasion for each ; for in that way they will be able to distinguish the uncompleted from the finished works, and the educational writings from those directed against swindlers."[54] He goes on to enumerate his writings in chronological order for one period of his life. In the second part of the work he gives a classified list of them under fifteen headings ; here, too, come personal references, for instance : " I have expounded my views on the problems of ethics in the following books."

The biographical section gives not only the external data of Galen's life but also an insight into the polemical publications and the teaching methods of these learned physicians. We are told, for instance, that when he was living in Rome as physician in ordinary to the emperor an eminent colleague of his—" an envious and quarrelsome person, though over seventy "—reacted to Galen's fame, which could no longer be ignored, with the question what was his authority as a teacher (that is to say, to what school of medicine he belonged), and Galen replied to this in public lectures (such as used to be improvised on passages from the old medical authorities) with attacks on the school to which his rival belonged. His claim to understand many new things in anatomy, or to understand it better than the earlier physicians, started malevolent comments which, when he took no notice of them, were thrust at him in the course of the everyday meetings of the doctors at a place called the Grove of Peace, until at last he issued a challenge to public debate.   We are also told of the typical attacks on scientific medicine, on the " theorist doctor " (λογίατρος), to which he was subjected.   These attacks led him to withdraw from public lecturing to the practice of his profession. Another book of his, ostensibly instructional, deals with his successes in treatment.[55]   But the author's philosophical interest carries him beyond such things : he wants to lay down the requirements of a course of scientific education, and here is the point from which, in various passages in both works,[56] Galen describes his own development by way of example ; here again, since his purpose is to offer a rational explanation, he draws from his experience what is typical.

He begins by explaining, from the philosophic antithesis between the attitude of a reflective mind and uncritical *laisser faire*, his own attitude and method : he attacks the traditional reliance on authority, under which physicians and philosophers allowed their choice of standpoint or school to be determined by " the presence in their city of fathers or teachers or friends or some eminent person " who represented the tendency in question.   In opposition to this he refers to a work of his own as representative of his scientific character—a work in which, he claims, instead of the usual self-advertisement, he showed his readers how, by means of logical training and unprejudiced thinking, to attain an independent and reasoned decision as to the right course to take.

He then deals with the demand that medicine and philosophy should be studied together ; he mentions, in Aristotelian fashion, the conditions for this, talent, instruction, and practice, and gives examples, " not merely incidentally ", from his own course of study : he was fortunate in having a well-to-do father with a general scientific culture, who helped him to gain an early mathematical education in addition to the usual schooling, so that at fifteen he was able to begin the study of philosophy, starting with logic, and to continue it under teachers of all four schools, transferring at seventeen to medicine ; he was able then to accomplish real achievements only because he concentrated his whole life on the practice of those branches of knowledge, instead of entering in the usual fashion into political activities.

Then at last he gives something of general importance.   In dealing with his writings on problems of logic, he throws light on them from his personal intellectual development ; and in this connexion he touches on an essential philosophical point characteristic of the intellectual situation of that time. He sought from the first for a criterion of truth of general validity, a " rule of demonstration " that would show its fruits in the recognition of truth or error not only in others' demonstrations but also in his own search for knowledge. Then comes the progress through the various schools of philosophy—including those of "all the Stoics and Peripatetics then famous "—with the discovery that their logic was of little applicability to his problems, and where applicable was open to objection and in some cases against " natural conceptions ". " And so, by the gods ! so far as my teachers were concerned, I, too, should have fallen victim to Pyrrhonian scepticism if I had not been able to hold by mathematics, in which I had made progress from the first, especially in my studies under my father, who had himself been taught by his father and grandfather." He draws attention also to the successes of mathematics in astronomy and technology, as well as its unanimous recognition in the logic of all the schools, which in other respects were at variance with one another and with themselves. He comes then, it is true, to too facile a conclusion : " Thus I realized that I must follow the type of the geometrical proof." But, however shallow the conception, these were nevertheless the essential stages—search for truth, dissatisfaction with conventional dogma, scepticism, discovery of a certainty—the stages that had been indicated in the past by Plato ; * and here they are presented to us for the first time in an express self-portrayal as the basis of the autobiographer's development. It is not by mere chance that he agrees with the Platonic Socrates in the conception of his intellectual development ; he had the biographical section of the *Phædo* in mind. This is shown in one of the autobiographical remarks which he liked to scatter through his educational works. He says in one place : " Even as a child I came in an extraordinary way—I do not know how, whether out of enthusiasm or in a sort of mania or whatever it may be called—to a contempt of the view of the ordinary man and to intolerance of all but truth and knowledge ; convinced that there is no finer or diviner possession for man." †

* See above, p. 106.
† Galen, at the beginning of Book 7 of his work on medical treatment (θεραπευτικὴ μέθοδος) : Ἐγὼ δὲ οὐκ οἶδ' ὅπως εὐθὺς ἐκ μειρακίου θαυμαστῶς, ἢ ἐνθέως, ἢ μανικῶς, ἢ ὅπως ἄν τις ὀνομάζειν ἐθέλῃ, κατεφρόνησα μὲν τῶν πολλῶν ἀνθρώπων δόξης, ἐπεθύμησα δὲ ἀληθείας καὶ ἐπιστήμης, οὐδὲν εἶναι νομίσας οὔτε κάλλιον ἀνθρώποις οὔτε θεώτερον κτῆμα.

Here we have the Platonic *motif* in Aristotelian guise ; and Galen's formulation of this fundamental *motif* of intellectual development was adopted by autobiographers of later times as their pattern.　The same applies to the stages he distinguished in his development.　We shall meet with them again and again in the autobiographical works of later antiquity and then in the humanist movements of modern times, until we come to Descartes' *Discours de la méthode*, the famous treatise of the great modern philosopher, which we may assign to the definite type of self-portrayal exhibited by Galen.　In ancient times it was to receive an important modification in Augustine's *Retractationes*, published two centuries after the essays of Galen ; there the fundamental idea at last appears of revealing the author's progress through the succession of his own works.

How far the realization of a writer's inner development went even in the pre-Christian, Hellenistic-Roman, epoch, is, however, ascertainable : we have Cicero's story of his education in his *Brutus*, which dates long before Augustine.　Here, too, Cicero treats of only one aspect of his life in his autobiography, but a most essential one, his art of oratory, based on his conception of the stateman's power of persuasion, formed by philosophic, philological, juristic, and historical schooling.　And as in this field he was the supreme master and expert, he was able here to give his self-portrayal with a sort of scientific authority ; thus it became an important link in the development of autobiography, although it was not expanded, like his political self-glorifications, into an independent work.　On the other hand, it was the first self-portrayal placed in a comprehensive historical setting.　The method, drawn from Peripatetic scholarship, of giving the collective history of the representatives of a particular field of intellectual production was here applied to his own person. But not as by the compilers of chronological epitomes of literary biographies who added their own name at the end of the collection.*　The plan of *Brutus*, that of describing the character of Roman eloquence from its beginnings, and following it through the generations,† was conceived by Cicero in a way that gives this series of character-sketches of orators the closest resemblance to what we call the history of literature.[57]

The essential historic idea that gives life to *Brutus* is that of

---

* This may be observed since St. Jerome. See below, chap. IV, iii.
† Cicero, *Brutus*, 19, 74 : *oratorum genera distinguere aetatibus* (" The task of distinguishing the categories of orators within their respective periods ").

the gradual but steady advance through which this national Roman art, in association with Greek literature, attained by stages with relative climaxes the perfection represented by Cicero himself. His theory, which he illustrated by the history of Attic oratory, and sought to make clear by a comparison with the continual advance of the plastic arts to moving fullness and truth and perfection,[58] was that the finest period of oratory was a relatively late product of the national culture, because it depended on a whole series of conditions. Thus he conceives his own achievement as the fulfilment of a long development on Roman soil, the slow progress of which he indicates by dealing among the rest with all the less distinguished names of Roman orators. Accordingly he considers the earlier stages in relation to the goals he had himself reached, sometimes directly measuring them against his own greatness ; thus in describing them he is able at the same time to show the conditions he had to satisfy and, on the other hand, to emphasize the specific value of those earlier products of Roman oratory, of which he was able to take advantage for his edification " when but a boy ".[59] The association becomes yet closer through the fact that, in consequence of the political upheaval under the influence of which the book was written (at the beginning of 46 B.C.), the art of oratory was in danger of losing its intrinsic importance as an element of statesmanship, so that Cicero had before his mind not only its perfection but the end of its practical importance. As for the latter element, he considered that in its recent flourishing state eloquence was " almost at its zenith ". What he found to surpass it was not so much this specifically oratorical element, as the deepening of the orator's true quality, attained, in his view, by a more universal culture, rooted in philosophy.[60]

Thus what we have here is not a mere boosting of his own person : on the contrary, it was because of the general historical plan of his work that now that, to conclude it, his own art was to be shown, Cicero no longer confined himself to discussing the style of his oratory, but gave the story of his education in order to provide a more detailed analysis of his development into a master of the art. This autobiographical section is governed by the same idea which underlay the whole book and gave it the character of a history of literature. He himself makes this clear, or, rather, lets Brutus do so in the dialogue, by showing his impatience " to hear about him himself " : " I don't mean about the merits of your oratory, which of course I know very well, as everyone else does, but I am eager to learn about the steps in your development.*

And now the procedure for solving this problem. Cicero describes his education with a scientific precision that promises a full explanation. This he is able to do because from his mastery of the field, already raised to so high an intellectual level that he developed a theory of his oratory, he surveys the causes that explained his ripe art : he now proceeds from these causes, in order to show how they had been working in the chronological sequence of his career. He begins with a picture of the first ten prentice years.[61] The contemporary eloquence surrounding the youth from time to time in the Forum, according to the changing political situation, the various types of his exercises in oratory, and in addition the comprehensive study with Roman jurists and with representatives of Greek philosophy and rhetoric, the incessant " labours in every branch of knowledge "—these are the formative elements he enumerates for that period, more or less year by year, simultaneously and successively according as they were in play together or in turn ; and especially as central element the energy of purposeful self-education, " work and industry ".† This integrating element corresponds to the characteristic self-assessment of writers representative of an age of enlightenment ; one is reminded, for instance, of Gibbon. Success in the ultimate appearance in public, still a little inhibited, is then simply represented as the outcome. This description seems more lifeless than it is, because the orators whose differing characters had already been indicated in the preceding narrative are mentioned here by name only, and because, on the other hand, Cicero's own giftedness is not expressly mentioned among the factors, though it is kept in the foreground throughout the book, especially through the dialogue form.

The next stage is introduced by the change in Cicero's style, which was perfected during his stay as a student in Greece and liberated him from the mannerisms of the time. Here, entirely in consonance with this pragmatic conception of intellectual development, but for the first time so far as autobiography is

---

* *Nec tam de virtutibus dicendi tuis . . . quam quod gradus et quasi processus dicendi studeo cognoscere* (65, 232).

† *Brutus*, 92, 318 ; *cf.* 65, 233 and elsewhere. " *Omni hoc sermoni propositum est non ut ingenium et eloquentiam meam perspicias unde longe absum, sed ut laborem et industriam* " (" My purpose in all this is not to parade my talent or my eloquence—far from it,— but just to let you see how hard I worked and how industrious I was ").

concerned, his physical constitution is taken into account—a
" long slender neck " above a frail, thin, tall body. To this
constitution, combined as it was with his boundless ambition to
acquire fame by his oratory, he attributes his endeavour to
attain a more moderate delivery ; and he explains this attain-
ment by his philosophical and rhetorical studies and practice ;
indeed, he attributes the result, through which he found himself
" almost transformed ", directly to the technical training by his
teacher. He is now very clever in showing his greatness. He
does not go on here to sum up those influences, lest his success
should appear to be their result ; he does so only later. He
starts afresh instead by presenting himself as the master he has
come to be. With subtle intent he does no more than briefly
recall the main features of his appearance in the Forum, pointing
to the arena of forensic speech, and to the quality of the rivals
with whom he had to contend ; on the other hand, he inserts
here a sketch of his official career, to increase interest in his person.
So one has the impression after all of a spontaneously ripened
quality when at last he reveals his self-confidence in face of the
critical contest : " It was apparent that whatever talent I
possessed had reached full development and a certain maturity." *

By parallel treatment with his rival in process of submergence,
Hortensius, he now brings his personal superiority into full light.
He illustrates the power of his oratory by its successes in bringing
him forward as a statesman ; only then does he give the integrating description of his ripe art,[62] assembling the various elements
of its formation. He refers to the philosophic studies underlying
his art, as well as to his oratorical and technical exercises,
emphasizing trait by trait that he accomplished something
unique. Finally comes the story of his activities since his
consulate, in the certainty of posthumous fame, but toned down
through the political tension amid which he wrote. For the
" destiny of the State " had made it impossible for him to show
himself as an orator at work in the life of a free community, and
with the cold self-analysis is mixed the painful feeling of the man
who, at the height of his capacity, sees the opportunity for his
best endeavours destroyed.

This autobiography, unique as it appears to us, may really
have been a pioneering achievement of Cicero's, much as the
idea probably belonged to him of employing the romantic style

---

* *Iam videbatur illud in me, quidquid esset, esse perfectum et habere maturitatem quamdam*
suam (Brutus, 92, 318).

of the writing of history for the story of his own career. His
method of approach, however, as seen through in his *Brutus*,
corresponds to the general intellectual situation of the time,
which made possible that objective attitude toward his own work ;
and the autobiographical portrayals in the parallel epochs of
modern times, especially in the European age of enlightenment
in the eighteenth century, confirm that we have here a definite
type of presentation of personality.

If we try to grasp this point more thoroughly, we have the
treatment of personality with which we made acquaintance first
and most plainly in the historical work of Polybius : this work,
compiled in accordance with the scientific attitude of the
Aristotelian school, carries us back to the origin of this whole
group of autobiographies.[63]   In Polybius' work Cicero, who
studied it, was able to find, here and there in the narrative,
personal statements of opinion by the great historian on the
scientific method applied by him.   But we also see in Polybius,
acutely expressed and formulated as a principle (IV, 8 ; IX, 22,
23), the characteristic attitude of the inquiring intelligence,
indeed of an intelligence touched by scepticism and trying to
overcome it.   He observes the various and often inconsistent
activities of the men of whom he has to tell ; he finds in them a
refutation of the idea that a man's character may be read
directly from his behaviour and actions, especially in situations
that seem to throw full light on it ; he seeks an explanation, on
the lines of the ancient Sceptic Protagoras, by conceiving the
spiritual, on the analogy of the physical, as something by nature
manifold and integrated (πολυειδές τι).   Thus, for instance, he
passes judgment on Aratus of Sicyon, a judgment of special
interest to us because he had access to Aratus' memoirs (IV, 8) :
" He had in general all the qualities that go to make a perfect
man of affairs.   He was a powerful speaker and a clear thinker,
and had the faculty of keeping his own counsel . . .   But this
very same man, when he undertook field operations, was slow
in conception, timid in performance, and devoid of personal
courage."   Then he generalizes :   " So true it is that there is
something multiform in the nature not only of men's bodies but
of their minds, so that not only in pursuits of a different class
the same man has a talent for some and none for others, but
often in the case of such pursuits as are similar the same man may
be most intelligent and most dull, or most audacious and most
cowardly." [64]

He holds nevertheless to the basic view that the nature of a human being is something clearly defined and permanent, so that inconsistencies cannot really exist. " We can hardly suppose that dispositions diametrically opposite exist in the same natures " (IX, 23, 4). Thus inconsistent behaviour must be understood as a perversion of the true character, due to external causes, a perversion that does not throw light on the character but conceals it. The circumstances, changing situations, and the influence of other persons, must be taken into account, explaining a changed or inconsistent course as due to the omission or the inability to make a free decision. Thus, for instance, in discussing Hannibal's character, he says with reference to the peculiar traits in it that were the subject of most dispute, such as cruelty and avarice (IX, 22) :

> It is no easy thing to state the truth about him, or in general about men who are engaged in public affairs. For some say that men's real natures are revealed by circumstances, the truth being brought to light in some cases by the possession of power, even if its possessors have hitherto managed to disguise it entirely, and in other cases by misfortune. But I cannot myself regard this view as sound. For it appears to me that, not in a few cases only but in most, men are compelled to act and speak contrary to their real principles by the complexity of facts and by the suggestions of their friends . . . The fact is that some princes are compelled to change with the change of circumstances and often exhibit to others a disposition that is quite the opposite of their real nature, so that, far from men's natures being revealed by such means, they are obscured.[65]

This view of men's nature governs the method which Polybius follows in his assessment of those of whom he writes. Proceeding carefully step by step in his judgment of the persons involved in his narrative, he interrupts it with critical reflections, and sums up his subjects' character from the conclusions suggested by the qualities revealed in the course of events, allowing for the influence to which each person is subjected. Unlike the style of exposition of great historical art such as that of Tacitus, who suggests to the reader a general estimate of the nature of an individual through the actual course of his life, and unlike the traditional [66] method of subjective explanation of history, which accompanies the appearance of great men with a general summing up of their character, by which they are established at the outset as among the unquestionably great, Polybius displays the significant characters without prejudice, as objects of study whose true nature can only gradually be revealed. His purpose is to confine the introductory statement of the character of the leading persons to the indication of their natural qualities, which yield the first particulars for the recognition of character ; then he stops in the course of his narrative at instructive points (in the case of complex characters, which he himself sets forth as politically instructive exemplars, this may be observed three times in the fragments), and, with reference to the actions related, mentions some particularly problematic characteristics of his hero and also any changes in his moral attitude, adoption of an evil course, continuance on that path, return of the man's better nature under the influence of misfortune ; [67] the usual comment after the departure of the historical person then serves for a critical summing-up.

We have here a gradual presentation of historical figures through the historian's judgment on them being formed step by step ; but with this gradualness of development is combined the process of change in those individuals themselves, observed by him from time to time and pursued stage by stage in the course of events. Here we have a pragmatic kind of analysis ; it presents that type of a history of development which proceeds from reflecting on the past, not from re-living and thereby re-animating it. We observed the same attitude to the object, more concentrated and more directed to the technical, in Cicero's autobiography. But that psychological pragmatism of Hellenistic historiography reaches further ; in some respects even the great spiritual autobiography represented by Saint Augustine's *Confessions* dates back to it.

NOTES

INTRODUCTION : SECTION I

1. *Cf.* Edmund Calamy, *An Account of my own Life*, introduction (written in 1727).

2. W. Dilthey, " Der Aufbau der geschichtl. Welt in den Geisteswissenschaften ", *Abhandl. Berliner Akad. d. Wissenschaften* (1911) ; *Ges. Schriften*, VII, p. 199. The translation of this passage is taken from *Wilhelm Dilthey. An Introduction*, by Professor H. A. Hodges (London, 1944), p. 28. Professor Hodges states that Dilthey considers autobiography to be " the stem from which the other human studies have all branched out ". With regard to this it may be mentioned that in his systematic and historically basic work, *Einleitung in die Geisteswissenschaften* (1883), Dilthey gave a classification of human studies in which at first he proceeded from biography as the basic form of historiography, without taking account of autobiography. He took account of it and accorded it primacy on the strength of the results of the prize offered by the Prussian Academy, as mentioned in the note on page vii.
The biologist J. Lionel Tayler expresses a similar view to that of Dilthey in his thoughtful book, *The Writing of Autobiography and Biography* (1926).

3. Charlotte Brontë, " Evening solace ". Quoted by Tayler, *The Writing of Autobiography*, p. 15.

4. Chopin is made to say this in Doris Leslie's biographical novel *Polonaise*, p. 95.

5. This fundamental notion of literary criticism, which is less current in England than in Germany, where it was introduced by Goethe, comes nevertheless from English æsthetics : Goethe took it over from Shaftesbury. *Cf.* M. Morris, *Der junge Goethe*, vol. 5, p. 344.

6. " Autobiography consists essentially of the reconsideration of recollections." E. Stuart Bates, *Inside Out. An Introduction to Autobiography* (2 vols., Oxford, 1936 and 1937).

7. De Quincey, *Reminiscences of the English Lake Poets.*

INTRODUCTION : SECTION II

1. *Cf.* A. Erman, *Die ägyptisehe Religion* (1905), pp. 137, 121, 87 *sqq.*

2. *Op. cit.*, p. 137.

3. *Op. cit.*, p. 140.

4. Inni and other autobiographies from records in Sethe, *Urkunden des äg. Altertums*, hrsg. v. Steindorff. IV Urk. der 18. Dyn. *Histor.-biogr. Urk.* (1905). Translations, e.g. *Zeitschr. f. äg. Sprache* (1873) (18. Dyn.). A. Erman, *Aeg. u. äg. Leben* (1885), pp. 415, 131. Brugsch, *Gesch. Aegyptens*, pp. 170, 246.

5. On the formula τά δε λέγει *cf.* Gerhard, *Untersuchungen zum Brief*, Philologus, LXIV (1905).

6. Funerary inscriptions from the twelfth and thirteenth dynasties. Those of Baba and Ameni according to the translation in Brugsch, *Gesch. Aegyptens*, pp. 245, 130 *sqq.*, and G. Maspero, *La grande inscription de Beni-Hassan, Recueil des travaux relatifs à la philol. égyptienne* (1870), I, pp. 174 *sqq.* Menuhotep in Erman, *Aeg. u. äg. Leben* (1885), p. 131.

7. Erman, *Die äg. Rel.* pp. 85-6.

8. Waitz, *Anthropologie der Naturvölker*, VI, 394.

9. Réville, *Histoire des Réligions*, II, 367–8, 175 *sqq.*, 245.   *Cf.* also Waitz, *op. cit.*, IV, 129, 307, 462.

10. Spiegel, *Avesta* III, 207-8 ; II, lviii, lix.

11. *Book of the Dead*, chap. 30, 1.   From the translation in Erman, *op. cit.*, p. 143.

12. Erman, pp. 104-5.   *Cf.* Maspero, *op. cit.*, p. 46.

13. The texts on the gold plates from Petelia and Thurioi (fourth and third centuries B.C.) are to be found in Diels, *Fragm. der Vorsokratiker*.   *Cf.* Diels, *Ein orphischer Demeterhymnus, Festschr. f. Gomperz* (1902).   A. Dieterich, *Nekyia*, pp. 84 *sqq.*, 128–9, 135–6.   Rohde, *Psyche*, II (2), p. 217–8.   Relation to Egyptian practice and suggestion of historical connexion in Th. Gomperz, *Griech. Denker*, I, pp. 106 *sqq.*

14. *Cf.* Erman, *Die äg. Rel.*, pp. 56, 44.

15. *Cambridge Ancient Hist.*, III, p. 194.

16. *Cf.* E. Meyer, *Gesch. des Altertums*, I, pp. 148, 345.   E. Bezold, " Die babyl.-assyr. Lit.", *Kult. d. Ggw.*, I, 7 (1906), p. 42.   *Cambridge Ancient Hist.*, III (1925), " The Assyrian Empire ", p. 194.

17. *Cf.* E. Meyer, *Entstehung des Judentums* (1896), p. 48, n. 1. H. Gunkel, " Die israel. Lit.", *Kult. d. Ggw.*, I, 7, pp. 73, 101.

18. This " Hofstil " with its influence on the eschatology of salvation and damnation, is discussed by Gressmann in Bousset u. Gunkel, *Forsch. zur Rel. u. Lit. des A. u. N.T.*, vol. 6 (1905), pp. 250 *sqq.*   Specimens from Egyptian songs on the king in Erman, " Die äg. Lit.", in *Kult. d. Ggw.*, I, 7, p. 35 ; *cf.* also, for instance, the passages in the Life of Sinuhe, in Erman u. Krebs, *Aus d. Papyrus der kgl. Museen*, pp. 18–19.

19. Erman, *Die äg. Rel.*, pp. 39–40, 70.

20. *Cf.* Rawlinson, *The Five Great Monarchies*, II, pp. 72–3.   Quoted in Maspero, *op. cit.*, p. 352.

21. H. Zimmern, *Babylonische Busspsalmen* (1885).

22. This text and the others according to the translation in *Keilinscriftliche Bibliothek* (ed. E. Schrader, 1889), etc.   *Cf.* also the translation in Sayce, *Records of the Past*.

23. *Cf.* Maspero, *op. cit.*, p. 430, and Sayce in *Records of the Past*, N.S., II, 132.

24. *Cf.* Maspero, *op cit.*, p. 430.

25. E. Unger, " Altorientalische Könige als Kulturbringer ", in *Forschungen und Fortschritte*, IX, no. 17 (Berlin, 1933).

26. *Cf. Cambridge Ancient Hist.*, III, p 88.

27. " Sardanapalus ", in *Keilinschr. Bibl.*, I, 141.

28. The translation is taken from the *Cambridge Ancient Hist.*, III, p. 127.

29. F. Hommel, *Geschichte Babyloniens u. Assyriens* (1885), p. 765.   *Cf. Keilinschr. Bibl.*, III, 2, pp. 11–12.

30. *Ezra Studies*, by Ch. C. Torrey (Chicago, 1910).   *A critical commentary on the works of Ezra and Nehemiah*, by L. W. Batten (Edinburgh, 1913).

31. *Cf.* Erman, *Aeg. u. äg. Leben*, p. 494.

32. " Das Leben des Sinuhe ", translated by Erman, in *Aus d. Papyrus der kgl. Museen*, pp. 14–29.   *Cf.* " Die äg. Lit.", *Kult. d. Ggw.*, I, 7, p. 31.   The beginning of the poem is given in Gardiner, " Eine neue Handschr. des Sinuhe-Gedichts ", *Sitzungs-Berichte Berl. Akad. der Wiss.* (1907), p. 146. English translation in *Egyptian Tales*, by Sir W. M. Flinders Petrie (1917).

33. In Erman, *Aus d. Papyrus der kgl. Museen*, pp. 43–6, " Die äg. Lit.," *loc. cit.*, p. 32.

34. With Erman, *cf.*, for example, Graf v. Schack, *Die Unterweisung des Königs A. I.* (Paris, 1883–4), p. 21 :   " There is no alternative but to believe the evidence of the papyrus, according to which Amen-em-het was the compiler."

35. *Cf.* A. Erman, " Eine Reise nach Phönicien im XI. Jahrh. v. Chr. (Papyrus aus der 21. Dynastie) ", *Zeitschr. f. Aegyptologie*, vol. 38.   G. Roeder, *Altägypt. Erzählungen* (1927).   Maspero and Wiedemann regard the story as fiction.

36. In Maspero, *Les contes populaires de l'ancienne Egypte*, p. 140. *Cf.* Erman, " Die äg. Lit.", pp. 30-1.   Flinders Petrie, *Egyptian Tales.*   Petrie's translation is here used.

37. *Cf.* E. Schwarz, *Fünf Vorträge über den griech. Roman.*

38. W. M. Flinders Petrie, *Egyptian Tales*, second series.   Also in the *Masterpiece Library of Short Stories*, edited by Sir J. A. Hamerton, vol. 1.   Use has here been made of both translations. *Cf.* also G. Roeder, *Altägypt. Erzählungen.*

39. The text of the inscription is in *Keilinschr. Bibl.*, III, 101. Fr. Lenormant, *Les premières Civilis.*, II, pp. 104–10, regards it as a reproduction of an inscription on a statue of the king.   So also Maspero, *Histoire ancienne*, pp. 188–9.   E. Meyer, *op. cit.*, p. 162, treats the text as the beginning of an annalistic inscription : a usurper could have sought to legitimize himself in this way.   According to Tiele, *Babylon.-assyr. Gesch.*, I, 114-5, the inscription is older than the reign of Sargon II (eighth century B.C.).

40. Gressmann, *loc. cit.*, pp. 269–70.

41. This supersession of " he " by " I " occurs with differing frequency in the three extant texts. *Cf.* E. de Rouge's translation, with notes quoting the variants. *Recueil des travaux rel. à la phil. ég.*, I (1870), pp. 1 *sqq.*

42. Another instructive example is to be found in one of the orally transmitted stories of the primitive race of the Ainu, mentioned at the end of this section.   In this story—no. 20 of the collection referred to—the narrator, who has chosen the first-personal method, frequently drops out of his part and changes to the third person.

43. The personal testimony of Otto Ludwig, quoted in Dilthey, " Die Einbildungskraft des Dichters " (*Philos. Aufs. Zeller gewidmet.*, 1887), p. 407.

44. *Materials for the Study of the Ainu Language and Folklore.   Collected by Bronislaw Pilsudski*, Cracow, 1912.   I am indebted to Dr. Arthur Waley for the mention of this book.

Part I : Introductory

1. Plato, *Rep.*, x, 604.

2. See Wilamowitz, in *Hermes*, XV, 515. *Cf.* F. Leo, *Die griech.-röm. Biographie* (1901), p. 86 *et al.*

3. *Cf.* Von Wilamowitz, " Die griech. Lit. des Altertums ", *Kult. d. Ggw.*, I, 8, pp. 114-5.

4. W. Dilthey, *Einleitung in die Geisteswissenschaften* (1883), p. 224 (*Ges. Schriften*, I).

Part I : Chapter I

1. *Cf.* Erich Schmidt, " Die Anfänge der Lit. und die Lit. der primitiven Völker ", *Kult. d. Ggw.* (1906), I, 7, p. 17.   H. M. Chadwick, *The Heroic Age* (1912).

.2. See above, p. 51.   Only one reference exists in an autobiography to the *Alkinou-apologoi*, the traveller's tales in Aelius Aristides : see below, Part II, chap. 3, 4.

3. *Cf.* E. Schmidt, *op. cit.*, where the instance is given of a Red Indian chieftain, and of a Basuto warrior who " after the fighting and a bath relates his glorious adventures to the seated audience, first talking and then singing ". —H. Gunkel, " Die israel. Lit." (*Kult. d. Ggw.* I, 7, p. 59), with reference to

Genesis iv., 23-4 : " When the hero of the most ancient times returned from combat, he sang his song of victory."

4. *Cf.* W. Dilthey, " Ideen über eine beschreibende und vergleich-ende Psychologie ", *S.-B. Berl. Akad. Wiss.* (1894), especially p. 1407 (*Ges. Schriften*, V).

5. W. Dilthey, " Der Aufbau der geschichtl. Welt in den Geisteswissen-schaften " (1910). *Ges. Schriften*, VII.

6. W. Dilthey, " Die Anthropologie im XVII. Jahrh." (1904). *Ges. Schriften*, IV, p. 437.

7. Karl Joël, *Der Ursprung der Naturphilosophie aus dem Geiste der Mystik* (Basle, 1903).

8. See Schwartz, *Charakterköpfe a. d. ant. Lit.*, 1903 ; *H's Erga*, erkl. v. Wilamowitz, 1928.

9. *Erga*, 654–62. These lines were regarded in the past, on the strength of a conjecture of Plutarch's, as an interpolation, but are now generally regarded as genuine. *Cf. Hésiode, Les travaux et les jours* (ed. Paul Mazon, Paris, 1914), p. 136.

10. *Cf.* R. Harder, in *Gnomon*, 1932 (review of the second edition of this book).

11. *Cf. Lyra Graeca*, newly edited and translated by J. M. Edmonds (1927), III, 631.

12. *Lyra Graeca*, III, 606, 667.

13. *Cambridge Ancient Hist.*, IV, 483.

14. Von Wilamowitz, " Die griech. Lit.", *Kult. d. Ggw.*, I, 8, p. 21.

15. Synesios, περὶ ἐνυπνίων, *Patrol. Migne*, vol. 66, p. 1316.

16. Plato, *Protagoras*, 342E.

17. *Cf.* Von Wilamowitz, *Aristoteles und Athen*, II.

18. Aristotle, Ἀθην. Πολιτεία, 5.

19. English translation from J. E. Edmonds, *Elegy and Iambos*, in Loeb's Classical Library, *Solon*, fr. 5, 36, 32, I, pp. 141, 149, 147.

20. *Cf.* Rohde, *Psyche*, especially II (2), pp. 62 *sqq.*, 113-4. Diels, *Parmenides' Lehrgedicht*, pp. 10 *sqq.*, and on Epimenides, *S.-B. Berl. Akad. Wiss.* (1891), pp. 393 *sqq.* A. Dieterich, *Nekyia*, especially pp. 126 *sqq.* Rohde, *Der griech. Roman*, p. 279, n. 2.

21. Diels, *Fragmente der Vorsokratiker* (5th ed., 1934). John Burnet, *Early Greek Philosophy* (Oxford, 1892).

22. K. Joël, *op. cit.*, p. 35.

23. Burckhardt, *Kultur der Renaissance* (5th ed.), I, 304.

24. Joel, *op. cit.*, pp. 29–30.

25. Diels, *Herakleitos von Ephesos* (1901), pp. vi *sqq.*

26. Dilthey, *Einleitung*, p. 192.

27. Fr. 24 and 63, with Diels' note on them, in opposition to Rohde, *Psyche* (2nd. ed.), II., p. 150, n. 1.

28. On fr. 88, 111, 125, *cf.* Rohde *op. cit.*, II, 148.

29. Ed. Meyer, *op. cit.*, IV, 249, 218. *Cf.* Rohde (2nd. ed.), II, p. 193.

30. *Cf.* Bruno Snell, " Die Auffassung des Menschen bei Homer ", in *Die Entdeckung des Geistes* (Hamburg, 1946).

Part I : Chapter II

1. Ed. Meyer, *op. cit.*, IV, p. 122.

2. For the " ideal of the citizen of the State " in classic art, *cf.* Julius Lange, *Die Darstellung des Menschen in der älteren griech. Kunst*. For the " ideal principle of order " in tragedy, W. Dilthey, " Beiträge zum Studium der Individualität ", *S.-B. Berl. Akad. Wiss.* (1896), pp. 317–18. *Ges. Schr.* V.

3. J. Bruns, *Das literar. Porträt des Griechen* (1896).

4. Von Wilamowitz, *Die griech. Lit.*, p. 55.

5. H. Nohl, *Sokrates und die Ethik*, p. 62.

6. *Cf.* J. Bruns, *op. cit.* ; von Wilamowitz, *op. cit.*, p. 80.

7. *Cf.* Ed. Meyer, *op. cit.*, IV, 120 ; V, 361.

8. Bernouilli, *Griech. Iconographie*, I, 118.

9. Ed. Meyer, *op. cit.*, IV, 260 *sqq.*

10. For the passages in the *Theaetetus* (especially 157B and 159B), *cf.* Laas, *Idealismus und Positivismus* (1879), I, esp. pp. 196 and 212 *sqq.* Also *Symposium*, 207D.

11. Thucydides I, 138. *Cf.* Bruns, *op. cit.*, pp. 68–9, and the corresponding assessment of Alcibiades, p. 512.

12. *Cf.* W. Dilthey, " Die Funktion der Anthropologie im 16. u. 17. Jahrh.", *S.-B. Berl. Akad. Wiss.* (1904), p. 5 (*Ges. Schriften*, II).

13. This version is taken (with some slight modifications), by the kind permission of the publishers and editor, from the translation by the Rev. W. G. Bury in the Leob Classical Library, *Plato*, vol. 7.

14. Von Wilamowitz (*Plato*, p. 644) takes this as certain. The translation is by W. R. Paton, in *The Greek Anthology* (Loeb Classical Library), II, Book VII, no. 99.

15. This is the view of von Wilamowitz, *Plato*, II, 295, I, 652.

16. *Cf.*, e.g., E. Howald, *Plato, Epistulae* (1923).

17. I. Bruns, *op. cit.*, pp. 443 *sqq.*

18. Von Wilamowitz, *Die griech. Lit.*, p. 73. *Cf.* Wendland in the *Göttinger gelehrte Anzeigen* (1906), pp. 356 *sqq.*

19. That the oration " On the Crown " was published by Demosthenes himself has been established by Wendland in *Anaximenes von Lampsakos* (1905), p. 12.

20. Von Wilamowitz, *op. cit.*, p. 73.

21. *Antidosis*, procemium, 6–7. In this and the following quotations use has been made of the translation by G. Norlin in the Loeb Classical Library.

22. On one occasion he had been entrusted by Timotheus with propaganda for a decision in Athenian policy, the renewal of the Athenian naval league in 378.

23. Plato, *Gorgias*, 452D, E. Translated by W. R. M. Lamb, in the Loeb Classical Library.

24. Aristotle, in *Rhet.* 19, 1358 a 17, disputed Isocrates' originality. *Cf.* von Wilamowitz, *Hermes* (1900), 35, p. 533. Leo, *op. cit.*, p. 91, takes the opposite view. The deciding authority was here again the Sophist Gorgias. See Seyffert, " Xenophons Agesilaus ", *Gött. Diss.* (1901).

25. *Cf.* J. Bruns, *op. cit.*

26. F. Leo, *Die griech.-röm. Biographie*, pp. 87–8, 235. *Cf.* also Wendland, *Anaximenes*, pp. 54 *sqq.*

27. Thucydides II, 34–6. *Cf.* von Wilamowitz, *Griech. Lesebuch*, pp. 135 *sqq.* In this connexion it is immaterial that we have no knowledge of the funeral oration actually delivered by Pericles.

28. *Cf.* Lehrs, *Popul. Aufsätze* : " Daemon und Tyche ".

29. *Cf.* Ivo Bruns, *op. cit.*, pp. 116 *sqq.*

30. Bruns, *op. cit.*, pp. 120 *sqq.* Leo., *op. cit.*, pp. 91–2. Wendland, *op. cit.*, pp. 54 *sqq.*

31. Καινότης, διαφορά, ἄτοπον. *Antidosis*, § 1.

32. The title *Antidosis* has reference to this lawsuit, which may really have taken place, in 355. In Athens men of the wealthiest class were called upon to perform the " liturgies " (public services), such as meeting the expense of training a chorus for a drama or of fitting out a warship. A citizen charged with a " liturgy " might call upon any other citizen whom he believed to be

richer than himself either to take over the duty or to exchange properties with him. This process was called *antidosis* (" exchange ").

33. *Cf.* J. Bruns, *op. cit.*, pp. 463, 465, 296 *sqq.*, 501–2, 521 *sqq.*

34. This was emphasized as long ago as 1570 by H. Wolf, argum., p. 455, annot. p. 705.

35. As in Bruns, *op. cit.*, pp. 527–8.

36. *Cf.* Wilamowitz, *Aristoteles u. Athen*, II, 380 *sqq.*

37. Leo, *op. cit.*, p. 92.

38. Plutarch, *Moralia*, περὶ τοῦ αὐτὸν ἐπαινεῖν ἀνεπιφθόνως.

39. *Aelius Aristides* (ed. Dindorf), II, 491 *sqq.*

PART II : INTRODUCTORY

1. *Cf.* von Wilamowitz, *Die griech. Lit.*, pp. 92 *sqq.* P. Wendland *Die hellenistisch-römische Kultur in ihren Beziehungen zu Judentum und Christentum* (1907) (*Handbücher z. N. T.*, hrsg. v. Lietzmann), pp. 19 *sqq.*, where authorities are quoted.

2. *Cf*, Usener, *Epicurea*, p. 405. Susemihl, *Gesch. der Griech. Lit.*, I, p. 92, n. Von Wilamowitz, *Aristoteles und Athen*, II, p. 415. Wendland, *Zeitschrift f. neutestamentl. Wiss.*, V., pp. 338 *sqq.* See also Seneca, *Ep. ad Lucil.*, 64, 9, and elsewhere ; Epictet. Diss., I, 4 etc. *Cf.* below, chap. III, III and IV.

3. *Cf.* W. Dilthey, " Ideen zu e. beschreib. Psychol.", *S.-B. Berl. Akad. Wiss.* (1894), p. 1390. *Ges. Schriften*, V.

4. *Cf.* von Wilamowitz, *Die griech. Lit.*, p. 194.

5. *Pro Archia Poeta*, XI, 26.

6. Cicero ad fam., V, 12, 8.

7. Cicero, *Pro Archia*, 23–30.

8. The Poetics of Aristotle, 39, 1451*b*.

9. *Cf.* H. Peter, *Die gesch. Literatur der Kaiserzeit*, II, pp. 180 *sqq.* Von Wilamowitz, *op. cit.*, p. 118. Reitzenstein, *Hellenist. Wundererzählungen* (1906). Further von Wilamowitz-Moellendorf, in his review of the 1907 edition of this book, *Internationale Wochenschrift für Wissenschaft*, &c. (1907), pp. 1905 *sqq.*

10. Von Wilamowitz, *op. cit.*, pp. 104–5. *Cf.* E. Schwartz, *Fünf Vorträge über den griech. Roman.*

11. *Cf.* Reitzenstein, *op. cit.*, I, § 3, pp. 83 *sqq.*

12. *Cf.* the quotations in Bonhöffer, *Die Ethik des Stoikers Epiktet*, pp. 248 *sqq.*

13. *Die griech. Lit.*, p. 2.

14. J. Kaerst, *Die Idee der Oikumene*, pp. 13–14, 20–1.

15. *Cf.* P. Wendland, *op. cit.*, pp. 73 *sqq.*, with the literature there quoted.

16. Lucretius, *De Nat. Rerum*, III, 302–18.

17. *Cf.* W. Dilthey, " Auffassung und Analyse des Menschen im 15. u. 16. Jahrh.", *Archiv f. Gesch. der Philos.* IV (1890), pp. 614 *sqq.*, 618. *Ges. Schriften*, II. A. Schmekel, *Die Philos. der mittleren Stoa* (1890).

18. Cicero *De Officiis*, I, 30, 107 ; 33, 121. See also R. Hirzel, *Unters. zu Ciceros philos. Schriften II*, pp. 430 *sqq.* A. Schmekel, *op. cit.*, pp. 195–6.

19. Cicero, *op. cit.*, 30, 107. *Cf.* Schmekel, *op. cit.*, pp. 212, 209–10. Hirzel, *op. cit.*, p. 434, n.

20. Dilthey, *op. cit.*, pp. 614 *sqq.*, and " Natürl. System der Geistesw. im 17. Jahrh.", *Archiv. f. Gesch. der Phil.*, VI (1893), pp. 256–7. *Ges. Schriften* II.

21. Dilthey's formula in his *Grundriss der Allgemeinen Geschichte der Philosophie.*

22. *Cf.* Schmekel, *op. cit.*, pp. 384 *sqq.*, 400–1, *et passim.*

23. Goethe, *Die Natur* (*Aufsatz, aphoristisch*, 1782). This famous dithyramb was not Goethe's own, but was only inspired : the author was Christoph

Tobler, a friend of Goethe and disciple of Lavater. Tobler made use in it of a Hellenistic model, the Orphic Hymn No. 10, addressed to the goddess Physis. *Cf.* demonstration in Fr. Schultz, *Festschrift für Julius Petersen*, 1938, and Dornseif in *Die Antike* XV (1939). The actual phrase translated above does not appear, however, in the Orphic Hymn, and is clearly Goethe's own.

PART II : CHAPTER I.

1. *Cf.* J. Kaerst, *Gesch. des Hellenist. Zeitalters*, I (1901), pp. 383 *sqq.*

2. *Cf.* the inscriptions on the marble throne of Adulis, Dittenberger, *Sylloge* 44 (Ptolemy III Euergetes, 285–247 ; in emulation of Rameses ?), and *Corpus Inscr. Gr.*, III, 5127*b*, the inscription of the founder of the Axumitic kingdom, probably about A.D. 50—*cf.* Dillmann, " Ueber die Anfänge des Axumitischen Reichs", *Abh. Berl. Akad. d. Wiss.* (1878), pp. 195 *sqq.*—where we also find the familiar phrase of Nebuchadnezzar, Darius, etc., " and all these are the races which I was the first and only one after the kings before me to subjugate ". *Cf.* Mommsen, *Histor. Zeitschr.*, 57, 1887, p. 395, and *Röm. Gesch.*, V, p. 599 n., where attention is drawn to the importance of these inscriptions for the understanding of the Monumentum Ancyranum and also of those of Nemrud-Dagh (see below).

3. Diodor., 27 ; similarly in Euhemeros' Ἱερὰ ἀναγραφή. *Cf.* Wendland, *op. cit.*, p. 70.

4. *Cf.* K. Humann and O. Puchstein, *Reisen in Kleinasien und Nordsyrien* (1890), pp. 216–345 ; especially pp. 272 *sqq.* and 328 *sqq.*

5. *The Histories of Polybius*, Book I, chap. 1 ; translation by W. R. Patton, in the Loeb Classical Library.

6. *Ibid.*, Book III, chap. 56.

7. *Ibid.*, chap. 33.

8. *Cf.* Polybius, Book III, chap. 20, and Corneliŭs Nepos, *Lives*, Hannibal, 13.

9. *Cf.* E. Schwartz, *Charakterköpfe aus der antiken Lit.*, pp. 71–2.

10. Wilamowitz, *op. cit.*, p. 117.

11. Cicero, *Pro Archia*, 24.

12. *The Histories of Polybius*, Book I, chap. 3. *Cf.* F. Jacoby, *Fragm. Gr. Hist.*, II, no. 231.

13. Polybius II, 40, 4. Plutarch, *Aratus* 3.

14. Plutarch, *Aratus* 32.

15. Polybius, Book II, chap. 47.

16. *Cf.* Wilcken, *Philologus*, LIII, pp. 80 *sqq.* E. Meyer, *Gesch. des Altertums*, III (1901), pp. 46–7. J. Kaerst on Alexander's *Ephimerides* in Pauly-Wissowa. On the connexion with the East, Friedländer, *Sittengesch. Roms* I (6th ed.), p. 199 ; for the link between the imperial diaries and those of the Macedonian court, Casaubonus on Sueton. August. c. 64 (*cf.* Friendländer, *op. cit.*). The imperial diaries were comprehensively dealt with as early as 1655 in Mascardi *Dell' Arte Historica*, Venice (" Effemeridi ", pp. 55 *sqq.*).

17. Mommsen, *Staatsrecht*, II (3rd ed.), p. 907, 1. Wilcken, *op. cit.*, p. 116, considers that there was no special court journal and regards the record under the emperors as a combination of " business and court journal ".

18. Mommsen, *Röm. Gesch.*, V, p. 3.

19. By Athenæus in his *Deipnosophistai*. The fragments are collected in Müller, *Fragm. Graec. Hist.* III, 186–9. There were twenty-four " books ", written in the first person. *Cf.* Felix Jacoby, *loc. cit.*, Part II C (1926), no. 234.

20. Athenæus, Book XIV, p. 654 C. Translated by Ch. B. Gulick, in the Loeb Classical Library.

21. Athenæus, Book X, p. 438 D.
22. Polybius, Book XXVI, chap. 10.
23. Josephus, *Antiq.*, XV, 6, 3. *Cf.* F. Jacoby, *loc. cit.*, II C, no. 236.
24. Plutarch, *Anton.*, 82, 2.
25. *Ibid.*, 83.
26. Evidence and fragments in H. Peter, *Historicorum Roman. Fragmenta*, (1883).
27. Cicero, *ep. ad Quintum*, fr. 1, 18, 23.
28. Cicero, *Brutus*, xxix, 112. Translated by G. L. Hendrickson, in the Loeb Classical Library.
29. The inscriptions confirm this view. Armstrong, *Autobiog. Elements*, pp. 224, 262.
30. H. Usener, *Götternamen*, pp. 75 *sqq.*
31. Marquardt, *Privatleben der Römer*, I (2nd ed.), pp. 241–2. Mommsen, *Staatsrecht*, I (2nd ed.), pp. 426 *sqq.*
32. Pirckheimer quotes in support of this Valerius Maximus, V, 8, 5.
33. Von Wilamowitz, *Die griech. Lit.*, p. 141.
34. H. Peter, " Der Brief in der röm. Lit.", *Abh. der Kgl. Sächs. Ges. der Wiss, philol.-hist. Klasse*, 41 (1901), p. 5.
35. Leo, *Die griech.-röm. Biographie*, p. 234.
36. Mommsen, *Staatsrecht*, I (2nd ed.), p. 497.
37. Mommsen, *Staatsrecht*, I, p. 617, 208, 105, n. 2 ; II, p. 128, n. 3.
38. Cicero, *De Finibus Bonorum et Malorum*, II, 22, 74.
39. Suetonius, *Tiberius*, c. 27.
40. *Cf.* Marquardt, *op. cit.*, pp. 340 *sqq.*
41. F. Vollmer, " Laudationum funebrium Rom. historia et reliq. editio ", *Fleckeisens Jahrb. f. klass. Phil.*, Supp.-Bd. xviii (1892), pp. 475 *sqq.*
42. Wilhelm Ihne, *History of Rome*, English edition IV (1882), pp. 316, 430.
43. Vollmer, *op. cit.*, pp. 466–7.
44. Leo, *op. cit.*, p. 225.
45. Cicero, *Pro Archia poeta*, IX, 22.
46. *Plinii Naturalis Historia*, Book VII, chap. 43, 139–41. Translation by H. Rackham, in the Loeb Classical Library.
47. Cicero, *De Orat.*, II, 11, 46, 84, 342–3, in Vollmer, *op. cit.*, pp. 475–6.
48. See Vollmer, p. 477, and the fragment on p. 480 from the *Laudatio L. Caecilii Metelli.*
49. H. Peter, *Hist. Rom. Fragm.*, p. 120. (Vollmer concurs.)
50. *Corp. Inscr. Lat.*, VI, 1527 and 31670 ; H. Dessau, *Inscriptiones selectae* 8393. *Cf. Notizie degli Scavi di Antichità* (1899), p. 413. W. Warde Fowler in *Class. Rev.*, XIX (1905).—The identification of the husband with Q. Lucretius Vespilio must be regarded as erroneous, in spite of Mommsen (*Abh. der Berl. Akad. d. Wiss.* (1863), pp. 456 *sqq.*), and consequently the name Turia must also be abandoned. According to Hirschfeld, *Wiener Studien*, XXIV (1902), pp. 233 *sqq.*, Acilius (Appian 4, 39), who was proscribed in 43 B.C., may be conjectured to be the writer.
51. U. von Wilamowitz-Moellendorff in his review of the first edition of the present work, *Internat. Wochenschrift für Wiss., Kunst, u. Technik*, I (1907), cols, 1107 *sqq.*
52. H. Dessau, " Mommsen und das Monumentum Ancyranum ", *Klio* (1928), XXII, pp. 270, 372.
53. Cicero, *Cato Major de Senectute*, vii, 21.
54. Seneca, *Ep. Morales*, 108. Another fragment is extant in Cicero, *De Legibus*, II, 57. *Cf.* Sandys, *Latin Epigraphy*, p. 7.
55. *Cf.* Armstrong, *Autobiog. Elements*, pp. 250 *sqq.*, 243. Sandys, *op. cit.*, p. 65.

56. *Cf.* F. Blumenthal, " Die Autob. des Augustus ", in *Wiener Studien*, XXXV and XXXVI (1913–14).

57. Petronius Arbiter, *Satyricon*, chap. 71. Translation by M. Heseltine, in the Loeb Classical Library.

58. Pliny, *Nat. Hist.*, XXIV, 4, 17.

59. Livy, Book XL, 34, 5.

60. Pliny, *Nat. Hist.*, XXXV, 12. *Cf.* Sandys, *op. cit.*, pp. 10, 95.

61. *The History of Rome*, by Wilhelm Ihne, IV, p. 317 (1882).

62. Livy, Book XLI, 28, 8. *Cf.* Ihne, *op. cit.*, III p. 426,.

63. Dessau, *Inscript. selectae*, no. 23. *Cf.* Armstrong, *op. cit.*, p. 262 ; Sandys, *op. cit.*, pp. 132, 137.

64. Probably the Popillius who was Consul in 132 ; but it may have been the Censor of 159 who bore the same name ; *cf.* Nissen, *Landeskunde* (1902).

65. Dessau, *op. cit.*

66. Marquardt, *op. cit.*, I, pp. 243–4. Mommsen, *Staatsrecht*, I (3rd ed.), pp. 5, 2 ; III, p. 1016. H. Peter, *Die geschichtl. Lit. über die röm. Kaiserzeit*, I, p. 223.

67. H. Peter, *Hist. Rom. Reliq.*, p. xxxiii. Teuffel, *Literaturgesch.* (3rd ed.), § 80. *Cf.* also Münzer, *Quellenkritik der Naturgesch. des Plinius*, pp. 351 *sqq.*

68. W. Ihne, *The History of Rome*, IV, p. 319.

69. Cicero, *Cato Maior de Senectute*, xi, 38.

70. Schanz, *Gesch. der Röm. Lit.*, I., p. 135. H. Peter, *Geschichtl. Lit. über die röm. Kaiserzeit*, I, pp. 136–4, 201–2.

71. Plutarch, *Æmilius Paulus*, xv, 3.

72. Plutarch, *Tiberius Gracchus*, viii.

73. *Cf.* Cicero, *De Divinatione*, I, 18, 36 ; II, 19, 62. Cicero mentions the letter only because of its account of the evil omen that forecast the death of the father of the Gracchi.

74. H. Peter, *Die geschichtl. Literatur über die römische Kaiserzeit*, Book II, chap. 2. (" Die vom Hof unabhängigen Denkschriften "), p. 201.

75. *Cf.* Pauly-Wissowa, *Real-Encyclopädie*, I (1894), p. 587.

76. Cicero, *Brutus*, xxix, 111.

77. Seneca, *Epistulæ morales*, xxiv, 4. Translated by R. M. Gummere, in the Loeb Classical Library.

78. Plutarch, *Sulla*, xxiii, 2.

79. Plato, *Republic*, I, 332*d*.

80. Cicero, *Ep. ad Atticum*, II, i, 1 and 2.

81. Cicero, *Brutus*, lxxv, 262.

82. *De Bello Gallico*, viii.

83. Eduard Schwartz, *Charakterköpfe aus der antiken Litteratur*, p. 72.

84. Hirtius, *Præfatio*.

85. Cicero, *Brutus*, xxix, 112 ; xxxv, 132.

86. Spartianus 16, 1. *Cf.* J. Plew, *Quellenuntersuchungen zur Geschichte des Kaisers Hadrian* (1890), p. 3.

87. Cicero, *De Rep.*, i, 11, 17 ; 8, 13.

88. Evidence in H. Peter, *Hist. Rom. Reliq.*, pp. cclxi *sqq.*

89. Cicero, *De Orat.*, ii, 5, 20.

90. Evidence in R. Büttner, *op. cit.*, especially pp. 135 *sqq.*

91. Cicero, *Brutus*, 35, 132. *Cf. De Orat.*, ii, 58, or. 32.

92. Ταῦτα περὶ τῆς θειότητος. Plutarch, Sulla, vi. 3–5 ; *cf.* xix, 5.

93. Translation quoted from the Loeb Classical Library.

94. Usener, *Götternamen*, esp. pp. 338–9.

95. K. Lehrs, *Dämon und Tyche. Populäre Aufs. aus dem Altertum* (1875), esp. pp. 187–8. *Cf.* E. Rohde, *Der griech. Roman*, pp. 276 *sqq.*

96. F. Leo, " Römische Poesie in der Sullanischen Zeit ", *Hermes*, II (1914), p. 165.

348 NOTES—PART II : CHAPTER I

97. Cicero, *De Divinatione*, I, 33, 72.
98. *Cf.* J. Plew, *Ueber die Divination in der Geschichtsschreibung der röm. Kaiserzeit. Festschrift für L. Friedländer* (1895), p. 360–1.
99. Plutarch, *Sulla*, 7. Also from Sulla's book in H. Peter, *Hist. Rom. Reliq.*, p. cclxxxii.
100. *Cf.* Gressmann, *op. cit.*, on the inscription of Sargon II.
101. Plutarch, *Sulla*, 6, 5 ; 9, 27. For the attribution of the last three passages to Sulla, *cf.* Peter, *op. cit.*
102. *Ibid.*, 19 and 28.
103. *Ibid.* 37.
104. Cicero, *Ep. ad Fam.*, v, 7. *Cf.* Zielinski, *Cicero im Wandel der Jahrhunderte*, p. 5.
105. Cicero, *Or. pro Archia*, 11, 28 ; *Ep. ad Att.*, 1, 16, 15.
106. Cicero, *ad Att.*, i, 19, 10.
107. Cicero, *ad Att.*, ii, 1, 1.2. ; ad Quintum, fr. ii, 15, 5. *Cf.* Peter, *Hist. Rom., Fragm.*, p. 208.
108. Cicero, *ad Att.*, i, 20, 6 ; ii, 1.
109. Cicero, *ad Att.*, ii, 1, 1. *Cf.* Nepos, *Atticus*, 18, 5.
110. On the *hypomnema* as source of Plutarch's *Cicero*, c. 10–23, *cf.* Weizsäcker, *Jahrb. f. Phil.*, iii, pp. 417 *sqq.*, and especially K. Buresch, " Die Quellen zu den vorhandenen Berichten von der catilinarischen Verschwörung ", in *Comment. philol.*, dedicated to O. Ribbeck (1888), pp. 219 *sqq.*
111. Buresch, *op. cit.*, p. 233.
112. Fragments in Cicero's Works (Müller), iv, 3, pp. 398–9. The reconstruction by Van Heusde in Suringar, *De Rom. Autobiographiis* (1846), p. 24, and in Ribbeck, *Gesch. der röm. Dichtung*, i, 296 *sqq.*, is not altogether exact.
113. Cicero, *De Divinatione*, I, 13, 22.
114. Cicero, *Ep. ad Quintum*, fr. ii, 7, 1 (55).
115. Cicero, *De Officiis*, i, 22, 77.
116. Cicero, *ad Att.* ii, 3, 3 (60).
117. Cicero, *ad Att.*, i, 19, 10.
118. Cicero, *De Oratore*, ii, xv, 62.
119. *Ibid.* II, xii, 51–3.
120. *Cf.* for what follows Reitzenstein, *Hellenist. Wundererzählungen* (1906), pp. 84 *sqq.* The present chapter was written before the appearance of Reitzenstein's book. This should be mentioned because it may serve as confirmation.
121. Cicero, *Ep. ad. Fam.*, V, XII, 5. Translated by W. Glynn Williams in the Loeb Classical Library.
122. Reitzenstein, *op. cit.*, pp. 90 *sqq. Cf.* above, p. 189.
123. Reitzenstein, *op. cit.*, p. 97.
124. Cicero, *Ep. ad Fam.*, V, 12.
125. *Cf.* F. Leo, " Die römische Lit. des Altertums ", *Kultur der Gegenwart*, I, 8, p. 334.
126. Dio's Roman History, Book XLIX, 4, 2–4.
127. *Ibid.*, LIV, 24, 7. *Cf.* Peter, *Die geschichtl. Litt.*, I, p. 205.
128. J. Plew, *Quellenunters. zur Gesch. des Kaisers Hadrian*, pp. 119–120.
129. Dio Cassius, xlviii, 34, 3.
130. *Cf.* H. Peter, *op. cit.*, I, 372 *sqq.*, 297 *sqq.* ; also J. Plew, *op cit.*, pp. 107 *sqq.*
131. Gardthausen, *Augustus*, I, p. 686.
132. Suetonius, *Aug.*, 86.
133. Fr. 11 ; *cf.* Peter, *op. cit.*, p. 372 n.
134. Suetonius, *Aug.*, 85.

135. F. Blumenthal, " Die Autob. des Augustus ", *Wiener Studien*, XXXV and XXXVI (1913 and 1914). *Cf.* Pauly-Wissowa, *Real-Encyclopädie*, X, 275 *sqq.*

136. Suetonius, *Aug.*, xiii, 1.

137. *Ibid.*, xv.

138. *Cf.* Blumenthal, *op. cit.*, p. 123.

139. *Cf.* the informative article by Richard Laqueur on Nicolaus Damascenus in Pauly-Wissowa, *Real-Encyclopädie*, XXXIII (1936), pp. 408 *sqq.* The article also gives the reference to Tacitus—*Dialogus De Oratoribus*, c. 28. Laqueur says of the biography of Augustus which Nicolaus compiled, making use of the emperor's autobiography, that it was " analogous in a certain sense to the Cyropædia ". Cicero said the same thing of the autobiography of Scaurus (see above, p. 210). Thus the pedagogical point of view need not date from the court " philosopher " Nicolaus, but may have been adopted by Augustus himself from the tradition of Roman autobiography.

140. Iliad, xviii, 89. Translated by A. T. Murray, in the Loeb Classical Library.

141. *Cf.* K. Fitzler and O. Seeck in Pauly-Wissowa's *Real-Encyclopädie*, X (1919), pp. 318, 322, 325.

142. Suetonius, *Divus Augustus*, ii, 4.

143. Pauly-Wissowa's *Real-Encyclopädie*, VII, 284 (Münzer).

144. *Antony and Cleopatra*, Act 1, Scene 2.

145. Martial, *Epigrams*, I, iv, 8.

146. Pliny, *Ep.*, IV, xiv, 4.

147. Suetonius, *Aug.*, lxviii, lxix.

148. *Cf.* Gardthausen, *Augustus*, I, 196, II, 93, and for the opposite view, Münzer in Pauly-Wissowa, VII, 284.

149. Essays, II, 12. *Cf.* the translator's note on Martial XI, xi, *op. cit.*

150. Suetonius, *Aug.*, lxii, 2.

151. Suetonius, 65. Dio Cassius, 55, 20, 14. Seneca *De Benef.*, 6, 32. Tacitus *Ann.*, I, 6. *Cf.* Peter, *op. cit.*, pp. 355–6.

152. A reliable collection of passages drawn from this autobiography may be culled from Spartian's *Vita Hadriani*, as these passages " stand out clearly through the absence of the rhythmical conclusion of the sentences ". Von Winterfeld, " Ziele u. Aufgaben der mittelalt. Philologie ", *Verh. der 47. Vers. deutscher Philol. u. Schulm.* (1904), p. 18.

153. On this *cf.* Peter, *op. cit.*, I, pp. 298 *sqq.*

154. In addition to the fragments, *cf.* Münzer, *Beitr. z. Quellenkritik*, etc., pp. 391–2.

155. *Libro de la vida y costumbres de Don Alonso Enriquez de Guzman, Caballero noble desbaratado.* See below, vol. III.

156. Sept. Severus, fr. 2, 5. Augustus, fr. 11 (on this see Plew, *op. cit.*, pp. 115 *sqq.*), 6, 7, 15, 9, etc.

157. On the fragments, *cf.* Plew, *op. cit.*, pp. 111 *sqq.*

158. Plutarch, *Moralia*, 207 ; Sayings of Cæsar Augustus, 10.

159. Gardthausen, *Augustus*, I, pp. 980–1, 1276 *sqq.* ; II, pp. 863 *sqq.*

160. Bormann, *Bemerkgn zum schriftl. Nachlass des Kaisers Augustus, Marburger Rektoratschrift 1884*, p. 6.

161. *Monum. Ancyr.*, ed. Mommsen (2nd ed.), pp. iv–v. But the detail is disputed by scholars.

162. Mommsen, " Der Rechenschaftsbericht des Augustus ", *Sybels Histor. Zeitschr. N.F.*, 21 (1887), p. 383. Von Wilamowitz recalls Hannibal's record of his deeds, set up alongside the Hera of Croton when he was leaving Italy.

163. *Cf.* Gardthausen, I, pp. 1276–7, 1345–6.

164. The various interpretations are collected in Gardthausen, I, pp. 1288 *sqq.*

165. As is done by Armstrong, *Autobiog. Elements*, etc., and even H. Dessau, " Mommsen und das Monumentum Ancyranum ", *Klio*, XXII (1928).
166. *Cf.* O. Hirschfeld, *Wiener Studien*, VII (1885), p. 174.
167. Following Mommsen, *Monum. Ancyr.* (2nd ed.), p. vi. Nissen, *Rhein. Mus. N.F.*, LXI, pp. 486–7, and von Wilamowitz, *Hermes*, 21, differ.
168. *Cf.* Ed. Meyer, " Kaiser Augustus ", *Histor. Zeitschr.*, 91, N.F. 55 (1903), pp. 405 *sqq.*
169. *Cf.* Bormann, *Bemerkungen*, etc., pp. 20 *sqq.*
170. *Cf.* Gardthausen, *Augustus*, I, pp. 1284 *sqq.*, 1337–8; II, 887–8.
171. *Cf.* Fr. Koepp, " Zum Mon. Ancyranum ", *Sokrates* (1920), pp. 289 *sqq.*
172. This had been done most thoroughly by J. Plew, *Quellenuntersuch.*, pp. 100–1.

PART II : CHAPTER II

1. *Cf.* H. Oldenberg, *Buddha*, (1st ed.), pp. 26, 158, 292, 351.
2. *Cf.* F. Leo, *Die griech.-röm, Biographie*, pp. 97 *sqq.*, 188 *sqq.*
3. *Cf.* H. Siebeck, *Gesch. der Psychologie*, I (1880), 2, pp. 104 *sqq.*
4. *Cf.* above, pp. 195–6, and A. Schmekel, *Die Philos. der mittleren Stoa*, pp. 336–7.
5. Leo, *op. cit.*, pp. 99 *sqq.*
6. Demonstrated in Leo's description of its history, *op. cit.*
7. Leo, *op. cit.*, p. 189.
8. *Cf.* von Wilamowitz, *Die griech. Lit.*, pp. 114 *sqq.*
9. *Cf.* P. Wendland, *Berliner philol. Wochenschr.*, 24 (1904), p. 292.
10. *Cf.* the author's article on the autobiographies of the French aristocracy of the seventeenth century, in *Deutsche Vierteljahrsschrift f. Litteraturwissenschaft*, I (1926).
11. *Cf.* F. Leo, " Das Schlussgedicht des ersten Buches des Properz ", *Nachr. Gött. Gel. Ges.* (1898), pp. 470 *sqq.*
12. On the first edition in *The Oxyrhynchus Papyri*, Part XVII (1927), *cf.* R. Pfeiffer, " Ein altersgedicht des Kallimachus ", *Hermes* (1928), and his new edition of the poet (Oxford, 1950).
13. English translation by A. S. Hunt, *Ox. Pap.*, modified to meet Pfeiffer, *op. cit.*
14. Crusius, *Rhein. Mus.*, XLIV, p. 455. Friedländer, *Sittengesch. Roms*, III (6th ed.), p. 39.
15. *The Epigrams of Martial*, Book I, i. Translated by Walter C. A. Ker in the Loeb Classical Library.
16. *Cf.* the conclusion of his so-called *Bios*, c. 76.
17. *Cf.* von Wilamowitz, *Antigonos von Karystos*. Leo, *op. cit.*, pp. 67–8, 129 *sqq.*
18. *Annaei Senecae oratorum et rhetorum sententiae divisiones colores*, rec. Bursian (1857). The comparison with the memoirs of Antigonus in von Wilamowitz, *op. cit.*, p. 82. A good example of characterization of distinguished friends is Seneca's portrait of Laberius, *Controv.*, I, 13–24.
19. Diogenes Laertius, IV, 46.
20. Leo, " Das Schlussgedicht ", *op. cit.*
21. For the literary form *cf.* L. Niedermeyer, " Untersuchungen über die antike poetische Autobiographie ", *Münchener Dissertation* 1919.
22. *Cf.* Aristotle, *Nic. Eth.*, IV, 11 : οἱ μὲν ὄργιλοι ὀργίζονται (irasci celerem) . . . παύονται δὲ ταχέως· οἱ καὶ βέλτιστον ἔχουσιν.
23. *Cf.* the analysis by A. Dieterich, *Rhein. Museum*, LV, pp. 207 *sqq.* The translations that follow are by H. F. Butler, in the Loeb Classical Library (Propertius).

24. *Cf.* R. Pfeiffer, *Ein neuer Altersgedicht des Kallimachus*, p. 322.
25. Cicero, *De Oratore*, IX, 32. *Brutus*, 92, 317 (*strepitus*).
26. Ovid, *Tristia*, I, 10. Translated by A. L. Wheeler, in the Loeb Classical Library.
27. *Cf.* Niedermeyer, *Untersuchungen zur antiken poet. Autob.*, p. 24.
28. Fragments in C. Müller, *Fragmenta Historicorum Graecorum*, III, 343. Jacoby, *F. Gr. Hist.*, II, 90.
29. Fr. 135 (Jacoby). See also R. Laqueur's article on Nicolaus in Pauly-Wissowa, XXXIII (1936), cols. 368 and 400.
30. Julianus Apostata, Letter to Themistius, 265D.
31. *Cf.* F. Leo, *Die Biographie, op. cit.*, pp. 190–1.
32. *Cf.* Müller, *F.H.G.*, III, p. 347.
33. *Nic. Eth.*, II, 7 ; *cf. Pol.*, VII, 14, 30, and *Rhet*, I, 9. For the individual virtues see the relevant chapters of *Nic. Eth.*, III, 9 *sqq.*
34. *Nic. Eth.*, VII, 1, 8.
35. *Cf.* H. v. Arnim, *Dio von Prusa*, pp. 112 *sqq.* E. Nordern, *Antike Kunstprosa*, pp. 670 *sqq.*
36. Varro *Sat.*, fr. 418–19. Epictetus *Diss.*, III, 23, 36–7. *Cf.* Norden, *op. cit.*, p. 671 n. with its reference to Philo *De Congr.*, 3. For the oriental picture of the soul's journeying, see below, chap. III, iv.
37. *Cf.* Julian, *epist. ad Themistium*, 265D (*Op.* ed. Hertlein, p. 343) : Θράσυλλος, Τιβερίῳ πικρῷ καὶ φύσει χαλεπῷ τυράννῳ ξυγγενόμενος, εἰ μὴ διὰ τῶν καταλειφθέντων ὑπ᾿ αὐτοῦ λόγων ἀπελογήσατο δείξας ὅστις ἦν, ὤφλεν ἂν εἰς τέλος αἰσχύνην ἀναπάλλακτον, οὕτως αὐτὸν οὐδὲν ὤνησεν ἡ πολιτεία. In Müller, *F.H.G.*, III, 501, this passage is overlooked.
38. Josephus, *Contra Apionem*, 29 *sqq.*
39. See above, Introduction, p. 17.
40. *Jewish War*, III, 108 ; *Cf.* H. St. J. Thackeray in his introduction, p. x.
41. *Life*, 17–19. The translation here and in the quotations that follow is from Thackeray, in the edition of Josephus in the Loeb Classical Library.
42. Thackeray in his introduction to the *War*, p. xxvi.
43. *Vita*, 357–8. *Cf.* also *Contra Apionem*, 45–6 and 53.
44. *Contra Apionem*, 37 *sqq.*
45. *Vita*, 6 ; *cf. Contra Apionem*, 30–31.
46. See Hölscher's article on Josephus, Pauly-Wissowa, *Real-Encyclopädie*, IX (1916), col. 1936.
47. *De Divinatione*, II, i, 2.
48. Cicero, *De Divinatione*, II, i, 1. Translated by W. A. Falconer in the Loeb Classical Library. The opening of Augustine's " Soliloquies " resembles this. Cicero : *Quaerenti mihi multumque et diu cogitanti, quanam re possem prodere . . .* Augustine : *Volventi mihi multa ac varia mecum diu ac per multos dies sedulo quaerenti memet ipsum ac bonum meum . . .* This deserves mention because a similar resemblance between the passage in Augustine and the beginning of Varro's *Bimarcus* has been pointed out in support of the contention that the source of the " Soliloquies " is to be found in Cynicism (Hirzel, *Der Dialog.*, I, pp. 446–7).
49. *De Divinatione*, II, ii, 6.
50. Sallust, *Bellum Catilinae*, III, 3 ; IV, 2.
51. *De Divinatione*, II, ii, 6–7.
52. *Ibid.*, II, ii, 5.
53. περὶ τῆς ταξέως τῶν ἰδίων βιβλίων. *Galeni scripta minora rec.* Marquardt, etc., II, 80–90. περὶ τῶν ἰδίων βιβλίων, *ibid.*, pp. 91–124. *Cf.* II, p. lxiii.
54. *Op. cit.*, p. 102.
55. περὶ τοῦ προγιγνώσκειν, *Op.* (ed. Kuhn), XIV, 599.

56. *Op. cit.*, pp. 80–1, 88–9, 115 *sqq.*
57. *Cf.* Leo, *Die Biographie, op. cit.*, pp. 219 *sqq.*
58. *Brutus*, 6, 25–6 ; 10, 39 ; 11, 44 ; 18, 70–1 ; 36, 138.
59. *Ibid.*, 31, 120–1 ; 40, 150–1 ; 43, 161 ; 44, 164 ; 87, 298.
60. *Ibid.*, 43, 161.
61. *Brutus*, c. 89 and 90.
62. *Brutus*, 93, 322.
63. *Cf.* J. Bruns, *Die Persönlichkeit in der Geschichtsschreibung der Alten.* (1898).
F. Leo, *Die Biographie, op. cit.*, pp. 242 *sqq.*
64. Polybius, *The Histories*, IV, 8, 7.   Translated by W. R. Paton in the
Loeb Classical Library.
65. Polybius, IX, 22, 7–8 ; 23, 4.
66. Leo, *op. cit.*, p. 248.
67. Polybius, XVIII, 33, 6.